BIOPOLITICS, GEOPOLITICS, LIFE

BIOPOLITICS, GEOPOLITICS, LIFE

Settler States and Indigenous Presence

RENÉ DIETRICH AND KERSTIN KNOPF, EDITORS

Duke University Press   *Durham and London*   2023

Designed by Courtney Leigh Richardson
Project Editor: Ihsan Taylor
Typeset in Portrait Text and IBM Plex Mono
by Westchester Publishing Services

Library of Congress Cataloging-in-Publication Data
Names: Dietrich, René, [date] editor. | Knopf, Kerstin, editor.
Title: Biopolitics, geopolitics, life : settler states and indigenous presence /
René Dietrich and Kerstin Knopf, editors.
Description: Durham : Duke University Press, 2023. | Includes index.
Identifiers: LCCN 2022043243 (print)
LCCN 2022043244 (ebook)
ISBN 9781478019763 (paperback)
ISBN 9781478017080 (hardcover)
ISBN 9781478024347 (ebook)
Subjects: LCSH: Indigenous peoples—Colonization. | Settler colonialism. |
Decolonization. | Biopolitics. | Geopolitics. | BISAC: SOCIAL SCIENCE / Indigenous
Studies | SOCIAL SCIENCE / Ethnic Studies / General
Classification: LCC JV305 .B56 2023 (print) | LCC JV305 (ebook) |
DDC 320.1/2089—dc23/eng/20221205
LC record available at https://lccn.loc.gov/2022043243
LC ebook record available at https://lccn.loc.gov/2022043244

Cover art courtesy of Deborah A. Miranda.

Duke University Press gratefully acknowledges the German Research Foundation
through the Universität Bremen, which provided funds toward the publication of
this book.

CONTENTS

FOREWORD

ALYOSHA GOLDSTEIN

Dead salmon are coming back to life, and the "Red Crow" Mi'kmaq reserve in so-called Québec is under siege by insatiable white settler zombies. Although immune from being turned into the living dead, Native peoples are nonetheless exposed to the relentless violence of the zombie onslaught and at risk of being disemboweled and devoured. The Mi'kmaw filmmaker Jeff Barnaby's feature *Blood Quantum* (2019) is a present past set in 1981, the explosive year when the Québec police invaded the Listuguj Mi'gmaq First Nation to impose new controls over Native fishing and when the proposed patriation of the Canadian constitution sought to eliminate Aboriginal treaty rights.[1] Barnaby's film evocatively stages elements of the biopolitical and geopolitical entanglement of Indigenous presence and settler-colonial occupation that are the focus and vital contribution of this volume. Envisioning an Indigenous futurity beyond the viral plague of the settler undead, the film tells a story of Native peoples defining their own relations with the human and more-than-human world beyond the terrors of colonization and its genocidal calculus of blood quantum deployed in the service of Indigenous displacement and dispossession.

While colonialism renders land an alienable thing to be possessed, passively available for capitalist market exchange, Barnaby's film, like many of the essays in this book, knows the Earth to be both animate and agential. According to Barnaby, "If you start looking at things like viral outbreaks as the planet's immune system, what would be better for our planet than just turning all these parasites into fertilizer? It's like it's turning the stupid fucking white man into something it could use."[2] In a soliloquy midway through the film, during a moment of reprieve from the carnage and struggle for survival, the Mi'kmaw character Moon (played by the iconic Cayuga actor Gary Farmer) declares, "The earth is an animal, living and breathing." Shifting from English to Mi'kmaw, he asserts, "White men don't understand this"; then, in English, "That's why the dead keep coming back to life." "Who says we're immune?" he asks rhetorically, switching to Mi'kmaw to muse that "maybe the earth just forgot about us." Alternating between Mi'kmaw and English throughout, the film underscores its address to a Mi'kmaq audience and, by inference, a Native viewership more broadly. *Blood Quantum*'s title itself explicitly attributes the colonial necropolitics of Indigenous generational attrition to the genre of horror. Yet its narrative, which ends with a child immune to zombification born of a Mi'kmaw father and white mother, insists on Indigenous futurity, emplacement, and kinship beyond the artifice of blood. Indigenous relations grounded in being claimed as kin ultimately prevail over and against the fabulation of blood quantum as the measure of biopolitical membership and a livable life.

In settler-colonial nation-states such as the United States and Canada, the doctrine of tribal sovereign immunity is a central if nonetheless beleaguered tenet of Indigenous sovereignty.[3] Although technically a juridical clause indemnifying legislative bodies, government agencies, and tribal commercial enterprises from being sued, sovereign immunity is in fact a matter of the very substance of sovereignty itself, reaffirming sovereign power as source of juridical authority and reserving the privilege to remain above the law for the sovereign. Sovereign immunity is a preemptive jurisdictional capacity that by extension can inoculate populations and territories. Tribal sovereign immunity is articulated and contested at the biopolitical and geopolitical limit of colonial authority while ultimately inscribed as a category of colonial law rather than originating in the jurisprudence of specific Indigenous nations and, in the United States, remaining nonetheless subordinate to congressional plenary power. For instance, among the most recent flashpoints of contestation over tribal sovereign immunity, the Saint Regis Mohawk Tribe patent deal with the pharmaceutical corporation Allergan in 2017 prompted strident non-Native condemnation of the tribe's ostensible abuse of immunity for profit. In 2019, the US Supreme Court upheld a lower court's decision that rejected the application of tribal sovereign immunity in the case, despite the tribe's contention that the proposed partnership with Allergan would generate revenue necessary to "address the chronically unmet needs of the Tribal community, such as housing, employment, education, healthcare, cultural and language preservation."[4] Colonial sovereign power, in this instance, reasserted its prerogative over the dispensation of immunity as superseding the Indigenous administration of life, death, and jurisdiction.

What Roberto Esposito calls the immunological paradigm casts the immune system as a military apparatus. This biomedical model, argues Esposito, imagines immunity as a means of "violent defense in the face of anything judged to be foreign."[5] At the same time, immunization as a mechanism of biopolitical governance entails introducing the virus in attenuated form to preempt a more virulent manifestation of the same contagion and thus "reproduces in a controlled form exactly what it is meant to protect us from."[6] With the biomedical model as a basis for juridical-political form, the body politic is imagined as a bounded space under siege and most effectively defended by this form of exclusion by inclusion. Such relations of inclusive exclusion take on starkly divergent valences depending on whether they are mobilized on behalf of the settler nation-state or negotiated by Indigenous peoples as an imposed condition that might possibly facilitate survivance.

Made just before the devastating emergence of COVID-19, *Blood Quantum* now seems eerily amenable to the lens of the pandemic, not least because of the long history of colonial biological warfare waged against Indigenous peoples, perhaps most notoriously through the weaponization of blankets infected with smallpox by the US military.[7] The proliferation of maps that chart the vectors and epicenters of contagion during the COVID-19 pandemic exemplifies the spatial calculus at work in the biopolitical coproduction of territory and population. Settler epidemiology and news coverage rendered Indigenous nations simultaneously within and beyond the pale of the settler nation-state. Settler news platforms reported the gruesome statistics of Indigenous infection and death as at once symptomatic of the most impoverished and vulnerable populations of the body politic and altogether foreign to the medical modernity and public health governance of the settler state. After suffering the highest rate of COVID-19 infections per capita in the United States during May 2020, the Navajo Nation instituted curfews for its citizens and established checkpoints at its borders to keep out visitors. These measures contributed to substantially reducing viral spread, hospitalization, and death.[8] For much of the pandemic, Pueblo Indian nations in so-called New Mexico also closed their borders. Surrounded by the settler state of South Dakota, the Cheyenne River Sioux Tribe likewise set up highway checkpoints in August 2020 in an effort to turn away the massive influx of people traveling to the Sturgis Motorcycle Rally. Yet more than 250,000 bikers ignored the tribe's blockade, gathering again in 2021, despite evidence that the previous year's rally had produced lethal outbreaks in neighboring states and Native reservations.[9] This volume supplies indispensable tools not only for contending with the politics of the immunological paradigm through which Indigenous life persists but for more broadly engaging the politics of life itself under and beyond settler-colonial occupation.

Biopolitics, Geopolitics, Life: Settler States and Indigenous Presence is a decisive contribution to contemporary debates on the politics of Indigenous life and colonial regimes of land, labor, and racialization. Refusing the separation of land and bodies through which settler colonization seeks to displace and replace, contributors to this volume ground their inquiry in the radical relationalities and interdependences of Indigenous world making. This is a crucial rebuke to the processes that Lisa Lowe critically analyzes as the "colonial divisions of humanity" in which, as Frantz Fanon observed, "the colonial world is a compartmentalized world."[10] Challenging the colonial capitalist division between land and bodies has substantial consequences. Rigid categorical distinctions between land as the principal target of settler colonization and coerced racialized labor as exclusively associated with chattel slavery obscure questions such as those having to do with Indigeneity in African and African diasporic contexts, Indigenous displacement and migration, and colonial regimes of confinement and carcerality. In the pages that follow, the authors trouble the normative "colonial divisions of humanity" in ways that demonstrate the potential for further developing analytic connections with how particular colonial uses of racialization not only are a means of undermining Indigenous sovereignty but also are sites of struggle over relations of reciprocity, social reproduction, and reproductive justice.[11] The volume's imperative to critically rethink the colonial logics of life, land, human, and more than human together likewise centers the necessarily inextricable realities of movement, multiplicity, and interrelation.

The ten incisive chapters assembled here, along with René Dietrich's astute introduction, generatively invite further inquiry and elaboration. Just as *Blood Quantum* vividly narrates colonial apocalypse and Indigenous futurity while potentially alluding to the expansive resonance of the zombie film as a subgenre of the anticolonial imaginary, *Biopolitics, Geopolitics, Life* is both a profound resource for thinking together in its own right and inspires ongoing study and critical projects yet to come.[12] Barnaby's film might evoke anticolonial and antiracist affinities by prompting viewers to recall the specific historical circumstances in which the figure of the zombie emerges not as embodying the insatiable hunger of colonization or capitalism but as bearing the viciously dehumanizing consequences of enslavement and the plantation economy in the Caribbean and the US South while also manifesting white fears of the Haitian Revolution. Contributors to this volume offer compelling insight into the differential distribution of life and value that are fundamental arenas of contestation under colonial racial capitalism with substantial implications. *Biopolitics, Geopolitics, Life* is invaluable for its sustained commitment to centering

Indigenous presence and persistence in its understanding of the biopolitical and geopolitical as constitutively, if also heterogeneously, enmeshed.

NOTES

1 On the Listuguj raids, see Alanis Obomsawin's documentary film *Incident at Resti-gouche* (1984). For more on the First Nations movement that responded to Canada's proposed constitutional changes, see Emma Feltes and Glen Coulthard, eds., "The Constitution Express: A 40-Year Retrospective," a special issue of *BC Studies: The British Columbian Quarterly* 212 (Winter 2021–2022).

2 Quoted in Jordan Crucchiola, "Jeff Barnaby Made an Apocalypse Movie to Watch the System Fall. Then a Pandemic Hit," *Vulture*, May 6, 2020, https://www.vulture .com/2020/05/jeff-barnaby-is-worried-white-people-wont-get-blood-quantum.html.

3 David E. Wilkins and K. Tsianina Lomawaima, *Uneven Ground: American Indian Sovereignty and Federal Law* (Norman: University of Oklahoma Press, 2002), 216–48.

4 Saint Regis Mohawk Tribe's Motion to Dismiss for Lack of Jurisdiction Based on Tribal Sovereign Immunity, *Mylan Pharmaceuticals Inc. v. Allergan Inc.*, proceeding no. IPR2016–01127 (September 22, 2017), 6. For an outstanding analysis of the case and its implications see Theresa Rocha Beardall, "Sovereignty for Sale? Tribal Patent Shelters and the Risky Business of Sovereign Derivatives," *Native American and Indigenous Studies* 9, no. 2 (Fall 2022): 3–37.

5 Roberto Esposito, *Immunitas: The Protection and Negation of Life*, translated by Zakiya Hanafi (Cambridge: Polity, 2011), 17.

6 Esposito, *Immunitas*, 8.

7 For further analysis of this history of biological warfare as rationalized by the colonial state's relentless criminalization of Indigenous peoples, see Joanne Baker, *Red Scare: The State's Indigenous Terrorist* (Oakland: University of California Press, 2021), xii–xiii.

8 Simon Romero, "Checkpoints, Curfews, Airlifts: Virus Rips through Navajo Nation," *New York Times*, April 9, 2020, https://www.nytimes.com/2020/04/09/us /coronavirus-navajo-nation.html. More broadly, see Matthew L. M. Fletcher, "Pandemics in Indian Country: The Making of the Tribal State," *University of St. Thomas Law Journal* 18, no. 2 (April 2022): 295–306.

9 Stephen Groves, "Sturgis Rally Expecting 250K, Stirring Virus Concerns," *Indian Country Today*, August 9, 2020, https://indiancountrytoday.com/news/sturgis-rally -expecting-250k-stirring-virus-concerns; M. J. Firestone, Haley Wienkes, Jacob Garfin, and Xiong Wang et al., "COVID-19 Outbreak Associated with a 10-Day Motorcycle Rally in a Neighboring State," *Morbidity and Mortality Weekly Report*, November 27, 2020, http://dx.doi.org/10.15585/mmwr.mm6947e1.

10 Lisa Lowe, *The Intimacies of Four Continents* (Durham, NC: Duke University Press, 2015), 7; Frantz Fanon, *The Wretched of the Earth*, translated by Richard Philcox (New York: Grove, [1961] 2004), 3.

11 The politics of adoption, foster care, and other forms of custodial supervision are especially significant as contested sites for the social reproduction of biopower.

See, for instance, Christina Firpo and Margaret Jacobs, "Taking Children, Ruling Colonies: Child Removal and Colonial Subjugation in Australia, Canada, French Indochina, and the United States, 1870–1950s," *Journal of World History* 29, no. 4 (December 2018): 529–62; Laura Briggs, *Taking Children: A History of American Terror* (Oakland: University of California Press, 2020); and Matthew L. M. Fletcher and Wenona T. Singel, "Lawyering the Indian Child Welfare Act," *Michigan Law Review* 120, no. 8 (June 2022): 1775–98.

12 For more on *Blood Quantum* and anticolonial zombie film and television, see Michael Truscello and Renae Watchman, "*Blood Quantum* and Fourth Cinema: Post- and Paracolonial Zombies," *Quarterly Review of Film and Video* (2022), https://doi .org/10.1080/10509208.2022.2026273.

ACKNOWLEDGMENTS

This book started as an international conference at the Institute for Transnational American Studies (since renamed the Obama Institute) at the Johannes Gutenberg University of Mainz in June 2015. As the organizers, we gratefully acknowledge the German Research Foundation (DFG) for its generous financial support of the conference. We give special thanks to the administrator of the Obama Institute, Anette Vollrath, and our staff members Tanja Ebner and Jan Kwiatkowski for making everything at the event run smoothly.

Moreover, we thank everyone who contributed to the gathering—all of the speakers, with their valuable presentations (unfortunately not all of them could be included in this volume), and all of the attendees who added to the conversation, including the students in the seminar "Settler Colonialism," who provided outstanding poster presentations. We also make special note of the Chumash and Esselen author Deborah Miranda, who not only allowed us to use her artwork for our flyer, poster, and book cover but also enthusiastically answered students' questions about her writing in a special class session and gave a reading at the Gutenberg Book Store in downtown Mainz. Thanks, Deborah! We also thank the bookstore's staff for their support of the reading.

In the years since the conference, many people and conversations helped to make this book come into being. First and foremost, we thank all of the contributors to this volume. They literally make this book what it is through offering in their chapters their important insights into the issues of bio- and geopolitics in settler states and forms of Indigenous presence contesting these means of colonial rule. We thank them for sharing their knowledge with us and the readers of this volume as well as for being diligent in their revisions and patient in this rather long process from conference to publication. We extend a special thanks to Alyosha Goldstein, whose thoughtful foreword opens the door to the volume while adding further perspectives and nuances to it. Alex Trimble Young was an early reader of the introduction, and his insightful attentiveness helped to hone some of its central arguments.

In Mainz, Alana Mazur was invaluable for her editorial assistance with the introduction and the overall volume, and in Bremen, Donia Labidi provided important support toward the end. At Duke University Press, we truly could not have found a better editor for this project than Courtney Berger, as she accompanied us on a path that included not only expected, but also the unexpected, difficulties, such as a global pandemic. That this book reached completion under these circumstances can in many ways be credited to her kind and steady guidance along the way. In addition, we thank everyone at Duke who helped: Sandra Korn, who had an answer to every question and paved the way especially at the finishing stage; Alejandra Mejía, for taking care of the final submission; Susan Deeks (copy editor) and Ihsan Taylor (project editor) for their diligent work up to publication; and Courtney Richardson for her beautiful book cover design. We thank the anonymous readers for their careful attention to the manuscript and their valuable comments and suggestions, which helped to make the volume stronger. Finally, we are thankful to everyone who has played a part in making this book into what we hope is a vital contribution to an important and ongoing conversation.

A note on the book cover: We are very grateful and proud to be able to feature the artwork of Deborah Miranda on the cover. The piece, "Blood Quantum: The Four Sacred Directions," was originally included in her mixed-genre work *Bad Indians: A Tribal Memoir* as part of the series "Things You Can Do with Your Chart for Calculating Quantum of Indian Blood." Referring to a US-specific context, it illustrates widespread settler colonial biopolitical techniques of racialization while creatively overwriting these with an assertion of Indigenous presence. As an indicator of Indigenous placemaking in spiritual, cultural, social, and political terms, the "Four Sacred Directions" of the piece manifest an understanding of geopolitics and relationality based in Indigenous ways of seeing and being in the world that refuse to be defined and contained by settler colonial restrictions.

THE BIO/GEOPOLITICS OF SETTLER STATES AND INDIGENOUS NORMATIVITIES

RENÉ DIETRICH

Twenty-First-Century Reports from Settler States

On November 21, 2016, water protectors at Standing Rock are attacked with water cannons, mace, tear gas, and rubber bullets by armed forces composed of several law enforcement agencies and private security firms. Earlier the same year, the Lenca Honduran environmental rights activist Berta Cáceres is assassinated. In November 2017, Australian Prime Minister Malcolm Turnbull rejects the Uluru Statement from the Heart, which calls for a "First Nations voice" in Australia's Constitution. On the same weekend, the detention centers for refugees on the islands of Nauru and Manus are dismantled, without offering the inhabitants refuge in the settler colony. In 2018, Indigenous people from Central American countries are among the most vulnerable of those seeking refuge in the United States, where they are subjected to the policy of immediate arrest and family separation; in June, a Maya-Mam woman from Guatemala is killed by a border patrol agent. In Canada, in the spring of 2018, both Gerald Stanley, in the case of his killing of Colton Boushie (Red Pheasant First Nation), and Richard Cormier, in the case of the murder of Tina Fontaine (Sagkeeng First Nation), are acquitted—in Stanley's case, by an all-white jury—which leads to nationwide demonstrations for reforming the justice system.[1]

All of these moments demonstrate the ongoing conditions of settler-state violence across the settler-colonial archipelago in the twenty-first century.[2] At the same time, they attest to the strength, determination, and resurgence of Indigenous peoples seeking to protect rights, bodies, lands, and waters as part of century-long anticolonial struggles against invasive settler forces. In centering Indigenous principles, politics, and practices of kinship and relationality, these Indigenous activists are living, as the Michi Saagiig Nishnaabeg scholar and writer Leanne Betasamosake Simpson describes it, "as we have always done."[3]

These are just a few examples of settler-colonial violence that have been deemed "newsworthy" by national and international outlets as well as by social media channels. There are many more moments that do not get registered in the news and social media. But in looking at these moments together, we seek to show what is regularly missed when they are reported as isolated and extraordinary occurrences—namely, how they are in fact related to one another as well as to a settler-colonial status quo of eliminatory dispossession that traverses the national specificities of each reported instance.

In this it is crucial to note what these reports show: militarized police brutality and orchestrated killings of those who oppose capitalist-extractivist interests and protect Indigenous land, waterways, and life; the violent and bureaucratic protection of nativist settler claims while disavowing Indigenous rights; the non-culpability of settlers killing Indigenous bodies; and the increased vulnerability of Indigenous peoples to violence as they move in the contexts of multiple settler regimes. Their newsworthiness might suggest that they are extraordinary, and in being reported as isolated instances, this impression is strengthened. However, looking at them together shows how often violence does not disrupt the status quo but is instead so ordinary an aspect of the settler state that it constitutes the status quo.

Ultimately, the tendency to see such events as isolated incidents rather than as reflective of long-standing structures of dispossession and colonization, or as divorced entirely from questions of settler colonialism and Indigeneity, leads to reports especially by major media outlets that are unable or unwilling to see, know, or name the ongoing condition of settler violence intensified in these moments. This, in turn, points to the larger patterns of invisibilizing and unknowing of settler colonialism that are endemic to it.[4] In other words, while the occurrences that appear to have breached the norm can become the object of news reports and analysis for major media outlets, the norm itself remains beyond analysis.[5]

For the purpose of this volume, these individual instances of state violence across multiple sites of settler-colonial formations in the twenty-first century are significant precisely in how they mark momentary intensifications of larger, violent patterns of colonial statist (capitalist, extractivist) non-Native settlement that are otherwise fully routinized, normalized, and unspectacularly habituated. Productive of ongoing dispossessing and unlawfully delegitimizing conditions, these patterns structure the un(re)marked quotidian as much as historically intensified moments in the archipelago of lands colonized via settlement. They signify some of the manifold ways in which, as Aileen Moreton-Robinson (Goenpul, Quandamooka First Nation) has importantly described it: "The relationship between Indigenous sovereignty and state sovereignty [figures] as relations of force located within a matrix of biopower."[6] Biopower, for Moreton-Robinson, functions as a normalizing force that "work[s] to produce whiteness as an invisible norm," making non-Native settlement the unchallenged geopolitical norm through which state sovereignty is constituted and upheld.[7] The perpetuated settler aggression visited on Indigenous bodies, lands, and lives functions as an enactment of such biopower to "make" the settler state "live" at the expense of Indigenous livelihood.

Constituting globally expansive geographies, these large territories subjected to settler colonialism are then representative, as Scott Morgensen has shown, of the "historical grounds for the globalisation of biopower" and instrumental in "producing biopower in the present that requires denaturalising critique."[8] By necessity, such "denaturalising critique" needs to be oriented toward an Indigenous-centered decolonization. In this sense, the instances of settler-state aggression portrayed earlier also figure, in the terms of the Ngāti Awa and Ngāti Porou scholar Linda Tuiwai Smith, as sites in "the struggle for decolonization."[9] As one of the "five conditions or dimensions" that frame this struggle, Smith lists "the concept of structure, the underlying code of imperialism, of power relations."[10] To us, this indicates that a close consideration of the bio- and geopolitical structures underlying the normativities of settler statism is not merely something that precedes forms of "struggle for decolonization" but can be mobilized as being integral to it. Taking this interplay of "structure" and "struggle" into account, this volume seeks to analyze the biopolitics and geopolitics of settler colonialism as they structurally manifest across distinct yet related international and transnational sites of Indigenous struggle over non-Native statist occupation, including nations across the Americas and the Pacific islands of Hawai'i as well as across Australia and Aotearoa/New Zealand. In doing so, *Biopolitics, Geopolitics, Life* focusses both on the quotidian aspect of settler state violence and on moments of historical intensification.

At the same time, the volume emphasizes Indigenous work within the interrelated spheres of activism and political and critical thought, along with the literary and visual arts, that can help to map, in Smith's term, "the conceptual terrain of struggle" as well as the everyday sites of struggle on the ground.[11] On the one hand, such work makes settler-colonial conditions visible, nameable, and knowable via their denaturalization. On the other hand, this work actively participates in what Smith has described as a further dimension in the "struggle for decolonization"—namely, "a way of reimaging the world" that draws on different epistemologies, thus "unleashing the creative spirit."[12] As our volume draws together different disciplines from the social sciences and humanities, we maintain that "a way of reimagining the world" through Indigenous-centered perspectives provides a shared lens.

The contributions to *Biopolitics, Geopolitics, Life* illuminate this work toward Indigenous decolonization from their distinct disciplinary standpoints while acknowledging the intersections of thought, practice, and action. We understand this work thus in its political potentiality as one possible path toward the dismantling of settler-colonial bio- and geopolitical conditions. The book thus highlights the Indigenous bodies and lives that continually help to make visible an ever-present and irreducible thinking and practicing that goes beyond and insists on Indigenous epistemologies and practices beyond settler logics.

The Normativities of Statist Settlement

We understand settler-colonial biopolitics and geopolitics as intersecting and coconstitutive paradigms of governance and governmentality. These paradigms ultimately produce settler-defined modes of life and forms of land use that are defined and perpetually reiterated both as a universalized self-evident norm and as normative demand placed on all peoples, including the ones dispossessed and regularized through the very same paradigms. Through this process, certain modes of life—such as the ideal of liberal individuated selfhood produced through the nuclear family or forms of land use, such as home ownership, surplus mass agriculture, or industrialized large-scale construction and extraction—are rendered self-evidently natural, "modern," or "civilized."

This volume sets out to analyze settler nation-states as geopolitical and biopolitical projects that initiate and perpetuate specific forms of land tenure, social practices, and governance, all of which operate in contradistinction to dimensions of embodied and spatialized Indigenous sovereignty. The analytical work of the volume is thus aimed at what David Scott has described as a central concern of colonial projects in "disabling old forms of life" and, in their stead, working to "enable—indeed, . . . to oblige—new forms of life to come into being."[13] Even more pointedly, the Yellowknives Dene theorist Glen Coulthard has observed "the ability [of settler colonialism] to produce *forms of life* that make settler-colonialism's constitutive hierarchies seem natural."[14]

We maintain that laying bare how settler-colonial social structures are normalized and naturalized can be a means of simultaneously denormalizing and denaturalizing them, which ultimately opens a new perspective on Indigenous lived presences and struggles in the settler state. Translating the socially specific into the natural obscures how certain bio- and geopolitical mechanisms derive from and are privileged by a particular non-Native model of governance and social organization. This model is, in turn, based on notions of the social and the political that are historically specific but become universalized. In this way, a specific political model becomes that which, in Mark Rifkin's words, comes to "to constitute a viable political form(ul)ation as such."[15] While formed through specific (classed, gendered, racialized, ableist, and heteronormative) power structures, the European-modeled settler state is made to seem as if it promotes the seemingly natural course and order of life—and within the US Constitution the state is even justified with the "right to life." It is made to appear to promote the *course* of life through its reproduction of nuclear family socialization and its *order* through a hierarchized model of apparently given anthropocentric dominance.[16] This framework calls to mind Michel Foucault's terminology of biopower. The settler state's naturalizing "technology of power centered on life itself" enables it to exclusively proclaim unabrogated sovereignty over the territory and all forms of life that inhabit it.[17] All the while, this is made to appear not as an ongoing invasion, but as integral to the normal processes of living. The consolidation of settler-colonial power is then turned into a means through which the state fosters not only its own well-being but that of (settler) life itself.

Following these considerations, the volume seeks to address two central questions: How do biopolitical and geopolitical techniques produce these normativities? And how are these settler-colonial normativities, in turn, upheld and invisibilized through intersecting forces of bio- and geopolitical logics, discourses, and practices? In asking these questions, we are specifically interested in how they relate to each other, as this indicates to us how intimately settler bio- and geopolitics are related to each other and are used to affirm each other.

This volume seeks to push forth an understanding of the interplay of a biopolitical logic of racialization, regularization, and naturalization with a geopolitical logic of dispossession and removal as a dialectical dynamic within the eliminatory logics of settler colonialism.[18] Instead of advocating the priority of one theoretical framework over another, we ask how a biopolitical perspective can enhance, or complicate, a geopolitical analytic, and vice versa. How can a biopolitical perspective shed light on dispossession, expropriation, extraction, and removal as a set of geopolitical practices that are not only racialized but also targeted particularly in terms of gender, sexuality, age, ability, and so on? And how can a geopolitical perspective productively inform a biopolitical analytic of racialization, subjugation, and regularization by more closely calling attention to how land itself is not merely a place *on* which biopolitical measures take place and manifest? How does the perspective change if land is also viewed as a configuration (of thought, practice, sociality, embodiment) *through* which biopolitical techniques become effective, particularly in their attempt to disable Indigenous peoples' lived relationships to land?[19] Probing these questions is ultimately at the heart of this introduction and guides the contributions to the volume.

How, then, do bio- and geopolitical techniques work together to target Indigenous peoples in specific ways? An important part of answering this question lies in how norms are constructed that relate to both spheres. Many scholars have shown that biopolitical attempts to regulate Indigenous peoples—in the Chickasaw scholar Jodi Byrd's words, via "the technologies of biopolitics that have defined the twentieth and twenty-first centuries," including removal, assimilation, education, administration, genealogical politics, surveillance, and disciplinary regimes—subject those peoples to settler-colonial rule by depoliticizing them into a population subjected to control.[20] In refusing to acknowledge Indigenous nations as sovereign polities in their own right, biopolitical practices subsume them under an imaginary racialized population denominated variously, for instance, as "Indians," "*índios*," or "Aborigines." The invented groups under these monikers vary only slightly from one another in their perceived qualities, assumed to be innate, that serve to distinguish them categorically from the (white) settler as the rightful member of the body politic proper.[21] The intimate links between biopolitics and geopolitics operative in settler states come into full view when one reads Giorgio Agamben's "bare life" together with Mark Rifkin's concept of "bare habitance." In this way, the "state of exception" foundational for Western sovereignty as a practice of "inclusive exclusion" becomes productively connected to the geopolitical operations of subsuming Indigenous lands within seemingly self-evident settler-state territoriality.[22]

Notably, this state of exception is again integral to and productive of the settler-colonial norm. This is not meant to disavow how the principle of "inclusive exclusion," which the "state of exception" enables, continues to produce actual situations of emergency for Indigenous peoples, predominantly in the starkly unequal manner of how they are exposed to but remain largely unprotected by settler law. The widespread violence against Indigenous women perpetrated by mostly non-Indigenous men, regularly with impunity, sharply conveys this principle for the present moment. At the same time, this can only be fully understood, as Sarah Deer (Muscogee), Joanne Barker (Lenape), Mishuana Goeman (Tonawanda Band of Seneca), and others have shown, within the larger historical continuities of devaluing Indigenous lives and sexualizing Indigenous women.[23] In a self-replicating manner, every present instance of violence is embedded in these histories and helps to entrench them further within the settler-colonial present.[24]

However, to the dominant white settler society, the very same structures register as the norm. Therefore, any Indigenous challenge to the existing power structures of settler rule registers only as an aberration from said norm. Hence, this challenge needs to be denied or contained in what Elizabeth Povinelli has recently called a "cramped space of maneuver."[25] As the settler state assumes to exhibit the self-evident norm of sociopolitical organization that best enables modes of living and land use that are to reflect a natural order of life, any "Indigenous interruption" of this norm does not appear as political opposition from a positionality of the subaltern.[26] Instead, it is read and dismissed as a deviance from the modern-life-affirming norm, a deviance that deserves to be targeted and marked for elimination. Registering as nothing but an aberration, Indigenous life itself in its multiple forms—political and social, collective and individual, embodied and representational, spectacular and quotidian—is what is marked for risk, injury, and elimination through bio- and geopolitical techniques to affirm and reiterate settler-colonial normativities.

With these observations we want to draw attention to how the devaluation and disregard of Native polities and Native lives are interdependent within dominant settler societies—and how this operates simultaneously on a biopolitical and a geopolitical level. As the logics of hierarchization integral to the biopolitical mechanisms of the settler nation-state interlock, they deny on a geopolitical level Indigenous peoples the status of autonomous polities existing on lands that are only imagined as settler territory, because settlers have imagined Indigenous people as being incapable of properly inhabiting land. These logics quickly and "naturally" extend to denying Indigenous people the right to existence and to life *itself* within the political formation of the settler state. While this formation is constituted from the start as a violation of Indigenous rights, this violation is neutralized by translating it into the naturalized narrative of non-Indigenous progress.

In this regard, Indigenous death, on any scale, does not signal a moment to question the settler order; rather, it functions as a confirmation of its premise and objective—to the point that the Indigenous body becomes legible only as dead, either already dead or always dying.[27] What becomes clear when submitting instances—both collective and individual, macro and micro—of settler-colonial violence to a bio- and geopolitical critique is that positioning Indigenous peoples within an Agambenian state of exception to the sovereign rule of settler nation-states is not distinct from exposing Native bodies to settler violence with seeming impunity. Instead, such positioning reproduces, on an individual and bodily level, the logic through which Indigenous peoples are perceived as existing in a state of legal exception. On both levels, Native bodies are rendered as available to settlers' desires, needs, or force, without this enforcement being registered as a violation of rights of either the individual body or the body politic of Indigenous peoples in their entirety.

By the same token, Indigenous life in its cultural, social, political, and spiritual dimensions represents the antithesis to settler-state rule and exposes the normalized structures of the settler state as designed to uphold an anti-Indigenous status quo. We hope to show, then, through the contributions to this volume, that a focus on Indigenous lived presences—within as well as alongside and, especially, opposed to settler nation-state formations that operate through a set of geo- and biopolitical logics—is not just a means to render visible some of these forms of life and practices that are otherwise invisibilized. Instead, we also want to present it as a way to open avenues for thinking and imagining the denaturalization of settler-colonial rule, something we consider a theoretical tool in service of the decolonial struggle to dismantle the settler-colonial norm.

The volume tackles questions of bio- and geopolitical racialized dispossession by refocusing *life* as a relational and expansive term for the critique of settler-colonial conditions that centers Indigenous perspectives, epistemologies, and ontologies. *Life*, understood as such—intimately related to land, to ways of being in the world that constitute and signal Indigenous peoplehood and sovereignty, to the lived political existence of Indigenous nations in relation to other polities, including settler states—we view as an analytical instrument to capture ways that disrupt or exceed biopolitical management and geopolitical organization. Beyond that, *life* signals crucial junctures of land and body, the emplaced and the embodied, through which to trouble the clear demarcations of geopolitics and biopolitics. A reconfigured notion of life in these terms works to challenge the premises through which settler-colonial geo- and biopolitics operate and thus suggests alternative normativities that disrupt the logics through which they function.

Settler-Colonial Analytics, Bio/Geopolitics, and Multiple Trajectories of Study

To analyze how biopolitics and geopolitics operate in tandem for the workings of settler-colonial formations, this volume adopts a theoretical perspective on settler colonialism that is relational, flexible, and self-reflexive. Most important, we see analytical approaches to the phenomenon, structures, and logics of settler colonialism as proceeding from multiple points of departure and moving along specific trajectories.

One approach lies in the Australian historian Patrick Wolfe's directing of the anthropological gaze back in the late 1990s at how anthropologists and other non-Native scientists have constructed a racialized and culturalized "Aboriginality"—divorced from Indigenous peoples' understanding of themselves as independent, sovereign polities—in ways that replicate and partake in settler societies' attempts to eliminate and replace Native societies. The dictums through which Wolfe described these structural qualities of settler societies as distinct from other forms of colonialism—"the logic of elimination," "invasion is a structure not an event"—became a main source of citation and adaptation of his work, in some cases too easily standing in for any serious engagement with both a settler-colonial and Indigenous studies framework.[28]

Preceding Wolfe's work, as Shannon Speed (Chickasaw) and others have recently pointed out, the interrogation of settler societies undertaken by largely female scholars in *Unsettling Settler Societies: Articulations of Gender, Race, Ethnicity, and Class* (1995), edited by Daiva Stasiulis and Nira Yuval-Davis, figures as another point of departure for us that, in turn, sketches a different trajectory for a settler-colonial analytic that we practice in this volume.[29] As Stasiulis and Yuval-Davis emphasize their "resistance to drawing an unambiguous line of demarcation between settler and other (colonial, postcolonial, metropolitan) societies" and instead draw attention to how settler societies establish "systems of exclusion and exploitation of both 'indigenous' and 'alien' peoples within," they offer a sense of the entanglements between different colonial regimes as well as between differentiated forms of racialization within a settler state.[30]

While their work has not circulated as widely as Wolfe's, revisiting it may help us grasp recent debates on the intersections of settler colonialism, empire, and race not only as critiquing a Wolfean approach to settler colonialism that more strongly emphasizes elements of distinction and binary relations but also as reasserting other trajectories of settler-colonial analytics, which we also want to exemplify in this volume.

This volume also engages with the long-standing, robust, and ever expanding work of Indigenous studies that straddles multiple disciplines. (Critical) Indigenous studies are clearly indispensable for a settler-colonial analytic in that they make conditions of ongoing (settler) colonial relations visible by centering Indigeneity as a sociopolitical category and a lived experientiality that contests heteropatriarchal, capitalist, extractivist structures endemic to settler-colonial realities. Indigenous studies thus bring to the fore a continuously emerging and evolving understanding of Indigenous-centered sovereignty and self-determination, including the prospect and potential of decolonization.[31]

A bio/geopolitical analysis of settler colonialism necessarily engages related forms of oppression. For example, Black and anti-imperial scholars have demonstrated the insufficiency of a rigid settler-Native binary to account for slavery and forms of forced migration and thereby worked strongly in revising and expanding a settler-colonial analytic. Offering insights that resonate with Stasiulis and Yuval-Davis's approach in *Unsettling Settler Societies*, these theorizations by Iyko Day, Manu Karuka (Vimalassery), Tiffany Lethabo King, and others pursue a better understanding of how settler states operate through their own, specific racialized regimes and are embedded within imperial assemblages that extend beyond the territory marked, and masked, as domestic.[32] In this sense, we see this volume's focus on the interconnectedness of bio- and geopolitics as offering one path to pursue what Alyosha Goldstein, Manu Karuka (Vimalassery), and Juliana Hu Pegues have recently termed "relations of study."[33]

Conceiving of Indigeneity within the biopolitically racialized, gendered, and sexualized regimes of settler states, this volume also seeks to open modes of inquiry toward other regimes of racialization and differently defined modes of subjection orchestrated through the same state. While Black, Indigenous, and other bodies that are excluded from the white settler biopolitical body may be subjected to what Wolfe has called "different regimes of race," these regimes clearly are not unrelated.[34] We maintain that if, in North American contexts, the Indigenous body is pathologized, abnormalized, and criminalized differently from the Black body, these techniques still share the same premise and aim. They seek to define an unmarked body as the universalized representative of a population that deserves to be nourished, fostered, and protected for the health of the nation while at the same time denying that this body's whiteness (and hetero cis-maleness) is the determining factor for its privileged position within the racialized state as the unmarked, universalized qualifier of "the people" as such.

These forms of settler-colonial racialization can be observed in other contexts, as well. Indigenous bodies in Australia codified as "Black" are confronted even more directly with what Moreton-Robinson has recently described as the "white possessive" of the settler state. And in Latin America, Indigenous bodies are to blend into the biopolitical regime of *mestizaje* as another form of Indigenous disappearance. In both cases, whiteness—even if only imagined or projected as a common Europeanness in origin or as a marker specifying degrees of national belonging—still remains a central reference point for what counts as the rightful population of the settler state and can be universalized as the qualifier of the fully human.[35] In this sense, Sylvia Wynter's theorization of "Man-as-Human" remains an important touchstone for us as it captures the main biopolitical current that traverses globally connected yet differentiated settler-state regimes.[36]

Wynter's notion of "Man-as-Human" brings to the fore how regimes of particularized subjection biopolitically produce the seemingly unmarked hetero-masculine white body as the definition of the universalized human. King then draws on Wynter, as well as on Hortense Spillers and Alexander Weheliye, to point out that dehumanizing the Native body by targeting it for extermination and the Black body by turning it into property, unmaking it through "parasitic and genocidal violence," is primarily done "in order for the white human to self-actualize."[37] In similar terms, Sherene Razack argues: "Viewed as abject bodies always on the brink of death, Indigenous people can be imagined as less than human, a dehumanization that gives birth to the settler as fully human."[38] Widening the geographical focus, Lisa Lowe, in her analysis of "the intimacies of four continents," also identifies how "the placement of peoples at various distances from liberal humanity" leads to "colonial divisions of humanity," which are not aberrations to but "integral parts of the genealogy of modern liberalism."[39]

For our volume, we seek to investigate these "colonial divisions of humanity" not as an addition to but as the defining starting point of a biopolitical inquiry. Arguably, the "genealogy of modern liberalism" Lowe describes is at the heart of a critical Foucauldian tradition of biopolitical thought, yet the sites from which to appraise the "colonial divisions of humanity" appear only as an afterthought in Foucault's analysis. Thus, a biopolitical approach that centers the varying and intersecting colonial contexts in which differently racialized peoples are not assigned a fully human status requires a critique of the orthodox biopolitical framework itself. What are the analytical consequences when foregrounding the otherwise marginalized or simply "added" sites as the decisive moments of modern biopolitical formation instead, and what new analytical vocabularies might need to be developed? To engage these questions and their significance for the work this volume sets out to do, we turn to Weheliye, who observes that Wynter's and Spillers's theorization of the "violently tiered categorization of the human species in western modernity" opens new insight as it proceeds "without denoting race and gender to the rank of the ethnographically particular, instead exposing how these categories carve from the swamps of slavery and colonialism the very flesh and bones of modern Man."[40]

In the first instance, Weheliye's project in *Habeas Viscus* focuses on the significance of Black studies for the figuration of humanity. Still, just as he points to the link between "slavery and colonialism," his vision of a liberation points to, following Wynter, the understanding of the "figure of Man as a racializing assemblage" and, beyond that, to "the terrain of humanity as a relational assemblage."[41] Weheliye displaces Man's universalization as human and indicates the relational itself as integral to the figure of the human. In this way, his project of Black liberation gestures beyond the notion of a liberal humanism, in which everyone is equally human and in which rights can be easily ascertained with reference to a human rights framework that functions by insisting on the same statist framework.[42] Instead, his project ultimately points more broadly toward the biopolitical mechanisms of the racialized settler state and the possibility of dismantling it. It holds a potential of liberation for differentially racialized peoples in the settler state, and thus for Black freedom and decolonial struggles alike. Arguably, the potential for the latter remains largely implicit, just as the link between slavery and colonialism is not fully argumentatively realized. However, we want to emphasize for the purposes of this volume that his work opens the space to activate this potential for the biopolitical rethinking of the human in and beyond geopolitical white settler contexts. The "violent conflation" of white heteromasculinity ("Man") with humanity—producing a status quo of Man as human inscribed in the legal framework of the racial settler state itself—has targeted African-descended and Indigenous peoples differently, yet relatedly, as marked for enslavement and elimination.[43]

From this vantage point, Weheliye's work opens a possibility to refuse the "colonial divisions of humanity" with the insistence "that Man's juridical machine can never exhaust the plentitude of the world."[44] If we thus read the critique of the colonial state within Weheliye's indictment of the racializing regime, it shows how the "plentitude of the world" can be made to bear on the project of liberation itself. *Habeas Viscus*'s emphasis on the necessity to unmake and radically reconfigure the racial regimes and colonial divisions of human-ness speaks to the shared space in which the varied struggles against the differentially racialized regimes of settler states—which includes but should not conflate Indigenous-centered decolonial struggles and Black freedom struggles—take place. Crucially, they need to take place together for possibilities of (political) sustained life resistant to white settler regimes to emerge.

With the idea of a shared space in mind, this volume seeks to understand differently inflected biopolitical regimes together with geopolitical imaginaries to address how Indigenous dispossessed lands are connected to other subaltern geographies. What Katherine McKittrick has called "black geographies"—particularly the geographies of Black women, on lands already marked by Indigenous dispossession—we see as an opportunity for thinking "Black resistance" through land that is in alliance with and in support of Indigenous anticolonial struggles rather than deferring or subsuming them.[45] McKittrick's objective to "make visible social lives which are often displaced, rendered ungeographic" speaks to how invaded spaces, defined by settler norms, are continuously whitened.[46] In addition, her work calls attention to how the processes that render some geographies legible and legally binding, and that render some lives "geographic" via their privileged position within these imaginaries, legitimizes exclusive white settler belonging on these lands in the first place. Her analysis offers a path, then, which we seek to further lay out in this volume, of thinking through the possibility of multiple geographies that struggle against the monolithic geopolitics of the white settler state—in her case, the United States—while countering the erasure of Indigenous forms of belonging to the land. Conversely, as Simpson outlines in *As We Have Always Done*, thinking McKittrick's theorization of "black geographies" together with struggles for Indigenous sovereignty can pave ways to address her question: "How am I accountable to the struggle of Black peoples . . . within the context of Nishnaabeg political and ethical systems?"[47] For Simpson, this accountability might manifest in an understanding of land-based governance that does not demand exclusive control over territory but, rather, allows for the possibility that access to it, as well as meeting obligations and responsibilities toward it, can be defined through relationships of sharing: "Within Nishnaabeg political thought, we have practices of sharing space with other nations and communities of peoples and respecting their autonomy to govern themselves over those lands."[48]

McKittrick and Simpson thus formulate potential ways of thinking beyond settler geopolitical regimes through figures of multiple political geographies in which land becomes a site of relation for coexistent forms of governance.

While this outlines the conditions for a thriving Indigenous (political) life, our volume also bears in mind the work of María Josefina Saldaña-Portillo, which sheds light on how the very geopolitical construction of specific settler states' borders, by contrast, relies on and reinforces differently imagined biopolitical "racial geographies," artificially separating Indigenous people of the same region.[49] More specifically, the construction of Indigenous people into the distinct racialized categories of "Indians" and "*índios*" serves to reinforce and naturalize the artificial border between the two settler states of the United States and Mexico.[50] Caught in racial imaginaries, the border both constitutes and divides the geopolitical entities of North America and Latin America as well as, arguably, the economic constructs known as the Global North and Global South. The border of the settler imaginary thus becomes a site through which the North seeks to protect its privilege, strongly configured through whiteness, and disavow its responsibilities in producing globally unjust structures. This, in turn, exposes Indigenous people on both sides of the settler-imposed border to increased vulnerability, as racialized Indigenous minority or racialized migrant population, or both. The ways in which the different imaginaries of race affect Indigenous peoples in bio- and geopolitical terms can be seen, for example, in how Mexican Indigenous communities are absorbed into a *mestizaje* nationalism while their counterparts in the United States are racialized as minorities, underlining a settler norm that is directly defined through whiteness.[51] Shona Jackson's *Creole Indigeneity* further illuminates how geopolitical internationalist relations are tied to the biopolitical production of Indigenous peoples within the racial imaginaries of settler states. Jackson's important theorization of how a subaltern nation-state such as Guyana appropriates Indigeneity as a means of national emancipation for the creolized population is work that she continues in this volume.[52]

Neoliberalism, Extractivism, and Defending Indigenous Life

To think beyond the biopolitics and geopolitics of race within settler states, we need a linked theorization of biopolitics and geopolitics that considers how life itself is valued (or discounted) within the exploitative and extractivist settler structures toward people and the land. What, then, would it mean to think about the late Lauren Berlant's notion of "slow death" and Rob Nixon's concept of "slow violence" alongside and in dialogue with each other when viewed as conditions of life under settler colonialism?[53] While the work of both does not engage directly with questions of Indigeneity, it does speak to the simultaneous pervasiveness and invisibility of settler colonialism as well as to the routine practices of Native erasure. The question that drives this critical dialogue is, then, not how these concepts outside of Indigenous studies can add to the field but, rather, how this scholarship is itself changed when viewed from the perspective of Indigenous studies.

Both Berlant's and Nixon's decelerated vocabulary of the gradual, incremental, and accretive speaks to how settler social structures are configured as stretched across time in a way that makes the condition of attrition and erosion for Indigenous peoples, directly affecting lands and bodies, appear to be woven into the temporal fabric itself, effectively closing off any alternative future possibility. "Slowness," then, offers a way to consider the simultaneous deprivation of Indigenous lands and bodies as a self-perpetuating structure that not only aims for the elimination of the Native (in Wolfe's terminology) but also employs bio- and geopolitical techniques for "settler time" to function as the erasure of futurities thought otherwise.[54]

Berlant states: "The phrase slow death refers to the physical wearing out of a population in a way that points to its deterioration as a defining condition of its experience and historical existence."[55] While Berlant's primary target is a neoliberal paradigm of self-optimization, we want to ask what new insights can be gained by considering through their writing intersecting (neo)liberal and settler-colonial logics. Under which conditions and to which end does this "deterioration" occur? And how is value-determining capital linked to the ongoing settler capitalization of Indigenous lands, bodies, and lives?

Asking these questions invites us to consider "deterioration" not so much as a "defining condition" for Indigenous peoples. Instead, it appears as a condition through which they become defined from the outside to provide and constantly secure the condition of possibility for the liberal settler state. The state may no longer actively or publicly encourage the killing of Indigenous peoples so as not to trouble its own democratic rights-based order. Yet providing evidence of the "deterioration" of Indigenous peoples as their "defining condition" clearly serves as a means to secure and foster what the Kahnawà:ke Mohawk theorist Audra Simpson has termed "the life of the state," a life imagined as everlasting and ever in the need of resources grabbed from Indigenous lands and lives.[56]

An investment in the belief of Indigenous "deterioration" fosters a pervasive sense of settler indifference to them, even in contexts couched in the benevolent terms of (neo)liberal care. For example, in investigating state responses to health-care emergencies among the Inuit in Canada, Lisa Stevenson has observed how "forms of care" administered by the settler welfare state remain indifferent to the specific Indigenous peoples cared for, an indifference that is accompanied by a sense of expectancy of their death. In response to the high rates of suicide among the Inuit, Stevenson contends that, within "the forms of anonymous care in the colonial/postcolonial context . . . , caregivers exhort Inuit to live while simultaneously expecting them to die."[57] She goes on: "Such forms of bureaucratic care, while working to maintain the physical life of Inuit *qua* Canadian citizens, may also manifest a form of indifference on part of the state—an indifference that is sometimes perceived by Inuit as murderous."[58] Inuit may perceive that indifference as murderous because it surfaces also in contexts that are less benevolent. In this case, that indifference manifests in the settler administration of care: caring for the continuity of Inuit life as such while not caring exactly *who* lives and *how* one continues to live under situations of colonialism, and not necessarily expecting Inuit to keep on living. Yet the same indifference and expectancy of Indigenous death through their "deterioration" takes on the form of neglect and aggression in different instances, maybe most notably in the long-lasting neglect by the Canadian state (and by the United States) of the large number of missing and murdered Indigenous women and girls.[59] While this neglect is once more bureaucratically regulated under the current Canadian government through the conduct of an official inquiry leading to Indigenous charges of race-based genocide, the same indifferent neglect, coupled with an aggressive attitude toward the victims of such violence, continues to manifest itself in the rulings of the court cases on the killings of Colten Boushie and Tina Fontaine in the spring of 2018.

In the cases of both Boushie and Fontaine, one might say that the slow death through settler colonialism—the conditions that make Indigenous bodies vulnerable to settler violence—accelerated rapidly to produce their sudden and violent deaths at the hands of settlers. However, in the widespread settler-colonial perception, the deeper causes lie not in a continuing historical system of social injustice, but in the "deterioration" as the defining condition of the teenagers' lives that make their violent deaths appear inevitable and as happening unavoidably. In this view, they merely occur, either by accident (in the defense of Gerald Stanley) or at the hands of any other man Tina Fontaine could have encountered (in the defense of Raymond Cormier). Both rationalizations make it possible to absolve the perpetrators of responsibility for Boushie's and Fontaine's deaths. With both cases resulting in acquittals, the deaths of Indigenous youth—purportedly brought about by a life inviting danger (Fontaine) or by posing an assumed danger to settler life (Boushie)—are both expected and indifferently accepted. Regarded as non-resourceful lives without benefits to the liberal settler state, neither Boushie nor Fontaine is assigned enough value for their families to receive justice for their violent deaths in settler courts. In this case, Berlant's idea of "cruel optimism" might mean to still expect "reconciliation" to move forward when being confronted with a situation in which justice and the value of Indigenous life is continually and habitually being denied.

When we move from the biopolitical administration of Indigenous life and death to the geopolitical use of land, rethinking Berlant's notion of "deterioration" as the defining settler perception of Indigenous life also shows how settler accumulation through excavating and exploiting Indigenous resources of life, most often tied to the land itself, can be justified. What is deteriorating can be improved only by settler intervention, whether Indigenous life through the administration of care or other state interventions or Indigenous land through construction or extraction.[60] In this way, monetary value is generated from the land, regularly with life-diminishing results for Indigenous peoples and lands, causing what Razack has called "dying from improvement."[61]

The "attrition of subjects" in Berlant's thought, then, connects to "attritional violence," which for Nixon is a decisive aspect of slow violence.[62] His concept of slow violence is clearly geopolitically oriented in the way it seeks to account for "slowly unfolding environmental catastrophes" that are characterized by "a violence of delayed destruction that is dispersed across time and space."[63] We want to highlight his thought, as we find it helpful for thinking of land-oriented settler temporalities alongside bodily slow death. This is specifically the case since settler colonialism clearly offers itself for analysis as an ongoing history structured through "slowly unfolding environmental catastrophes," along with moments that intensify these particular forms of violence (toward the land as well as toward the human and other-than-human forms of being that inhabit it).

The centrality of environmental catastrophe to the Indigenous experience of settler colonization also makes environmental justice a key Indigenous issue. At the same time, as Dana Gilio-Whitaker (Colville Confederated Tribes) points out, environmental justice needs to be rethought for the situation of Indigenous peoples so that it takes into account issues of sovereignty, acknowledges the "colonial condition," and frames "decolonization as a potential framework within which environmental justice can be made available."[64]

The "colonial condition" assumes the irreversibility of these catastrophes, thereby creating the conditions for slow death that structure Indigenous life under settler rule, a condition that functions precisely by foreclosing all futurities imagined otherwise. Kristen Simmons has written of "settler atmospherics" that stifle the very breath of Indigenous people struggling under these conditions—conditions that are ubiquitous and in which the air itself can be weaponized against Indigenous peoples in moments of intensified state violence. Simmons's notion that "breathing in a settler atmosphere is taxing," commenting on the violent militarized response with tear gas and pepper spray to the water protection at Standing Rock, also helps us to make sense of the large number of Inuit suicides dealt with only through a care of indifference and the poisonous effects of air pollution through extraction industries, such as the toxic clouds emitted by oil sand production to which Indigenous communities are disproportionately exposed.[65]

How slow violence is an indicator of and contributor to the quotidian attrition of subjects being exposed to slow death becomes visible in the varied forms of extractive capitalism that operate on Indigenous lands. These include mineral mining, oil drilling, and as Macarena Gómez-Barris states, other "technologies that mark out regions of 'high biodiversity' in order to reduce life to capitalist resource conversion."[66] Indigenous lands are recoded as part of what Gómez-Barris terms the "extractive zone," in which the forms of life it harbors are targeted for profit. While "Indigenous peoples often multiply rather than reduce life possibilities" in these regions, they are still marked not only by deterioration but also by expendability.[67] Disposability comes to define settler conceptions of Indigeneity. Overall, this places the "destructive path that is extractive capitalism" close to the possible destination of "wastelanding," which Traci Brynne Voyles analyzes with reference to the history of uranium mining in Navajo country.[68]

It is only when settler-colonial attacks on Indigenous lands and bodies are intensified that non-Indigenous publics pay attention to them and to the direct Indigenous response and resistance. Oftentimes, though, such settler-colonial attacks and forms of Indigenous resistance are read merely through environmentalism, ignoring how they are embedded in wider and long-lasting forms of violence. Beyond that, highly visible movements to protect Indigenous life and defend Indigenous lands and waters should not detract from a long history of geographically widespread, diversified, and often less publicized struggles. Gómez-Barris reminds us: "The Sioux and trans-confederation struggle contesting the Dakota pipeline is only one example of continual Indigenous land defense in the Américas," which always entails a defense of the Indigenous rights to this land.[69] In this sense, it is not sufficient to think of these as environmental causes that are distinct from Native struggles for decolonization. Instead, we want to emphasize for the work of this volume how Indigenous dispossession functions as the condition of possibility for practices and discourses that exploit and violate the land. Understood in bio- and geopolitical terms, the extractive zone continues to be vital to settler-colonial structures that capitalize on Indigenous bodies, lands, and lives.

What the struggles against these structures hold in common is how they counter the seeping of slow violence and slow death into the lands and bodies of Indigenous peoples. In doing so, they center a different temporality of continuities; emphasize enduring relationships to the land reactivated through collective practices, activism, and ceremony; and rearticulate a sense of continual resurgence. Disrupting any conventional self-perpetuating and self-complacent settler fantasy of changelessness as a given in its habituated perpetration of slow violence, such a sense of resurgence calls back to earlier moments of anticolonial struggles and looks toward different possible futurities. Specifically, it highlights the potential of an Indigenous and decolonized futurity rooted in "the invisible, the inanimate, and the non-human forms that creatively reside as afterlives of the colonial encounter," as Gómez-Barris puts it, all the while pointing to the political significance of Indigenous-centered epistemologies that conceives of all forms of life and being in relationality.[70]

Land, Water, and Indigenous Normativities of Political Life

"Land is life," posits Patrick Wolfe in his essay "Settler Colonialism and the Elimination of the Native" (2006). Notably, he modifies his own statement immediately by adding, "at least, land is necessary for life," from which follows that "contests for land can be—indeed, often are—contests for life."[71] From his initial statement, Wolfe develops the premise that settler colonialism's focus on "territoriality" as its "irreducible element" is inevitably genocidal, as well.[72] The theft of land equals, and is regularly accompanied by, the taking of lives. In his formulation, then, "land is life" or is "necessary for life" functions through how he defines its negation. Having no land, or being dispossessed of land equals death, and orchestrated acts of dispossession constitute genocidal practices.[73]

If we approach the statement from a perspective that centers Indigenous epistemologies, however, it resonates in quite a different manner in addition to indexing the genocidal impetus of dispossession. This becomes clear when we read it alongside *mni wiconi*, Lakota for "water is life," the central call of the water protectors at Standing Rock. This call was taken up on many different occasions and at many different locations to show solidarity. Yet the levels of meaning that were more readily evoked, especially connected to a non-Indigenous environmentalism, could be quite comfortably translated to, or integrated within, a liberal-humanist framework, possibly more so than the parallel statement "land is life." *Mni wiconi* tended to be read, then, as "water is the source of life" or "without water there is (literally) no life."

Within these accounts, however, the "life" of "land" and "water" appears immediately and solely in service of human and nonhuman populations. It seems, then, that the "life" that land and water embody is meaningful only to the degree that both are a source of life and a necessity for life for other beings—humans, other-than-human animals, plants—who are in need of their life-giving qualities. In that sense, the "life" of land and water always registers as secondary to the forms of life that need to be nourished by it.

Indigenous scholars discussing the movement at Standing Rock and what Melanie K. Yazzie (Diné) and Cutcha Rising Baldy (Hupa, Yurok, Karuk) call "the politics of water," though, make clear that *mni wiconi* is not that easily reducible.[74] They assert instead an expansive view of nonhuman life and relations that has epistemological and political dimensions. Nick Estes (Lower Brule Sioux) states that *mni wiconi* "is also an affirmation that water is alive" and that Mnisose—the Missouri River, which the resistance to the Dakota Access Pipeline sought to protect—is best understood as a "nonhuman relative, who is alive, and who is also of the Mni Oyate, the Water Nation."[75] Relatedly, Craig Howe (Oglala Sioux) describes Mnisose as a "living being" and frames the resistance at Standing Rock in terms of relationality: "Standing Rock is where the people are gathered to protect their relative right now."[76] Extending this thought, but also emphasizing water's own autonomy, Edward Valandra (Oceti Sakowin Oyate/Sicangu Titunwan) writes: "We . . . recognize water as having personhood, independent of humans 'giving' that standing or status."[77] For Yazzie and Baldy, this notion of water's autonomy is coupled with a focus on "water view," the perspective that water itself has on the world, which ultimately not only highlights water's agency but also puts a demand on human action in relation to water: "Our theoretical standpoint is one that foregrounds *water view*, (re)claiming knowledges not just for the people, but also for the water; not just looking at our relationship to water, but our accountability to water view."[78]

When taking these water views from Indigenous scholars into account, it appears that *mni wiconi* (water is life) and "land is life" do not so much assert that life is equal to water and land or that land and water are important for the continuation of life. Instead, they articulate the dynamic forms of existence, the ways of being in the world that inhere to land and water in themselves as being meaningful in their own right, not solely because they nourish other forms of life. This shift entails viewing how water extends beyond itself toward nonhuman and human bodies without reducing this to a resource that functions in support of a body's life. Instead, it can be appreciated as a form of communal interaction between humans and what Zoe Todd (Métis/otipemisiw) has called their "watery kin."[79] Furthermore, it points to a means of establishing, manifesting, and affirming relations among all forms of being that makes present a structure of kinship crucial to the social and political life of Indigenous communities.

In these readings of *mni wiconi*, what is at stake is more than the ascription of life and agency to an entity that is, in non-Native epistemologies, largely regarded as inanimate. For merely expanding the definitions of what is alive beyond the more conventional parameters always allows the possibility of redrawing the border between life and nonlife at another moment, thus simply reproducing the system that *mni wiconi* challenges. In that sense, the force of *mni wiconi* might not come so much from an expanded definition of life as from a refusal to accept the rules of a system of governance that operates by insisting on the division of what it regards as life and nonlife. The Australian scholar Elizabeth Povinelli has recently analyzed this system—in analogy to biopower—as "geontopower," which she specifies as "the management of existents through the separation of that which has and is imbued with the dynamics of life (birth, growth, finitude, agency, intentionality, self-authored, or at least change) and that which settler liberalism treats as absolutely not."[80]

In *Geontologies: A Requiem to Late Liberalism*, Povinelli investigates six "forms of existence often referred to as Dreaming or totemic formations" for whose maintenance her "Indigenous friends and colleagues" of the social collective Karrabing in the Northern Territory of Australia struggle "within a cramped space of maneuver."[81] In accordance with her definition of *geontopower*, she asks how these forms of existence could "have standing before the public, law, and market as a political subject."[82] Ultimately, this question does not depend so much on extending the parameters of life to include, as Povinelli puts it, these "existents" within it. For her, such a move would confine the existents and Indigenous people engaged with them "to the imaginary of the Animist, a form that has been made compatible with liberal states and markets."[83]

According to Povinelli, the figuration of the "Animist" is one of liberal recognition in which "Indigenous people agree to participate as an Animist voice in the governmental order of the people."[84] Instead of challenging the order of "late liberal approaches to geontology," such a measure allows settlers to remain comfortable in that order by affirming their assumption that Indigenous people have "a cultural belief about things rather than a probing analytics of their existence."[85] Accordingly, opening the political discourses and spaces for nonlife forms of existence does not mean to assert their liveliness and include them within a "biontology."[86] Instead, it means to register them as "geontological, meteorontological, econtological statements [that] refuse to abide by any fundamental difference between Life and Nonlife."[87] Through this mode of refusal Povinelli unmasks how "the division of Life and Nonlife as a division of givenness" is itself the crucial sovereign act of late liberal settler governance.[88] This act seeks to confine Indigenous people to the "social tense" of the "primitive" in that their "cultural belief" appears as an anachronistic aberration to this norm of "givenness." By presenting a state of "givenness" that manifests in the "division of Life and Nonlife" as something that is installed through a sovereign act instead of being merely described in a neutral assessment of what self-evidently *is*, though, Povinelli raises another issue—namely, she poses the question of what it means not to make transparent the political reasoning of establishing such a division, especially by acting as if there was no such political reasoning in the first place.[89] Asking this question becomes particularly salient in the current moment when "the self-evident distinction of Life and Nonlife" is "crumbling" under the "conceptual impact" of the Anthropocene.[90]

The call *mni wiconi* (and Wolfe's offering that land is life) draws our attention to how settler governance over bodies of water as nonlife, objects for use, and resources to be exploited is already premised on and constructs a seemingly "self-evident distinction" into *bios* and *geos* as relevant separate categories of governing difference. As a form of colonial violence in and of itself, this distinction produces a "cramped space of maneuver" as the defining condition for all ensuing struggles of Indigenous people and the existents they care for and maintain to "*manifest and endure* in contemporary settler late liberalism."[91]

What does it mean, then, to assess the colonial violence of this division as the point of departure for any settler geo- and biopolitical analytics going forward? In "Indigenizing Agamben," Rifkin influentially and importantly argues that "the biopolitical project of defining the proper 'body' of the people is subtended by the geopolitical project of defining the territoriality of the nation," emphasizing the geopolitical quality of the state of exception to which Indigenous peoples are exposed.[92] Yet by analytically connecting settler biopolitical to geopolitical rule and ultimately stating that the latter has primacy over the former, he still suggests that the distinction between geo- and biopolitical rule can be meaningfully construed, even if only for analytical purposes. His argument implies that the means through which these specific forms of governance, bio- and geopolitical, are employed are decisive for indicating particular forms of settler-colonial governance, not that their operation is premised on having produced this distinction itself.

The question, then, is whether an analysis of settler-colonial bio- and geopolitics as distinct, yet related, modes of settler governance reproduces, necessarily and inevitably, on an analytic level "the division of Life [bios, zoe] and Nonlife [geos] as the division of givenness" that Povinelli critiques as a sovereign act of settler governance itself. In this sense, the division of bios and geos becomes a lens through which to interrogate settler-colonial operations (particularly in the way they exceed an Agambenian biopolitical framework) instead of being viewed as a settler-colonial operation in itself. This division itself is thus not viewed as a fundamental sovereign act that discounts Indigenous analytics of (political) existence and casts settler-colonial impositions on this analytic as an assertion of what is always already a condition of "givenness." If that is the case, however, what would an analytic look like that refuses this violent reproduction of division between life and nonlife while not, at the same time, reproducing the liberal recognition of animism as "cultural belief"? And what role could the call *mni wiconi* play, if not necessarily in formulating that analytic, yet still in orienting the theoretical parameters toward it?

When one reconsiders Povinelli's analysis of geontopower in this respect, her work does not so much suggest new ways to connect a bio- and geopolitical analytics through a focus on late liberal settler governance as offer a shift in the parameters of inclusion and exclusion central to all biopolitical inquiries from life and death to life and nonlife. She thereby draws attention to how a definition of population and of territory as distinct entities to be governed—without accounting for all forms of existence that inhabit and make up the land that contribute to Indigenous forms of place-based sociality—shows this form of governance to be fundamentally premised on disregarding Indigenous people's "analytics of their existence."[93] This disregard includes willingly ignoring the impact these analytics exercise on what constitutes societies and polities for Indigenous peoples. So settler forms of governance violently impose, affirm, and institutionalize this disregard while simultaneously insisting on its self-evident quality.

Instead of asking how we might define such Indigenous analytics of being across the constructed divisions of life and nonlife, it might be more useful to consider the forms of being settler-colonial impositions target when they seek to establish and perpetuate their own "givenness." Goeman's analysis of settler colonialism as a gendered spatial violence is helpful in this regard, as she writes: "Colonialism is not just about conquering Native lands through mapping new ownerships, but it is also about the conquest of bodies," so that "the making of Indian land into territory required a colonial restructuring of spaces at a variety of scales," including "Native bodies" themselves.[94] What emerges from this scalar analysis is, then, not so much a division of bios and geos as a continuum of spatial relationships that extends across Native lands and bodies in interaction. Through measures of "colonial restructuring of spaces," which include "abstracting lands and bodies into territories and citizens," this continuum of relationships is also targeted as such.[95] Moving from relationships to abstractions thereby instantiates the division that is to enable clear-cut geo- and biopolitical techniques to be known as the norm of governance.

Importantly, Indigenous political theory and practice contest just such a norm. What Povinelli terms an "antinormative normativity" that could emerge from an engagement with formations "refusing to abide by any fundamental difference between Life and Nonlife" resonates with Coulthard's concept of "grounded normativity."[96] He characterizes grounded normativity as "living our lives in relation to one another and our surroundings in a respectful, nondominating, and nonexploitative way."[97] He elaborates: "Within this system of relations human beings are not the only constituent believed to embody spirit or agency. Ethically, this means that humans held certain obligations to the land, animals, plants, and lakes in much the same way that we hold obligations to other people."[98] Likewise, Jeannette Armstrong (Syilx Okanagan) and Richard Atleo (Nuu-chah-nulth) show that North West Coast land ethics are based on the notion that humans, animals, plants, and land coequally and interdependently form a life force together; that resources are "shared" according to certain "contracts" and protocols; and that such knowledge is contained in seminal oral accounts.[99]

What marks land as life and water as life, then, might not be so much an ascription of biologically defined lifelike qualities to entities that follow different patterns of being and becoming. In this case, it would reaffirm the premise of a division of bio and geos on which settler-colonial bio- and geopolitics ultimately rest rather than tracing ways, as this volume is interested in, of disrupting or running counter to such a premise. Instead, calling water and land life might be best captured as a naming of the obligations, commitments, reciprocal arrangements, and mutual attachments or affections that constitute lived relationships and relational modes of living between certain forms of human life and other-than-human lives as well as between specific bodies of land and water and other formations of nonlife that are constitutive of, integral to, and interwoven in the social fabric and political life of community and peoplehood.

While Coulthard talks about "grounded normativity" in general terms, he speaks clearly from a Yellowknives Dene perspective; the "land, animals, plants, and lakes" also need to be reflected in their specificity and specific relevance for Yellowknives Dene communities. In that sense, *mni wiconi* as a statement in Lakota (rather than in English) has significance that exceeds the more general connotation of water being life. Resisting the "power of abstracting land and bodies," as Goeman puts it, into neatly divided categories means to attend to the specific relationships Indigenous people engage with particular bodies of land and water in the mutual and shared making of social and political life in a specific place. The particular instances of commitment, maintaining, and caring that define the relationships—as between the Byulen and their Dreaming, which move through Povinelli's *Geontologies*—might then form the ground from which a specific kind of normativity can be articulated. Fundamentally, the very act of biopolitically defining and regulating a people as a solely human population, simply happening to exist on a specific piece of land with given environmental characteristics, already attacks the principle of Indigenous place-based relational peoplehood in that it silently excludes, as Todd states, "land, water, plants, animals and other more-than-human beings *as political agents* in their own right."[100]

Mni wiconi, read in this way, is not a means to communicate Indigenous causes to a broader non-Native public. More to the point, it articulates Indigenous resistance, resurgence, and refusal that is grounded within the normativities of distinct Indigenous conceptions of political formations defined by a specifically place-based relationality. It is not so much an act of resistance that falls into any of the categories—such as environmental protection or cultural preservation—through which Indigenous struggles are largely made legible and relatable to non-Native contexts as an act of refusal that is oriented toward the decolonial imperative of a relational politics. Such a politics seeks to exceed the confines set by each parameter of knowing and governing Indigenous difference by foregrounding the principle of relationality as a mode of refusal. As Simpson argues, "'Refusal' rather than recognition is an option for producing and maintaining alternative structures of thought, politics and traditions away from and in critical relationship to states."[101] She goes on: "'Refusal' holds on to a truth, structures this truth as stance."[102] Reading the relational politics of Indigenous sociality as a mode of refusal points to the "alternative structures of thought, politics, and traditions" and the "truth as stance" brought forth as a denaturalizing force to the settler politics of division (into bios and geos) and the resultant governing of difference. Insisting on the "truth" of Indigenous political life structured through all forms of existence—including what is categorized as human and nonhuman, life and nonlife—as dynamic positions of kinship unearths or activates anew alternative structures of the polity that remain irreducible to settler terms of liberal recognition.[103] They turn Leanne Betasamosake Simpson's descriptions of precolonial treaty relationships between human and nonhuman nations into a challenge to the state by tracing the political orders beyond it: "Animal clans were highly respected and were seen as self-determining, political 'nations' (at least in an Indigenous sense) with whom the Nishnaabegs had negotiated ritualized, formal relationships that required maintenance through an ongoing relationship."[104]

With this, the claim, assertion, act of refusal, and call to resurgence of *mni wiconi* cuts through settler-colonial techniques of bio- and geopolitical rule by exposing their fictitious divisions as part of the work of dividing Indigenous claims to political life, claims that remain irreducible to the imaginaries inscribed within the legal frameworks of settler states. *Mni wiconi* disrupts these modes of colonial division in that it insists on a political epistemology of relationalities that contains a decolonial imperative. In this understanding, Mnisose, the Missouri River, does not just constitute an object or part of a national geography (Indigenous or non-Indigenous) or a point of reference for the resistance to state power. Instead, it marks a form of political life that exists not merely within the settler state but also alongside it, beyond it, and in opposition to it. Engaged, in Audra Simpson's words, in a "critical relationship to the state" in which it refuses to be absorbed by modes of settler rule, such life is embodied and emplaced within a position that holds on to "a truth" and is "a stance" opening up new political possibilities.

Attending to Indigenous Lands, Lives, and Bodies across Settler States

Within this volume, the analysis of settler-colonial formations extends across the hemisphere of the Americas and via the Pacific to noncontinental territories claimed by the United States, exemplified by Hawai'i, as well as to Australia and Aotearoa/New Zealand. In offering such an expansive perspective on the geographies of settler colonialism, we seek to comprehend it as it appears in its various forms, not just as a singularly defined project. We do not want to normalize rhetoric that sees some settler states as more prototypical than others. Instead, we want to foster an approach that more fully engages the complexities and relationalities of colonial statist settlements. Moving across (trans)nationally constituted sites of settlement that proceed on historically differentiated trajectories, this volume seeks to draw out points of mutual recognizability across geographical ranges in their parallelized techniques of instituting ongoing Indigenous dispossession and delegitimization as the status quo of statist formation.

The essays in this volume approach these issues from a variety of disciplinary perspectives, including literary and cultural studies, political theory, age studies, and visual culture as well as film studies. This variety underscores how the questions and concepts of biopolitics, geopolitics, and life cut across disciplinary and methodological borders. It further illustrates the inter- and transdisciplinarity of Indigenous studies as a field that intersects multiple areas of scholarship—from social sciences, natural sciences and legal sciences to the humanities—to address the diversity of Indigenous peoples as well as to interrogate how settler conditions pervade all areas of life and inquiry.

Within this interdisciplinary framework, the contributions from within literary, cultural, and film and media studies take on a specific significance. Within the realm of the speculative and imaginary, they foreground the bio- and necropolitical conditions of living under settler colonialism that are rendered invisible in dominant discourse and unsettle the limits of the thinkable within settler society by broadening the range of the possible within the imaginative, thus opening a path toward a decolonial imaginary. The volume demonstrates that Indigenous and settler-colonial studies not only inhabit a vital place within the humanities. Beyond that, they also significantly add to humanities' discourses and focuses by making a necessary claim to think decolonization and the liberation of settler bio- and geopolitical rule as a possibility and imperative within our cultural, social, and political imaginary.

The volume opens with an essay by Mishuana Goeman on the violence against Native women as a form of extirpation and the role of Indigenous literatures as paving new paths toward justice. Doing so, her essay already displays the particular social and political function of literature by arguing for its capacity as a form of testimony for the otherwise unsaid and underreported. Goeman denounces the use of the term *epidemic* to describe the widespread violence against Native women in the United States and Canada because it makes assault appear to be linked to innate biological traits, veils culpability of (white) male subjects, and deflects responsibility from the historical and systemic causes of such violence. Moving away from the resulting inadequacies of the settler-colonial justice system, she analyzes Native women's writing as a form of witnessing to violence in two senses: a victim's witnessing of the crime that is also a form of violence affecting Indigenous communities and witnessing as storytelling, giving testimony to occurred (and ongoing) crimes that can provide new paths for justice in combating violence against Native women beyond settler law.

The two essays that follow continue this conversation on normalized violence against Indigenous bodies while extending it to different contexts of institutionalization and exploring its critique as a possibility to emphasize Indigenous-centered normativities. To this extent, Sandy Grande (Quechua) addresses "age" as a phenomenon and category of life that, particularly in how its management affects Indigenous communities and contradicts as well as alters understandings of age widespread in Indigenous societies, makes visible the mechanisms of a settler-capitalist biopolitics of disposing (as well as physically removing from sight) those modes of life that are not productive to upholding the colonial capitalist status quo. She shows how such mechanisms are countered by the gesturing toward an "Indigenous elsewhere." She outlines it as a space of being that transcends the mode of productive functionality as well as opposes the narrative of physical and mental decline that accompanies European/settler accounts of aging with accounts of accessing ways of being and inhabiting (mental) space that exceed the commonly shared surfaces of everyday twenty-first-century life in settler states.

Addressing another form of institutionalized containment in distinct yet related ways, Robert Nichols asks how the analysis of the Canadian prison system can be productively rethought by considering its racism in not only the disproportionate numbers of various racialized populations being imprisoned but also the "colonialism of incarceration" itself. The prison system operating from claims of territorialized sovereignty of the nation-state forms the point of departure for its fundamental critique from an Indigenous perspective in Nichols's argument. The essay thus intersects bio- and geopolitical critique by asserting Indigenous normativities as it examines how a biopolitical form of regulating populations' lives according to certain norms and nation-state laws can be unsettled through a geopolitical critique of the state's legitimacy to exert these laws. Doing so, it opens a pathway for activating the decolonial potential in critical prison studies.

As Nichols's chapter demonstrates, settler state violence is inscribed within the institutions that govern regimes of the everyday—whether they constitute daily processes of law enforcement, legal systems, or age administration. This focus on the institution links Nichols's chapter to the next two contributions, which investigate techniques that assert the legal framework of the settler state while advocating a rhetoric of recognition and emancipation. Moving beyond the continental possessions of what is today the United States, the Kanaka Maoli scholar David Uahikeaikalei'ohu Maile provocatively asks, "Are Hawaiians Indians?" (thereby repurposing an attack on the Indigeneity of Native Hawaiians by the then attorney Brett Kavanaugh) to connect an analysis of racializing settler-colonial biopolitics to a critique of liberal state recognition. Drawing on the strategy of the US Department of the Interior outlined in the 2014 Notices for Proposed Rule Making to consider the possibility and terms of the federal recognition of a Kanaka Maoli governing entity (and thereby reestablishing a government-to-government relationship between it and the United States), Maile elucidates how these notices constitute "notices of settlement" that seek to perpetuate US settlement in Hawai'i by eclipsing Kanaka Maoli sovereignty through recognition. In response, the rejection of these notices by Kanaka Maoli representatives documents for Maile an "archive of refusal" to ongoing settler-state imposition.

As the volume's geopolitical scope further widens, the repurposing of another Indigenous archive becomes the point of departure for Shona Jackson's important exploration of postcolonial biopolitics in Guyana: the Guyanese airport, located and temporarily named for the town Timehri, which is known for Indigenous petroglyphs (pictographic rock carving), represents these as hieroglyphs (prelinguistic signs). In Jackson's reading, this shows how the signs of a sovereignty prior to and independent of the colonial as well as the postcolonial state (petroglyphs) are reproduced as simulacra of an Indigeneity that anticipates and prefigures the emancipation of the postcolonial state as being itself always already protonational (hieroglyphs). As her essay argues for the difference between the postcolonial, nonwhite, involuntary settler state and the dominant white settler state, Jackson expands her discussion to the Amerindian Act in the iterations of 1977 and 2006 to show how the Guyanese state continues to produce Indigenous peoples as a body to be governed in service of the postcolonial state while denying them any rights they could claim as sovereign peoples not restricted to the state's juridical space.

While the Creolized Black peoples of Guyana constitute the privileged biopolitical body in contrast to Indigenous peoples, Jackson's contribution crucially attests that the Amerindian Act also signifies a struggle of Black peoples against ongoing histories of being reduced to bare life, which the Guyanese state wards off by relegating Indigenous peoples to this status instead. This strategy does not, however, change Guyana's own subaltern position as a nonwhite postcolonial state. The exploration of complex Black-Indigenous relations continues in Mark Rifkin's chapter, which addresses for the US context the possible incommensurability between Black freedom and Indigenous sovereignty struggles, with the former being largely cast in terms of fungibility of the flesh and the latter in terms of dispossession of land. Attending to this possible impasse, Rifkin considers the role that speculative genres, explicitly creating what-if scenarios, can play in thinking "imaginaries of the flesh and the land" in relation to each other. While Afro-pessimistic thought on Indigenous sovereignty as a reactionary investment in "propertied selfhood," for Rifkin, shows the difficulties of overcoming this impasse, his reading of the Afrofuturist author Octavia Butler offers new possibilities to think through it, including the tensions that arise when attempting to subsume a territorial geopolitics of Indigeneity under a biopolitical imaginary of the racialized body.

Rifkin's essay not only accompanies Jackson's in exploring the complexities of Indigeneity and Blackness but is also the first of a cluster focusing on the position and potential of literary writing to negotiate and challenge settler bio- and geopolitical frameworks. After Rifkin's exploration of Afrofuturist writing, Sabine Meyer focuses on Native fiction, taking Diane Glancy's novel *Pushing the Bear* as an example of Native Removal literature that renders the Cherokee expulsion of the 1830s, known as the Trail of Tears, as a biopolitical experience that seeks to reduce the Cherokee to the Agambenian status of "bare life." (We follow Meyer's practice of capitalizing *Removal* to denaturalize it.) At the same time, in her reading the novel brings to the fore the close intertwining of biopolitics and geopolitics manifest in Removal, with the settler-colonial production of the Cherokee as nomadic people facilitating their dispossession and Cherokee slaveholding practices doubly depriving Black enslaved people of the right to life and reducing them to the status of property to be removed. Ultimately, though, Meyer suggests that the novel brings to the fore the category of "Indigenous lives" that counters biopolitical reduction by rehumanizing and repoliticizing the Cherokee through the powers of storytelling and language, oral and written. Within this cluster on literary writing as a contestation of settler bio- and geopolitics, this chapter thus highlights the potential of Native literatures to formulate the dimensions of political and transnational lives for Indigenous peoples beyond reductive settler definitions.

If Rifkin points out how speculative genres can open "political possibilities," the normalized reception of other genres appears to foreclose such possibilities, such as when magical realism is connected to a Third World postcolonial context and the magic it employs appears to originate solely from non-Western cultures. Precisely at this juncture, Michael R. Griffiths's contribution makes an important intervention as he proposes through Daniel Heath Justice's concept of "wonderwork" a decolonization of what is read as magical realism in the works of the Noongar author Kim Scott and the Māori author Witi Ihimaera. Through a reading strategy that puts magical realism under erasure, what is viewed as "magic" no longer appears simply as an othering device for Indigenous cultures but is reappraised by Griffiths as an effect that is produced at the intersection of two competing forms of empiricism in a situation of ongoing colonization. In detailed readings of both writers, Griffiths draws out how such a decolonial reassessment of magical realism through a trans-Indigenous reading is able to make visible the colonial archive as an investment in the invasive magic of biopower that seeks to erase Indigenous peoples through their ordering into hierarchized colonial systems of belief. At the same time, such a perspective ultimately works to re-presence Indigenous knowledges as both autonomous and necessarily interacting with colonial modes of power in their own dynamic of Indigenous modernity and relationality.

For Griffiths, the colonial archive is the product and the means of settler desire to index and target Indigenous difference, but he also notes that the archive can be turned into a space of resistance (which for Maile, as noted earlier, even extends into an "archive of refusal" of Native people defying colonial power). At this intersection of the archive as colonial instrument and possible site of subversion, Jacqueline Fear-Segal's contribution is positioned to investigate the visual archive of one of the most (in)famous biopolitical institutions of the United States: the Carlisle Indian Industrial School. The first government-run boarding school complementing the assimilationist efforts of allotment, Carlisle produced a visual archive that documents its erasure of Indigeneity, as Fear-Segal outlines. At the same time, however, Fear-Segal traces in the archive manifestations of visual sovereignty straining against the official narrative of erasing any sense of Indigenous autonomy. Using photography and painting to their own end, students exerted sovereign forms of self-expression that point to visual art as a means of signifying Native belonging and survivance. At the same time, Fear-Segal's analysis indicates the close link between a defiant mode of self-representation and the political activism some pursued after Carlisle, as exemplified by the portraits of Luther Standing Bear.

Fear-Segal's chapter is the first of two essays toward the end of this book that focus on visual representation as a means of engaging settler geo- and biopolitics. Following it, the final contribution to this volume, by Kerstin Knopf, focuses on how filmic representations can capture Indigenous struggles over space and its signification by visually rendering how space can be differently produced, possibly simultaneously across multiple layers, as either colonial space or sites of ongoing Indigenous belonging. In an analysis of the Brazilian Italian coproduction *Birdwatchers* (*Terra Vermelha*), which depicts the land-reclamation struggles by the Guaraní-Kaiowá, Knopf modifies the Deleuzian-Guattarian framework of "deterritorialization" and "reterritorialization." Specifically, she adapts it to an Indigenous framework to describe the ongoing dispossessive and acquisitive processes and structures through which Indigenous people and settler culture become simultaneously de- and reterritorialized and Indigenous homelands thus are redefined as post/colonial space. While the film illustrates these processes by showing that the Guaraní-Kaiowá community struggles on places marginal to its original homelands (reserves, roadways), it also indicates how a production of post/colonial space is never complete and how, through cultural practices and displays of resistance, the continuing sense of Indigenous belonging to the land can be reactivated and asserted.

Clearly pointing beyond the level of representation to the actual struggles portrayed, this final chapter to the volume also shows how these efforts at reclaiming land expose the necropolitics of settler geopolitics. The main character leading the reclamation movement is closely modeled on the actor portraying him, and just like the main character in the film, the actor himself is killed shortly after the film is completed in an effort to quell this moment of anticolonial struggle. As one Indigenous activist's death among many, it adds one more instance to the settler-state violence listed at the outset of this introduction, violence committed to preserve the colonial status quo. At the same time, the Guaraní-Kaiowá keep resisting this violence as they and other Guaraní communities struggle for land demarcation in the south of Brazil.

One point of departure for the analyses performed by the essays in this volume is the settler states' invariable production of Indigenous lives as vulnerable, exposed to violation, or endangered. Inevitably, though, this notion is traced back to some defect within Indigenous peoples themselves, not viewed as a call to analyze the violence inherent to any settler-colonial project. Conversely, this volume is equally interested in how Indigenous life always has been and remains irreducible to the logics of bio- and geopolitical settlement. Acting in the sense of a "being with" that does not engage the oppositional and binary logics of settler bio- and geopolitics, Indigenous people's lived experiences, epistemologies, ontologies, embodiments, and relationalities continually help to make present spaces whose ordering principles are indifferent to any assumed settler parameter of definitional containment.[105] If they seem irresponsible, excessive, or improper to the liberal settler mind, then because they do not exist to respond to colonial imposition, they are always excessive to the colonial order, and they do not adhere to the propertied claims by settler states.

As the Laguna Pueblo author Leslie Marmon Silko puts it in her memoir, *The Turquoise Ledge*, the Laguna Pueblo never corrected the Spanish for falsely dating their establishment to 1698 because this colonial perception "made no difference to their reckoning of the world."[106] Together with Coulthard's grounded normativity, diminishing such colonial falsehoods as inconsequential links to what Shiri Pasternak has called "grounded authority."[107] This authority always exists within and against a situation of colonization and, at the same time, is oriented toward parameters that continually exceed all that seeks to limit, contain, or otherwise "fix" it. In contrast to a desire to "fix" Indigenous life according to one specifically defined norm or within one register of significance, this volume seeks to trace Indigenous life across multiple sites as an evolving, emergent, ever present, and ever changing practice, constellation, and relation that moves forward while continually constituting manifold ways of being in the world. These ways of being present an otherwise to what is fixable and to what allows fixture in the limited terms of set(tled) theoretical bodies or colonial logics. Out of this tension, the following conversations on settler bio- and geopolitics and Indigenous lived presence gain their dynamic.

NOTES

1   For news outlets reporting of these incidents, see, on Standing Rock, Julia Carrie Wong, "Dakota Access Pipeline: 300 Protesters Injured after Police Use Water Cannons," *Guardian*, November 21, 2016, http://www.theguardian.com/us-news /2016/nov/21/dakota-access-pipeline-water-cannon-police-standing-rock-protest; and Jonah Engel Bromwich, "Sixteen Arrested at North Dakota Pipeline Protest," *New York Times*, January 20, 2018, https://www.nytimes.com/2016/11/21/us/dakota -access-pipeline-protesters-police.html. On the assassination of Berta Caceres, Elisabeth Malkin, "Who Ordered Killing of Honduran Activist? Evidence of Broad Plot Is Found," *New York Times*, March 3, 2018, https://www.nytimes.com /2017/10/28/world/americas/honduras-berta-caceres-desa.html; on the Stanley verdict, Guy Quenneville and Jason Warick, "Gerald Stanley Found Not Guilty in Colten Boushie's Death," CBC *News*, February 10, 2018, http://www.cbc.ca/news /canada/saskatoon/gerald-stanley-colten-boushie-verdict-1.4526313; on the Cormier verdict, Lyle Stafford, "Missing, Mourned, Unresolved: Cormier's Acquittal Leaves Tina Fontaine's Family Searching for Answers," *Globe and Mail*, February 22, 2018, https://www.theglobeandmail.com/news/national/tina-fontaine-raymond-cormier -verdict/article38062879; on the killing of Claudia Patricia Gómez Gonzáles, Nina Lakhani, "'Immigration Killed Her': Guatemalan Woman Shot Dead by US Border Patrol," *Guardian*, May 25, 2018, https://www.theguardian.com/us-news/2018/may/25 /woman-shot-dead-border-patrol-rio-bravo-texas-identified; on Indigenous families migrating to the United States from Central America, Tristan Ahtone, "Indigenous Immigrants Face Unique Challenges at the Border," *High Country News*, June 24, 2018, http://nmpolitics.net/index/2018/06/indigenous-immigrants-face-unique-challenges -at-the-border.

2   This introduction was written before the COVID-19 pandemic and its disproportionate impact on Indigenous communities. Like many crises around the world, COVID-19 exposes how the violence of settler-colonial biopolitics is indelibly woven into the social fabric of Indigenous life. This stresses the fact that Indigenous peoples are exposed to the pandemic more seriously than any other group in, for instance, North America, unveiling the crisis in its entanglement with settler colonialism as such.

3 Leanne Betasamosake Simpson, *As We Have Always Done: Indigenous Freedom through Radical Resistance*, Indigenous Americas (Minneapolis: University of Minnesota Press, 2017).

4 On the notion of "unknowing" as integral to colonial conditions, see Manu Vimalassery, Juliana Hu Pegues, and Alyosha Goldstein, "Introduction: On Colonial Unknowing," *Theory and Event* 19, no. 4 (2016), https://muse.jhu.edu/article/633283. They write, "This ignorance—this act of ignoring—is aggressively made and reproduced, affectively invested and effectively distributed in ways that conform the social relations and economies of the here and now."

5 As a case in point, a major treatise in the *New York Times Magazine* on the Indigenous youth who launched the water protection at Standing Rock analyzes the black snake from Lakota mythology not only as standing in for the pipeline but also as symbolizing, as Dallas Goldtooth put it, "a darkness, a sickness, whose only intention is to sow dysfunction and loss of life in our community." However, subsequently the article ties this larger reference solely to social problems on the reservation—"alcoholism, suicide, and abuse"—instead of to the larger social condition of ongoing settler colonialism as causing "dysfunction and loss of life": Saul Elbein, "The Youth Group That Launched a Movement at Standing Rock," *New York Times Magazine*, January 31, 2017, https://www.nytimes.com/2017/01/31/magazine/the-youth-group-that-launched-a-movement-at-standing-rock.html.

6 Aileen Moreton-Robinson, *The White Possessive: Property, Power, and Indigenous Sovereignty* (Minneapolis: University of Minnesota Press, 2016), 131.

7 Moreton-Robinson, *The White Possessive*, 130.

8 Scott Lauria Morgensen, "The Biopolitics of Settler Colonialism: Right Here, Right Now," *Settler Colonial Studies* 1, no.1 (2011): 73.

9 Linda Tuhiwai Smith, *Decolonizing Methodologies: Research and Indigenous Peoples*, 2d ed. (London: Zed, 2012), 201.

10 Smith, *Decolonizing Methodologies*, 201.

11 Smith, *Decolonizing Methodologies*, 201.

12 Smith, *Decolonizing Methodologies*, 201.

13 David Scott, "Colonial Governmentality," *Social Text* 43 (Autumn 1995): 193.

14 Glen Coulthard, *Red Skin, White Masks: Rejecting the Colonial Politics of Recognition* (Minneapolis: University of Minnesota Press, 2014), 152.

15 Mark Rifkin, "Indigenizing Agamben: Rethinking Sovereignty in Light of the 'Peculiar' Status of Native Peoples," *Cultural Critique* 73, no. 1 (2009): 91.

16 For the former, see, among others, Beth H. Piatote, *Domestic Subjects: Gender, Citizenship, and Law in Native American Literature*, Henry Roe Cloud Series on American Indians and Modernity (New Haven, CT: Yale University Press, 2013). For the latter, see Billy-Ray Belcourt, "Animal Bodies, Colonial Subjects: (Re)Locating Animality in Decolonial Thought," *Societies* 5, no. 1 (2014): 1–11. I elaborate on the function of settler colonialism to normalize and hierarchize in René Dietrich, "The Biopolitical Logics of Settler Colonialism and Disruptive Relationality," *Cultural Studies—Critical Methodologies* 17, no. 1 (2017): 67–77.

17 Michel Foucault, *The History of Sexuality,* vol. 1: *An Introduction,* translated by Robert
    Hurley (New York: Pantheon, 1978), 144.

18 For the logic of elimination, see Patrick Wolfe, *Settler Colonialism and the Transformation
    of Anthropology: The Politics and Poetics of an Ethnographic Event* (London: Cassell, 1999), 27:
    "Settler-colonialism consists in a negative articulation between invaders and the land.
    The cultural logic which is organic to a negative articulation is one of elimination."

19 For discussions of geopolitics in settler-colonial contexts, see, among others, Ikuko
    Asaka, *Tropical Freedom: Climate, Settler Colonialism, and Black Exclusion in the Age
    of Emancipation* (Durham, NC: Duke University Press, 2017); Joanne Barker, ed.,
    *Sovereignty Matters: Locations of Contestation and Possibility in Indigenous Struggles for
    Self-Determination* (Lincoln: University of Nebraska Press, 2005); Brenna Bhandar,
    Colonial Lives of Property: Law, Land, and Racial Regimes of Ownership (Durham, NC:
    Duke University Press, 2018); Lisa Tanya Brooks, *The Common Pot: The Recovery of
    Native Space in the Northeast,* Indigenous Americas Series (Minneapolis: University
    of Minnesota Press, 2008); David A. Chang, *The World and All the Things upon It:
    Native Hawaiian Geographies of Exploration* (Minneapolis: University of Minnesota
    Press, 2016); Mishuana Goeman, *Mark My Words: Native Women Mapping Our Nations,*
    First Peoples: New Directions in Indigenous Studies (Minneapolis: University
    of Minnesota Press, 2013); Elizabeth Hoover, *The River Is in Us: Fighting Toxics in a
    Mohawk Community* (Minneapolis: University of Minnesota Press, 2017); Carole
    McGranahan and John F. Collins, eds., *Ethnographies of U.S. Empire* (Durham, NC:
    Duke University Press, 2018); Dana E. Powell, *Landscapes of Power: Politics of Energy
    in the Navajo Nation,* New Ecologies for the Twenty-First Century (Durham, NC:
    Duke University Press, 2018); Alice Te Punga Somerville, *Once Were Pacific: Māori
    Connections to Oceania* (Minneapolis: University of Minnesota Press, 2012).

20 Jodi A. Byrd, "Introduction to the Indigeneity's Difference: Methodology and
    Structures of Sovereignty Forum," *J19* 2, no. 1 (2014): 131–36. For discussions of
    settler-colonial biopolitics from a variety of perspectives, see Joanne Barker, *Native
    Acts: Law, Recognition, and Cultural Authenticity* (Durham, NC: Duke University
    Press, 2011); Jodi A. Byrd, *The Transit of Empire: Indigenous Critiques of Colonialism,*
    First Peoples: New Directions Indigenous (Minneapolis: University of Minnesota
    Press, 2011); Sarah Deer, *The Beginning and End of Rape: Confronting Sexual Violence
    in Native America* (Minneapolis: University of Minnesota Press, 2015); Michael R.
    Griffiths, ed., *Biopolitics and Memory in Postcolonial Literature and Culture* (Farnham,
    UK: Ashgate, 2016); J. J. Kēhaulani Kauanui, *Hawaiian Blood: Colonialism and the
    Politics of Sovereignty and Indigeneity,* Narrating Native Histories (Durham, NC:
    Duke University Press, 2008); Dian Million, *Therapeutic Nations: Healing in an
    Age of Indigenous Human Rights,* Critical Issues in Indigenous Studies (Tucson:
    University of Arizona Press, 2013); Aileen Moreton-Robinson, "Towards a New
    Research Agenda?: Foucault, Whiteness and Indigenous Sovereignty," *Journal of
    Sociology* 42, no. 4 (2006): 383–95; Scott Lauria Morgensen, *Spaces between Us: Queer
    Settler Colonialism and Indigenous Decolonization,* First Peoples: New Directions in
    Indigenous Studies (Minneapolis: University of Minnesota Press, 2011); Sherene
    Razack, *Dying from Improvement: Inquests and Inquiries into Indigenous Deaths in Custody*

(Toronto: University of Toronto Press, 2015); Rifkin, "Indigenizing Agamben"; Mark Rifkin, *When Did Indians Become Straight? Kinship, the History of Sexuality, and Native Sovereignty* (New York: Oxford University Press, 2011); Audra Simpson, *Mohawk Interruptus: Political Life across the Borders of Settler States* (Durham, NC: Duke University Press, 2014); Kimberly TallBear, *Native American DNA: Tribal Belonging and the False Promise of Genetic Science* (Minneapolis: University of Minnesota Press, 2013).

21 For constructions of the Indian, *índio*, and Aboriginal, see, respectively, Byrd, *The Transit of Empire*; María Josefina Saldaña-Portillo, *Indian Given: Racial Geographies across Mexico and the United States*, Latin America Otherwise (Durham, NC: Duke University Press, 2016); Elizabeth A. Povinelli, *The Cunning of Recognition: Indigenous Alterities and the Making of Australian Multiculturalism*, Politics, History, and Culture (Durham, NC: Duke University Press, 2002).

22 As Giorgio Agamben argues at length in *Homo Sacer: Sovereign Power and Bare Life* (Stanford, CA: Stanford University Press, 1998), bare life is the status produced for populations that are exposed to the force of sovereign power but not protected from it through law. The status of "inclusive exclusion" and the "state of exception" assigned to the production of bare life is simultaneously the legal space in which sovereign power constitutes itself. "Not simple natural life, but life exposed to death (bare life or sacred life) is the originary political element": Agamben, *Homo Sacer*, 88. Drawing on and revising Agamben through an Indigenous studies perspective, Rifkin coins *bare habitance* as the legal "status of the reservation, a space that while governed under 'peculiar' rules categorically is denied status as 'external,' or 'foreign.'" Similar to the status of bare life, the production of "bare habitance" is constitutive for the exercising of geopolitical sovereignty "in the (re)production and naturalization of national space": Rifkin, "Indigenizing Agamben," 94. Agamben himself draws strongly on Carl Schmitt for his theorization of inclusive exclusion, state of exception, and "nomos." For a critical reappraisal of Schmitt in the context of contemporary anticolonial and anticapitalist insurgent politics, see Federico Luisetti, John Pickles, and Wilson Kaiser, eds., *The Anomie of the Earth: Philosophy, Politics, and Autonomy in Europe and the Americas* (Durham, NC: Duke University Press, 2015).

23 See, among others, Joanne Barker, ed., *Critically Sovereign: Indigenous Gender, Sexuality, and Feminist Studies* (Durham, NC: Duke University Press, 2017); Deer, *The Beginning and End of Rape*; Mishuana Goeman, "Ongoing Storms and Struggles: Gendered Violence and Resource Exploitation," in *Critically Sovereign: Indigenous Gender, Sexuality, and Feminist Studies*, edited by Joanne Barker (Durham, NC: Duke University Press, 2017), 99–126; Sherene H. Razack, "Gendering Disposability," *Canadian Journal of Women and the Law* 28, no. 2 (August 2016): 285–307. See also Mishuana Goeman's essay in this volume.

24 Lorenzo Veracini, *The Settler Colonial Present* (London: Palgrave Macmillan, 2015).

25 Elizabeth A. Povinelli, *Geontologies: A Requiem to Late Liberalism* (Durham, NC: Duke University Press, 2016), 26.

26 The term is from Simpson, *Mohawk Interruptus*.

27   Razack, *Dying from Improvement*. See also Audra Simpson, "The State Is a Man: Theresa Spence, Loretta Saunders and the Gender of Settler Sovereignty," *Theory and Event* 19, no. 4 (2016): http://muse.jhu.edu/article/633280: "Canada requires the death and so called 'disappearance' of Indigenous women in order to secure its sovereignty."

28   For some of the most influential work by Wolfe, see *Settler Colonialism and the Transformation of Anthropology*; Patrick Wolfe, "Settler Colonialism and the Elimination of the Native," *Journal of Genocide Research* 8, no. 4 (December 2006): 387–409; Patrick Wolfe, *Traces of History: Elementary Structures of Race* (London: Verso, 2016). For scholarship on settler colonialism that engages Wolfe's premises and advances the field, especially with a comparative and transnational perspective, see Fiona Bateman and Lionel Pilkington, *Studies in Settler Colonialism: Politics, Identity and Culture* (Basingstoke, UK: Palgrave Macmillan, 2011); Bruno Cornellier and Michael R. Griffiths, "Globalizing Unsettlement: An Introduction," *Settler Colonial Studies* 6, no. 4 (October 2016): 305–16; Lisa Ford, *Settler Sovereignty: Jurisdiction and Indigenous People in America and Australia, 1788-1836* (Cambridge, MA: Harvard University Press, 2010); Margaret D. Jacobs, *White Mother to a Dark Race: Settler Colonialism, Maternalism, and the Removal of Indigenous Children in the American West and Australia, 1880-1940* (Lincoln: University of Nebraska Press, 2009); Lorenzo Veracini, *Settler Colonialism: A Theoretical Overview* (Houndmills, UK: Palgrave Macmillan, 2010); Veracini, *The Settler Colonial Present*. For a critical discussion of Wolfe's work, an approach to settler colonialism in the line of Wolfe's analysis, or the simplified reception of Wolfe's analysis (that runs the danger of occluding other approaches and perspectives), see Manu Vimalassery, Juliana Hu Pegues, and Alyosha Goldstein, "Introduction: On Colonial Unknowing," and contributions to *Theory and Event* 19, no. 4 (2016), https://muse.jhu.edu/article/633283; Alex Young, "A Response to 'On Colonial Unknowing,'" *Theory and Event* 20, no. 4 (2017): 1035–41, http://muse.jhu.edu/article/675630; Manu Vimalassery, Juliana Hu Pegues, and Alyosha Goldstein, "Colonial Unknowing and Relations of Study," *Theory and Event* 20, no. 4 (2017): 1042–54, http://muse.jhu.edu/article/675631. See also Cynthia G. Franklin, Njoroge, and Suzanna Reiss, eds., "Tracing the Settler's Tools: A Forum on Patrick Wolfe's Life and Legacy," *American Quarterly* 69, no. 2 (2017): 235–47. And in response to each other, see J. Kēhaulani Kauanui, "'A Structure, Not an Event': Settler Colonialism and Enduring Indigeneity," *Lateral* 5, no. 1 (2016), https://doi.org/10.25158/L5.1.7; and Beenash Jafri, "Ongoing Colonial Violence in Settler States," *Lateral* 6 no. 1 (2017), https://doi.org/10.25158/L6.1.7.

29   Shannon Speed, "Structures of Settler Capitalism in Abya Yala," *American Quarterly* 69, no. 4 (2017): 783–90.

30   Daiva K. Stasiulis and Nira Yuval-Davis, eds., *Unsettling Settler Societies: Articulations of Gender, Race, Ethnicity and Class*, Sage Series on Race and Ethnic Relations, vol. 11 (London: Sage, 1995), 3–4.

31   For the purposes of this volume, the development of Native and Indigenous studies termed critical Indigenous studies is most relevant. For an overview of theoretically, critically, and politically oriented Native studies, see Audra Simpson and

Andrea Smith, eds., *Theorizing Native Studies* (Durham, NC: Duke University Press, 2014). For a definition and genealogy of critical Indigenous studies (cis) in the United States and Canada, see Barker, *Critically Sovereign*, 9 ("Cis distinguished itself through questions about Indigenous sovereignty, self-determination, and citizenship. Indigenous peoples' efforts to secure collective rights to sovereignty and self-determination as provided for within international and constitutional law was differentiated from the efforts of 'minority' people—including immigrant and diaspora communities and their descendants—to claim citizenship and civil rights within their nation-states"). See also Chris Andersen, "Critical Indigenous Studies: From Difference to Density," *Cultural Studies Review* 15, no. 2 (2011): 80–100; Danika Medak-Saltzman, "Empire's Haunted Logics: Comparative Colonialisms and the Challenges of Incorporating Indigeneity," *Critical Ethnic Studies* 1, no. 2 (2015): 11–32; Aileen Moreton-Robinson, ed., *Critical Indigenous Studies: Engagements in First World Locations*, Critical Issues in Indigenous Studies (Tucson: University of Arizona Press, 2016).

32 Iyko Day, *Alien Capital: Asian Racialization and the Logic of Settler Colonial Capitalism* (Durham, NC: Duke University Press, 2016); Iyko Day, "Being or Nothingness: Indigeneity, Antiblackness, and Settler Colonial Critique," *Critical Ethnic Studies* 1, no. 2 (2015): 102–21; Manu Karuka, "Black and Native Visions of Self-Determination," *Critical Ethnic Studies* 3, no. 2 (2017): 77; Tiffany Lethabo King, "In the Clearing: Black Female Bodies, Space and Settler Colonial Landscapes" (PhD diss., University of Maryland, 2013); Justin Leroy, "Empire and the Afterlife of Slavery: Black Anti-imperialisms of the Long Nineteenth Century" (PhD diss., New York University, 2014). For an investigation of settler colonialism and racial capitalism, see Jodi A. Byrd, Alyosha Goldstein, Jodi Melamed, and Chandan Reddy, eds., "Economies of Dispossession: Indigeneity, Race, Capitalism," a special issue of *Social Text* 36, no. 2 (June 2018). Much of this work challenges the settler/native binary implicit in some of settler-colonial scholarship and explicitly affirmed in Patrick Wolfe, "Recuperating Binarism: A Heretical Introduction," *Settler Colonial Studies* 3, nos. 3–4 (2013): 257–79. Byrd's employment, borrowed from the Barbadian poet Kamau Brathwaite, of *arrivant*, or a variation thereof, has proved helpful in theorizing processes and the violence of diaspora in connection to settler-colonial modes of dispossession. See also Cornellier and Griffiths, "Globalizing Unsettlement," in which they ask, "Might the relation between diaspora and indigeneity, native and *arrivant* be thought through intersectional solidarities beyond the binarism of the settler/native paradigm, while nonetheless continuing to insist on the sovereignty of indigenous rights to their traditional territories? . . . [O]ur point is to challenge Wolfe's binarism while acknowledging that to do so is to nonetheless accept that insurmountable salience of Wolfe's central notion of elimination as the founding premise of settler colonialism."

33 Vimalassery et al., "Colonial Unknowing and Relations of Study," 1042.

34 Wolfe, *Traces of History*, 2.

35 Moreton-Robinson, *The White Possessive*. See also, among others, Speed, "Structures of Settler Capitalism in Abya Yala." For the "racial dynamics" within settler colo-

nialism and whiteness as central for the position of the settler, see Day, "Being or Nothingness," 107.

36 Katherine McKittrick, *Sylvia Wynter: On Being Human as Praxis* (Durham, NC: Duke University Press, 2015), 3. Sylvia Wynter herself talks of the present ethnoclass (i.e., Western bourgeois) conception of the human that overrepresents itself as if it were "the human itself": Sylvia Wynter, "Unsettling the Coloniality of Being/Power/ Truth/Freedom: Towards the Human, after Man, Its Overrepresentation—An Argument," *CR: The New Centennial Review* 3, no. 3 (2003): 257–337. How racialization affects settler belonging beyond the settler-Indigenous relation shows also in Australia's casting the refugees from largely Muslim countries as a threat to be violently detained while inviting non-persecuted fellow-settler white South African farmers as an easily fitting and enriching group with values similar to Australia—or, more specifically, white settler Australia.

37 Tiffany Lethabo King, "New World Grammars: The 'Unthought' Black Discourses of Conquest," *Theory and Event* 19, no. 4 (2016), http://muse.jhu.edu/article/633275. See Hortense J. Spillers, "Mama's Baby, Papa's Maybe: An American Grammar Book," *Diacritics* 17, no. 2 (1987): 65–81. For additional research in Black studies focusing on the biopolitics of race and racialization, see, among others, Denise Ferreira da Silva, *Toward a Global Idea of Race*, Borderlines 27 (Minneapolis: University of Minnesota Press, 2007); Saidiya V. Hartman, *Lose Your Mother: A Journey along the Atlantic Slave Route* (New York: Farrar, Straus and Giroux, 2007); Saidiya V. Hartman, *Scenes of Subjection: Terror, Slavery, and Self-Making in Nineteenth-Century America*, Race and American Culture (New York: Oxford University Press, 1997); Sharon Patricia Holland, *Raising the Dead: Readings of Death and (Black) Subjectivity* (Durham, NC: Duke University Press, 2000); Christina Sharpe, *In the Wake: On Blackness and Being* (Durham, NC: Duke University Press, 2016); Michelle M. Wright, *Physics of Blackness: Beyond the Middle Passage Epistemology* (Minneapolis: University of Minnesota Press, 2015).

38 Razack, *Dying from Improvement*, 59.

39 Lisa Lowe, *The Intimacies of Four Continents* (Durham, NC: Duke University Press, 2015), 7–8.

40 Alexander G. Weheliye, *Habeas Viscus: Racializing Assemblages, Biopolitics, and Black Feminist Theories of the Human* (Durham, NC: Duke University Press, 2014), 30.

41 Weheliye, *Habeas Viscus*, 136.

42 For a critique of the human rights framework from an Indigenous perspective, see Peter Kulchyski, *Aboriginal Rights Are Not Human Rights: In Defence of Indigenous Struggles* (Winnipeg: ARP Books, 2013); Shannon Speed and Jane F. Collier, "Limiting Indigenous Autonomy in Chiapas, Mexico: The State Government's Use of Human Rights," *Human Rights Quarterly* 22 (2000): 877–905.

43 Weheliye, *Habeas Viscus*, 136.

44 Weheliye, *Habeas Viscus*, 131.

45 Katherine McKittrick, *Demonic Grounds: Black Women and the Cartographies of Struggle* (Minneapolis: University of Minnesota Press, 2006), xi.

46 McKittrick, *Demonic Grounds*, x.

47   Simpson, *As We Have Always Done*, 230.

48   Simpson, *As We Have Always Done*, 230.

49   Saldaña-Portillo, *Indian Given*, 7.

50   For these questions, see also Maylei Blackwell, Floridalma Boj Lope, and Luis Ur-rieta Jr., eds., "Critical Latinx Indigeneities," a special issue of *Latino Studies* 15, no. 2 (July 2017): 126–37; as well as M. Bianet Castellanos, ed., "Settler Colonialism in Latin America," *American Quarterly* 69, no. 4 (2017).

51   Saldaña-Portillo, *Indian Given*, 26–27.

52   Shona N. Jackson, *Creole Indigeneity: Between Myth and Nation in the Caribbean*, First Peoples: New Directions in Indigenous Studies (Minneapolis: University of Minnesota Press, 2012).

53   Lauren Berlant notably does not reference conditions of settler colonialism directly in *Cruel Optimism*; instead, settler colonialism and Indigeneity remain a lacunae and silence in their thought. See Lauren G. Berlant, *Cruel Optimism* (Durham, NC: Duke University Press, 2011); Byrd, *The Transit of Empire*, 34–38. Rob Nixon speaks more directly to Third World postcolonial conditions, but also creates a link to US expansion and dispossession of Native peoples when he mentions how the ongoing movement of settler colonialism has produced "scars of displacement in American history" that have further inflicted "ecological, spiritual, and communal damage": Rob Nixon, *Slow Violence: The Environmentalism of the Poor* (Cambridge, MA: Harvard University Press, 2013), 243. While neither work thoroughly engages questions of settler-colonial bio- and geopolitics and Indigeneity, we want to consider the implications of their analysis of the contemporary moment for life under settler colonialism and think across both terms to represence the settler structures that they forgo in their own analysis.

54   Mark Rifkin, *Beyond Settler Time: Temporal Sovereignty and Indigenous Self-determination* (Durham, NC: Duke University Press, 2017).

55   Berlant, *Cruel Optimism*, 95.

56   Simpson, "The State Is a Man."

57   Cf. Marie-Hélène Cousineau and Susan Avingaq, dirs., *Sol* (documentary film, Arnait Video Productions, 2014). Lisa Stevenson, *Life beside Itself: Imagining Care in the Canadian Arctic* (Oakland: University of California Press, 2014), 7.

58   Stevenson, *Life beside Itself*, 73.

59   Cf. Audrey Huntley, dir., *Go Home, Baby Girl* (documentary film, Canadian Broadcasting Corporation, 2005); Christine Welsh, dir., *Finding Dawn* (documentary film, National Film Board of Canada, 2006); Matthew Smiley, dir., *Highway of Tears* (Finesse Films, 2015).

60   See also Jaskiran K. Dhillon, *Prairie Rising: Indigenous Youth, Decolonization, and the Politics of Intervention* (Toronto: University of Toronto Press, 2017).

61   Razack, *Dying from Improvement*.

62   Nixon, *Slow Violence*, 2.

63   Nixon, *Slow Violence*, 2.

64   Dino Gilio-Whitaker, *As Long as Grass Grows: The Indigenous Fight for Environmental Justice, from Colonization to Standing Rock* (Boston: Beacon, 2019), 25.

65 Kristen Simmons, "Settler Atmospherics," *Society for Cultural Anthropology*, Dispatches, November 20, 2017, https://culanth.org/fieldsights/1221-settler-atmospherics. The oil sand extraction completely destroys the targeted boreal forest and bog land in northern Alberta and continually leaks toxins into the environment through tailing ponds; draws immense amounts of water from local rivers; pollutes local water systems; and continuously emits a cloud of small-particles pollutants, secondary organic aerosols, into the atmosphere comparable to that emitted in the larger Toronto area. See Tzeporah Berman, "Canada's Most Shameful Environmental Secret Must Not Remain Hidden," *Guardian*, November 14, 2017, https://www.theguardian.com/commentisfree/2017/nov/14/canadas-shameful-environmental-secret-tar-sands-tailings-ponds; Ivan Semeniuk, "Oil Sands Found to Be a Leading Source of Air Pollution in North America," *Globe and Mail*, May 25, 2016, https://www.theglobeandmail.com/news/national/oil-sands-found-to-be-a-leading-source-of-air-pollution-in-north-america/article30151841. This industry provides jobs for local Indigenous people, but it also destroys livelihoods and life itself with polluted food sources. Cf. Warren Cariou and Neil McArthur, dirs., *Land of Oil and Water* (documentary film, 2009).

66 Macarena Gómez-Barris, *The Extractive Zone: Social Ecologies and Decolonial Perspectives* (Durham, NC: Duke University Press, 2017), xvi.

67 Gómez-Barris, *The Extractive Zone*, xix.

68 Gómez-Barris, *The Extractive Zone*, 2. See also Traci Brynne Voyles, *Wastelanding: Legacies of Uranium Mining in Navajo Country* (Minneapolis: University of Minnesota Press, 2015).

69 Gómez-Barris, *The Extractive Zone*, xvii.

70 Gómez-Barris, *The Extractive Zone*, xx.

71 Wolfe, "Settler Colonialism and the Elimination of the Native," 387.

72 Wolfe, "Settler Colonialism and the Elimination of the Native," 388.

73 When Wolfe's statement is cited, the equation of land with life through its negation is usually adapted, as well. A case in point for an argument that defines Wolfe's "land is life" through its negative is in Roxanne Dunbar-Ortiz's *An Indigenous Peoples' History of the United States*, in which the quote from Wolfe's essay precedes a statement outlining the intersection of US settler colonialism, white supremacy, and genocide. Roxanne Dunbar-Ortiz, *An Indigenous Peoples' History of the United States* (Boston: Beacon, 2014), 2.

74 Melanie K. Yazzie and Cutcha Risling Baldy, "Introduction: Indigenous Peoples and the Politics of Water," *Decolonization: Indigeneity, Education and Society* 7, no. 1 (2018), 1.

75 Nick Estes, *Our History Is the Future: Standing Rock versus the Dakota Access Pipeline, and the Long Tradition of Indigenous Resistance* (London: Verso, 2019), 15.

76 Craig Howe and Tyler Young, "Mnisose," *Society for Cultural Anthropology*, Fieldsights: Hotspots, December 22, 2016, https://culanth.org/fieldsights/mnisose.

77 Edward Valandra, "Mni Wiconi: Water Is [More than] Life," in *Standing with Standing Rock: Voices from the #NoDAPL Movement*, edited by Nick Estes and Jaskiran Dhillon (Minneapolis: University of Minnesota Press, 2019), 81.

78 Yazzie and Baldy, "Introduction," 2.

79 Zoe Todd, "Protecting Life below Water: Tending to Relationality and Expanding Oceanic Consciousness Beyond Coastal Zones," American Anthropologist, October 17, 2017, http://www.americananthropologist.org/2017/10/17/protecting-life-below-water-by-zoe-todd-de-provincializing-development-series.

80 Povinelli, *Geontologies*, 20.

81 Povinelli, *Geontologies*, 26.

82 Povinelli, *Geontologies*, 35.

83 Povinelli, *Geontologies*, 28.

84 Povinelli, *Geontologies*, 35.

85 Povinelli, *Geontologies*, 46.

86 Povinelli, *Geontologies*, 52.

87 Povinelli, *Geontologies*, 102.

88 Povinelli, *Geontologies*, 75.

89 Povinelli, *Geontologies*, 75.

90 Povinelli, *Geontologies*, 14.

91 Povinelli, *Geontologies*, 26, 28.

92 Rifkin, "Indigenizing Agamben," 94.

93 Povinelli, *Geontologies*, 46.

94 Goeman, *Mark My Words*, 33.

95 Goeman, *Mark My Words*, 32.

96 Coulthard, *Red Skin, White Masks*, 60; Povinelli, *Geontologies*, 102, 148.

97 Coulthard, *Red Skin, White Masks*, 60.

98 Coulthard, *Red Skin, White Masks*, 61.

99 Jeannette C. Armstrong, "Constructing Indigeneity: Syilx Okanagan Oraliture and tmixʷcentrism" (PhD diss., Universität Greifswald, Germany, 2009), http://ub-ed.ub.uni-greifswald.de/opus/volltexte/2012/1322; Richard E. Atleo, *Tsawalk: A Nuu-chah-nulth Worldview* (Vancouver: University of British Columbia Press, 2004); Richard E. Atleo, *Principles of Tsawalk: An Indigenous Approach to Global Crisis* (Vancouver: University of British Columbia Press, 2011).

100 Zoe Todd, "Commentary: The Environmental Anthropology of Settler Colonialism, Part I," *Engagement* (blog), April 11, 2017, https://aesengagement.wordpress.com/thematic-series/life-on-the-frontier-the-environmental-anthropology-of-settler-colonialism.

101 Audra Simpson, "The Ruse of Consent and the Anatomy of 'Refusal': Cases from Indigenous North America and Australia," *Postcolonial Studies* 20, no. 1 (2017): 2.

102 Audra Simpson, "The Ruse of Consent and the Anatomy of 'Refusal,'" 9.

103 Kyle Whyte addresses many of these issues. He writes, for instance, "The water protector's morality flows, then, from Indigenous governance systems that support cultural integrity, economic vitality, and political self-determination and the capacity to shift and adjust to the dynamics of eco-systems": Kyle Whyte, "The Dakota Access Pipeline, Environmental Injustice, and U.S. Settler Colonialism," *Red Ink* 19, no. 1 (2017): 154–69. We want to propose that the governance systems do more than "adjust to the dynamics of eco-systems"; they are also formed by

structuring these ecosystems as part of the polity themselves for which Indigenous governance systems are responsible.

104 Leanne Betasamosake Simpson, "Looking after Gdoo-Naaganinaa: Precolonial Nishnaabeg Diplomatic and Treaty Relationships," *Wicazo Sa Review* 23, no. 2 (2008): 29–42.

105 Stefano Harney and Fred Moten, *The Undercommons: Fugitive Planning and Black Study* (Wivenhoe, UK: Minor Compositions, 2013).

106 Leslie Marmon Silko, *The Turquoise Ledge* (New York: Penguin, 2011), 21.

107 Shiri Pasternak, *Grounded Authority: The Algonquins of Barriere Lake against the State* (Minneapolis: University of Minnesota Press, 2017).

1

"YOU TELL ME YOUR STORIES, AND I WILL TELL YOU MINE"

Witnessing and Combating Native Women's
Extirpation in American Indian Literature

MISHUANA GOEMAN

Over the course of the past several years, American Indian, Indigenous, and First Nation activists and scholars have been able to draw attention to two issues that are deeply affecting Indigenous communities in North America: (1) the issue of resource extraction—in particular, in the social movement of Idle No More in 2013 and, most recently, Standing Rock in 2016; and (2) the so-called epidemic of sexual assault on American Indian Reservations. As Sarah Deer makes clear in her book *The Beginning and End of Rape*, this is not an epidemic; the term *epidemic* is misleading, as it implies "that the problem is biological, that the problem originated independent of a long-standing oppression, that it has infected our society, twisting human relations. . . . Using the word epidemic deflects responsibility."[1] All too often the press has jumped on these issues in a salacious way. The common approach to settler violence is to decontextualize it from history and from the present political moment, without any aim to change the settler structure that supports the violence it purports to "feel bad" about. The settler public wants a particular kind of story. The statistics, the political rhetoric, and the lack of addressing issues in Indian Country or with Indian populations are colonial statecraft. As Joanne Barker states at the beginning of the introduction to *Critically Sovereign*: "It is a genuine challenge not to be cynical, given the relentlessness of racially hyper-gendered and sexualized appropriations. . . . It is also a challenge to take seriously the apologies that follow."[2] I use extirpation here to move us forward in thinking through the violence against Native women and the lack of justice in these moments. There are three meanings of *extirpation*, all of which relate to these issues. The first is to obliterate; the second is to root out; and the third is to conduct the removal of parts with surgical precision. The goal of settler colonialism is found in the first two positions of the definition, and the third is the goal of governmentality of Native lands and bodies, as will be discussed throughout.

Thus, Diane Sawyer reports on the poverty and violence at Pine Ridge while leaving out the legalities that set up poverty on reservations; the mainstream media reports on extremely high rates of rape on reservations but not the long-standing exploitation and lack of funding for criminal investigations or the protection of tribal citizens; environmental destruction by a pipeline runs through unceded territory is bemoaned only as cultural and spiritual loss rather than as an illegal infraction; or Hollywood makes a movie addressing sexual violence on reservations but has a white male hero as the main character rather than highlighting the massive amount of labor and love that Native women have undertaken to address this issue. All of these instances fail to accept how Canada and the United States benefit from the structures of colonialism and, at its core, the assault on Native women. As the report *A Roadmap for Making Native America Safer*, presented to the US president and Congress, illuminates throughout its three-year collection of data and evaluation: "The institutionalized federal under-funding and over-control of tribal justice systems has resulted in unacceptable high rates of violent crime and social alienation whose tragic effects extend well beyond Indian Country into every state in the Union."[3] Too often in addressing sexual violence against Native women or environmental racism, the relegation of Native space as separate, obsolete, over there, and of a different time drives the narrative. In other words, in this settler grammar of place, Indian Country and Indian bodies are criminalized.[4] Indians are understood by the wider public as far removed, both temporally and spatially; Indian people are gawked at as rare, not encounters with the real but, rather, those always bereft of "real" Indianness, or ghosts not quite tangible or in focus. Joyce E. King defines *dysconscious racism* as "a form of racism that tacitly accepts dominant white norms and privileges. It is not the absence of consciousness (i.e., unconsciousness) but an impaired consciousness or distorted way of thinking about race as compared to, for example, critical consciousness."[5] It is the "uncritical habit of mind" that enables mainstream America and Canada to believe and act in that belief system as though Native people are in another place that does not have a subsequent impact on the rest of society. It is a consistent placement of Native people in the imagination and in everyday actions as an irrelevance that then manifests itself in a tone of toxic care or a savior complex or completely ignores the structural issues that make possible the violence.

And yet I find myself, too, repeating the statistics that reach out and grab one's attention: one in three Native women experience sexual violence. Eighty-six percent of those rapes will involve a non-Indian and will also involve battering. These are just the contemporary and reported statistics. There are all other kinds and forms of sexual abuse and violence that occur in their wake that have been ongoing against Native peoples across centuries and in various spaces, from assault on tribal lands to constructed reservations, boarding schools, urban centers, border towns, and college campuses. Native feminist scholars and activists have done the lion's share of work acknowledging these issues and thus changing the material realities on the ground and in planning for the future. The first part of this chapter speaks to key interventions of critical sovereignty in Indigenous women's praxis. To demonstrate the long line of interventions of Indigenous women, I turn to stories told and retold in communities, stories that clearly link dispossession to the immiserating of Native women over the decades. In particular, I discuss *Bad Indians: A Tribal Memoir*, by Deborah Miranda, and her work to disrupt stories of pathology and pure loss while recognizing the generational effects of gendered violence. In the second part of the chapter, I turn to thinking about the witnessing that occurs and the violence that witnessing inflicts to extend the call for alternatives to these issues. In particular, I examine what the work of Louise Erdrich's *The Roundhouse* accomplishes in relation to a less well-known novel: *Elsie's Business*, by Frances A. Washburn (Lakota). The discussion of witnessing complements the work of scholars I discuss in the first part by thinking about these abuses with and beyond the law. A witness can be one who testifies that the crime took place; the witness can also be a victim. In *Elsie's Business*, Washburn's character Oscar, an older gentleman who tells Elsie's story of survival and death as well as traditional Deer woman stories, states: "How about this. You tell me your stories, and I'll tell you mine."[6] How does storytelling offer an alternative to the legal witnessing? How does it reach beyond and find an alternative to our current justice system? For laws, especially those applied in Indian Country, do not protect the threads and fabric of the community.

For the Record

Deborah Miranda labels the first section of her tribal memoir "The End of the World: Missionization 1776–1836," incorporating various genres to tell alternative narratives to colonization. The witnessing is archived, reworded, and repositioned as evidence. The title demands that there be a recognition of California Indian life and vitality—a whole world system that was not living in despair, neglect, or even the too often touted "primitive state." It was a complex world system containing science and knowledge of ecosystems, trade markets extending over large regions, political systems based on kinship and responsibility, and songs and cultural art that flourished throughout the regions. This California Indian history is too often erased, neglected in a larger American story of its own birth in Manifest Destiny or violently flattened as history becomes mythologized as a peaceful endeavor. Her titling of the chapter situates the story of America's California as one of loss that begins with colonial violence—and this takes a decidedly gendered form. It is an intervention into the use of the word *epidemic* by the media. It is a tracing, a California haunting, of how this world of California Indians came to an end. Yet unlike the "poverty porn" or creation of the happenstance tragedy spoken of above, she clearly is encouraging us all "to make story again in the world," which is the title of her last chapter.[7] She links a history of colonization *and Native peoples' survival* to the present moment. She witnesses not only the effect of violence but also the strength of her people in these stories. As Vicenta reminds us in the story, women's voices "are the antidote to lies" (xx). They are evidence of harm, cruelty, and inhumanity; this is evidence that has no statute of limitations. It moves to justice that extends beyond a courtroom.

In a genealogical chart form encompassing a whole page, Miranda lays out the development of California in all its brutality. She begins with Spain (the state) and Catholic Church (the cultural arm of colonization), marrying them together and linking the offspring of subjugation of bodies (Soldiers and Rape) to that of land theft (Franciscans and Missionization). The chart of these different generations of violent colonial policy clearly links gendered violence to that of land dispossession. It also links compulsory heterosexuality and heteropatriarchy through the forms of marriage, rape, and colonial masculine power. Furthermore, the chart ends with all the "problems" that are reported in damage-centered research on Native peoples.[8] In each subsequent generation of violence, expanded on throughout the tribal memoir in poetry, short story, photographic essay, lesson plan, and diagram, Miranda makes clear the power of gendered violence as she fleshes out the story of colonialism by incorporating Native experiences.

"Los Pájaros," the poem that follows the chart, speaks to "seeing your people [the Spanish] come through the fields" and the "fleeing" and fear that ensues as "the soldiers, clever as they are at lassoing cows/preyed upon the women for their unbridled lust" (3). Rape was a common occurrence and, in fact, an intentional part of colonization. Yet Miranda handles it with humanizing care: "Indian men defended their wives—/prey for the unbridled lust—/only to be shot down with bullets" and, in the next stanza, "The Indian men tried to defend their wives/ of various and beautifully blended colors" (3). The poetic scene, riffing off the firsthand account of the recently sainted Junipero Serra in May 1773 and May 1774, retells a story of expunged resistance and the great violence it took to conquer what is now California. Also of note in this moment is the double entendre of the word *Pájaros*, which is slang for LGBTQ. In times of colonial exertion of heteropatriarchy, rape and the killing of non-gender-conforming tribal peoples were common and documented by Bartolomé de las Casas and others. The fear of death and punishment forced a gender and sexual binary, quite literally manifested in the setup of the *monjerío*, which provided easy access to all women. The oral histories of this layout are well known by tribal members across California and the consequences of such architecture understood intergenerationally. The *monjerío*, set apart and with little light, were sturdy buildings that contained only the women. These carceral gendered spaces were a mapping of violent pre-state practices that made vulnerable generations of California Indian women.[9] Ben Madley, quoting Father Luis Jayme in 1772, relates a story from a firsthand account of sexual violence: "Very many of them deserve to be hanged on account of the continuous outrages which they are committing in seizing and raping of the women. There is not a single mission where the gentiles have not been scandalized."[10] The systemic nature of rape and lack of acknowledgment of the trespasses on land and bodily sovereignty has continued unabated for centuries and is part of a disciplinary process of dehumanizing Native populations. While it may seem a historical leap from the past to the present, the system that has set up and enabled injustice began at contact. Native women writers witness the trajectory of history, testifying to the ways these structures impact their everyday.

Reflecting the chart, the next piece is also a poem that tells the story of colonial desire and violence from the religious point of view. In "Fisher of Men," Miranda cleverly repeats the lines, "Before long, they will be caught/

in the apostolic and evangelical net," as we see the ruminations based on the now sainted Junipero Serra reverberate throughout the poem. The tone is one of desire, as over and over, in religious fervor of sin, the nakedness of California Indians is repeated: "They are naked as Adam/in the garden before sin." Yet as the pope declared in the early years of colonization of the Americas, the Indigenous people of the Americas had no souls and all were sinners; thus, no one was worthy of saving, and all were "ripe/for the reapers" (4–5). Here, in the marrying of these back-to-back poems, Miranda exposes the link between the soldiers' rape and the desire at play by the priests, concepts that made the pope declare that these non-Christians were without souls and thus without rights to the land that they had occupied since time immemorial.

These are early manifestations of hierarchies that would support the enactment in law of terra nullius (translated as no-man's-land) and doctrine of discovery whereby title could be passed only between Christian nations. In the 1830s, this maneuvering would set up federally recognized American Indian nations as domestic dependent nations in the US Supreme Court's Marshall Trilogy and drive the push west forward—and, with this settler avarice, a now legal consumption of Native land. The Supreme Court would invoke the Doctrine of Discovery based on terra nullius, a concept that denies and extirpates complex Indigenous societies, and a Catholic papal bull to claim land as property. A gendered process of acquiring and domesticating land and law took hold, as did, in connection to land dispossession, compulsory heterosexuality and a racially gendered legal morass. As Beth Hege Piatote (Ni:mi:pu: [Nez Perce]) comments on early nineteenth-century literature: "The national domestication projects of settlement and expansion corresponded with the proliferation of domesticity as an ideology."[11] Piatote carefully unpacks the family and home in tribal communities as sites of resistance to citizenship and land acquisition. Miranda, in her tribal memoir, also works to weave together a shattered family and tribe through bits and fragments in the archive, choosing to tell the story not only of domestication but also of extirpation. Extirpation, while not fully achieved, shattered California tribal communities who faced state-propelled genocide. Invested with many resources, as meticulously documented by Ben Madley, those who settled participated in the extermination of California Indians.[12]

Let us return to the statistics and the touting of an epidemic or the ways in which the media are creating a crisis, as though sexual violence against Native women is a momentary rise in assaults. Miranda opens up her letter to her ancestor, Vicenta, by speaking of Vicenta's rape at the hands of priests as well as of her own rape as a child. "I could try to be funny," Miranda writes, "That's how I've learned to deal with it. I mean it happens all the time right? It's not just that we're women, we're Indian women . . . poor Indian women" (23). The feminist letter genre, coupled with jokes seemingly in bad taste, demands a response to the statistics on the page, even if the "statistics . . . are predictable. Thirty-four percent of us raped; one in three! And ninety percent of the rapists are non-Indian" (23). Humor collapses the moments between a construction of a sad isolated past of rape through the *conquistadores*, temporally distanced from present-day settler national identities, and the seemingly more progressive present time with knowledge about the evils of sexual violence and a legal order that protects bodily sovereignty of all—post-slavery, post–civil rights, and post–sexual revolution. Miranda's following words unravel this presupposition of a time when the legal system and the nation-state instituted safety for American Indians: "Well, I shouldn't complain. Those are stats from my day and age. For you, it's probably more like 100 percent" (23). Unlike a linear narrative of history, Miranda is able to trace these early histories into her present-day status as an Indian and how the legal system and an ethos of violence against Native women evolved from these early moments of contact. This form of witnessing in Native women's literature is not about the event; she is witnessing the structure of colonialism through settler and spatial temporalities.

Miranda moves quite easily in her tribal memoir between her Ohlone-Costanoan Esselen Nation and the racial category of "Indian," as do many who grow up Indian. As Jodi Byrd states, the Indian is a "transit"—that is, not only those who stand in the way of empire building and must thus be eliminated, but also those through which empire moves or those who make up the "living dead of empire."[13] How does this resonate with the attention and the energy garnered around the "Stolen Sisters," the murdered and missing Indigenous women in Canada, and the subsequent countermovement, or with the attention finally being paid to rape statistics in Indian Country? Why is it that, no matter how much activists and scholars pull in place-based political analysis of these assaults, backed by historical and statistical facts, the front line of communities are still flattened and specificity is still erased under the structural statecraft of colonialism? This obscuring and racial homogenizing of Indians renders Native people, particularly women, deficit subjects. To continue with Byrd: "Any assemblage that arises from such horizons [that of savage alterities] becomes a colonialist one, and it is the work of indigenous critical theory both to rearticulate indigenous phenomenology and to provide (alter)native interpretative strategies through which to apprehend the colonialist nostalgias that continue to shape affective liberal democracy's investment in state sovereignty as a source of violence, remedy, memory, and grievability."[14] How then, is the sexual violence of empire still moving through the transit of Indian? What are some of the ways to strategize a solution to the issue of sexual violence against Native women without, yet again, blaming the racialized victim, pathologizing and uprooting her from history, her land, her now pathologized community in the name of rescuing? Thus far, there has been a tendency to racialize the matter in reporting the statistics, to find solutions that continue to diminish sovereignty through the legal means that caused many of the issues to begin with. Byrd laments that the "racialization in the United States now often evokes colonization as a metonym," and "this conflation masks the territoriality of conquest by assigning colonization to the racialized body."[15] Moving from Byrd's work with "Indian" as a transit through which empire moves, Audra Simpson speaks to the flesh of transit and its formation in the politics of willful ignorance of the violence against Native communities. In speaking of the relationship between the state and heteropatriarchy, she makes the following claim:

> As well, [the state] seeks to destroy what is not. The state does so with a death drive to eliminate, contain, hide and in other ways "disappear" what fundamentally challenges is [sic] legitimacy: Indigenous political orders. And here is the rub, Indigenous political orders are quite simply, first, prior to the project of founding, of settling, and as such continue to point, in their persistence and vigor, to the failure of the settler project to eliminate them, and yet are subjects of dispossession, of removal, but their polities serve as alternative forms of legitimacy and sovereignties to that of the settler state.[16]

Native women, in addressing the issue of sexual violence, consistently use their place-based geographies to persevere against extirpation. It is my intention in the next section of this chapter, to examine how that literature presents alternatives for dealing with colonial structures that render Native women vulnerable, invisible, and incoherent in discourses of justice.

Witnessing

Many of the Native women who have come to me in my various roles as relative, friend, teacher, and mentor have spoken of the violence they have endured and the violence they have borne witness to in their various roles. A person who experiences a violent crime can also be a witness to its occurrence, providing evidence and material to form a case. Native women have been witnessing for hundreds of years, providing evidence long before the court systems set up what Amnesty International frames as a "maze of injustice," from a report of the same name that called attention to legal loopholes.[17] Since this report and the massive organizing across the Americas, multiple books, research projects, and organizations have formed to address the conditions that promulgate these statistics. Some are small, local organizations focusing on Indigenous feminist practices of care, and others work to inform policy. Witnessing stories are written in archives; written in oral traditions as communities used stories to adjust to the brutality of colonization; written in contemporary fiction and poetry; written in social media and blogs; and beautifully addressed in the richness of art practices in all mediums. Yet even with the thousands of stories and patterns of sexual violence laid bare, justice has not come.

In my teaching of *Sharing Our Stories of Survival*, a key community-based resource for dealing with sexual assault and its aftermath, I often ask my students why they believe that Charlene Ann LaPointe begins her article "Sexual Violence: An Introduction to the Social and Legal Issues for Native American Women" with stories of her family and weaves in the discussion of community, family, and culture as it intersects with settler structures of state-imposed violence throughout her writing. Rather than the state being an overarching, distant structure, LaPointe pulls it in close, drawing on the ways it creates a formidable intimacy from her childhood onward. Even with this maneuver, however, the students respond by relegating responsibility for rape and lack of justice to "Indian" culture. In part, this returns to an ethos of sexual violence created through intersectional representation; they have had years of a faulty socialization that pathologizes Indians. Regardless of how often I repeat that 86 percent of rapes of Native women are committed by non-Natives, which makes the racialized violence markedly different from that of other groups who experience similar crimes, or remind them that there is no such thing as *the* Indian culture, this pathologizing of the Indian becomes the settler blanket of comfort.

I in no way wish to ignore or turn away from the Indian male rapist, either, that LaPointe so bravely confronts in this moment. As Sarah Hunt conveys: "Colonialism relies on the widespread dehumanization of all Indigenous people—our children, two-spirits, men and women—[then] colonial violence could be understood to impact all of us at the level of our denied humanity. Yet this dehumanization is felt most acutely in the bodies of Indigenous girls, women, two-spirit and transgender people, as physical and sexual violence against us continues to be accepted as normal."[18] It is on the complexity of focusing on the conditions set forth by an ethos of sexual violence, by a continual witnessing, and by the lack of expectations around bodily sovereignty that the witnessing pivots.

In LaPointe's important article we find the story of one woman's experience with violence that moves through various life cycles. In fact, throughout this very important anthology, many of the essays weave together the personal, the legal, and the hopes and aspirations the Native women are putting forth; they tell of their specific stories of horrific violence not as confession but, rather, to keep future generations safe. They tell of the landscape, of the specificity of their belief systems, of the particularity of institutions that enable the violence against them to continue. LaPointe's encounters with settler institutions—from the school to the police—and those before her become the site of violence. As Laura Kwak states, "It is through the bureaucratic governance over life that violence reinvigorates liberal democracy, remakes nations, reinscribes binaries, and renarrates mythical stories about a clash of civilizations."[19] Violence is not a racially inherited trait but part of the outcomes of violent policies. To bear witness to the story is an important part of what Native women attempt in telling their stories. LaPointe expounds on this: "Using my own experience as a victim of sexual violence in childhood and young adulthood is an attempt to follow the trauma through its lifecycle and to describe the unseen trash that we carry into different phases of our lifecycles, sometimes right to our very death bed."[20] It is the witnessing, the acknowledgment of Native women's carrying a brunt of colonization, that is key to a larger discussion of addressing sexual violence. The overemphasis on crisis and epidemic ignores the witnessing in the scholarly articles, the as-told-to stories, the archive that provides documented evidence of the fact of this violence, and the stories shared. Witnessing is strength, and we should not strip bare the living experiences of American Indian and Indigenous women as purely victims. In fact, it is in the passing of stories that Native women have survived and fought further immiseration. Yet we also must recall Dian Million's words on the difficulties associated with bearing witness, "The same stories collectively witnessed the social violence that was and is colonialism's heart. . . . [T]o 'tell' called for a reevaluation of reservation and reserve beliefs about what was appropriate to say about your own family, your community."[21] In the novels that follow, the authors attest to the duality, the difficulties in witnessing, as they "balanced the necessity to change things and constraints to 'silence' their pain and experience."[22]

I say this with a caveat. I in no way wish to conflate witness with survivor in this moment. To conflate the witnessing with the pain of endurance undermines the pain of violence in the material. Rather, I contend that the witnessing of intergenerational forms of violence directed at gendered Indigenous bodies has created an ethos of violence from the mundane everyday of being denied who we are or being appropriated—casually named an S-word or "Chief" or relegated to the uncomfortable spaces of settler imagination—to the more serious life-and-death situations of border-town violence, being targeted for sexual violence and sex trafficking, and the very denial of our bodily integrity. It is not just Indians who witness the hierarchy of bodily integrity in the news, film, literature, and media, as we see throughout the literature discussed here. The mainstream has learned that our subjecthood was always meant to be discarded. We must unlearn and problematize how racialized violence against Indians is tolerated. Witnessing and telling the stories are at once strength, but they do accumulate to lay a burden on certain doorsteps and not others. The awe-striking statistics are one thing, but if we consider witnessing as an ongoing form of violence—and one that Native women experience at alarming rates and at alarmingly young ages—we then delve into the ways that sexual violence against Native women and communities in the form of witnessing can also be used to discipline women and subject them to continued violence. It is important in our approaches to avoid the trap of victimizing while recognizing the harm of witnessing violent events. As Deer comments in "Decolonizing Rape Law," "It becomes important, then, for tribal governments to construct rape not only as an attack on an individual woman—but also an attack on the entire community."

Here I turn briefly to address the Pulitzer Prize–winning novel *The Roundhouse*, by Louise Erdrich (Chippewa), and how it provides a platform to discuss the various laws at play in Indian Country. It is a fictional book that brought much attention to the crimes being committed in Indian Country. The book animates write-ups in the *New Yorker*, *Huffington Post*, and the *New York Times*; on National Public Radio; and in all manner of mainstream media. The book itself rests on a form of witnessing—a witnessing of the aftermath of a brutal rape and its effect on a family and a community. It is told in a coming-of-age narrative of a boy in the midst of early puberty and contains a mystery of sorts. *The Roundhouse* begins with the following scene driven by emotion, letting us know that the story is about the controversy of lack of justice in Indian Country: "I put my hands on his hands and looked into his eyes. His leveling brown eyes. I wanted to know that whoever had attacked my mother would be found, punished, killed. My father saw this. His fingers dug into my shoulders."[23] In the same breath, this normal reaction to the hurt inflicted on a loved one is complicated with the father's knowledge of federal Indian law:

> He tapped his watch, bit down on his lip. Now if the police would come. They need to get a statement. They should have been here.
>> We turned to go back to the room.
>> Which police? I asked.
>> Exactly, he said. (15)

When the tribal, state, and federal police arrive at the hospital to take a statement—an actual component of what happens in rape and violence against Indian women—there is confusion about who has jurisdiction. The questions that arise are: Where did the rape take place? and Was the perpetrator Indian or non-Indian? Another issue that comes into play with Geraldine's rape is the extent of brutal violence (see 41, 160–61). Geraldine's rapist's intent to kill her to hide the secret of a different murder would make this a federal case. However, she cannot speak—or, rather, she refuses to identify her rapist, knowing through her work in the tribal court system that justice will not be served.

This sets Joe's life in motion as he turns to figuring out what happened to his mother. Eventually, we find out that the event happened on the border between tribal and nontribal land and that the perpetrator was not a member of the tribe. Again, the pathologizing of Indians manifested in law and order makes for a vulnerable population. The court "recognize[s] that some Indian tribal court systems have become increasingly sophisticated and resemble in many respects their state counterparts. . . . They have little relevance to the principles which lead up to conclude that Indian tribes do not have inherent jurisdiction to try and punish non-Indians."[24] The US Supreme Court has overwhelmingly ruled against full exercise of tribal sovereignty in the past few decades as a means to address the disparities of administering justice for crimes committed by nonmember, non-Native actors.[25] The concluding remark in Justice William Rehnquist's written opinion in the heavily cited case *Oliphant v. Suquamish Indian Tribe* (1978) should force readers to question the very foundations on which the decision was based: "Finally, we are not unaware of the prevalence of non-Indian crime on today's reservations which the tribes forcefully argue requires the ability to try non-Indians. . . . They have little relevance to the principles which lead us to conclude that Indian tribes do not have inherent jurisdiction to try and punish non-Indians."[26]

In this moment, Chief Justice Rehnquist operates from the premise that primitive governments cannot handle the prosecution of those deemed full citizens—the non-Native—for fear they will not be judged justly by their Indian peers. The experience and witnessing of violence is forgone as the court regulates testimony to location, race, and other forms of evidentiary procedures. A Native woman bearing witness to the crime is not enough to bring US forms of justice.

Erdrich takes up these unjust legal matters and quickly problematizes them in relation to justice and liberal democracy. For Indians, the law is much like the weather. Erdrich, through her protagonist, is clear about the precarious and unsettled ground of legal democracy in settler courts: "My father could out-weather anybody. Like people anywhere, there were times when it was the only topic where people here felt comfortably expressive, and my father could go on earnestly, seemingly forever" (110). Her pointed critique of the law as a comfort is clear. It cajoles and makes one feel protected and thus we acquiesce to the sovereign state. Yet for Indians, forced to submit through colonization, this has never been an easy placation. The law has always been violent and not a grantor of protection to territorial or bodily sovereignty. Erdrich continues to expound on the weather and its unpredictability: "When the current weather was exhausted, there was all the weather that had occurred in recorded history, weather lived through or witnessed by a relative, or even heard about on the news. Catastrophic weather of all types. And when that was done, there was all the weather that might possibly occur in the future. I'd even heard him speculate about weather in the afterlife" (110). This tongue-in cheek metaphor speaks to the acute awareness American Indians (and here I am intentionally using the racial category as it matters in law) have of the everyday impact of settler structures in their lives. Again, it is an intimacy with institutions and awareness that makes witnessing a form of violence and a form of strength.

In the end, however, Joe's best friend kills Lark, the rapist who was also trying to gain land claims. We see a grappling with an unjust system. The priest tells Joe to ask for forgiveness; Joe seeks to end the rapist's life; and his dad resigns himself resolutely to the law to which he has devoted his life, a law he recognizes as deeply flawed: "Any Judge knows there are many kinds of justice—for instance, ideal justice as opposed to the best-we-can-do-justice, which is what we end up with in making so many of our decisions. It was no lynching. There was no question of his guilt. He may have even wanted to get caught and punished. We can't know his mind. Lark's killing is a wrong thing which serves an ideal justice. It settles a legal enigma. It threads the unfair maze of land title law by which Lark could not be prosecuted. His death was the exit" (306).

So what is Erdrich suggesting in the wake of this settler predicament? What does it mean that Native women's stories and witnessing are not enough in relation to legal proceedings? What are the ongoing implications of ignoring sexual violence against Native women? How do we account for justice? How might we question the use of law as the primary recourse in the context of settler colonialism? Are there other forms of justice? Knowing the limits of law is crucial. Geraldine, in her refusal to name, to speak, to settle through American courts, is key to this discussion.

Previous to the publication of *The Roundhouse*, *Elsie's Business* addressed the high rates of sexual violence in Indian Country. The novel is set in 1969–70 during what has come to be known as "the reign of terror" in plains Indian

Country. This novel is set eight years before the *Oliphant* decision, yet the issues of jurisdiction, race, and settler violence weave threads through these different temporal, societal, and spatial geographies. The novel begins with Elsie's rape by three young white men who target her as a Native women walking down a cold, isolated road. Elsie's personhood is clearly disregarded, moving from derogatory words spewed to rape to the finale, which results in her being run over as the assailants seek to leave the crime scene. She is left to die on the side of the road. The violence these young men commit is not extraordinary; rather, it is part of the everyday practice in the border town in which the novel is set.[27] The opening scene is intense; in it, we hear our first inaudible words from Elsie, who symbolizes and reflects the Deer Woman stories throughout the novel. After that witnessing of the events, Elsie's story takes a communal turn: "If you want to know more about Elsie's story than just the official reports, you have to ask one of the grandfathers because they know all the old stories as well as the new ones, the latest gossip, and sometimes it's all the same stories happening over and over."[28] The Deer Woman signifies sexual transgression and its consequences for an entire community, or, according to Oscar, the traditional storyteller and community pivot in the text, "Men who see the deer woman go crazy, but women who see her are rewarded with the ability to make beautiful things—maybe beadwork or quillwork" (39). Men who violate women and thus create an imbalance in community are doomed to perish. Women who are enticed from their homes and do not attend to community are also at risk. The witnessing of Deer Woman in relation to sexual violations as not an individual act but as one that the community must address arises in Frances Washburn's use of myth around which the story pivots. These stories around which the novel is set remind the readers of tending to important relationships. The consequence of rape and transgression is harsh, as we see throughout the novel. Just as in Miranda's tribal memoir, this particular story involves a turn toward the traditional: the Deer Woman stories, a critique of limiting forms of justice that appeal to US law, and a wrestling with what to do about sexual violence.

Official reports, the fodder of law, do not suffice. As the novel's title implies, the small town sets about telling the young woman's business, and in a sense it is implied that Elsie's business should, in fact, be all of our business. So while the story is told to her estranged father after her death and through various people whom Elsie encounters in her travels, it is a story in which all partake; thus, all become responsible for answering the conditions that set up the sexual violence Elsie endured. We never actually hear Elsie's story; she does not testify. Rather, the narrator sets about gathering testimony from the town. In Vancouver, Jaskiran Dhillon contextualizes Washburn's work in a historical milieu, thus exposing the state's move to individualize violence and resistance to it: "Colonial violence, then, is always deliberately attached to an agenda of individual subjectification that functions to sublimate collective resistance and reinforce self-rule in the name of settler sovereignty."[29] *Elsie's Business* uses storytelling in this small-town setting to produce a collective path forward and to expose the power relations involved. The bits and pieces of Elsie's story and murder filter through the lens of people's position vis-à-vis power in the text. The community witnesses what the lack of attention to sexual violence can do.

After the rape and her mother's subsequent death while she is healing, Elsie is whisked away to a neighboring town to hide the savage violence committed by the prominent white prodigy in the town. Even though the boys meet their death in a car accident shortly after the rape, the local sheriff still burns Elsie's clothes (evidence) to keep his job. It is an election year, after all. In a scene set at the hospital, the doctor assumes the sexual violence was committed by another Indian: "I want to know just as soon as you can tell me somehow, someway, just who the hell did this to you. . . . I also want to know when you goddamned Indians are going to quit trying to kill each other" (87). In this series of conversations, the doctors, nurses, and sheriff are not neglectful or without feeling. Rather, they are tied up in a system that diminishes Indians' humanity. At one point, before he burns Elsie's clothes so as not to "sully" his rich patron's name during the election year, a nurse asks the sheriff: "What about justice?" The question is left to settle in the conversation, to trail off. When she asks, "What about Elsie?" the response does not change. Her removal from the Standing Rock area—and here we can further think about long lines of Indigenous dispossession and removal from their home territories—is used to protect the status quo of the border town. As Simpson clarifies in theorizing gendered violence in relation to the state, grievability of violence against Indians is necessary to "governability."[30] Indian deaths, rapes, and removal are part the everyday in this era. Unfortunately, the statistics have not improved much in border towns.

When attempting to build a new life in another border town near a related Lakota reservation, a series of events happens, and Elsie is raped and murdered three years later. This reflects the peril of *being* an Indian woman in the spaces controlled by the settler state. Throughout the story, we comprehend, as do the characters in the text, the constant risk of rape and violence under which Elsie lives. During this time, she befriends a churchgoer and resolute Catholic named Nancy Marks, who makes it her mission to "save" Elsie. Unfortunately, Elsie and Nancy have many misunderstandings, and in the end Nancy admits she learned more about herself through knowing Elsie than she ever knew about Elsie as a human. The Indian community also avoids Elsie; thus, she also misses that particular safety net: "It wasn't that they were unkind to Elsie but that they were a little afraid of her, being as she was, the embodiment of past transgressions, living proof of what happens when people upset the social order of things" (68). Washburn pointedly looks at kinship and its obligations throughout the novel, seeking kinship ties as a way to set right the balance of sexual violence. Kinship and governance are entangled for Native people: in terms of relationality, the sexual violence against Elsie moves beyond the individual and affects the entire Indian community. The Deer Woman appears here as a community out of balance and a reminder to pay attention to relationships.

However, the border town and its daily operations are deeply invested in the individual. The individual, however, is defined by racial divisions—divisions that do not apply the law equally. Washburn makes this pointedly clear in the novel: when the mayor is found to be publicly drunk, he is taken home by the police, whereas jailing Indians is common practice: "The usual high number of Indians were arrested for drunk and disorderly, public intoxication or just GPV-general principals violated. Most of them were unable to pay their fines, so, as usual, they worked it off by laboring at five dollars a day (less the cost of their two scanty meals per day) serving as helpers for the city garbage collection. Except for the Indians themselves, no one else talked about the Indian arrests. It was too commonplace" (67). Similar to the labor and incarceration in the case of the California racialized system, there was a correlation between private morality and public condemnations of Indians in vague principle laws. The pathologizing of Indians as alcoholics, lost and bereft of morals, results in high rates of incarceration that continue today. It also results in the ethos of sexual violence and ethos of disposability of Native women. The arrest and unfair jailing practices, rates of poverty, and lack of infrastructure at this time was well known throughout the Dakotas. The same language used to justify the small infraction is employed at the point of violent rape. Elsie is referred to as a "goddamned slippery whore," "bitch," "squaw," "dirty old skin," and "cow" throughout her beating and rape. This reflects the statistic that, "when asked whether the aggressors physically hit them during the assault, over 90 percent of Native women victims report their perpetrator(s) used a weapon, compared to 9 percent of white women."[31] This witnessing of the event moves beyond the statistics, divulging the dehumanization that lies at the foundation of settlement in the seemingly safest of towns. The doctor, in response to Elsie's condition and the death of the three assailants, proclaims: "Whoever said nothing happens in small towns ain't never been here" (28). Washburn paints a clear picture of settler towns and the maintenance of racial hierarchies in rural America that are far from idyllic.

The final murderer is never revealed, but an acute awareness of the divergence zones and the lack of intercommunity reconciliation following these unfortunate events develops throughout the novel. The power relations that have been set in place fail to address the very issue that leaves "Nancy wonder[ing] why young Indian women seemed the center of so much tragedy" (86). This is reminiscent of the other logics of elimination: those of the dead and a colonial ordering or a settler grammar of place where Native people are continually positioned as always dying or dead. In many ways, it is an axiom of itself when paired with the rates of death of Native people in custody or on the streets. Nancy's abrasive words puncture the naturalness of Elsie's death, as the reader has come to know full well the settler structures that led to her death.

In the last pages of *Elsie's Business*, we realize that we will never know who murdered Elsie. We will not know the reason—whether it was to silence her; whether it was a refusal of sexual advances; or even whether it was being in the wrong body at the wrong place. The reader is left unsatisfied. The reader is left without a full story. As in so many rapes and murders in Indian Country and beyond, Native women do not receive the recourse of justice, and there are no answers for their communities. Rather, we witness the aftermath of the loss. While some, such as Mason, the prominent landowner and father of the boys who raped Elsie at the start of the novel, would like to cover up these individualized indecencies, as he "never taught [his] boys to be killers or rapists, either. . . . Christ, you try raising two boys up here," the stories are witnessed and shared (209). The stories refuse the narrative of erasing the collective violence. His own dehumanizing words show that Mason wishes Native people were gone and no longer a burden to white settlers: "Yeah, I admit, I never had any use for an Indian, and I still don't" (209). This moment in the text is indicative of the conversation around sexual violence in the United States that Mason tells Elsie's father: *"I want that dead girl and you to hell and gone out of our lives. . . .* Can I tell my wife it's over? It ain't never going to come up again?" (209) Elsie's story did not die, nor will it. Neither will the story of sexual violence as long as it continues. It is a violence that will not be suppressed in the logics of the elimination of Native people in a settler context. Elsie's father tells the white settler, "I can't promise what else or who else might bring this up again. You never know what bones someone might dig up" (209). And this is the power of story. While records may be lost, evidence incinerated, and power used to bury the violence it takes to maintain a colonial order, the story will be there to voice and refuse. So we know that, despite people like Mason, who will "do everything in [his] power to keep those bones buried" (209), there are alternative stories.

Conclusions

In discussing the three texts—*Bad Indians*, *The Roundhouse*, and *Elsie's Business*—
I point to three very different place-based communities dealing with the very
real assaults on Native women. While Erdrich's novel revolves around a clearly
delineated federally recognized tribe, Miranda must and does address the
specificity violence takes on for California Indians who faced Spanish and US
colonization and did not have their treaties ratified by Congress. Thus, many
California Indian tribes were not able to keep their territorial sovereignty and
go unrecognized by the law. However, high rates of sexual violence still exist.
The ethos of colonial violence does not disappear at the borderlines. This is
also evidenced in the border-town rape of Elsie. As she travels to and from
work, across reservation and county boundaries, these imaginary and mapped
lines determine her recourse to justice or lack thereof. What she does not escape is who she is as a mixed Indigenous and Black woman in South Dakota.
Kristin Simmons reminds us that "the settler colonial project of US Empire
is, after all, to place indigenous nations and bodies into suspension"; to do so,
those bodies must be constructed "as crisis or colonial residue," or what I refer
to here as creating an ethos of violence.[32] These spaces, governed by specific
jurisdictions, still govern bodies. We find the importance of bearing witness in
each of these texts, an importance that counters the state as a site of justice.

Whether the space is the reservation, the urban, or the rural, we need to
address the ethos of sexual violence against Native women by critically listen-
ing to the stories, the accounts of witnessing, to provide a path for a healthy
future. In the case of California, Cutcha Baldy relates the importance of seeing
Indigenous futurity as deeply tied to promoting healthy Native women's bodies and understanding them as necessary to our collective futures. Her book
We Are Dancing for You (2018) provides a witnessing of renewal and respect for
the power of the body as it dances, as it does so in community, and thus understanding one's worth and place. It also undoes the power of the story created
by anthropologists, historians, and all others who demean that power: "Song,
stories and research—they come to you. They say, 'This is what you will do
now.'"[33] A form of Native feminist witnessing is proactive and attests to settler-
state power as an intimate form of violence. In its report, the Tribal Law and
Order Commission emphasizes the need to uphold tribal sovereignty and seek
"alternatives": "From the tribal viewpoint, this finding is neither surprising nor
new. Tribes are long-time advocates for alternative approaches."[34] As pipelines
and fracking are established, so, too, are man camps and places of already deep
heteropatriarchal power. These "settler atmospherics" must be accounted for,

as they are part of a much wider breadth of the population. Simmons moves us to the following question: "What would it take for individuals to reconceptualize the embeddedness in which we all already are with and have the potential to be for—to stage the grounds for a collective reimagining, a conspiration, an atmospheric otherwise?"[35] While I speak to fiction in this essay, the fiction itself is written from the experience of those who know and understand all too well how violence and terror of assault impacts the intimacies of daily life, and they are asking for a reconceptualizing of colonial violence.

In closing, I think through the words of Deborah Miranda, who asks the pivotal question: "But where to start? What's the best way to kill a lie? Like bad spirits they are notoriously immune to arrows—in fact, they are often known to rise after being killed, even after being buried. We must know where to aim, pick our targets, remain clear-sighted" (xx). I argue that the telling of Miranda, Erdrich, and Washburn unburies the bones of violence and pulls all into the story of colonialism. We all are accountable in the telling and thus must be moved to action. In this chapter, I hope I have made clear that it is not enough to tell statistics, to present the facts, to apologize for a past, or to provide testimony in a court of law that does not hear women's voices. We must listen to the witnessing of violence and, once we hear the stories, do more than pity or pathologize. Instead, we must take aim at that which is buried. No matter how difficult, Native and non-Native people alike must engage with how the world is constructed through the brutal and immiserating power of gendered violence directed at Native women.

NOTES

1 Sarah Deer, *The Beginning and End of Rape: Confronting Sexual Violence in Native America* (Minneapolis: University of Minnesota Press, 2015), x.

2 Joanne Barker, *Critically Sovereign: Indigenous Gender, Sexuality, and Feminist Studies* (Durham, NC: Duke University Press, 2017), 1–2.

3 Indian Law and Order Commission, *A Roadmap for Making Native America Safer: Report to the President and Congress of the United States*, November 2013, 90, https:// www.aisc.ucla.edu/iloc/report/files/A_Roadmap_For_Making_Native_America_ Safer-Full.pdf.

4 See Mishuana Goeman, "Disrupting a Settler-Colonial Grammar of Place: The Visual Memoir of Hulleah Tsinhnahjinnie," in *Theorizing Native Studies*, edited by Audra Simpson and Andrea Smith (Durham, NC: Duke University Press, 2014), 235–65.

5 Joyce E. King, "Dysconscious Racism: Ideology, Identity and the Miseducation of Teachers," *Journal of Negro Education* 60 (1991): 135.

6   Frances Washburn, *Elsie's Business* (Lincoln: University of Nebraska Press, 2006), 120.

7   Deborah A. Miranda, *Bad Indians: A Tribal Memoir* (Berkeley, CA: Heyday, 2013), 207 (hereafter, page numbers from this work are cited in parentheses in the text).

8   For a call to end damage-centered research, see Eve Tuck, "Suspending Damage: A Letter to Communities," *Harvard Educational Review* 79, no. 3 (2009): 409–27.

9   Jackie Teran, "The Violent Legacies of the California Missions: Mapping the Origins of Native Women's Mass Incarceration," *American Indian Culture and Research Journal* 40, no. 1 (2016): 19–32.

10 Benjamin Madley, *An American Genocide: The United States and the California Indian Catastrophe, 1846–1873* (New Haven, CT: Yale University Press, 2016), 17.

11 Beth H. Piatote, *Domestic Subjects: Gender, Citizenship, and Law in Native American Literature* (New Haven, CT: Yale University Press, 2013), 5.

12 Madley, *An American Genocide.*

13 Jodi A. Byrd, *The Transit of Empire: Indigenous Critiques of Colonialism* (Minneapolis: University of Minnesota Press, 2011), 226.

14 Byrd, *The Transit of Empire,* 21.

15 Byrd, *The Transit of Empire,* xxiii–xxiv.

16 Audra Simpson, "The State Is a Man: Theresa Spence, Loretta Saunders and the Gender of Settler Sovereignty," *Theory and Event* 19, no. 4 (2016).

17 Amnesty International USA, *Maze of Injustice: The Failure to Protect Indigenous Women From Sexual Violence in the USA* (New York: Amnesty International USA, 2007).

18 Sarah Hunt, "More Than a Poster Campaign: Redefining Colonial Violence," *Decolonization: Indigeneity, Education and Society* (blog), February 14, 2017, https://decolonization.wordpress.com/2013/02/14/more-than-a-poster-campaign-redefining-colonial-violence.

19 Laura Kwak, "Introduction to Section One," in *At the Limits of Justice: Women of Colour on Terror,* edited by Suvendrini Perera and Sherene Razack (Toronto: University of Toronto Press, 2014), 19.

20 Charlene Ann LaPointe, "Sexual Violence: An Introduction to the Social and Legal Issues for Native Women," in *Sharing Our Stories of Survival: Native Women Surviving Violence,* edited by Sarah Deer, Bonnie Clairmont, Carrie A. Martell, and Maureen L. White Eagle (Lanham, MD: AltaMira, 2008), 38.

21 Dian Million, "Felt Theory: An Indigenous Feminist Approach to Affect and History," *Wicazo Sa Review* 24, no. 2 (Fall 2009): 56.

22 Millin, "Felt Theory," 56.

23 Louise Erdrich, *The Round House* (New York: HarperCollins, 2012), 14 (hereafter, page numbers from this work are cited in parentheses in the text).

24 *Oliphant v. Suquamish Indian Tribe,* 435 US 191 (1978).

25 *United States v. William S. Rogers,* 45 US 567 (1846); *Oliphant v. Suquamish Indian Tribe; United States v. Lara,* 541 US 193 (2004).

26 *Oliphant v. Suquamish Indian Tribe.*

27 Nick Estes, Melanie K. Yazzie, Jennifer Nez Denetdale, and David Correia, *Red Nation Rising: From Bordertown Violence to Native Liberation* (Oakland, CA: PM Press, 2021).

28 Washburn, *Elsie's Business*, 1 (hereafter, page numbers from this work are cited in parentheses in the text).

29 Jaskiran Dhillon, *Prairie Rising: Indigenous Youth, Decolonization, and the Politics of Intervention* (Toronto: University of Toronto Press, 2017), 83.

30 Simpson, "The State Is a Man," n.p.

31 Deer, *The Beginning and End of Rape*, 4.

32 Kristen Simmons, "Settler Atmospherics," *Society for Cultural Anthropology*, Fieldsights, November 20, 2017, https://culanth.org/fieldsights/1221-settler-atmospherics.

33 Cutcha Risling Baldy, *We Are Dancing for You: Native Feminisms and the Revitalization of Women's Coming-of-Age Ceremonies*, Indigenous Confluences (Seattle: University of Washington Press, 2018), 6.

34 Indian Law and Order Commission, *A Roadmap for Making Native America Safer*, 131.

35 Simmons, "Settler Atmospherics," n.p.

2

THE BIOPOLITICS OF AGING

Indigenous Elders as Elsewhere

SANDY GRANDE

In what sense does a life unfold?—MICHEL FOUCAULT, *The History of Sexuality, Volume 1* (1978)

What if staying alive has something to do with witnessing the death in life? What if dying, and being borne along by those who love you, is also a way of being alive? How might we care for life that is constitutively beside itself, life that could never be full itself?—LISA STEVENSON, *Life beside Itself* (2014)

While the notion of *precarity* as a social condition marked by economic insecurity has been in circulation since the 1970s, it came into wider usage in the United States after September 11, 2001, a dilatory effect of the increased surveillance and austerity measures implemented by the George W. Bush administration.[1] The concept "expresses [not only] the sense that the state has broken its ideological promise (what Polanyi posited in *The Great Transformation*) to ameliorate the misery capitalism necessarily generates" but also the embodied experience of living in a time of permanent and irregular war, marked by rising authoritarianism, increased militarization, and environmental destruction.[2] While theorized as an effect of contemporary conditions, I understand precarity as an extension of the structures of settler colonialism—its ever expanding modes of dispossession whereby "people and places" are "remade as things in the service of the accumulation of wealth and the exercise of geopolitical power."[3]

Indeed, over the past ten years I've gained a deeper, more visceral understanding of the ways in which precarity is a state manifested through the settler "logics of elimination."[4] In 2005, I joined the growing legion of 65.7 million family caregivers in the United States, most of whom are women and, disproportionally, women of color. First, my ever stoic dad suffered a mild heart attack and then a stroke, which precipitated aortic valve replacement surgery. A couple of years later, he was diagnosed with stomach cancer, for which he underwent two surgeries, the second resulting from a surgical error committed in the first. Around the same time, my beloved mom (already a breast cancer survivor) began to suffer a succession of chronic and acute illnesses. Eventually, her struggles through pulmonary fibrosis, glaucoma, rheumatoid arthritis, and dementia contributed to a series of falls, the last of which was catastrophic and ultimately fatal. While my parents were never sick at the same time, their turn-taking extended the experience of precarity across the decade in a manner that seemed to mirror the unremitting spate of crisis and disaster in the external world: one after the next after the next.[5]

Because of the association of precarity with crisis, the work of caregiving is often constructed as a subtractive experience, self*less* work riddled with material and spiritual costs for both the caregiver and care receiver. But while it was very difficult at times, there was nothing about my experience that felt like an evisceration or lessening of self. Most of the time I felt only that I was gripping tightly to a shared experience of *mutuality*, a life of togetherness that I was unwilling to trade for its absence, its void. Together we pushed back, resisted and refused the indignities of a system intent on apprehending the end of my mother's life. For me, the experience of caregiving (doing the work to let live), as well as hospicing (doing the work to let die), was deeply meaningful and transformative. So while the weight of impending loss loomed heavy, the overall experience was unexpectedly redemptive in its resistances, refusals, and acquiescences.

In its broadest sense this chapter examines the ways in which settler discourses encode a particular episteme that reflects the logics and imperatives of capital (i.e., dispossession, extraction, accumulation) and white supremacy in ways that ultimately "eliminate" other knowledges and ways of being. For instance, within the logics of settler capitalism, the elderly are legible only as a population of aging bodies that ignite a crisis of decreased labor power and increased social expenditure. I am also interested in the processes by which biopolitical-bureaucratic forms of caretaking, insistent on indifference and anonymity, work to remove/replace Indigenous modes of caregiving as defined through relations of mutuality and responsibility that are deeply intimate, generational, and land-based.[6] Within their communities, Indigenous elders are valued well beyond their "productivity" and hold places of distinction as knowledge keepers; spiritual and political leaders; and attendants of past, present, and future generations. They are poignant reminders of the failures of "elimination" and living witnesses to the multitude of crimes committed against Indigenous humanity. Which is to say, they persist as the inconvenient truths, the undead, the mnemic traces and "ciphers" of the "absent but seething presence" of more than five hundred years of settler domination.[7]

Given their place of distinction, one might assume that Native American and Indigenous studies would be replete with scholarship on elders and aging. But as it stands, relatively little work is being produced within the field.[8] This absence helps to perpetuate the lack of understanding of how Indigenous elders constitute a distinctive population and how colonialist constructions of aging as crisis continue to eliminate, displace, dispossess, and commodify. Insofar as the aged are a site of governmentality, decolonial theories and analyses of aging are important to discerning and disrupting the contours of the settler project. Thus, this chapter represents both an intervention and a searching. Specifically, it *intervenes* in analyses of aging that rely on settler logics at the same time it *searches* for alternatives, an Indigenous "elsewhere" of aging wherein health and well-being are defined through relations of care and mutuality.

Toward this end, I begin with a discussion of the geopolitics and biopolitics of aging and the ways in which they shape understandings of what it means to be "elderly" as well as how we understand relations of care. I end with a discussion of Indigenous perspectives of aging as they arise within and across different communities. Grounded in Indigenous ontologies, I argue that a decolonial theory and politics of aging is critical not only to the projects of Indigenous resistance and resurgence but also to imagining life beyond the limits of settler precarity.

The Geopolitics of Aging

According to the Administration on Aging, by the year 2030 the ratio of "older adults" (sixty-five and older) to "adults" (twenty-four to sixty-four) will increase by 80 percent in the United States, which is to say that in a little under a decade, one in every five adults will be sixty-five or older.[9] The global population of older adults will similarly skyrocket, rising from 680 million to 2 billion by the year 2050; doubling from 11 to 22 percent.[10] Such unprecedented demographic shifts have activated the world's superpowers, who anxiously measure national and global rates of longevity against falling birthrates in an ongoing effort to forecast the impact of aging on the labor force. The resulting calculus fuels the discourse of aging as crisis.

Indeed, the World Bank began forecasting geopolitical decline nearly twenty years ago. Its report *Averting the Old Age Crisis: Policies to Protect the Old and Promote Growth* frames the "crisis" in terms of decreased productivity and its suggestions for "averting" the crisis in terms of the sustainability of government-funded entitlement programs (i.e., Social Security and Medicaid).[11] In other words, the World Bank posits "old age" and "economic growth" along the crude capitalist binary of either people *or* profits. Nevertheless, findings from the report set the stage, and soon demographers and policy analysts started to reference "the 2050 problem" as a kind of fiscal cliff of aging, with the coming "demographic storm" situated as the harbinger of a dystopic future marked by "zero GDP growth," "stagnating entrepreneurship," and even a "generational war."[12] For example, in its report on the global aging crisis, the Center for Strategic and International Studies predicts that, when governments are "faced with the choice between economically ruinous tax hikes and politically impossible benefit cuts," they will ultimately choose a third option: "cannibalizing other spending on everything from education and the environment to foreign assistance and national defense."[13] While not all reports are equally alarmist, nations across the globe are increasingly shifting modes and structures of governmentality to more closely arrogate the "management" of the elderly.

Economists and policy makers have an easier time imagining massive global decline than they do reimaging work beyond the bounds of capitalist modes of production. This, despite the fact that "ideas about the nature of work, productivity and the life cycle" were "forged in an earlier era of industrial capitalism" and are quickly becoming outmoded.[14] This fundamental failure forecloses an opportunity to reconceptualize the aging population as a site of possibility, of perceiving the aged as a conceptual opening for rethinking the central dichotomies and contradictions of the settler colonialism and capitalism: disentangling the centrality of work to existence, of economic growth to production, of production to wage labor, of age to declining yield, and, ultimately of life beyond the productivist logics of capital.

Instead, current research and scholarship on aging evidences a continued conflation with conditions of deficit and decline, animating lines of inquiry such as: How do we maintain global dominance under conditions of a declining work force and increased social expenditures? Is the future behind us? How can we reconfigure aging and the aged as the next frontier for capital? How can science isolate and treat the "disease" of aging, and what new technologies can be developed to "cure" it?[15] Clearly such questions refract settler logics of accumulation and dispossession that inform not only how populations are managed but also how individuals are perceived and treated. In this instance, the aged are perceived as post-productive subjects and thereby treated as threats to the capitalist state. The discourse of crisis underscores their incommensurability, providing the staging ground for policies of elimination.

In the United States, recent threats to subsidized housing, Meals on Wheels, Medicaid, and Social Security are justified through the coming "demographic storm," while globally some states have already parlayed the crisis into regressive policies such as mandating the privatization of retirement savings (e.g., Australia). But perhaps the most disturbing among such developments is the emergence of "pay for success" (PFS) programs or social impact bonds (SIBs). The dream child of philanthrocapitalists, SIBs function as a mechanism by which the state can outsource the responsibility for social welfare to private companies, aiming to leverage private capital toward persistent social ills where government has "failed" (e.g., homelessness, prison recidivism, teen pregnancy). As such, SIBs perform more like equity investments than bonds, promising a return on investment (ROI) only once and if a program achieves its agreed-on outcomes. Typical contracts are devised among government agencies, venture capitalists, nongovernmental organizations, and private evaluation firms that coordinate the terms of service and schedule for earnings. Social impact bonds are aggressively marketed as both socially necessary and socially conscious, a benevolent and charitable means for reinvigorating capitalism and, as such, hark back to the nineteenth-century American Indian civilization programs aimed at "saving" the Indian.[16]

The Rikers Island recidivism PFS project implemented in 2012 serves as a case in point. According to the contract, Goldman Sachs served as the funder; the Manpower Demonstration Research Corporation (MDRC) was the social service provider; and the Vera Institute designed and performed the evaluation.[17] The goal of the program was to reduce recidivism among incarcerated sixteen- to eighteen-year-old male youth through a focus on "personal responsibility, education, training, and counseling," otherwise known as Moral Reconation Therapy (MRT). Goldman would garner a return on its initial investment of $9.6 million once, and if, the program achieved an 8.5 percent reduction in recidivism with rates greater than 10 percent triggering returns between $500,000 and $2.1 million.[18] According to an analysis conducted by *Nonprofit Quarterly*, this translates into a potential ROI of 87.5 percent, raising the ethical question of how much socially conscious business ventures should be able to earn—particularly since, even in the instance of failure, Goldman Sachs stood to gain as a result of the complex structure of tax loopholes, write-offs, charitable donations, and Community Reinvestment Act credits.

Despite the feel-good discourse, SIBs mark a new and dangerous border in the neoliberal restructuring of the public sphere by furthering the reach of private for-profit capital into the realm of social services, essentially situating business as a proxy for government. In so doing, vulnerabilized populations are financialized, not simply treated as surplus but literally commodified into private assets. In her article "Pre-Black Futures," Katharyne Mitchell exposes such strategies as enactments of a racialized biopolitics, whereby nonwhite populations are prefigured as morally, physically, or intellectually incapable of embodying the traits that "distinguish the proper economic subject."[19] Zenia Kish and Justin Leroy similarly contextualize SIBs as a form of racial capitalism in "Bonded Life: Technologies of Racial Finance from Slave Insurance to Philanthrocapital."[20] They argue that, "like the financial incentives sustaining slavery . . . , life bonds generate profit by revaluing racialized life," not only restructuring "life into debt" but also creating a market of "subprime subjects" whose vulnerabilities are exploited as opportunities for capital accumulation (633). In summary, SIBs propose a new technology of biopolitical control through which (1) governments are permitted to pay private investors for services they are obligated to provide; (2) persons are fully amortized, whereby the body is reconstituted as a potential investment and future dividend; and (3) "subprime" populations are tied to profit making in ways that are even more brazenly premised on the continuation of racist and colonialist forms of subjugation.

As a vulnerabilized population, the aged are prime targets for SIBs, and as a racialized population, Indigenous elders are even more so. Corporations are not only racing to capitalize on the "ageing mega-trend" and "silver economy"; they are also vying to gain access to their "share of elderly people."[21] As investors compete to expand their portfolios, they work to minimize risk, enacting sorting and selecting strategies of settler logics. That is, they differentiate between surplus and redeemable subjects who can be recuperated into worth for the settler state. Similar in spirit to General Richard Pratt's "Kill the Indian, Save the Man" campaign, modern philanthrocapitalists imagine their own benevolence as they "save" the elderly by converting them from public threat into private asset. In the next section, I discuss how this geopolitical framing informs not only biopolitical regimes of care but also the parameters—the shape—of life itself.

The Biopolitics of Aging

Though a contested construct even within Foucault's own writing, the "birth of biopolitics" is widely understood as marking the entrance to modernity and rupture from "the sovereign" as the locus of power.[22] Whereas the sovereign once held the absolute right to "make die or let live," modern expressions of disciplinary power aim to maximize life through controlling bodies and effectively administering populations—to "make live and let die."[23] In the aftermath of 9/11, Foucault's analyses served as the theoretical ground for new trajectories and formations of biopolitics. Most notably, Giorgio Agamben's insertion of a politics of death (*thanatopolitics*)—made legible through the ancient figure of the *homo sacer*—addressed the post-9/11 (re)production of American sovereignty through the deprecation and abandonment of others. Michael Hardt and Antonio Negri's analysis takes biopolitics beyond the geographic bounds of the nation-state into the metaphysical and social fields of power in their construction of biopolitics as *biopotenza*, an analysis that spurned debate on the modes and possibility of resistance in the authoritarian state.[24] Perhaps most relevant to this analysis is Achille Mbembe's work on *necropolitics*, which examines how the social and political space of neoliberal, global capitalism is managed and organized by the logic of death, shifting the central problematic of biopolitics from "make live and let die" to "let live and make die."[25] That is, contemporary forms of subjugation and cruelty have conferred on whole populations "the status of living dead," blurring the "lines between resistance and suicide, sacrifice and redemption, martyrdom and freedom."[26]

These critiques and nuances of the contemporary biopolitical turn are similarly reflected within the hard sciences, deliberating the impact of neoliberalism on the management of illness, health, and vitality and the shifting modes of power and governmentality between bodies and populations. The work of Paul Rabinow and Nikolas Rose is foundational to this understanding.[27] Following Gilles Deleuze, they are concerned with examining the relationship between the "molar and molecular," which is to say, toggling between "the emphases and relations on ways of thinking and acting at the level of population groups and collectivities" and "the individualization of biopolitical strategies."[28] They argue that, in the era of the welfare state, "the molar was privileged," with states providing "mechanisms of security" such as subsidized housing and health care, but that the neoliberal state ushered in a molecular turn.[29] More specifically, Rose argues that, in this context, "biopolitics no longer pertains to the life of populations but, instead, to 'the politics of life itself.'"[30] They further suggest that the molecular sciences themselves are part of a "general movement of power away from a concern with populations" toward a neoliberal preoccupation with extraction and accumulation, which is to say, the production of biocapital.[31]

According to Rose, the "intense capitalization" of the sciences has given rise to "a new molecular ontology of life" wherein the elements of life itself (i.e., DNA, stem cells, embryos) are being "accorded a new mobility" through capitalization: "decomposed, stabilized, frozen, banked, stored, commoditized, accumulated, exchanged, traded across time, across space, across organs and species, across diverse contexts and enterprises in the service of both health and wealth."[32] This mobility, in turn, has created a transnational "political economy of vitality" with supra- and multinational institutions and corporations regulating "flows of knowledge, cells, tissues and intellectual property."[33]

The shared nexus of interest among global corporations, scientists, and the settler state is the desire to compress morbidity, which means to shorten the length of time between an individual's ability to live at full capacity (i.e., without chronic illness or disability) and death. Consider, for example, the recent formation of the research-and-development biotech company Calico (short for California Life Company). Launched in 2013 by Larry Page, the chief executive of Google Inc., and Arthur Levinson, the chief executive of Apple and Genentech, Calico set out to "cure death," illness, and the "disease of aging."[34] Once operating as a secret division of Google, Calico began by formalizing partnerships with leading scientists, universities, and biotech and genetic technology industries (including Ancestry.com) to build the largest genomic database in the world. Since its inception, tech titans from Facebook, eBay, PayPal, and Oracle have all invested hundreds of millions of dollars in solving the "problem" of human finitude. While framed as the new frontier of biotechnology, Kevin Bruyneel notes, the desire to possess and extend life is constitutive of the settler state. That is, primitive accumulation is the process of making Indians die in order for settlers to live.[35]

In this ongoing "theater of cruelty," Peter Thiel, the cofounder of PayPal, emerges as one of the most outspoken and messianic of patrons. For the self-professed libertarian, accepting the inevitability of mortality is a failure not only of the imagination but also of the "constraints" placed on scientists by institutional review boards and other regulatory bodies.[36] Thiel is not alone in his opinion that traditional research protocols unnecessarily inhibit scientific innovation. As noted by Melinda Cooper, since "President Ronald Regan implemented a series of reforms designed to mobilize a 'revolution' in the life sciences, public health and biomedicine," every administration has narrowed the distinction between biological (re)production and capital accumulation.[37] Indeed, under the Trump administration, the circumvention of traditional research protocols resulted in a major shift in funding practices. Whereas the federal government once funded two-thirds of scientific and medical research, now two-thirds is funded by private industry—corporate agents accountable to nothing and no one but bottom lines and profit motives.

The particular liaison between venture capitalists and the biotech industry around the shared ambition to "cure death" raises ominous questions: How might the meaning of life (and death) be denigrated if it is no longer considered finite? How will immortality impact compromised ecosystems? How much will eternal life cost? Who will have access to the necessary technologies? How will the extension of life among the world's elite exacerbate the crushing inequality across the life span? In other words, who will need to die in order to let live?

Such developments are reviving debates about the meaning and value of life and engendering new forms of politics in order to understand them (e.g., biocapitalism, posthumanism). Brett Neilson names the central tension between the "massive capital investment in the vitality of molecular life" and the "marked social divestment" in social welfare as the "immortalization of the flesh and the amortization of the body."[38] This analytic infrastructure is, of course, not only ageist and ablest but also deeply classed and racialized. That is, insofar as state divestments in health and welfare disproportionately impact Black, brown, and poor communities at the same time that they situate white elites as the target market for antiaging technologies, they resuscitate eugenicist ideologies. The sciences have a long history of being implicated in imperialist processes of making race and nation, serving as one of the central apparatuses of biopolitical control for the settler state. From the specious science of blood quantum to racial classification systems, the sciences have remained integral to processes of "making live and letting die," granting legitimacy to the selection of bodies marked as profit and marking others as surplus.

At the heart of this chapter, however, are questions about how such capitalist intensifications impact the organization and administration of care, particularly of the elderly. Foundational to the biopolitical shifts discussed earlier is the settler logic of individualism, which allows for the atomization and mobilization not only of life but also of the structures of care. Under the Fordist-Keynesian order, the state invested in the upkeep of the (white, male) worker's body (i.e., through pensions, health care, housing, etc.), enabling discourses of older men as a deserving class, a "greatest generation" that worked hard for self and country and earned their social security in later life. As noted by Bruyneel, however, Keynesian prosperity is part of the broader American "mythos" built on "settler-colonial logic, practices, and structures."[39] In this instance, the "promise" of the New Deal was largely waged on a series of "nonpromises" to Blacks, with programs such as Fair Housing and Social Security excluding and discriminating against them to garner support, especially from Southern Democrats.[40] The "threat" of the new racial order proposed by the Civil Rights Movement contributed to the recasting of state-sponsored entitlements as costs, if not debts, as well as to the general turn toward neoliberalism.

Not surprising, along with the rise of neoliberalism came the discourses of "self-care" and "successful aging," both of which trade upon the myth of the autonomous individual.[41] Exemplified in the work of John W. Rowe and Robert L. Kahn, "successful aging" is rooted in biomedical indicators and reflects one's capacity to live independently and free of disease and disability.[42] Such "positive" models of aging were ostensibly advocated as a counter to stereotypes of the elderly as passive and dependent, but the reality is that they emerged through "particular political and biomedical networks in the U.S." that were aligned with corporatist agendas to raise the retirement age and lessen government expenditure.[43] Indeed, the notion of "successful aging" led to advocacy for "aging in place," wherein older adults stay in their homes and out of state subsidized institutional care. "Success" is clearly equated with an overall reduction in public expenditure and increased rates of in-home care with individuals and families not only assuming all the responsibility for aging but also the risks.

Thus, as older adults suffered the consequences of federal and corporate divestment in their care, they were also made to endure a system that defined them as "successful" only if they could negotiate a complex health-care system on their own. Those who could not were, by default, failures at aging.[44] Thus, the notion of self-care has served as a critical accomplice to the structural adjustments and management of biopolitical forms of care. The net effect is an economic and ideological system that reifies individualism as synonymous with health and success—a course originally set in motion more than five hundred years ago.

Indigenous Relations of Care and Responsibility:
In Search of Elsewhere

Insofar as the intensification of biopolitics under neoliberalism represents an extension of the settler project, Indigenous perspectives on aging are crucial—not in the liberal sense of adding culturally relevant models for the sake of pluralism but, rather, as a rupturing of the dehumanizing logics of capitalism; as the decolonial turn toward Indigenous resurgence. Relations of responsibility, collectivity, mutuality, and reciprocity are foundational to Indigenous protocols and practices as well as to distinctive ontologies of life, death, and beingness that, as noted by Stevenson, are not bracketed by the material or the "known."[45] The rising population of Native American and Indigenous elders present a unique opportunity to consider how their "collective continuance" informs the project of Indigenous resurgence. The result of this could move us closer toward a decolonial existence that is more squarely rooted in elders' experience and knowledge.

To begin, aging in Indigenous communities is generally experienced or understood not as a "crisis" but, rather, as a particular location within the broader cycles of life. Conducting research on aging in Indigenous communities, thus, presents a particular challenge since older adults are not viewed as a distinctive population. This means that research that begins with gathering data on Indigenous adults aged sixty-five and older ends up trafficking in the same deficit discourses as research among other aging populations. Studies of Indigenous *elders*, however, garner different results and point to distinctive paradigms of aging.

As previously noted, Indigenous elders are those persons identified by their communities as knowledge keepers and resources of generational and traditional continuities. Across the few studies of Indigenous elders that exist, there emerges a pattern of belief around a view of aging as neither temporally ordered nor linear in relation to the life span. For instance, as Jordan P. Lewis found in his work among Alaska Natives, the definition of *elder* is not based on chronological age; rather, it is a designation or honor bestowed by the community, a status earned through "unspoken rules" regarding wisdom, experience, and contribution to community. As distinguished by one woman in the study, "Some of us merely become elderly," but others become elders.[46]

Even more distinctive, elders are viewed as a product of the *social imaginary*, not necessarily ontologically located in the body or the mind. Consider, for example, Wendy Hulko and her colleagues' work among Secwepemc First Nations peoples wherein elders are described this way: "On the medicine wheel . . . infants sit beside the elders . . . [and] may be considered teachers. Elders and infants are both close to the spirit world; the infants arriving from it, and the elders traveling to it. This closeness to the spirit world may bring a spiritual strength, but it may also bring a physical vulnerability and sensitivity to environmental disturbance."[47] In addition to illustrating the fluidity of life's cycles, this passage suggests a conceptual opening for rethinking biomedical conceptions of life and death through its depiction of elders as moving back toward the creator and the spiritual realm.

Similarly, research on dementia and other so-called diseases of the mind within Indigenous communities suggests competing ideas of what it means to be of sound mind. For example, in their work with the Oklahoma Choctaw, J. Neil Henderson and L. Carson Henderson report that there is no word for the "loss of one's mind or intellect" in the Choctaw language. In fact, memory loss is not considered a loss at all but rather a condition where the person's mind is simply perceived as being "*elsewhere.*"[48] The researchers surmise that cultural contexts that include supernatural connections to the spirit world as "a matter of routine life experience" demonstrate a greater tolerance, if not value, for what appears to be "irrational" behavior, developing alternative explanations for dementia-related conditions as being in "communication with 'the other side.'"[49] In other words, the fluid and dynamic systems of "cognitive travel between the empirical and non-empirical environments" within many Indigenous communities serve as a counterfactual against deficit frameworks, generating "a positive specialness" about what is going on with their elders.[50]

Among conditions associated with aging, I am particularly interested in Indigenous views of mental capacity not only because my mom (Ona) was diagnosed with dementia but also because of the potential insights into how settler logics are transited through the constructions of reason, the mind, and its supposed loss. In 2012, the World Health Organization identified dementia as a "public health priority," seemingly casting elders with memory loss as a greater sociopolitical risk than the historical amnesia of the settler state, even as it increasingly suffers the relentless animus of its own denial. As noted by Manu Vimalassery and colleagues, the state of "colonial unknowing" is more than a simple act of forgetting or ignorance; it is instead "aggressively made and reproduced" to maintain the settler order.[51] Thus, to the degree that normative theories of democracy and the apologue of modern liberalism situate reason— or, more specifically, the reasonable man—as the *topos* of sovereignty, it needs to be acknowledged as a key site of settler hegemony. In this sense, the aged—as vessels of diminished reason—represent a different kind of crisis for the settler state. The thought of a society with skyrocketing populations of centenarians is so disturbing to a system built on the myths of rationality that it is already developing strategies of containment.

Sadly, settler logics are so hegemonic that they are beginning to supplant these more traditional understandings of what it means to be 'old' in Native communities. In his research, Lewis found generational distinctions between older adults (non-elders) who place a greater emphasis on health status in aging and elders who emphasize "well-being," a state understood as the ability to give back, to be able "to share, be happy . . . and pass on what you know."[52] Similarly, the work of Hulko and her colleagues suggests that, as biomedical models of disease infiltrate communities (either through dislocation or out-reach programs), what was once perceived as a spiritual state of being *elsewhere* is increasingly being understood as an effect of disease and in need of medi-cal care. As a result, families are becoming convinced that they can no longer care for their elders, setting in motion yet another removal: of elders out of homes and into institutional care. The notion of communities without elders, without the critical connective tissue between generations, to ancestors and the spirit world, is an unimaginable loss. Indeed, elders are so critical to the political project of Indigenous resurgence that we may need to enter them into witness protection programs. But at minimum, questions and concerns presented by elders and aging call for our urgent and collective attention and thus need to figure more centrally in Native American and Indigenous studies: "Indigenous futures are entirely dependent on what we do now . . . with our Ancestors and those yet unborn."[53]

It was a privilege to be by Ona's side as she journeyed *elsewhere*. She reported regularly, in great and vivid detail, about her travels to and from the spirit world. During the Ukrainian crisis, she recounted her visit to the Oval Office and the advice she gave to President Barack Obama. She also often traveled back home to Peru, talking about her school and "working so hard" to please the nuns. Across her cognitive excursions she was reflective, powerful, and instrumental. In her final days, she spoke in all of her languages—English, Spanish, and Que-chua—as she moved effortlessly through her entire life span. She even relived, in quite dramatic and visceral fashion, the experience of giving birth. Across all of it, as the so-called disease of dementia progressed, she gained a deeper sense of herself, becoming ever more cognizant of where she had been and where she was going—until, eventually, she went.

In her lifetime, Ona was a thoroughly syncretic being who agilely and duti-fully traversed across her traditional and Catholic faiths. It was one of her life dreams to go to the Vatican and visit the Pope. As it happened, my first-ever trip to Rome coincided with the first anniversary of her passing. So I took her ashes with me, thinking I'd leave some at the Vatican and fulfill her wishes. Once I got there, however, it didn't feel right—too much exhibition, surveillance, spectacle, and ostentation for Ona's liking—so I didn't leave any behind. As the trip came to a close, I felt remorseful about not finding a place for her ashes. To clear my head, I took one last meandering walk through the streets of Rome, on which I came upon the Pantheon, the nearly two thousand-year-old monument to the gods. It was both magnificent in its splendor and resilience and unremarkable in its location, nestled among bars, restaurants, and supermarkets. I knew immediately—this was the place. I sprinkled her ashes at the vestibule, under the sculpture of the Madonna del Sasso, and on the floor beneath the oculus to the sky. In the end and in the beginning, Indigenous peoples come from and return to land—a site of perpetual and perennial memory that is never lost.

NOTES

Parts of this chapter were previously published in "Aging, Precarity, and the Struggle for Indigenous Elsewhere," *International Journal of Qualitative Studies in Education* 31, no. 3 (2017): 168–76, https://doi.org/10.1080/09518398.2017.1401145. They are reprinted here with permission of the publisher, Taylor & Francis Ltd.

1 The notion of precarity in reference to the insecure working conditions brought about by neoliberal reforms emerged in the 1970s as an effect of working-class politics.

2 Rob Horning, "Precarity and 'Affective Resistance,'" *New Inquiry* (blog), February 14, 2012, https://thenewinquiry.com/blog/precarity-and-affective-resistance; Karl Polanyi, *The Great Transformation: The Political and Economic Origins of Our Time* (Boston: Beacon, 2001).

3 Alyosha Goldstein, ed., *Formations of United States Colonialism* (Durham, NC: Duke University Press, 2014), 2.

4 For further discussion of this concept, see Patrick Wolfe, "Settler Colonialism and the Elimination of the Native," *Journal of Genocide Research* 8, no. 4 (December 2006): 387–409, https://doi.org/10.1080/14623520601056240.

5 For me, the demands of caregiving were most intense across the years 2004–14, a decade that included the Indian Ocean tsunami, Hurricane Katrina, the earthquake in Haiti, the subprime mortgage crisis, and Fukushima, among others.

6 For further articulation of "anonymous care," see Lisa Stevenson, *Life beside Itself: Imagining Care in the Canadian Arctic* (Oakland: University of California Press, 2014).

7 Jong Bum Kwon, "Forging a Modern Democratic Imaginary: Police Sovereignty, Neoliberalism, and the Boundaries of Neo-Korea," *Positions: Asia Critique* 22, no. 1 (December 2014): 73, https://doi.org/10.1215/10679847-2383858.

8 Much of the research on Indigenous elders and aging is being produced in the sciences and comports with biomedical models of health and well-being, as is noted in Jordan P. Lewis, "Successful Aging through the Eyes of Alaska Natives: Exploring Generational Differences among Alaska Natives," *Journal of Cross-Cultural*

Gerontology 25, no. 4 (December 2010): 385–96, https://doi.org/10.1007/s10823-010-9124-8; Karina L. Walters, Ramona Beltran, Tessa Evans-Campbell, and Jane M. Simoni, "Keeping Our Hearts from Touching the Ground: HIV/AIDS in American Indian and Alaska Native Women," *Women's Health Issues* 21, no. 6 (November 2011): S261–65, https://doi.org/10.1016/j.whi.2011.08.005.

9 This is surmised to be the result of a declining birthrate and a rise in the average life expectancy, from 47 years in 1900 to 78 years today, and projected to be 84.5 years by the year 2050. Moreover, much of the upsurge is attributed to the aging seventy-seven million baby boomers, the first generation of whom became eligible for retirement in 2011.

10 In the year 2050 one in every eight people in the world will be sixty-five or older. It is also worth noting that as the national and global community ages, it is becoming less white and more female. The ratio of women to men older than eighty-five is forecast to be 100:49.

11 World Bank, *Averting the Old Age Crisis: Policies to Protect the Old and Promote Growth* (Washington, DC: World Bank, 1994), http://documents.worldbank.org/curated/en/973571468174557899/Averting-the-old-age-crisis-policies-to-protect-the-old-and-promote-growth; John A. Turner, "Book Review: Income and Social Security and Substandard Working Conditions: *Averting the Old Age Crisis: Policies to Protect the Old and Promote Growth*," *Industrial and Labor Relations Review* 48, no. 4 (July 1995): 862–63, https://doi.org/10.1177/001979399504800426.

12 Kenneth W. Gronbach, *The Age Curve: How to Profit from the Coming Demographic Storm* (New York: American Management Association, 2008). In their report "Global Aging and the Crisis of the 2020s," Neil Howe and Richard Jackson equate the "crisis of aging" with issues of national security and a Pax Americana redux: Neil Howe and Richard Jackson, "Global Aging and the Crisis of the 2020s," *Current History* 110, no. 732 (2011): 20.

13 Howe and Jackson, "Global Aging and the Crisis of the 2020s," 20.

14 Diana Coole, "Reconstructing the Elderly: A Critical Analysis of Pensions and Population Policies in an Era of Demographic Ageing," *Contemporary Political Theory* 11, no. 1 (February 2012): 62, https://doi.org/10.1057/cpt.2011.12.

15 See, for example, Egon Diczfalusy, "An Aging Humankind: Is Our Future behind Us?" *Aging Male* 1, no. 1 (January 1998): 8–19, https://doi.org/10.3109/13685539809148598; Peter G. Peterson, "Gray Dawn: The Global Aging Crisis," *Foreign Affairs*, January 1, 1999, 42–55, https://www.foreignaffairs.com/articles/1999-01-01/gray-dawn-global-aging-crisis; Helena E. Restrepo and Manuel Rozental, "The Social Impact of Aging Populations: Some Major Issues," *Social Science and Medicine* 39, no. 9 (November 1994): 1323–38, https://doi.org/10.1016/0277-9536(94)90364-6.

16 Michael E. Porter and Mark R. Kramer, "The Big Idea: Creating Shared Value, Rethinking Capitalism," *Harvard Business Review* 89, nos. 1–2 (2011): 62–77.

17 In 1974, the Ford Foundation and six government agencies created the Manpower Demonstration Research Corporation with the purpose of implementing and documenting the results of new programs intended to help the poor. It formally adopted MDRC as its registered corporate identity in 2003.

18 The ROI was figured based on the fact that, while $7.2 million of Goldman's initial $9.6 million investment was guaranteed by Bloomberg Philanthropies, its actual risk was only $2.4 million, on which it stood to earn $2.1 million.

19 Katharyne Mitchell, "Pre-Black Futures," *Antipode* 41 (January 2010): 365–66. Mitchell also argues that the landscape of risk, and its avoidance, is highly racialized through structures that create differential access to various social protections such as credit and insurance, safe working environments, and preferential or predatory mortgage lending.

20 Zenia Kish and Justin Leroy, "Bonded Life: Technologies of Racial Finance from Slave Insurance to Philanthrocapital," *Cultural Studies* 29, nos. 5–6 (September 3, 2015): 630–51, https://doi.org/10.1080/09502386.2015.1017137.

21 Stephanie Petrick, Arne Kroeger, and Carola Knott, *Impact Investing in Ageing*, Impact in Motion and Social Venture Fund, January 2014, http://www.impactinmotion.com/wp/wp-content/uploads/2014/02/Impact-investing-in-ageing_final_20140127.pdf, 3.

22 While a variety of presuppositions circulate under the sign of biopolitics, Michel Foucault's analysis serves as an anchor among complex and, at times, contradictory mappings of postsovereign and antisovereign forms of power. Specifically, his groundbreaking text, *The History of Sexuality, Volume 1: An Introduction* (New York: Vintage, 1990) and his subsequent lectures *Security, Territory, Population: Lectures at the Collège de France, 1977–78*, edited by Arnold I. Davidson (New York: Palgrave Macmillan, 2009) and *The Birth of Biopolitics: Lectures at the Collège de France, 1978–79*, edited by Michel Senellart (New York: Palgrave Macmillan, 2010), remain touchstones in a vast array of scholarship across multiple fields, examining the relationship among politics, life, the state, and the body.

For further mappings of the contradictions and complexities in use of the term *biopolitics*, see Timothy C. Campbell and Adam Sitze, eds., *Biopolitics: A Reader* (Durham, NC: Duke University Press, 2013); Mathew Coleman and Kevin Grove, "Biopolitics, Biopower, and the Return of Sovereignty," *Environment and Planning D: Society and Space* 27, no. 3 (June 2009): 489–507, https://doi.org/10.1068/d3508; Jakob Nilsson, ed., *Foucault, Biopolitics, and Governmentality*, Södertörn Philosophical Studies, 14 (Huddinge, Sweden: Södertörn University, 2013).

23 Foucault, *The History of Sexuality, Volume 1*, 136.

24 Coleman and Grove, "Biopolitics, Biopower, and the Return of Sovereignty."

25 Marina Grzinic, "Biopolitics and Necropolitics in Relation to the Lacanian Four Discourses," Simposium Art and Research: Shared Methodologies, Politics and Translation, Barcelona, 2012, http://www.ub.edu/doctorat_eapa/wp-content/uploads/2012/09/Marina.Grzinic_Biopolitics-Necropolitics_Simposio_2012.pdf; Achille Mbembe, "Necropolitics," *Public Culture* 15, no. 1 (January 1, 2003): 11–40, https://doi.org/10.1215/08992363-15-1-11.

26 Mbembe, "Necropolitics," 40.

27 Paul Rabinow and Nikolas Rose, "Biopower Today," *BioSocieties* 1, no. 2 (June 2006): 195–217, https://doi.org/10.1017/S1745855206040014.

28 Rabinow and Rose, "Biopower Today," 204.

29 Rabinow and Rose, "Biopower Today," 204.

30 Claire Blencowe, *Biopolitical Experience: Foucault, Power and Positive Critique* (New York: Palgrave Macmillan, 2012), 127.

31 Blencowe, *Biopolitical Experience*, 127.

32 Nikolas Rose, "Molecular Biopolitics, Somatic Ethics and the Spirit of Biocapital," *Social Theory and Health* 5, no. 1 (2007): 4.

33 Rabinow and Rose, "Biopower Today," 215.

34 For full text of the press release, see Jay Yarow, "Google Is Launching a Company That Hopes to Cure Death," *Business Insider*, September 18, 2013, http://www.businessinsider.com/google-is-launching-a-company-that-hopes-to-cure-death-2013-9?IR=T.

35 Kevin Bruyneel, personal communication with the author, Columbia University Indigenous Peoples Forum, April 25, 2018.

36 Theil came under fire for giving $1.25 million to the Trump campaign, as reported by David Streitfeld, "Peter Thiel to Donate $1.25 Million in Support of Donald Trump," *New York Times*, October 15, 2016, https://www.nytimes.com/2016/10/16/technology/peter-thiel-donald-j-trump.html.

37 Melinda Cooper, *Life as Surplus: Biotechnology and Capitalism in the Neoliberal Era*, In Vivo (Seattle: University of Washington Press, 2008), 3.

38 Brett Neilson, "Ageing, Experience, Biopolitics: Life's Unfolding," *Body and Society* 18, nos. 3–4 (2012): 44–71.

39 Kevin Bruyneel, "The American Liberal Colonial Tradition," *Settler Colonial Studies* 3, nos. 3–4 (November 2013): 316, https://doi.org/10.1080/2201473X.2013.810700.

40 See, for example, Ira Katznelson, *When Affirmative Action Was White: An Untold History of Racial Inequality in Twentieth-Century America* (New York: W. W. Norton, 2006).

41 This discourse of "self-care" is, of course, different from that articulated by Audre Lorde and other Black radical feminists.

42 John W. Rowe and Robert L. Kahn, "Human Aging: Usual and Successful," *Science* 237, no. 4811 (July 10, 1987): 143–49, https://doi.org/10.1126/science.3299702.

43 Heather E. Dillaway and Mary Byrnes, "Reconsidering Successful Aging: A Call for Renewed and Expanded Academic Critiques and Conceptualizations," *Journal of Applied Gerontology* 28, no. 6 (2009): 702–22.

44 Neilson, "Ageing, Experience, Biopolitics," 45.

45 Stevenson, *Life beside Itself*, 2.

46 Lewis, "Successful Aging through the Eyes of Alaska Natives, 390.

47 First Nations Centre, *Ownership, Control, Access and Possession (OCAP) or Self-determination Applied to Research: A Critical Analysis of Contemporary First Nations Research and Some Options for First Nations Communities* (Ottawa: National Aboriginal Health Organization, 2005), cited in Jeffrey Lawrence Reading, Valerie Gideon, and Andrew Martin Kmetic, *First Nations Wholistic Policy and Planning Model: Discussion Paper for the World Health Organization Commission on Social Determinants of Health* (Ottawa: Assembly of First Nations, 2007), http://www.deslibris.ca/ID/214703, quoted in Wendy Hulko, Evelyn Camille, Elisabeth Antifeau, Mike Arnouse, et al.,

"Views of First Nation Elders on Memory Loss and Memory Care in Later Life," *Journal of Cross-Cultural Gerontology* 25, no. 4 (December 2010): 330, https://doi.org/10 .1007/s10823-010-9123-9.

48 J. Neil Henderson and L. Carson Henderson, "Cultural Construction of Disease: A 'Supernormal' Construct of Dementia in an American Indian Tribe," *Journal of Cross-Cultural Gerontology* 17, no. 3 (September 1, 2002): 208, https://doi.org/10.1023 /A:1021268922685.

49 Henderson and Henderson, "Cultural Construction of Disease," 208.

50 Henderson and Henderson, "Cultural Construction of Disease," 208.

51 Manu Vimalassery, Juliana Hu Pegues, and Alyosha Goldstein, "Introduction: On Colonial Unknowing," *Theory and Event* 19, no. 4 (October 12, 2016), https://muse.jhu .edu/article/633283.

52 Lewis, "Successful Aging through the Eyes of Alaska Natives," 392.

53 Leanne Betasamosake Simpson, *As We Have Always Done: Indigenous Freedom through Radical Resistance*, Indigenous Americas (Minneapolis: University of Minnesota Press, 2017), 246.

3

THE COLONIALISM OF INCARCERATION

ROBERT NICHOLS

Despite common perception to the contrary, the Canadian prison population is disproportionately large relative to that of other, comparable societies, the result of a dramatic increase over the past twenty-five years. In the 1990s alone, federal prison populations increased by 25 percent and provincial prison populations by a further 15 percent. The number of young people in the country's correctional institutions has increased by nearly 30 percent since 1986.[1] A large omnibus crime bill recently passed into law by the Conservative government, which promotes further ideologically driven, yet demonstrably dysfunctional, "tough on crime" policies ensures that these trends will only expand and compound over time.[2]

This reality has been somewhat obscured by the hyperbolic violence of prison expansion and carceral power in the United States. Nevertheless, just as is true of the US case, prison expansion north of the border has been highly racialized, especially targeting Indigenous peoples. In 2010–11, Aboriginal peoples made up 27 percent of the total adult population in provincial or territorial custody and 20 percent in federal custody in Canada. Since Aboriginal peoples account for only 3–4 percent of the total Canadian population, this incarceration rate is seven to eight times higher than the general average. This discrepancy is particularly striking when considered in conjunction with a gendered analysis: Aboriginal women make up the single fastest growing imprisoned population and now account for 33.6 percent of all federally sentenced women in Canada.[3] In addition, Aboriginal inmates are subject to what the head federal correctional investigator refers to, rather euphemistically, as "routine over-classification." This means that Indigenous peoples are commonly classified as higher risk and more likely to reoffend; thus, they are released later in their sentences and are more often subjected to highly intense forms of incarceration, such as maximum security prisons and "administrative segregation" (otherwise known as solitary confinement). Partially as a result of this intensification, Aboriginal peoples are more likely to be involved in incidents involving harm to self or others while in custody, including 45 percent of all documented cases of self-injury.[4] Significant discrepancies in incarceration rates between Indigenous and non-Indigenous people can be found consistently across all provincial and territorial jurisdictions in Canada, but the degree of disproportion increases significantly in the west (Alberta, Manitoba, and Saskatchewan) and in the territories of the north. Moreover, just as with the US case, racial disproportionally is increasing over time. As the Office of the Correctional Investigator recently put the matter: "Aboriginal over-representation has grown in recent years: between 1998 and 2008, the federal Aboriginal population increased by 19.7 percent. Moreover, the number of federally sentenced Aboriginal women increased by a staggering 131 percent over this period."[5]

Critical prison studies—and the various forms of radical, grounded praxis out of which it has emerged, been transformed, and subsequently reinvigorated with conceptual and practical tools—has insufficiently attended to the centrality of colonialism to the origins, scope, scale, and legitimation techniques of carceral power in North America. As a result, it has, by and large, deprived itself of the energy and force of Indigenous critique. With the aim of contributing to a positive interjection and reinvigoration of the *decolonizing* possibilities latent within this field, then, this essay seeks to expand and refocus this framework. I argue that, although the incarceration of Indigenous peoples is closely related to the experience of other racialized populations in North America (especially African Americans) with regard to its *causes*, it is importantly distinct with respect to the *normative foundation* of its critique. Indigenous critique is first and foremost a political critique, related but not reducible to causal explanations rooted in economic and sociological developments. It is a form of critique that challenges the prevailing paradigm of "overrepresentation" in critical prison studies by calling into question the biopolitical category of "racialized population" itself. It also challenges the ideological distinction between the logic of war and the logic of social pacification on which carceral expansion depends; situates critical prison studies within the broader horizon of settler colonialism and territorialized sovereignty; and offers alternative normative grounds from which to launch a general critique of these processes.

I

The single most important set of tools available to any contemporary critical prison analysis in North America comes to us from decades of work in African American and women of color feminism, broadly defined. Academic activists such as Angela Davis and Ruth Gilmore are central to this debate, but so are organizations such as Incite! Women of Color against Violence, Critical Resistance, and the Sylvia Rivera Law Project.[6] Since these thinkers and organizations are building their analysis and critical praxis out of the US experience, they have been particularly focused on the centrality of anti-Black racism to understanding prison expansion in that country.[7] This has taken the form of drawing a line of continuity between the contemporary prison system and the long history of slavery, either by way of a causal link or via argument by analogy. The former attempts to demonstrate how the proliferation of Black Codes in the wake of formal abolition was directly and causally responsible for the turn to incarceration as a primary mechanism of social control over racialized populations (but especially African Americans). Such causal explanations have been difficult to establish with sufficient certainty, however, and can tend toward reductive, "single variable" forms of analysis that may improperly bracket out alternative explanations. Of late then, critical prison studies in the United States has tended toward a looser analogizing structure of argumentation, making the case that contemporary forms of imprisonment are *functionally equivalent* to antebellum slavery or Jim Crow legislation in the post-Reconstruction era, even if they are not causally determined by these antecedents.[8]

Any critique of Indigenous incarceration will have to grapple with similar ambiguity when it links imprisonment to colonialism, and in this we can no doubt learn from Critical Race Theory, women of color feminism, and their related domains. However, we will as fundamentally require some departure from them. For just as any properly grounded critical praxis would be, these other fields are rooted in a historical experience that, while intersecting with settler colonialism and Indigenous struggles, also diverges from them in relevant ways. Although some important literature exists that focuses on the specificity of Indigenous incarceration—most notably, work by Patricia Monture-Angus and Luana Ross—to date this dimension of the field remains relatively occluded from view.[9]

One feature of prevailing discourses on prisons that serves to propagate a certain occlusion of its colonial dimension is the persistent language of *overrepresentation* and *racial disproportion*, an idiom one can find even in the most critical camps. In this framework, empirical evidence is presented just as is given earlier in this chapter. The standard narrative structure begins with a recitation of statistical evidence pertaining to demographics, specifically comparing the racial organization of society at large with that of the incarcerated population. Any incongruity or discrepancy between the two is noted, commonly named overrepresentation, and then employed to offer tacit or overt condemnation of the system. This rhetorical strategy is, not surprisingly, most evident in mainstream organizations and academic research, but it is also startlingly widespread in critical and radical literature. To offer but one influential example of the former, in April 2011 the National Association for the Advancement of Colored People released a major report titled *Misplaced Priorities: Over Incarcerate, Under Educate*.[10] This meticulously detailed report documents the rapid growth of racialized incarceration in the United States, with a particular focus on its impacts on African American communities and the detrimental effects it is having on state capacities in other areas of investment and service delivery (especially education). Nevertheless, the primary critical thrust of the report rests with the idea of *disproportionality*, or the *overrepresentation* of racialized populations. As the title attests, it is primarily about *over*-incarceration, not imprisonment per se.

Overrepresentation is a highly ambiguous and malleable idiom, susceptible to multiple interpretations and easily rendered into diverse programs for action. For instance, disproportion may be construed as the result of economic or social pathologies exogenous to the criminal justice system itself. In this formulation, the overrepresentation of racialized populations in prisons merely *makes visible* broader social pathologies, albeit in a highly dramatic way. For instance, criminality is correlated to poverty, which in turn is correlated to racialization and marginalization. Thus, the overrepresentation of certain populations in penal institutions may be thought a function of racism, but only in a highly mediated manner. On a different reading, however, we also know that the judicial system *itself* is rife with racialized violence and injustice. Such relatively unmediated mechanisms of racism operate endogenously to the system and have been found to directly contribute to overrepresentation—for instance, in the manner in which racial bias operates at various stages of interaction with criminal justice officials, from being stopped for routine infractions (especially "stop and frisk" policies) to sentencing and treatment by prison officers. Returning to the Canadian context, then, both of these (external and internal) factors have been central to understanding the expansion of Indigenous incarceration. To cite but one example, a study conducted in 2004 found that Aboriginal women in maximum security were involved in security incidences at a rate (28.6 percent) comparable to that of female inmates in minimum and medium security institutions (26.8 percent), and the correlation between the Security Risk Score (based on previous criminal history) and involvement in such incidences was found to be practically zero: 0.01 for violent incidences and 0.05 for nonviolent incidences. The report drew the following conclusion from this evidence: "Aboriginal women are thus more routinely placed into tighter security settings despite the fact that their *criminal history has no predictive value* for whether they are genuinely a risk to other inmates or staff."[11] In other words, racial bias is demonstrably impacting internal prison operations, a key factor in understanding divergence between Aboriginal and non-Aboriginal experiences of incarceration (in terms of scope, scale, and intensity).

Analysis of the racism both exogenous and endogenous to the criminal justice system is clearly indispensable to a comprehensive analysis of imprisonment. It remains therefore the focus of much critical prison studies, as analysts seek to provide causal explanations for recent carceral expansion. However, this focus has its limits. While discriminatory implementation is undoubtedly important to the overall operation of penal power in North America, it is limited as an explanatory device in relation to prison expansion. For racial discrimination to serve this explanatory function, one would need to demonstrate not merely its contemporary extent and operation but also its dramatic *increase* since the 1970s. However racist the operation of the criminal justice system today may be (and no credible position can deny this generally), it another thing altogether to suggest that the system prior to the 1970s was significantly *less* so.[12]

As numerous works have documented, understanding the expansion of prisons in North America requires not merely a *social* analysis—that is, one rooted in the sociology of criminal justice officials in their interactions with targeted populations—but also a *political* one. This is to say that carceral mutation and expansion are explainable principally as a political strategy that links up with a variety of social and economic transformations that have taken place over the past few decades (especially neoliberal economic "adjustments" and the deregulation and dissolution of social welfare networks) without being entirely reducible to these other factors.[13] In other words, while these social and economic forces produced the relevant context, multiple responses to these transformations were nevertheless possible. Carceral expansion was not so much the necessary, automated effect of these various causes. It was (and is) a political choice adopted from within a range of possible responses. This point is punctuated by the fact, made repeatedly in the literature, that carceral expansion is not a function of increased crime. In fact, as volumes of work attest, there is little connection between crime and punishment in North America: technologies of punishment (and their ideological justifications) grow and morph quite independently of changes in crime trends.[14] Nor are such punitive transformations a function of economic demands in any simple, straightforward manner. Despite a continued emphasis in activist literature on privatization, for-profit motives, prisoners as surplus labor, or even the somewhat misleading "prison-industrial complex" neologism, prisons remain overwhelmingly public institutions, and carceral expansion remains a function of state imperatives. So the growth of prisons is not straightforwardly a function of either an increase in crime or unmediated profit motives. This is not to say that privatization has not increased or that it is not a central component of many contemporary prison systems in the Western world. However, such phenomena are more properly understood as the effects of prison expansion rather than its causes.[15] This indicates, then, that prison expansion is a distinctly *political* phenomenon.

Gilmore theorizes the politics of carceral expansion in terms of "surplus state capacity," which she defines as a "quality that can emerge over time as a result of the difference between what states can do *technically* and what they can do *politically*."[16] Thus, while the surplus state capacity mobilized toward carceral expansion is about technical power, it equally pertains to and has its roots in discourses of legitimation—namely, social pacification and managerial democracy. Political elites push "law and order" ideologies and carceral expansion because they recognize that these work to solidify hierarchical chains of authority and control over the state apparatus, and this functions primarily because large swaths of middle-class white people, driven by fear and racist fantasies, support such policies even in the face of overwhelming evidence that they do not operate to reduce crime. By bringing forward this political circuit of violence and legitimation, we can thus break from the kind of social critique proffered by the prototypical exasperated criminologist who throws up her hands in frustration that governments continue to pursue legal reforms that are not only ineffective but actively counterproductive (i.e., they fail to reduce crime rates and may actual increase them). For unlike those who adopt this naïve approach, we can see that such policies may not be designed to reduce crime in the first place. They can be viewed as failures only if one adopts the view that they are enacted primarily to make communities safer. Once we see that this is not the case—once we realize that such policies are first and foremost devised to maintain a system of state violence, racialized hierarchy, and, as I argue, continuous colonial reterritorialization—then we must confront how effective and successful they truly are.

Thus, carceral expansion as a *political formation* has been increasingly grasped as a function of the emergence and consolidation of a new "penal ethos" in North America over the past twenty to thirty years.[17] This entails the deliberate dismantling of the social welfare state (however inadequate and uneven its institutions were); a corresponding growth and glorification of the penal state; and an internal transcription of the very terms of the penal state toward an increasingly moralized, punitive approach that prioritizes the isolation, segregation, and politically symbolic (though functionally ineffective) performance of castigating criminals (overwhelmingly the racialized poor). In other words, it is not merely that the state punishes *more*. It does so *differently*, with a new penology that emphasizes highly intense socio-spatial isolation.[18] As Loïc Wacquant reminds us, "The expansive and expensive penal system is not just a consequence of neoliberalism . . . but an *integral component of the neoliberal state itself.*"[19] The ritualized morality of punishment has ensured that even those remnants of the social welfare state that persevere have been effectively integrated into and subordinated to carceral rhetoric and imperatives—for instance, in so-called workfare programs.[20] The horizontal spread of carceral governmentality thus exceeds its limited institutional manifestation in the prison itself, confirming yet exceeding one of Michel Foucault's central insights from *Discipline and Punish*.

II

Much of the survey earlier in the chapter is known. Although the general trajectory of critical prison studies has been driving toward the kind of distinctly *political* critique of carceral expansion outlined here, the field nevertheless remains fixated primary on causal explanations. To be clear, I am not suggesting that explicating the sociological causes of prison growth over the past thirty years or so is unworthy of time and attention. However, no causal explanation, however complex and nuanced, can satisfy our need for a normative critique. In this regard, historically and in the present, the Indigenous peoples of North America provided indispensable tools since their critical praxis (decolonization) has always *primarily* focused on a robust normative critique of state sovereignty *as such*, and only secondarily on its racist implementations. The focus of Indigenous peoples' struggles has always been the imposition of the Euro-American state apparatus itself. This critique imports a broader perspective that activists from various other traditions (Indigenous and non-Indigenous) can learn from and must contend with.[21]

In light of this perspective, sociological and demographic analysis of racialized incarcerated populations is inadequate when thinking about the political form of carceral power in North America. The colonial violence of carceral power in North America is not exclusively, or even predominantly, a function of the *number* or *proportion* of racialized bodies within institutions. Moreover, framing the matter in this way may exacerbate the problem. When the critique of incarceration rests on the overrepresentation of racialized bodies within penal institutions, this tacitly renders carcerality as a *dehistoricized* tool of state power—even if distorted by the pathological effects of a racist society—displacing an account of the continuity and linkages among carcerality, state formation, and territorialized sovereignty.

As Indigenous scholars such as Taiaiake Alfred, Joanne Barker, Glen Coulthard, and Audra Simpson (*inter alia*) have consistently argued, unlike other racialized populations in North America, Indigenous peoples constituted self-governing political communities prior to the imposition of European state and market forms.[22] Their *continued* sovereign presence on the North American continent attests not only to the failure of a series of projects of racial population management; it also fundamentally calls into question the very legitimacy of Euro-American states themselves. The central role of policing, prisons, and the criminal justice system in the maintenance and reproduction of the state form is therefore challenged in a manner that exceeds the paradigm of overrepresentation. Moving beyond the overrepresentation model, then, means asking after the political function of the carceral system as a whole, beyond that of racialized bodies within. In so doing, we confront a series of new questions: How can we analyze carceral power in the context of an ongoing denial of Indigenous peoples not merely as individuals or even as "populations" but as self-organizing, self-governing political collectivities? How are we to apprehend the cataloguing and deploying of statistical evidence in this situation, especially when the evidentiary record is itself so indebted to a state apparatus of monitoring, tracking, and documenting Indigenous bodies?[23] How do we draw on such statistical evidence while recognizing that these numbers constitute bodies as "populations" in a context of a depoliticizing biopolitics of surplus humanity and human management?[24]

Returning once more to the Canadian case, Indigenous peoples do not merely represent racialized bodies produced by a biopolitics of population management. Rather—and this is the radical actuality that must always be held at bay by the state—they constitute alternative political, economic, ecological, and spiritual systems of ordering, governing, and relating. In the context of ongoing occupation, usurpation, dispossession, and ecological devastation, *no* level of representation in one of the central apparatuses of state control and formalized violence would be proportionate. Instead, Indigenous sovereignty itself calls forth an alternative normativity that challenges the very *existence* of the carceral system, let alone its internal organization and operation.

III

Before turning more centrally to the question of alternative normativities, consider how Indigenous critique recasts another, related theme currently circulating in activist-academic literature—namely, the contemporary concern over a collapse between military and police operations. We are repeatedly reminded that, at present, foreign policy objectives described explicitly in terms of "war" are advanced not through the traditional confrontation of armed combatants, but through police-like operations over a globe envisioned as one large domestic space of surveillance and pacification. As we repeatedly hear from critics and defenders alike, US-led empire functions as a "global policeman." The corollary development is the increased militarization of traditional, domestic policing. Policing is thought to be militarized either when (1) it begins to employ certain technologies of intense violence normally not deployed against civilian citizenry (e.g., the use of armed personal carriers, drones, aerial surveillance, etc.); or (2) when it begins to serve overtly political aims, exceeding its traditional mandate to "serve and protect" the citizenry.[25] In such situations, the police risk being viewed as a force imposed externally by a government that the subjugated population does not recognize or authorize or that does not have effect participation within.[26] Criminal control bleeds into war.

Assertions that the logic of war and that of social pacification can still be effectively disentangled are belied by our reality. In the current climate no attempt to fully insulate these two logics from each other can succeed. Yet while recent commentators have expressed great dismay at the nakedly fluid boundary between military and policing operations today, viewed from the vantage point of settler colonialism and Indigenous critique, there is nothing new about this permeability. In the history of Anglo-American settler colonialism, for instance, the extension of criminal jurisdiction has long been central to the subjugation and displacement of Indigenous polities.[27] Existing in the "third space of sovereignty," Indigenous nations have always subverted distinctions between foreign and domestic as well as attempts to distinguish war decisively from crime management.[28] The largest and most important domestic policing organization in Canada, the Royal Canadian Mounted Police, emerged from its predecessor organization, the North-West Mounted Police. The latter was modeled on the Royal Irish Constabulary and expressly intended to function as a paramilitary organization, meant simultaneously to defeat Indigenous resistance politically and pacify it criminally.[29] In the United States, as well, although the Office of Indian Affairs, created in 1824, was very symbolically relocated from the War Department to the Department of the Interior in 1849, from that point forward, including Wounded Knee and the complex and tense relationship between American Indians and the Federal Bureau of Investigation (FBI), Indigenous peoples have always doubly subjected to these two logics of violence and control.[30] As a result, they are well positioned to observe that these are not, and never have been, fixed and parallel logics but have always intersected with each other. Indigenous critique thereby discloses the oscillation of these forms of state violence as *constitutive* of territorialized sovereignty in a colonial context rather than extraneous and novel.

The deep challenge posed by Indigenous peoples does not merely consist in their doubly subjected position here, however. Rather, it resides in the delegitimizing of the war-crime dichotomy in the first place, for Indigenous peoples in North America are in precisely the position mentioned earlier: experiencing policing itself as a force imposed externally by a government that the subjugated population does not recognize or authorize or does not have effect participation within.[31] In short, the *state itself* is apprehended as the primary vehicle for the collective organization of violence toward Indigenous peoples, historically and in the present. Indigenous politics is founded on this existential challenge. As the Indigenous (Mohawk) scholar Patricia Monture-Angus points out, in the Canadian context study after study has demonstrated that "Aboriginal people do not view the criminal justice system as a system that represents or respects them"; as a result, "the perceptions of Aboriginal peoples (while keeping in mind their diversity) thus thoroughly challenge the perspective of those who regard Canada to be a free and democratic state."[32] In this context, reforming the penal system to produce less "disproportionality" in racial demographics (between the inside and the outside of prisons) will continue to fail to take into account Aboriginal justice traditions, which are "a clear component of the inherent right to self-government."[33] While Indigeneity consistently avoids reduction to any fixed or determinate content, the condition of possibility for continued creative reinvention and reproduction of culture, tradition, spirituality, and life itself *as* Indigenous peoples has meant a persistent refusal to acknowledge the dehistoricized naturalization of domestic-versus-foreign distinctions meant to legitimize state violence.

Although this has a centuries-long history, what has changed is that, unlike in previous eras (unlike even the 1970s [e.g., Pine Ridge]), the incarceration of Indigenous peoples is increasingly dehistoricized—and thus depoliticized—through its representation as the general extension of racialized criminality. Even though far more Indigenous peoples are incarcerated today than, say, when Leonard Peltier was convicted in 1977, incarceration is more effectively and smoothly enacted because it has been routinized, bureaucratized, and detached from the longer colonial history of the state. By attending to the colonial function of carceral expansion today, we are cautioned against too hastily accepting the supposed radical novelty of the present, not to mention the story of neoliberalism's hollowed-out states or empire's virtuality. Indeed, we are even cautioned against too hastily accepting one of the prevailing narratives of Indigenous studies—namely, that North American settler states have moved from openly coercive and violent relations with Indigenous communities toward a more flexible, docile, politics of recognition and assimilation, a move away from the "hard infrastructure" of military operations and residential schools to the "soft infrastructure" of public apologies and cultural accommodation. While this transition to soft tactics has certainly occurred in some fields of governance, it is coeval with the growth of a whole shadow system of hard infrastructure that is every bit as material, physical, and coercive as ever. The settler-colonial state has not gone away at all or even become less of a physical, material presence. It has merely shifted its site of operation, perhaps most symbolically from the residential school to the prison. Read against this larger backdrop, we can begin to read the vast network of prisons in North America in terms of its ideological function relative to settler colonialism—that is, the manner in which it functions strenuously to depoliticize this ongoing material violence and erect a strict separation between *criminal control* and *conquest*, despite Indigenous societies' continued insistence that externally imposed coercive control over their members (for whatever reason) is an affront to the inherent right to self-government.

IV

Gilmore has persuasively argued that if we are to understand and properly subject carceral power to an effective critique, then we must not only "develop complex understandings of how prisoners became so massively available as carceral objects"—a matter surely deeply rooted in processes of racialization—but also "figure out how the ground the prisons stand on becomes available for such a purpose."[34] In thinking about how this ground becomes available, Gilmore has in mind the manner in which a permanent crisis in the workfare-welfare state has been literally displaced onto the landscape of relatively low-density, rural communities, which has produced new opportunities and demands for land grabbing. However, highlighting the colonialism of incarceration further draws our attention to the territorial foundation of prison expansion in a deeper and longer history. It forces consideration of the politics of territoriality in North America in a variety of forms, including the ways in which territorialized sovereignty aspires to impose an exclusivity and singularity of command and control that obliterates alternative normative orders beneath and beyond its aegis.

At the most immediately level, criminalized capture by the state is about management of "disorderly populations" through isolation. As Allen Feldman famously put it: "Arrest is the political art of individualizing disorder."[35] Of course, isolation and sequester are always already geospatial and thus implicated in territoriality in a general sense. Prisons are a spatial and territorialized matrix of punishment and control inasmuch as they attempt to provide geographical solutions to socioeconomic and political contradictions (in the form of cages, walls, and other technologies of isolation and segregation). As Gilmore forcefully put this point: "Incapacitation doesn't pretend to change anything about people except where they are. It is in a simple-minded way, then, a geographical solution that purports to solve social problems by extensively and repeatedly removing people from disordered, deindustrialized milieus and depositing them somewhere else."[36] Prisons certainly operate through geospatial media in this general sense, sharing a certain continuity with other technologies of spatial control such as "ghettoization." As a result, there is overlap here with other importance experiences of, for instance, African American subjugation and control. Prisons, ghettos, and other tools of capture and separation exhibit a revealing morphological continuity.[37] Attending to the historical experience of Indigenous peoples, however, these general geospatial formations are refocused through another lens of territoriality—settler colonialism and land acquisition—reframing Gilmore's considerations on the territorial foundation of the prison apparatus.

The Indigenous political theorist Glen Coulthard (Dene) provides a succinct and precise definition from which we can begin to bring the colonial-
territorial politics to the fore here. He designates a "colonial relationship" in
terms of the distinct form of domination it engenders. Colonialism is

> a relationship where power—in this case, interrelated discursive and non-
> discursive facets of economic, gendered, racial, and state power—has been
> structured into a relatively secure or sedimented set of hierarchical so-
> cial relations that continue to facilitate the *dispossession* of Indigenous
> peoples of our lands and self-determining authority. In this respect, Can-
> ada is no different than any other settler-colonial power: in the Canadian
> context, colonial domination continues to be structurally oriented around
> the state's longstanding commitment to maintain—through force, fraud,
> and more recently, so-called "negotiations"—ongoing access to the land
> that contradictorily provides the material and spiritual sustenance of
> Indigenous societies on the one hand, and the foundation of colonial
> state-formation, settlement and capitalist development on the other.[38]

Coupling Coulthard's work with the emergent field of settler-colonial studies
brings into focus the extent to which state and market formation in North
America has always been intimately bound up with *land acquisition* and *resettlement*, and that these have called forth distinct ideologies rooted in notions of
agrarianism, territorial possession, and improvement. The defining feature
of this particular political formation is not the appropriation of labor or the subjugation of Indigenous self-governing powers (although both of these are also
present). Rather, as James Tully reminds us, "The ground of the relation is the
appropriation of the land, resources, and jurisdiction of Indigenous peoples,
not only for the sake of resettlement and exploitation . . . but *for the territorial
foundations of the dominant society itself*."[39] Or as Patrick Wolfe states rather more
bluntly: "Territoriality is settler colonialism's specific, irreducible element."[40]

Contemporary critical theory has largely evaded an analysis of territoriality
and its relationship to classical colonial formations, oftentimes staking much
on a supposed movement toward a decentered, deterritorialized, virtual or
"postmodern" Empire thought to have succeeded the older, land-based form
of colonial power that held sway over an era now imagined as distant to us.[41]
However, viewed from the vantage point of Indigenous struggles, settler colonialism and—our focus here—carceral power as it is subtended by colonialism,
predictions of a neoliberal hollowed-out state, or a deterritorialized empire appear not merely premature but inattentive to the dialectical inversion of these
tendencies—that is, to the processes of concretization and the persistence of

fixity, rigidity, and *territoriality*. Thinking through carceral power and Indigenous incarceration, we can here, instead, ask after the continuation of classical building practices by the state, including its hard infrastructure, as well as the continuation of classical colonial relationships to land acquisition and dispossession that have provided the literal terrain on which biopolitical population management techniques such as segregation and sequester rest, observing not only that these remain central to the global organization of capital and biopower but also that such forces are in fact advancing rather than melting away.

Work by the political theorist Wendy Brown stands as an exception to this general occlusion inasmuch as she has attended to the paradoxes of the territoriality of contemporary sovereignty by highlighting the continuing importance of walls, fences, borders, and barriers to the organization of political space. Brown notes that what we have come to call "globalization" in fact "harbors fundamental tensions between opening and barricading, fusion and partition, erasure and reinscription. These tensions materialize as increasingly liberalized borders, on the one hand, and the devotion of unprecedented funds, energies, and technologies to border fortification, on the other."[42] In other words, while capital and military technology is increasingly deterritorialized and fluid, it is so only through the reassertion of rigidity, fixity, and territorial segmentation for certain populations. And, quite rightly, Brown draws a line of continuity between the contemporary resurgence of concrete barriers and the historical lineage of settler colonialism and land appropriation. In this way, she provides tools for understanding how the regulation of political space is not merely about the construction (or removal) of any specific walls, fences, or cages. It is, more properly, "a technology of separation and domination in a complex context of settler colonialism and occupation."[43]

In so-called Indian Country, there is nothing new about this paradoxical relationship of segregation and fluidity. Indigenous peoples are well acquainted with what Ann Laura Stoler has termed (following and building on Foucault) the carceral archipelago of empire, which has always combined spatial isolation and confinement with linkages and connectivity—in this particular case, highlighted most dramatically by the circuit many Indigenous peoples traverse today between the reserve or reservation and the prison, two sites of physical and spatial containment that are intertwined in each other.[44] In settler-colonial societies today, however, this reality is obscured not only by the ideological depoliticization of carceral expansion in general but also by the delinking of prison abolitionism from decolonialism and the "land question" specifically. To speak of the colonial violence of carceral power in North America is precisely to focus attention on how incarceration facilitates dispossession in this time and in this place.

In the final analysis, then, Indigenous critique launches its evaluation of carceral power by attending to the ways in which this apparatus of capture operates as one armature of territorialized colonial sovereignty, a continuous process of dispossession that (always imperfectly) undermines Indigenous practices of self-government by severing peoples from their historical relationship to the land. This critique already speaks of alternative normative relationships of governance, sociality, and ecology.

With regard to this latter question, consider again the work of Monture-Angus. Drawing on extensive work with Aboriginal women's associations across Canada, she points us directly to the ultimate normative foundation of the critique proffered here. In 1989, the Aboriginal Women's Caucus submitted a brief to the Solicitor General of Canada, making clear the status of Indigenous women as multiply subjected by sexist, racist, and colonial forms of governance and yet firmly rooted in an alternative ethic that precludes their legitimate incorporation into the criminal justice system, whatever their "level of representation" therein. The brief stated: "All Aboriginal, First Nations citizens are in conflict with the law. We are First Peoples with an inherent right to exercise our own systems of justice and the values these systems represent. The issue of Aboriginal women and the criminal justice system is merely the most blatant example of the oppression of First Nations People under a system of laws to which we have never consented."[45] Reflecting on this and other examples, the conclusion Monture-Angus draws is that "the foundational ideas of current correctional philosophy"—namely, punitive power and risk management—are "incompatible with Aboriginal cultures, law and tradition."[46]

This presents a unique and important challenge to the new penal ethos, since it cannot be easily resolved even through a "de-racialization" process or the reorganization of demographics. Even attempts to incorporate the alternative ethical systems of Indigenous peoples will fall short under such conditions. The inclusion of Healing Lodges and other Aboriginal-centered correctional facilities cannot conceal the fact that these institutions remain "within the legal and bureaucratic structure of the Canadian prison system . . . no matter how much Aboriginal culture and tradition inspires their contour, shape and form."[47] Whereas "racialization" approaches tend to focus on the racist operation of correctional institutions, Indigenous critique focuses attention on the normative critique of carceral power within a broader horizon, especially insofar as it functions as a principal apparatus of colonial-state power. This deep, territoriality-grounded normative vision is not reducible to the more prevalent antiracist analysis of critical prison studies (however indispensable the latter remains) and cannot be overlooked or ignored.

V

Theorizing and interrupting Indigenous incarceration means attending to more than the overrepresentation of racialized bodies.[48] It calls for an analysis of the colonial function of the carceral form in the here and now. To recapitulate: the concern here is not with a general notion that all imprisonment, regardless of time and place, is inherently colonial merely due to its form or mode of operation. The concern is, rather, with the fact that, in *this* context, carceral power takes on a colonial function as a result of its central role in manifesting and managing the territorialized violence of *these* states.[49] If sovereignty can be said to comprise the continual practice of asserting the singularity of political control in a given territorial space—thus combining exclusion and absolute decision—colonialism is the practical mediation of the external and internal boundaries of this process. It is the means by which sovereignty extends outward and is then reterritorialized through continual internal reorganization—hence, the association of colonization as an outward expansive force and an internal reorganization through containment, capture, and divisive social organization. In the contemporary Anglo-American world, this colonization is predicated by its *settler* form, as so many important interventions in Native American studies have demonstrated.

Settler colonialism is a distinctive ideological and material formation, and it should be clear here that the prison-industrial complex in North America is one technique in its operation today. Set alongside that other archipelago of spatial containment—the Indian reservation and reserve system—the contemporary carceral system colonizes and recolonizes in a classical sense: by providing a solution to that which exceeds and destabilizes sovereignty via a spatial reorganization of populations and a depoliticization of that process. While this apparatus is currently situated within empire and manifests itself in fully racialized terms of articulation, it cannot be reduced to these other formations. Settler colonialism aims not primarily at exogenous domination or the extraction of surplus value from an enslaved and subjugated population but, first and foremost, at the acquisition and maintenance of territorialized sovereignty through continual spatial containment, reorganization, and pacification—a process that both undermines and is continually challenged by the plurality of Indigenous normative worlds. Thus, the story of the rise of carceral power in the Anglo-American world cannot be told without attending to the history of settler colonialism, and it is only on the basis of this reframing that prison abolition can properly announce itself as decolonization.

NOTES

With minor changes, this chapter was previously published as "The Colonialism of Incarceration" in *Radical Philosophy Review* 17, no. 2 (2014): 435–55, https://doi.org/10 .5840/radphilrev201491622. It is reprinted here with permission of the publisher, the Philosophy Documentation Center.

1   Unless otherwise indicated, statistical information on Aboriginal incarceration in Canada is from Mia Dauvergne, "Adult Correctional Statistics in Canada, 2010–2011," *Juristat* (October 11, 2012); Samuel Perreault, "The Incarceration of Aboriginal People in Adult Correctional Services," *Juristat* (July 2009). The majority of statistical evidence on the incarceration of Indigenous people in Canada derives from *Juristat*, a periodical published by Statistics Canada, which advertises itself as "of interest to all those who plan, establish, administer and evaluate justice programs and projects as well as to anyone who has an interest in Canada's justice system": *Juristat*, Statistics Canada, accessed October 26, 2013, http://www.statcan.gc.ca/pub /85-002-x/index-eng.htm.

2   The controversial bill, traveling under the equally bloated and mangled title *An Act to Enact the Justice for Victims of Terrorism Act and to Amend the State Immunity Act, the Criminal Code, the Controlled Drugs and Substances Act, the Corrections and Conditional Release Act, the Youth Criminal Justice Act, the Immigration and Refugee Protection Act and other Acts (Safe Streets and Communities Act)*, passed into law in September 2013: see LegisInfo, Parliament of Canada, http://www.parl.gc.ca/LEGISInfo/BillDetails.aspx ?Mode=1&billId=5120829&Language=E.

3   Government of Canada, *Annual Report of the Office of the Correctional Investigator 2012–2013*, sec, IV, 30, https://www.oci-bec.gc.ca/cnt/rpt/annrpt/annrpt20122013-eng.aspx#sIV.

4   Government of Canada, *Annual Report of the Office of the Correctional Investigator 2012–2013*, 30.

5   Office of the Correctional Investigator, *Good Intentions, Disappointing Results: A Progress Report on Federal Aboriginal Corrections* (Ottawa: Office of the Correctional Investigator, 2009), 6, cited in Patricia A. Monture, "The Need for Radical Change in the Canadian Criminal Justice System: Applying a Human Rights Framework," in *Visions of the Heart: Canadian Aboriginal Issues*, edited by David Long and Olive Patricia Dickason (Don Mills, ON: Oxford University Press, 2011), 238. For a study on the imprisonment of women in Canada (but with little specific attention to Aboriginal women and no mention of colonialism), see Kelly Hannah-Moffat, *Punishment in Disguise: Penal Governance and Federal Imprisonment of Women in Canada* (Toronto: University of Toronto Press, 2001).

6   Two of the most frequently cited works in contemporary critical prison studies are Angela Davis, *Are Prisons Obsolete?* (New York: Seven Stories, 2003); and Ruth

Wilson Gilmore, *Golden Gulag: Prisons, Surplus, Crisis, and Opposition in Globalizing California* (Berkeley: University of California Press, 2007).

7   In the section that follows, I speak frequently of "racism" and "racialization." My specific understanding of these terms is highly indebted to Gilmore's definition of racism as "state-sanctioned or extralegal production and exploitation of group-differentiated vulnerability to premature death": Gilmore, *Golden Gulag*, 28.

8   See, e.g., Michelle Alexander, *The New Jim Crow: Mass Incarceration in the Age of Color-blindness* (New York: New Press, 2012).

9   Monture, "The Need for Radical Change in the Canadian Criminal Justice System"; Patricia Monture-Angus, "Aboriginal Women and Correctional Practice: Reflections on the Task Force on Federally Sentenced Women," in *An Ideal Prison? Critical Essays on Women's Imprisonment in Canada*, edited by Kelly Hannah-Moffat and Margaret Shaw (Halifax: Fernwood, 2000); Luana Ross, *Inventing the Savage: The Social Construction of Native American Criminality* (Austin: University of Texas Press, 1998). See also Jane Dickson-Gilmore and Carole La Prairie, eds., *Will the Circle Be Unbroken? Aboriginal Communities, Restorative Justice, and the Challenges of Conflict and Change* (Toronto: University of Toronto Press, 2005); Joyce Green, "From Stonechild to Social Cohesion," *Canadian Journal of Political Science* 39, no. 1 (2006); Patricia Monture-Okanee and Mary Ellen Turpel, "Aboriginal Peoples and Canadian Criminal Law: Rethinking Justice," *University of British Columbia Law Review* 26 (1992): 239–77. On incarceration as a theme in Indigenous literature, see Deena Rymhs, ed., *From the Iron House: Imprisonment in First Nations Writing* (Waterloo, ON: Wilfred Laurier University Press, 2008).

10 National Association for the Advancement of Colored People, *Misplaced Priorities: Over Incarcerate, Under Educate* (Baltimore, MD: NAACP, 2011), https://www.prisonpolicy .org/scans/naacp/misplaced_priorities.pdf.

11 David Milward, "Sweating It Out: Facilitating Corrections and Parole in Canada through Aboriginal Spiritual Healing," in *Windsor Yearbook of Access to Justice* 29, no. 1 (2011): 43.

12 As Loïc Wacquant puts this point, "True, discrimination in sentencing remains a reality at the final stage of the criminal justice process . . . , but discrimination clearly has not *increased* since the mid-1970s and so it cannot account for the spectacular worsening of 'racial disproportionality' in prison administration in the recent period": Loïc Wacquant, *Prisons of Poverty* (Minneapolis: University of Minnesota Press, 2009), 156.

13 Cf. Joe Soss, Richard Fording, and Sanford Schram, *Disciplining the Poor: Neoliberal Paternalism and the Persistent Power of Race* (Chicago: University of Chicago Press, 2011).

14 For example, in the same year that the Conservative government of Canada announced sweeping new "tough on crime" laws, Statistics Canada reported that the crime rate was the lowest in decades: "Canada's Crime Rate Lowest since 1972," CBC, July 25, 2013, accessed December 11, 2013, http://www.cbc.ca/news/canada /canada-s-crime-rate-lowest-since-1972-1.1334090.

15 For criticism of the "new slavery" arguments and the idea that capitalist labor exploitation is the primary driver of prison expansion, see Gilmore, *Golden*

Gulag, 21; James Kilgore, "The Myth of Prison Slave Labor Camps in the U.S.," *Counterpunch* (August 9, 2013), https://www.counterpunch.org/2013/08/09/ the-myth-of-prison-slave-labor-camps-in-the-u-s/.

16 Gilmore, *Golden Gulag*, 113.

17 Wacquant has meticulously documented how this new "penal common sense" has been actively exported by the United States to Western Europe (and beyond) through neoliberal think tanks, policy experts, and lobbying groups. It is reasonable to expect that the appearance of many of the same trends in Canada can be attributed to the adoption of this new kind of "Washington Consensus": see Wacquant, *Prisons of Poverty*, esp. 54.

18 For a powerful political-phenomenological critique of solitary confinement, see Lisa Guenther, *Solitary Confinement* (Minneapolis: University of Minnesota Press, 2013).

19 Wacquant, *Prisons of Poverty*, 175–76.

20 See Soss et al., *Disciplining the Poor*.

21 I offer this as a complement to the rich new body of work that explores the deep imbrications of Indigenous studies and Black political thought, some of which I explore in greater detail in Robert Nichols, *Theft Is Property! Dispossession and Critical Theory* (Durham, NC: Duke University Press, 2019), esp. chap. 4. For other work at this nexus, see Shona Jackson, *Creole Indigeneity: Between Myth and Nation in the Caribbean* (Minneapolis: University of Minnesota Press, 2012); Barbara Krauthamer, *Black Slaves, Indian Masters: Slavery, Emancipation, and Citizenship in the Native American South* (Chapel Hill: University of North Carolina Press, 2013); Tiya Miles, *The House on Diamond Hill: A Cherokee Plantation Story* (Chapel Hill: University of North Carolina Press, 2010); Tiya Miles, *Ties That Bind: The Story of an Afro-Cherokee Family in Slavery and Freedom* (Berkeley: University of California Press, 2005).

22 Joanne Barker, ed., *Sovereignty Matters* (Lincoln: University of Nebraska Press, 2005); Glen Coulthard, *Red Skin, White Masks: Rejecting the Colonial Politics of Recognition* (Minneapolis: University of Minnesota Press, 2014); Audra Simpson, *Mohawk Interruptus* (Durham, NC: Duke University Press, 2014).

23 For instance, consider the role of *Juristat* in the Canadian context: see *Juristat*, Statistics Canada, accessed October 26, 2013, http://www.statcan.gc.ca/pub/85-002 -x/index-eng.htm.

24 Statistical evidence of overrepresentation is not irrelevant or useless as a tool of argumentation. However, due to the inherent ambiguities of "overrepresentation," it has never been a sufficient tool for a robust normative critique of carceral power. Consider that between 1967 and 1991 thirty major studies were commissioned on Aboriginal peoples and justice in Canada that, on some accounts, have resulted in some 1,800 recommendations for reforming the Canadian justice system. In 1996, the Report of the Royal Commission on Aboriginal Peoples (RCAP) included a separate volume on Indigenous peoples and criminal justice, *Bridging the Cultural Divide*, which provided fifteen major new findings on the matter and seventeen additional recommendations. Almost none of these have been implemented, and in the time since the RCAP was released, the problem has only compounded:

Monture, "The Need for Radical Change in the Canadian Criminal Justice System," 239.

25 For examples from mainstream and journalistic work of spreading fear related to the former development (but that completely overlooks the colonial and racial dimensions of these questions), see Radley Balko, *The Rise of the Warrior Cop: The Militarization of America's Police Forces* (New York: Public Affairs, 2013); Arthur Rizer and Joseph Hartman, "How the War on Terror Has Militarized the Police," *Atlantic*, November 7, 2011, http://www.theatlantic.com/national/archive/2011/11 /how-the-war-on-terror-has-militarized-the-police/248047; Sarah Stillman, "Swat Team Nation," *New Yorker*, August 8, 2013, http://www.newyorker.com/online/blogs /comment/2013/08/swat-team-nation.html.

26 See Wacquant, *Prisons of Poverty*, 19.

27 For historical work documenting this fluidity, see Sydney Harring, *White Man's Justice: Native People in 19th Century Canadian Jurisprudence* (Toronto: University of Toronto Press, 1998).

28 Kevin Bruyneel, *The Third Space of Sovereignty* (Minneapolis: University of Minnesota Press, 2007).

29 Harring, *White Man's Justice*; R. C. Macleod, "Canadianizing the West: The North-West Mounted Police as Agents of the National Policy, 1873–1905," in *The Prairie West: Historical Readings*, edited by R. Douglas Francis and Howard Palmer (Edmonton: Pica, 1992), 225–38.

30 The FBI shares jurisdiction with the Bureau of Indian Affairs, Office of Justice Services (BIA-OJS) and has primary law enforcement responsibility on nearly two hundred Indian reservations. The Department of Justice traces its authority over law enforcement to treaty responsibilities established in *Cherokee Nation v. Georgia*, 30 US (5 Pet.) 1, 17 (1831), which set out the US government's duty to "protect" Indian tribes as "domestic dependent nations": see http://www.fbi.gov/about-us /investigate/vc_majorthefts/indian/indian_country_crime; and US Department of Justice, Office of Tribal Justice, accessed June 2014, http://www.justice.gov/otj. Perhaps the locale most symbolically associated with the overlap of military and policing powers as they relate to American Indians is Alcatraz, which initially functioned as a military prison where Indigenous political opponents were routinely incarcerated and, as a result, was later the target of Indigenous (re)occupation, from 1969 to 1971, by the United Indians of All Tribes. See Paul Chaat Smith and Robert Warrior, *Like a Hurricane: The American Indian Movement from Alcatraz to Wounded Knee* (New York: New Press, 1997).

31 This article does not attempt to extend the comparison beyond Canada and the United States to include other Anglo-settler polities, such as Australia and New Zealand. No doubt, however, such comparative work is possible and needed. For an example of such analysis, see Lisa Ford, *Settler Sovereignty: Jurisdiction and Indigenous Peoples in America and Australia, 1788–1836* (Cambridge, MA: Harvard University Press, 2010).

32 Monture, "The Need for Radical Change in the Canadian Criminal Justice System," 244.

33 Monture, "The Need for Radical Change in the Canadian Criminal Justice System," 240. See also RCAP (Royal Commission on Aboriginal Peoples), *Bridging the Cultural Divide: A Report on Aboriginal People and Criminal Justice in Canada* (Ottawa: Minister of Supply and Services, 1996), 289.

34 Gilmore, *Golden Gulag*, 130.

35 Allen Feldman, *Formations of Violence* (Chicago: University of Chicago Press, 1991), cited in Gilmore, *Golden Gulag*, 235.

36 Gilmore, *Golden Gulag*, 14.

37 See Wacquant, *Prisons of Poverty*, 82.

38 Glen Coulthard, "From Wards of the State to Subjects of Recognition? Marx, Indigenous Peoples, and the Politics of Dispossession in Denendeh," in *Theorizing Native Studies*, edited by Audra Simpson and Andrea Smith (Durham, NC: Duke University Press, 2014), 57–58.

39 James Tully, "The Struggles of Indigenous Peoples for and of Freedom," in *Political Theory and the Rights of Indigenous Peoples*, edited by Duncan Ivison, Paul Patton, and Will Sanders (Cambridge: Cambridge University Press, 2000), 39, emphasis added.

40 Patrick Wolfe, "Settler Colonialism and the Elimination of the Native," *Journal of Genocide Research* 8, no. 4 (2006): 388.

41 Important exceptions to this rule include Michel Foucault, *Security, Territory, Population* (New York: Palgrave Macmillan, 2007); and the work of Stuart Elden, especially *The Birth of Territory* (Chicago: University of Chicago Press, 2013).

42 Wendy Brown, *Walled States, Waning Sovereignty* (New York: Zone, 2010), 7–8.

43 Brown, *Walled States, Waning Sovereignty*, 30.

44 Ann Laura Stoler, *Along the Archival Grain: Epistemic Anxieties and Colonial Common Sense* (Princeton, NJ: Princeton University Press, 2009). Stoler is building on, while critically provincializing and decentering, Foucault's classic genealogy of carceral power in *Discipline and Punish*, but especially the symbolic function of the Mettray institution. While Foucault employs the opening of the Mettray penal colony in January 1840 to "fix the date of the completion of the carceral system," Stoler rightly points out that the institution was in fact part of a global, imperial formation that "connected strategies of confinement from metropole to colony and across the imperial world": Stoler, *Along the Archival Grain*, 131; see also Michel Foucault, *Discipline and Punish*, 2d ed. (New York: Vintage, 1995).

45 *Report of the Task Force on Federally Sentenced Women: Creating Choices* (Ottawa: Ministry of the Solicitor General, 1990), 23, cited in Monture-Angus, "Aboriginal Women and Correctional Practice," 57. The Aboriginal Women's Caucus was a group of Aboriginal women working in the Canadian criminal justice system.

46 She goes on to elaborate, writing, "People (or any 'thing' with a spirit) were not intended to be managed but rather respected. The conclusion is that one of the foundational ideas of current correctional philosophy is, in my opinion, incompatible with Aboriginal cultures, law and tradition": Monture-Angus, "Aboriginal Women and Correctional Practice," 56.

47 Monture-Angus, "Aboriginal Women and Correctional Practice," 53. This principled, deep normative critique of prisons as institutions of violence displaces

and eclipses work whose primary aim is to diagnose the manner in which carceral expansion is "antagonistic to democratic participation" and "inspires negative orientations toward government": Vesla M. Weaver and Amy E. Lerman, "Political Consequences of the Carceral State," *American Political Science Review* 104, no. 4 (November 2010): 817–33.

48 For work that carefully avoids the generalized "racialization" framework in favor of a rich historical analysis of the intertwining of anti-Black racism and settler colonialism, see Jackson, *Creole Indigeneity*.

49 This leaves open the question of how to relate the specificity of the carceral-colonial linkage in North America to other Anglo-settler colonies or other occupied lands (which is beyond the scope of this particular essay).

4

ARE HAWAIIANS INDIANS?

DAVID UAHIKEAIKALEI'OHU MAILE

The political status of Native Hawaiians in US law is precarious, and attempts to experiment with this precarious position have intensified in the past two decades. The US Supreme Court decision in *Rice v. Cayetano* (2000) generated much of this momentum.[1] It is a landmark case that continues to frame federal and state law in ways that constrain rights for Native Hawaiians as well as other Indigenous peoples under US regulation yet without formal recognition. I begin with *Rice v. Cayetano* to unravel a neglected thread in its legal genealogy. In his lawsuit, Harold "Freddy" Rice alleged that the State of Hawai'i violated the Fourteenth and Fifteenth Amendments of the US Constitution because he was restricted from voting in a state election on the basis of race. In 1978, the State of Hawai'i, caving to pressure by the modern Hawaiian sovereignty movement, created the Office of Hawaiian Affairs (OHA) as an agency to be led by Native Hawaiian trustees elected by Native Hawaiians.[2] When Rice, a US citizen born in Hawaiʻi and non-Native Hawaiian resident of the State of Hawaiʻi, was restricted from voting for OHA trustees, he brought the suit against Governor Ben Cayetano. Rice lost in lower courts but found solace with the US Supreme Court. The Supreme Court ruled, viewing the qualification of Native Hawaiian ancestry to be a proxy for race, that OHA elections instituted race-based voting—the State of Hawaiʻi had violated the Fifteenth Amendment.

Now, all residents of the State of Hawaiʻi, not just Native Hawaiians, vote in OHA elections and shape how OHA administers resources, programs, and services expressly for Native Hawaiians. It was a devastating decision for advocates of Native Hawaiian rights, self-determination, and sovereignty. Critically though, a core debate in the case pivoted on whether the legal category "Hawaiian" was a political or racial status. Before arguments were heard by the court, an amicus brief filed on May 27, 1999, in support of the plaintiff, raised serious legal and political concerns. The brief had an enduring impact and lingers as a nagging trace within biopolitical operations of US settler-state geopower. Brett Kavanaugh, an attorney and partner at Kirkland and Ellis LLP at the time, argued in the brief that "Hawaiian" is a racial classification. He suggested that Hawaiians do not share the political status of Indians because the Commerce Clause of the US Constitution recognizes the sovereignty only of Indian tribes. "Hawaiians," the brief noted, "do not and could not qualify as an American Indian tribe." The Supreme Court eventually agreed and blighted Hawaiian rights to self-determination and sovereignty.

A few months after submitting the brief, Kavanaugh published an op-ed titled, "Are Hawaiians Indians?"[3] I was hesitant to use this as my chapter's title, especially since it was intended to be reductive, offensive, and divisive. But taking great care to redirect it, I repurpose and inhabit the question because, as I show, it permeates the management of Hawaiian life by the federal government. The op-ed resurfaced in 2018 when Kavanaugh was nominated to replace Supreme Court Justice Anthony Kennedy, who inauspiciously wrote the majority opinion in *Rice v. Cayetano*. It circulated as damning evidence during his confirmation hearing before the Senate Judiciary Committee. Democratic Senator Mazie Hirono from Hawaiʻi was a member of the committee and pressed him: "Your view is that Hawaiians don't deserve protections as indigenous people under the constitution and your argument raises a serious question on how you would vote on the constitutionality of programs benefiting Alaska natives."[4] Hirono connected how Kavanaugh's anti-Hawaiian view contained pernicious consequences for other Indigenous communities, such as Alaskan Native Corporations with special programs created from congressional legislation like the Alaska Native Claims Settlement Act. Not only did the confirmation hearing put Kavanaugh's perpetration of sexual assault, performance of toxic masculinity, and perspective on abortion on full display, it also illustrated his white supremacist and colonial desire to dismantle affirmative action protections.[5] Sexual, gendered, and racialized violence became indelibly linked to colonial conquest. Kavanaugh's op-ed and discussions about it elucidate how questioning whether Hawaiians are Indians can be weaponized as a calculated test that perpetuates settler colonialism in Hawai'i.

Rather than providing an answer, I am greatly concerned with the work this question executes. My analysis does not forward a definition of the category "Indian" to determine whether or not Hawaiians fit. Instead, I question what kind of discursive work the question performs. My chapter stews on how the question and answers to it marshal a biopolitical management of Native Hawaiians that can serve the US settler-state's geopower in Hawai'i. Returning to the op-ed illuminates why the question is so nefarious. Further, it elucidates why the question is necessary for understanding "colonial governmentality," which Glen Coulthard discusses in the context of Canadian settler-state practices for managing First Nations, and I examine in US settler-state techniques for managing Kanaka Maoli (Indigenous people of Hawai'i).[6] My analysis here offers fresh insight about particular operations of colonial governmentality in Hawai'i.

Kavanaugh inquires "Are Hawaiians Indians?" to hypothesize that Native Hawaiians are indeed not Indians. What ensues in the op-ed is a dizzying exhibition of colonial racism. Severely misrepresenting conceptualizations of Indigeneity, nationality, race, ethnicity, and immigration, he describes Rice's legal claim and suggests there is an unconstitutional "naked racial-spoils system" that unfairly privileges and benefits Native Hawaiians.[7] Doing so, Kavanaugh mocks a brief, filed by the US Department of Justice supporting the defendant in *Rice v. Cayetano*, that contends the Native Hawaiian community is an Indigenous population equivalent to American Indian tribes. Ridiculing the claim, he opines that only federally recognized Indian tribes are entitled to special political benefits, and neither Congress nor the US Department of the Interior (DOI) has acknowledged Native Hawaiians as an Indian tribe. This contention comes into clearer focus in my analysis. "Hawaiians," Kavanaugh rambles, "have never even applied for recognition as an Indian tribe. The reason is obvious. They don't have their own government. They don't have their own system of laws. They don't have their own elected leaders. They don't live on reservations or in territorial enclaves. They don't even live together in Hawaii. Native Hawaiians are dispersed throughout the state of Hawaii and the United States. In short, native Hawaiians bear none of the indicia necessary to qualify as an Indian tribe."[8] Dripping in alternative facts, he contrives that Hawaiians are ineligible for the special political benefits available to Indigenous people in the United States because Hawaiians are not federally recognized like an Indian tribe. The Supreme Court listened to Kavanaugh so much so that he now sits as a justice on the court. The court concurred in *Rice v. Cayetano* with a conservative decision that harmed affirmative action protections for Native Hawaiians as well as Indigenous Oceanic people more broadly.[9] Nonetheless, the decision sparked a liberal race to federally recognize Native Hawaiians. The question of whether or not Hawaiians are Indians oozes from the lips and writings of conservative American politicians and, simultaneously, it pervades liberal US policies for federal recognition of Native Hawaiians framed like the vaccine rather than a mutation of the virus.

Progressive politicians, even those who are Kānaka Maoli (Native Hawaiians), have been hailed by the question and compelled to pursue federal recognition. Former Democratic Senator Daniel Akaka from Hawai'i began introducing legislation in 2000, immediately following *Rice v. Cayetano*, to establish a federal process to reestablish a government-to-government relationship between the United States and the Native Hawaiian community. The idea was that this could protect Native Hawaiian self-determination over resources, programs, and services bestowed by the United States. Although liberal politicians supported what became known as the Akaka bill, conservative politicians opposed it and mimed Kavanaugh's arguments concerning *Rice v. Cayetano*. Many Kanaka Maoli activists rejected it, too. Some suggested that Kanaka Maoli have never relinquished national and territorial sovereignty and the sovereignty offered would be limited under plenary power. Some posited further that Kanaka Maoli are not Indians and do not want to be recognized as an Indian tribe. Kavanaugh's question started seeping into criticisms of federal recognition. Along with advocates from OHA and elsewhere, Akaka labored in Congress over the next decade to get his bill passed, without success. Picking up where he left off, the DOI launched a campaign in 2014 to reestablish a government-to-government relationship with Native Hawaiians. The question of whether Hawaiians are Indians appears more and more like a structural pattern, not an isolated, past utterance. In this chapter, I show how the DOI experimented with whether or not Hawaiians are Indians by testing the biopolitical status of Native Hawaiians to legitimate the US settler-state's geopower over Hawai'i. Although the federal government is anxiously seeking to incorporate Hawaiians as Indians without land, I argue that Kānaka Maoli have rejected and refused the new colonial governmentality for federal recognition through articulations of 'a'ole (no) that expose the precarity of settler sovereignty in Hawai'i.

Advancing Reconciliation

On June 20, 2014, the DOI published an Advanced Notice for Proposed Rule-making (ANPRM) to propose an administrative rule to federally recognize a reorganized Native Hawaiian government. The primary purpose was to solicit input on a possible rule. Five threshold questions were provided to guide the content of feedback:

1 Should the Secretary propose an administrative rule that would fa-cilitate the reestablishment of a government-to-government relation-ship with the Native Hawaiian community?
2 Should the Secretary assist the Native Hawaiian community in reor-ganizing its government, with which the United States could reestab-lish a government-to-government relationship?
3 If so, what process should be established for drafting and ratifying a reorganized Native Hawaiian government's constitution or other governing document?
4 Should the Secretary instead rely on the reorganization of a Native Hawaiian government through a process established by the Native Ha-waiian community and facilitated by the State of Hawaii, to the extent such a process is consistent with Federal law?
5 If so, what conditions should the Secretary establish as prerequisites to Federal acknowledgement of a government-to-government rela-tionship with the reorganized Native Hawaiian government?[10]

Input could be submitted in written and oral formats. Verbal comments would be collected during testimony at public meetings. A key mandate, the ANPRM declared the DOI would conduct meetings across the Hawaiian archipelago and in Indian Country on the continent. The first meeting was scheduled three days after publication of the ANPRM. This executive process, perhaps by design, was rushed. The ANPRM forged a legal history for advancing reconciliation by reestablishing a government-to-government relationship with Native Ha-waiians. In it, re-establishment of a government-to-government relationship would reconcile past wrongs done to Kanaka Maoli. Creating a new pathway for federal recognition, distinct from prevailing mechanisms of congressional legislation and current executive procedures, the ANPRM emphasized that a special political relationship with trust responsibilities already exists between the federal government and Native Hawaiians. This legal history, claiming wrongdoing to engineer a special trust relationship for legitimating juridical authority, undergirds the entire rulemaking process.

The legal history described three narratives that rationalize federal recognition. First, congressional statutes created a special political and trust relationship with the Native Hawaiian community. Reiterating that Native Hawaiians are an Indigenous people who governed the Hawaiian Kingdom, the ANPRM identified that throughout the nineteenth century and until 1893 the United States "recognized the independence of the Hawaiian Nation . . . [and] extended full and complete diplomatic recognition to the Hawaiian Government."[11] This initial legal relationship was without special trust obligations; it was diplomacy between two independent nation-states. However, this relation was supplanted with another. Discussing that the Hawaiian Kingdom was overthrown by Americans with US military forces, the ANPRM asserted that a Joint Resolution passed by Congress in 1898 to annex Hawai'i crafted a new relationship. This inaugurated the federal government's original recognition of a domestic relationship with Hawaiians as a community claiming prior belonging to US territory. Subsequently, the ANPRM discussed that Congress instituted the Hawaiian Organic Act in 1900 to create the Territory of Hawai'i and acquire "ceded lands" that had been seized from the Hawaiian Kingdom by the Provisional Government and later transferred to the Republic of Hawai'i, inasmuch as a portion of proceeds from the lease and sale of these lands would come to benefit inhabitants of Hawai'i, including Kanaka Maoli. It then mentioned that Congress passed the 1920 Hawaiian Homes Commission Act (HHCA) to "rehabilitate the native Hawaiian population" after their decline, "by some estimates from several hundred thousand in 1778 to only 22,600," by designating approximately 200,000 acres of "ceded lands" for "native Hawaiians" to reestablish traditional lifeways. J. Kēhaulani Kauanui posits that the HHCA "institutionalized a trust agreement, constituting a special legal relationship."[12] Finally, the ANPRM reflected that, through the 1959 Admissions Act, Congress vested authority in the State of Hawai'i to manage and administer the lands set aside for rehabilitating "native Hawaiians" under the HHCA. Hence, the ANPRM argued, "Congress has enacted more than 150 statutes recognizing and implementing a special political and trust relationship with the Native Hawaiian community."[13] These statutes constitute a legal relationship that the DOI invokes to classify the US-Hawaiian relation as politically special and premised on trust. However, this relationship is not recognized as one between governments.

Second, congressional statutes instituted federal programs and services for the benefit of Native Hawaiians. A number of the listed statutes—the American

Indian Religious Freedom Act, National Museum of the American Indian Act, and Native American Graves Protection and Repatriation Act—categorize Hawaiians as Indians. This is where the ANPRM began to evacuate Hawaiian national sovereignty by including Kanaka Maoli in a framework of civil rights and affirmative action protections. "Congress," as the ANPRM phrased it, "has consistently enacted programs and services expressly and specifically for the Native Hawaiian community that are, in many respects, *analogous to, but separate from*, the programs and services that Congress has enacted for federally recognized tribes in the continental United States."[14] Such language is deliberate to interpellate Kanaka Maoli as domestic subjects of federal law. This maneuver, suggesting Native Hawaiians are analogous to but separate from Native Americans, is a sly technique of settler-state power.

Third, federal recognition of Native Americans represents a formal government-to-government relationship. This government-to-government relationship imparts self-determination, sovereignty, and other benefits to American Indian tribes. "Yet," according to the ANPRM, this has "long been denied to one place in our Nation, even though it is home to one of the world's largest indigenous communities: Hawaii."[15] On the one hand, the benefits of a government-to-government relationship have been denied to Kanaka Maoli. Exclusion rationalizes new instruments for inclusion that get signified as equality, justice, and reconciliation. On the other hand, acknowledging that Native Hawaiians constitute a large community of Indigenous people, Hawai'i is claimed as "one place in our Nation." Hawai'i has been *geographically included* within the territoriality of the US settler state, but Kanaka Maoli are *politically excluded* from a legal status and set of rights bestowed to tribes.

In 2001, a group of Native Hawaiian individuals and organizations filed a lawsuit that challenged the DOI's Procedures for Federal Acknowledgement of Indian Tribes, in Part 83 of Title 25 in the Code of Federal Regulations, which excluded Native Hawaiians from eligibility. In *Kahawaiolaa v. Norton* (2004), the DOI's procedures were upheld. The ANPRM noted that this case "upheld the *geographic limitation* in the part 83 regulations, 'concluding that there was a rational basis for the Department to distinguish between Native Hawaiians and tribes in the continental United States.'"[16] Yet the ANPRM proposed to bypass the geographic limitation because the ruling in *Kahawaiolaa v. Norton* expressed that the DOI may apply its expertise to determine whether Native Hawaiians could be recognized on a government-to-government basis. Flagging the administrative rule for federal recognition as an accommodating gesture of political inclusion, the ANPRM continued, "Reestablishing a government-to-government relationship with a reorganized sovereign Native

Hawaiian government that has been acknowledged by the United States could enhance federal agencies' ability to implement the established relationship between the United States and the Native Hawaiian community, while strengthening the self-determination of Hawaii's indigenous people and facilitating the preservation of their language, customs, heritage, health, and wealth."[17] Recognition would re-establish a formal government-to-government relationship that could ameliorate federal enforcement of the special trust affiliation and therein strengthen the self-determination necessary to preserve Indigenous language, customs, heritage, health, and wealth in Hawai'i—these were the so-called benefits offered in the deal.

But the ANPRM is not the first proposal to federally recognize Kanaka Maoli. The Akaka bill was an earlier attempt. Kauanui disentangles key legal developments that configured advocacy for the recognition offered by the Akaka bill.[18] She says that *Rice v. Cayetano* opened up programs and services for Native Hawaiians to attack. In its wake, lawsuits emerged alleging that state and federal policies implementing programs and services for Native Hawaiians were racially discriminatory. As the result of raiding civil rights and affirmative action protections, the political status of Hawaiian Indigeneity was reduced to a racial identification. "Within the broader context of these legal assaults, which deem any indigenous-specific program racist," Kauanui explains, "many Native Hawaiians and their allies support Akaka's proposal for federal recognition, since he pitched the legislation as a protective measure against such lawsuits."[19] Federal recognition therein developed into a protective response. Kauanui notes that when Akaka introduced the bill, he referenced the 1993 Apology Resolution as the legal footing for pursuing reconciliation. "In the post-*Rice* climate," she writes, "he suggested that the apology provided the foundation for reconciliation and that the Akaka Bill was the means by which a resolution was best served."[20] The resolution has offered the ultimate opportunity in federal law for advancing reconciliation with Native Hawaiians via recognition.

The ANPRM invoked the apology to justify federal recognition. "In 1993," it stated, "Congress enacted a joint resolution to acknowledge the 100th anniversary of the overthrow of the Kingdom of Hawaii and to offer an apology to Native Hawaiians."[21] Turning to Congress's words, the ANPRM identified that the federal government "express[ed] its commitment to acknowledge the ramifications of the overthrow of the Kingdom of Hawaii, in order to provide a proper foundation for reconciliation between the United States and the Native Hawaiian people." Restaging the apology for overthrowing the Hawaiian Kingdom, this manipulated US admission of culpability to demonstrate that "there has been no formal, organized Native Hawaiian government since 1893, when the United States overthrew the Kingdom of Hawaii," and thus suggest that re-establishing a government-to-government relationship could reconcile this.[22] Significantly, the ANPRM acknowledged that the United States thwarted Hawaiian rights to national and territorial sovereignty. As the Apology Resolution outlines, "The indigenous Hawaiian people never directly relinquished their claims to their inherent sovereignty as a people or over their national lands to the United States, either through their monarchy or through a plebiscite or referendum." This is a remarkable law because it holds that Kanaka Maoli have never surrendered sovereignty of the Hawaiian Kingdom's national lands. But the apology is surreptitious, and the ANPRM mimicked its furtiveness. The resolution went on: "Nothing in this Joint Resolution is intended to serve as a settlement of any claims against the United States." The ANPRM echoed that the United States is a "sorry state," borrowing Kauanui's phrasing.[23] It did so by weaponizing apology: "Promulgating a rule would not (1) alter the fundamental nature of the political and trust relationship established by Congress between the United States and the Native Hawaiian community; (2) authorize compensation for past wrongs; or (3) have any direct impact on the status of the Hawaiian homelands."[24] The apologetic settler state, pretending to want to cure harms it perpetrated, opens up legal mechanisms for federal recognition under a veil of reconciliation to complete legal settlement over territory. Commenting on the settlement process enacted through federal recognition, Maivân Clech Lâm, in an interview with Julian Aguon, refers to this as "the red carpet the assassin lays out before the murder takes place."[25] Settling Kanaka Maoli legal claims against the United States and acquiescing to American settlement of Hawai'i, in this way, could perhaps be the final nail in the coffin.[26]

Articulating 'A'ole

When the DOI held public meetings in 2014 to solicit feedback on whether and how the United States should re-establish a government-to-government relationship with Native Hawaiians, Kānaka Maoli overwhelmingly said no. It was explicit and unequivocal. At the initial meeting in Honolulu, Juanita Kawamoto politely told DOI representatives, "No, thank you." She stressed: "I'd like to be clear, all the things that you're doing here today are completely inappropriate, and I'm speaking in clear English so that all of you can understand, this is very inappropriate, to the point of absolutely disrespectful to our people here."[27] On the same day, Shane Pale generously addressed each threshold question at the Waimānalo meeting: "The short answer, again no, no, no, no and no."[28] With little notice, Kānaka Maoli mobilized quickly. Kawamoto and Pale declined recognition unapologetically, and others followed suit. The official transcripts of recorded oral testimony from these meetings are peppered with Kanaka Maoli voices rejecting federal recognition and refusing the US government's gift of reconciliation. Repudiating the executive rulemaking and proposed rule was articulated through the utterance "'a'ole," which means no.[29] This expression became part of a larger mo'okū'auhau (genealogical succession) of Kanaka Maoli resistance to American imperialism, empire, colonialism, and settler colonialism in Hawai'i. The 'a'ole to federal recognition was articulated in relation to histories, discourses, and embodiments of Hawaiian national and Indigenous sovereignties, contributing to what I call an archive of Kanaka Maoli refusal.

Testimony from the meetings illuminates that Kanaka Maoli overwhelmingly disapproved of a new rule to reestablish a government-to-government relationship. In Kapa'a, James Alalan Durest tackled the ANPRM's threshold questions: "For you guys' answers for the questions, hell no."[30] For Durest and many others, disapproval was vehement and explicit. But it was much more than an answer of no. Opposition was distinctively vocalized as 'a'ole. At the same meeting in Kapa'a, Puanani Rogers posited, "I protest and oppose the advance notice proposed rulemaking . . . and say 'a'ole, which means no in English."[31] Those testifying against the DOI and its ANPRM wielded this concise word with commanding meaning in 'ōlelo Hawai'i (Hawaiian language) to reject settler-state recognition. Gale Ku'ulei Baker Miyamura Perez attended the meeting in Waimea and told the DOI, "I'm here to say 'a'ole, or no, to all of your questions."[32] Although five threshold questions oriented input, nineteen procedural questions regarding governmental reorganization and drafting and ratifying a constitution were tucked into the ANPRM's conclusion that Kanaka Maoli such as Perez answered. E. Kalani Flores also testified in Waimea: "We say 'a'ole, no, to all the questions. What it's been is occupation, and the occupation has caused destruction, desecration to our lands."[33] Flores juxtaposed the symbolic proposition of recognition with realities of military occupation and environmental desecration. Re-establishing a government-to-government relation does not and cannot address the materiality of settler-state violence toward the 'āina (land) and that which feeds. Building on these comments, Mitchell Alapa noted in Kapa'a, "All I got to say to you folks is 'a'ole. All these things is 'a'ole."[34] The 'a'ole went even farther. It suggested that the DOI leave or, as Heali'i Kauhane phrased it in Keaukaha, "Go away."[35] Queries about whether and how the DOI should create an administrative rule for federal recognition were not turned down mildly.[36] The rejection vigorously asserted that the federal government retreat. Lawrence Aki issued an order in Kaunakakai: "You need to go home."[37] "These hearings," Walter Ritte summarized at the same meeting, "represent an honest reaction from the Hawaiian community. The majority is in no mood to continue our subservient relationship with the United States."[38] This was "a politicized expression of Indigenous anger and outrage directed at a structural and symbolic violence that still structures our lives, our relations with others, and our relationships with land."[39] According to a quantitative study led by Healani Sonoda-Pale on the ANPRM oral feedback, approximately 95 percent of Kanaka Maoli testifiers opposed the proposed rule.[40] The honest reaction, in the words of Ritte, was qualitatively and quantitatively significant. It communicated an unquestionable disapproval of federal recognition and contempt, disgust, and resentment for the colonial relations of subordination the settler-state desires to continue.

'A'ole emerged in relation to an intergenerational history of resistance. "Oh, honest Americans," Lākea Trask joshed in Keaukaha, "I stand before you today empowered by the nearly 40,000 who signed the Kū'ē Petitions and said no to annexation, the hundreds who testified already on their behalf. I stand here, humbled, ha'aha'a, that you folks have come all this way to meet us face to face, alo to alo. And I stand before you, angered and outraged at your motives for being here, for trying once again to steal our identity."[41] Many at the Arizona meeting, including me, testified that their ancestors had authorized the Kū'ē Petitions to fight against US annexation of Hawai'i in 1897, illustrating a truth that the Hawaiian Kingdom never consented to submit to US sovereignty and the Indigenous people of Hawai'i continue to refuse consent. As Trask remarked, the proposal represented a contemporary iteration of prolonged efforts to burgle Kanaka Maoli Indigeneity and steal Hawaiian sovereignty. The Kū'ē Petitions successfully protected against this in the late nineteenth century, and they provide a genealogical context and rationale for resistance to the US settler state. "Refusal holds on to a truth," Audra Simpson asserts, "structures this truth as stance through time, as its own structure and comingling with the force of presumed and inevitable disappearance and operates as the revenge of consent."[42] So in Kahului, Napua Nakasone stood firm on her truth: "Just as my kupuna wahine's signature proudly sits on the Kū'ē Petition of December 1897. I want my children, and my children's children, and their children after that to know beyond a shadow of a doubt that I wholeheartedly oppose the United States' occupation of my Hawai'i."[43] In the spirit of ancestors who opposed the commencement of US occupation, Kānaka Maoli testifying against the DOI refused to reconcile by re-establishing a government-to-government relationship because federal recognition obfuscates the unabated occupation of Hawai'i.

The 'a'ole was produced through and furthers an archive of Kanaka Maoli refusal. On one hand, 'a'ole to federal recognition had been established through an enduring history of refusals. On the other, these expressions contribute to a genealogical archive of Kanaka Maoli refusal. The archive is full of mo'olelo (histories, stories, and accounts) of our steadfast refusal. "The past is referred to as *Ka wa mamua*, 'the time in front or before.' Whereas the future, when thought of at all, is *Ka wa ma hope*, or 'the time which comes after or behind.' It is as if the Hawaiian stands firmly in the present," Lilikalā Kame'eleihiwa says, "with his back to the future, and his eyes fixed upon the past, seeking historical answers for present-day dilemmas."[44] With 1,795 pages of transcripts from twenty meetings, the official record is overflowing with, and haunted by, 'a'ole. My analysis does not explore the video recordings of meetings, which are available online, or in situ observations. What I am arguing is that this archive of refusal, documenting explicit articulations of 'a'ole, is based on and perpetuates mo'olelo to overturn the US settler state in Hawai'i as a domain of knowledge that shapes truth for Kanaka Maoli in the ongoing struggle over federal recognition.

Nevertheless, some testimony against recognition turned anti-intersectional. I want to unpack one testimony that is particularly revealing. In Keaukaha, Mililani Trask opposed the colonial relationship that the US settler state extended to Kanaka Maoli: "When the federal government and the state agreed to impose upon our peoples the yoke of perpetual wardship, this yolk, we break. We cannot accept it any further."[45] Trask then conveyed specific disapproval: "Our response to the interrogatories that are posed by [the Department of the] Interior are all no. And the reason why is because we are capable of being self-governing. But we are not capable of expressing our right to self-determination because federal policy limits this. We are not Indians. We will never be Indians and the federal Indian policy is inappropriate for our peoples."[46] Although Kauanui has critically probed this statement, I want to say something slightly different about it.[47] The comment is an example of what Amy Brandzel terms anti-intersectionality.[48] Brandzel suggests that the settler state does not desire intersectionality but refutes it by proliferating anti-intersectionality, or "epistemologies of identity that are normative, single-axis, and comparatively valued against other categories of identity."[49] They argue, "Hegemonic anti-intersectionality renarrativizes the naturalness and idealization of normative categories and reenacts violence to non-normative categories by renaturalizing their inhumanity."[50] Reflecting on the DOI meetings, they identify that the US settler state uses disciplinary powers of racialization to pass through and divide Indigenous populations regulated by its colonial power: "Kanaka Maoli argued that they are 'not Indians,' and that the offer to recognize a 'government to government' relationship on the U.S. nation-state's terms was a process of transforming Kanaka Maoli into 'tribes' and 'Indians.'"⁵¹ While some Kanaka Maoli opposed federal recognition in solidarity with Native Americans and tribal governments, Brandzel asserts that testimony equating Indianness with an inability to be self-determining in governance hindered possibilities for intersectional coalitions within the identificatory category of Indigeneity. Trask concluded her testimony: "You can braid my hair and stick feathers in it, but I would never be an Indian. I will always be a Hawaiian."⁵² This anti-intersectional rhetoric, reifying gendered colonial racism, is scattered throughout transcripts. In so doing, Kanaka Maoli have renarrated "'Indian' as sign within U.S. colonial discourse," which, Jodi Byrd says, "serves as a deracinated supplement that signifies the underside of imperial dominance."⁵³ My hope in this discussion is to name rather than silence, to denaturalize instead of normalize, an anti-Indian rhetoric in the moʻokūʻauhau of our resistance to US settler colonialism. Otherwise, paradigmatic Indianness will continue to fuel American colonialism and empire. "Because 'Indianness' serves as the ontological scaffolding for colonialist domination," Byrd writes, "anticolonial resistances, which align themselves against 'Indianness' as a manifestation of empire," such as the protest of Trask and others, "risk reflecting and reinscribing the very colonialist discourses used to possess and contain American Indian nations back onto the abjected 'Indian' yet again."⁵⁴ Instead of challenging recognition through paradigmatic Indianness, I suggest that ʻaʻole can offer an intersectional framework to filter the cacophony of settler-state techniques of racialization and colonization. Testifying ʻaʻole to federal recognition in (racialized) abjections of the Indian testifies ʻae (yes) to material conditions of (colonial) violence to which Indigenous peoples are subjected through federal Indian law. This is a dialectic orientation to consider the contradictions within what refusal rejects and what it may affirm. ʻAʻole thus is a critical framework for asserting ʻaʻole to federal recognition without saying ʻae to the conquest of other Indigenous peoples.

Notices of Settlement

Despite explicit opposition to the proposed rule by Kanaka Maoli, the DOI issued a Notice for Proposed Rulemaking (NPRM) on October 1, 2015. It suggested that a majority of written comments submitted for the ANPRM supported a rule. Exactly 5,164 written comments had been received, "more than half of which were identical postcards submitted in support of reestablishing a government-to-government relationship through Federal rulemaking."[55] Privileging written comments over verbal testimony was a blatant dismissal of input from Kanaka Maoli. Consequently, the DOI claimed that the general public favored federal recognition for Native Hawaiians. I contend that the ANPRM and NPRM were published as notices of settlement. The ANPRM and NPRM were legal notices that announced the federal government was attempting to settle the precarious biopolitical position of Hawaiians to geopolitically settle Hawai'i. The NPRM was the second component in this process. What the DOI garnered from public input was that federal law should open a door for Native Hawaiians to choose to walk through or not. The so-called choice is ours. When the NPRM addressed fourteen thematic responses to the ANPRM, it scorned opposing responses that objected to US jurisdiction over Kanaka Maoli and Hawai'i. "Comments about altering the fundamental nature of the political and trust relationship that Congress has established between the United States and the Native Hawaiian community," the DOI retorted, "were outside the ANPRM's scope and therefore did not inform the development of the proposed rule."[56] The rulemaking process openly omitted these comments, these choices. The NPRM subsequently posited, "The Department is bound by Congressional enactments concerning the status of Hawaii. Under those enactments and under the United States Constitution, Hawaii is a State of the United States of America."[57] Any opposition based in claims that the federal government and State of Hawai'i do not maintain jurisdiction over Kanaka Maoli and Hawai'i would be dismissed from the rulemaking. Valuing written comments, the NPRM did not hold public meetings. Feedback was accepted only in writing, which in the case of the ANPRM supported federal recognition vis-à-vis identical postcards that were repeatedly submitted and uniquely counted.

The NPRM manipulated the ANPRM's legal history to rationalize that plenary power over Native Americans extends to Native Hawaiians, and a new administrative rule for federal recognition would not alter that juridical power but strengthen its territorial sovereignty in Hawai'i. Whereas the ANPRM pronounced a legal history for advancing reconciliation, the NPRM suggested that legal history is a settled matter under congressional authority. "The existing body of legislation makes plain that Congress determined repeatedly, over a period of almost a century," the NPRM said, "that the Native Hawaiian population is an existing Native community that is within the scope of the Federal Government's powers over Native American affairs and with which the United States has an ongoing special political and trust relationship."[58] In such logic, reestablishing a government-to-government relationship with a reorganized Native Hawaiian government would not mirror the nation-to-nation association developed between the United States and Hawaiian Kingdom. The NPRM asserted, "The Native Hawaiian Governing Entity would remain subject to the same authority of Congress and the United States to which those tribes are subject and would remain ineligible for Federal Indian programs, services, and benefits."[59] Kanaka Maoli would be further denationalized as subjects of the Hawaiian Kingdom and, not formally constituting a tribe eligible for federal Indian programs and services, regulated as an Indigenous population subject to US juridical and territorial sovereignty. The language that Native Hawaiians are "analogous to but separate from" Native Americans provided an answer about whether Hawaiians are Indians to settle the territoriality of Hawai'i as geographically within the United States. The NPRM blatantly argued, "Reestablishment of the formal government-to-government relationship will not affect title, jurisdiction, or status of Federal lands and property in Hawaii. This provision does not affect lands owned by the State of Hawaii or provisions of State law. . . . And nothing in this proposed rule would alter the sovereign immunity of the United States or the sovereign immunity of the State of Hawaii."[60] The proposed rule would confirm the federal government's avowed special trust relationship, pulling Kanaka Maoli deep into the undertow of plenary power, and could formally recognize a new Native Hawaiian government as a ward of the settler state without a land base. The notices acknowledged, discussed, and rationalized that the legal status of Native Hawaiians would be settled, and Hawai'i would become settled as territory possessed by the settler state.

Rule of Recognition

The DOI's final rule strengthens the geopower of US settler-colonial biopolitics, and, I argue, it institutionalizes a new colonial governmentality for federal recognition that seeks to incorporate Hawaiians as Indians without land. The DOI created an administrative rule on October 14, 2016, to facilitate federal recognition for Native Hawaiians. Now the choice is either to submit an application for federal recognition of a Native Hawaiian Governing Entity (NHGE) or maintain the juridical status quo with an existing special trust relationship. The exercise of federal law on Indigenous people purports to provide a liberal democratic freedom of choice while deceitfully working in practice to fortify the disciplinary and regulatory jaws of the settler state's vice grip. Interrogating the rule, I demonstrate that it is the US assertion of sovereignty in Hawai'i that is indeed precarious. Looking again at meeting testimony, I track how Kanaka Maoli refusal of federal recognition exposed the incoherence of US settler sovereignty upon the 'āina of Hawai'i. I end the chapter by explicating the biopolitical animus aimed at Native Hawaiians for geopolitical settlement of Hawai'i and the ways in which Kanaka Maoli disrupt the sovereign nucleus of US settler-colonial biopower.

The biopolitical and geopolitical schematics within the settler state's offer of recognition employ colonial techniques of race, gender, and sexuality. In the final rule, the rhetorical maneuver that previously marked Native Hawaiians as "analogous to but separate from" Native Americans transforms into a discursive formation. Regarding programs and services provided to Native Hawaiians as analogous to but separate from those bestowed on Native Americans in federally recognized Indian tribes, the rule regulates Kanaka Maoli as an Indigenous group akin to Native Americans, which stands in for a racialized categorization of populations subject to US settler sovereignty. Referencing plenary power over Indian affairs and support in case law, the DOI suggests that the rule flows from and enforces Indian law and policy. For example, the rule cites the Federally Recognized Indian Tribe List Act of 1994 to explain that, because statutes already acknowledge a special trust relationship with Native Hawaiians, "the language of the List Act's definition of the term 'Indian tribe' is broad and encompasses the Native Hawaiian community."[61] Here, Hawaiians are considered Indians who constitute a tribe. Discussing *Johnson v. M'Intosh* (1823), *Cherokee v. Georgia* (1831), and *Worcester v. Georgia* (1832), Joanne Barker observes that the US settler state "asserted that tribes were weaker—uncivilized races living as barbarians in a permanent state of nature."[62] The rule reifies, as Barker puts it, US national narrations that racialize Indigenous peoples as perverse primitives, merciless savages, domestic dependents, and childlike wards—racializing monikers of inferiority that are gendered and sexualized—which are tropes of white supremacist and heteropatriarchal settler colonialism.

The rule of recognition that suggests Hawaiians are Indians is, however, limited through logics of land. To be clear, the federal government is seeking to assimilate Hawaiians as Indians without land. Institutionalizing a dangerous archetype for colonial dispossession in federal Indian law and policy, the rule attempts to absorb new tribes that are without jurisdiction over territory and resources, which the settler state and its settler citizenry can then call its own. For instance, it interprets the Indian Reorganization Act of 1934, delimiting the geographic scope for definitions of "Indian," to suggest that "Indian land" cannot be taken into trust for an NHGE. It similarly deciphers the Indian Gaming Regulatory Act of 1988 and declares the NHGE would not be eligible to conduct gaming due to definitions of "Indian lands" for "Indian tribes." The Gaming Act "was enacted to balance the interest of states and tribes and to provide a framework for regulating gaming on 'Indian lands.' There are no such lands in Hawaii."[63] Here, Hawaiians are considered Indians but without Indian land. Other measures such as the Indian Child Welfare Act and Violence against Women Act would also not apply, since "Congress provides a parallel set of benefits to Native Hawaiians within the framework of legislation that also provides programs to other Native groups."[64] These legal instruments— an inclusive biopolitical exclusion of Native Hawaiians that runs parallel to, but is premised on, the peculiar juridical status of Native Americans—pivot on the logical extension of settler-state territoriality. *"Because there is no Indian country in Hawaii,"* the rule elaborates, "upon reestablishing a government-to-government relationship with the United States, *the Native Hawaiian Governing Entity would not have territorial jurisdiction."*[65] Barker laments, "The rub as it were, for Native peoples, is that they are only recognized as Native within the legal terms and social conditions of racialized discourses that serve the national interest of the United States in maintaining colonial and imperial relations with Native peoples."[66] The biopolitical management of Native Hawaiians as a racialized, gendered, and sexualized population like Native Americans manufactures a discursive formation that, in turn, creates rules and limits according to "analogous but separate" legal logics that shore up the geopower of US settler-colonial biopolitics. Settling the biopolitical status of Kanaka Maoli not only functions to settle the geopolitical status of Hawai'i but, concomitantly, fashions a fresh liberal paradigm for federal Indian law and policy that desires to recognize and incorporate tribes without land or territorial jurisdiction. This new colonial governmentality is quite perilous and should be studied further.

In testimony against the rule, Kānaka Maoli disrupted these biopolitical and geopolitical calculations. In Kahului, Kaleikoa Kaʻeo exclaimed, "No consent, never. No, Department of the Interior. No treaty, never. No, Department of Interior. No cession of our citizenship. No, Department of Interior. No justice for our people for 120 years. No to the Department of Interior. No lawful authority to sit upon our people and step upon our necks. No to the Department of Interior."[67] His words illustrated how the US settler state exercises heteropatriarchal colonial power by disregarding Kanaka Maoli consent. Furthermore, Kaʻeo extended consent's revenge to assert that a treaty of annexation was never signed, Hawaiian national citizenship has never been resigned, and the federal government does not have juridical authority to regulate Kanaka Maoli. "I am not American, I am not American," Guy Hanohano Naehu declared on Molokaʻi, "and shame on you guys for perpetrating the illegality. Shame on you guys for perpetrating the fraud."[68] Naehu stated that he is not American; that Kanaka Maoli are not US citizens; and that the rule of recognition perpetuates a fraudulent construction that

Kanaka Maoli are Americans because of a special trust relationship stemming from an unlawful occupation of Hawaiʻi. These moʻolelo combined the rejection of recognition through Indigenous resurgence with a refusal of US settler-state sovereignty. "Indigenous peoples' individual and collective expressions of anger and resentment," Coulthard writes, "can help prompt the very forms of self-affirmative praxis that generate rehabilitated Indigenous subjectivities and decolonized forms of life in ways that the combined politics of recognition and reconciliation has so far proven itself incapable of doing."[69] The archive of Kanaka Maoli refusal represents a collective self-affirmation that seeks decolonization and deoccupation in the same step. Tisha-Marie Beattie responded on Maui to questions from the DOI: "Your answer from me is no. . . . You cannot give me back something I never gave up. . . . [T]ake your thing you wanna give us, throw 'em in the trash."[70] Moʻolelo combated recognition by challenging how the settler state was attempting to solidify its geopower through biopolitics. National and territorial sovereignty could not be given back to Kanaka Maoli because they have never been relinquished. The offer of recognition is trash, a thing to be thrown away. "We don't want it," Beattie concluded. "We sovereign."[71]

Assertions of Hawaiian sovereignty expose and upend a settler state of exception. Rather than amending the process for acknowledgment, the rule manufactured a new administrative procedure to facilitate federal recognition for Native Hawaiians. It instituted an exception to the geographic limitation barring Kanaka Maoli from acknowledgment under Part 83 of Title 25 in the Code of Federal Regulations. Hence the rule should be viewed as a US settler state of exception. The executive branch declared an exception to existing legal frameworks of formal acknowledgment to create new law for federal recognition that precariously attempts to signify sovereign power through the extension of law in its suspension.[72] Building on theorizations by Michel Foucault and Giorgio Agamben, the (sovereign) rulemaking includes Hawaiians (biopolitically) within existing regulations of Indian affairs only insofar as we are excluded from territorial authority and jurisdiction (geopolitically).[73] Mark Rifkin suggests that Indigenous claims of sovereignty can unmask and antagonize the emptiness of settler sovereignty as it nervously attempts to stabilize through settler states of exception.[74] Kānaka Maoli did just this. On Kauaʻi, Kaʻiulani Lovell told the DOI, "We're not part of your state. We're not here to create something where we're working together. We don't need to be recognized by you. We know who we are."[75] Kanaka Maoli articulating ʻaʻole unveiled federal recognition to be a sham of settler sovereignty, attempting to cohere US geopower in Hawaiʻi by answering the question of whether or not Hawaiians are Indians. Amid the biopolitical sleight of hand, Kanaka Maoli have responded that we are not part of the US settler state. Kanaka Maoli do not wish to collaborate with the federal government. And Kanaka Maoli do not need to be recognized by the US settler state because we know exactly who we are.

NOTES

1   See Chris Iijima, "Race over *Rice:* Binary Analytical Boxes and a Twenty-First Century Endorsement of Nineteenth Century Imperialism in *Rice v. Cayetano,*" *Rutgers Law Review* 53, no. 1 (2000): 91–125; J. Kēhaulani Kauanui, "The Politics of Blood and Sovereignty in *Rice v. Cayetano,*" *PoLAR: The Political and Legal Anthropology Review* 25, no. 1 (2002): 110–28; Judy Rohrer, *Staking Claim: Settler Colonialism and Racialization in Hawai'i* (Tucson: University of Arizona Press, 2017).

2   See Noelani Goodyear-Ka'ōpua, introduction to *A Nation Rising: Hawaiian Movements for Life, Land, and Sovereignty,* edited by Noelani Goodyear-Ka'ōpua, Ikaika Hussey, and Erin Kahunawaika'ala Wright (Durham, NC: Duke University Press, 2014).

3   Brett Kavanaugh, "Are Hawaiians Indians? The Justice Department Thinks So: Rule of Law," *Wall Street Journal,* September 27, 1999, http://www.wsj.com/articles /SB938365458335869648.

4   "Hirono Calls Supreme Court Nominee's Views on Hawaiians 'Offensive,'" *Hawaii News Now,* September 5, 2018, http://www.hawaiinewsnow.com/story/39034607/sen -hirono-releases-confidential-kavanaugh-documents.

5   Christine Hauser, "The Women Who Have Accused Brett Kavanaugh," *New York Times,* September 26, 2018, http://www.nytimes.com/2018/09/26/us/politics/brett -kavanaugh-accusers-women.html; Charlie Savage, "Leaked Kavanaugh Documents Discuss Abortion and Affirmative Action," *New York Times,* September 6, 2018, http://www.nytimes.com/2018/09/06/us/politics/kavanaugh-leaked-documents .html.

6   Glen Coulthard, *Red Skin, White Masks: Rejecting the Colonial Politics of Recognition* (Minneapolis: University of Minnesota Press, 2014), 15.

7   Kavanaugh, "Are Hawaiians Indians?"

8   Kavanaugh, "Are Hawaiians Indians?"

9   Aaron John Spitzer, "'A Wolf in Sheep's Clothing': Settler Voting Rights and the Elimination of the Indigenous Demos in US Pacific Territories," *Postcolonial Studies* 22, no. 2 (2019): 131–49.

10 US Department of the Interior, "Procedures for Reestablishing a Government-to-Government Relationship with the Native Hawaiian Community, 1090-AB05," *Federal Register* 79, no. 119 (June 20, 2014): 35296.

11 US Department of the Interior, "Procedures for Reestablishing a Government-to-Government Relationship with the Native Hawaiian Community," 35298.

12 J. Kēhaulani Kauanui, "Precarious Positions: Native Hawaiians and US Federal Recognition," *Contemporary Pacific* 17, no. 1 (2005): 5.

13 US Department of the Interior, "Procedures for Reestablishing a Government-to-Government Relationship with the Native Hawaiian Community," 35298.

14 US Department of the Interior, "Procedures for Reestablishing a Government-to-Government Relationship with the Native Hawaiian Community," 35299, emphasis added.

15 US Department of the Interior, "Procedures for Reestablishing a Government-to-Government Relationship with the Native Hawaiian Community," 35298.

16 US Department of the Interior, "Procedures for Reestablishing a Government-to-Government Relationship with the Native Hawaiian Community," 35299, emphasis added.

17 US Department of the Interior, "Procedures for Reestablishing a Government-to-Government Relationship with the Native Hawaiian Community."

18 J. Kēhaulani Kauanui, "Resisting the Akaka Bill," in *A Nation Rising: Hawaiian Movements for Life, Land, and Sovereignty*, edited by Noelani Goodyear-Kaʻōpua, Ikaika Hussey, and Erin Kahunawaikaʻala Wright (Durham, NC: Duke University Press, 2014), 312–30.

19 Kauanui, "Resisting the Akaka Bill," 316.

20 Kauanui, "Resisting the Akaka Bill," 317.

21 Department of the Interior, "Procedures for Reestablishing a Government-to-Government Relationship with the Native Hawaiian Community," 35299.

22 US Department of the Interior, "Procedures for Reestablishing a Government-to-Government Relationship with the Native Hawaiian Community," 35298.

23 Kauanui, "Resisting the Akaka Bill," 313.

24 US Department of the Interior, "Procedures for Reestablishing a Government-to-Government Relationship with the Native Hawaiian Community," 35299.

25 Julian Aguon, "The Commerce of Recognition (Buy One Ethos, Get One Free): Toward Curing the Harm of the United States' International Wrongful Acts in the Hawaiian Islands," *ʻOhia* 1, no. 1 (2012): 64.

26 Uahikea Maile, "The US Government Has Always Given Native Hawaiians a Raw Deal," *Guardian*, March 4, 2021, http://www.theguardian.com/commentisfree/2021/mar/04/us-government-native-hawaiians-raw-deal.

27 Jessica Perry, "Public Meeting Regarding Whether the Federal Government Should Reestablish a Government-to-Government Relationship with the Native Hawaiian Community," transcript of public comments, June 23, 2014, 76–77.

28 Perry, "Public Meeting Regarding Whether the Federal Government Should Reestablish a Government-to-Government Relationship with the Native Hawaiian Community," transcript of public comments, June 23, 2014, 67.

29 Mary Kawena Pukui and Samuel H. Elbert, *Hawaiian Dictionary* (Honolulu: University of Hawaiʻi Press, 1986), 27.

30 Terri R. Hanson, "Public Meeting Regarding Whether the Federal Government Should Reestablish a Government-to-Government Relationship with the Native Hawaiian Community," transcript of public comments, July 1, 2014, 18.

31 Hanson, "Public Meeting Regarding Whether the Federal Government Should Reestablish a Government-to-Government Relationship with the Native Hawaiian Community," transcript of public comments, July 1, 2014, 46.

32 Kristen Rehanek, "Public Meeting Regarding Whether the Federal Government Should Reestablish a Government-to-Government Relationship with the Native Hawaiian Community," transcript of public comments, July 3, 2014, 18.

33 Rehanek, "Public Meeting Regarding Whether the Federal Government Should Reestablish a Government-to-Government Relationship with the Native Hawaiian Community," transcript of public comments, July 3, 2014, 57.

34 Hanson, "Public Meeting Regarding Whether the Federal Government Should Reestablish a Government-to-Government Relationship with the Native Hawaiian Community," transcript of public comments, July 1, 2014, 88.

35 Elsie Terada, "Public Meeting Regarding Whether the Federal Government Should Reestablish a Government-to-Government Relationship with the Native Hawaiian Community," transcript of public comments, July 2, 2014, 32.

36 See Maile Arvin and Stephanie Nohelani Teves, "Recognizing the Aloha in 'No,'" *Hawaii Independent*, July 7, 2014, http://www.hawaiiindependent.net/story/recognizing-the-aloha-in-no.

37 Kathryn Plizga, "Public Meeting Regarding Whether the Federal Government Should Reestablish a Government-to-Government Relationship with the Native Hawaiian Community," transcript of public comments, June 28, 2014, 11.

38 Plizga, "Public Meeting Regarding Whether the Federal Government Should Reestablish a Government-to-Government Relationship with the Native Hawaiian Community," transcript of public comments" June 28, 2014, 61.

39 Coulthard, *Red Skin, White Masks*, 109.

40 "Protest Na'i Aupuni," accessed September 21, 2018, http://protestnaiaupuni.com.

41 Terada, "Public Meeting Regarding Whether the Federal Government Should Reestablish a Government-to-Government Relationship with the Native Hawaiian Community," transcript of public comments, July 2, 2014, 45.

42 Audra Simpson, "Consent's Revenge," *Cultural Anthropology* 31, no. 3 (2016): 330.

43 Jeanette W. Iwado, "Public Meeting Regarding Whether the Federal Government Should Reestablish a Government-to-Government Relationship with the Native Hawaiian Community," transcript of public comments, July 8, 2014, 88.

44 Lilikalā Kameʻeleihiwa, *Native Land and Foreign Desires: Pēhea Lā e Pono ai?* (Honolulu: Bishop Museum, 1992), 22–23.

45 Terada, "Public Meeting Regarding Whether the Federal Government Should Reestablish a Government-to-Government Relationship with the Native Hawaiian Community," transcript of public comments, July 2, 2014, 27.

46 Terada, "Public Meeting Regarding Whether the Federal Government Should Reestablish a Government-to-Government Relationship with the Native Hawaiian Community," transcript of public comments, July 2, 2014, 27.

47 J. Kēhaulani Kauanui, *Paradoxes of Hawaiian Sovereignty: Land, Sex, and the Colonial Politics of State Nationalism* (Durham, NC: Duke University Press, 2018).

48 Amy L. Brandzel, *Against Citizenship: The Violence of the Normative* (Urbana: University of Illinois Press, 2016).

49 Brandzel, *Against Citizenship*, 23.

50 Brandzel, *Against Citizenship*, 24.

51 Brandzel, *Against Citizenship*, 101.

52 Terada, "Public Meeting Regarding Whether the Federal Government Should Reestablish a Government-to-Government Relationship with the Native Hawaiian Community," transcript of public comments, July 2, 2014, 28.

53 Jodi A. Byrd, *The Transit of Empire: Indigenous Critiques of Colonialism* (Minneapolis: University of Minnesota Press, 2011), 157.

54 Byrd, *The Transit of Empire*, 157–58.

55 US Department of the Interior, "Procedures for Reestablishing a Government-to-Government Relationship with the Native Hawaiian Community," 59118.

56 US Department of the Interior, "Procedures for Reestablishing a Government-to-Government Relationship with the Native Hawaiian Community," 59120.

57 US Department of the Interior, "Procedures for Reestablishing a Government-to-Government Relationship with the Native Hawaiian Community," 59120.

58 US Department of the Interior, "Procedures for Reestablishing a Government-to-Government Relationship with the Native Hawaiian Community," 59120.

59 US Department of the Interior, "Procedures for Reestablishing a Government-to-Government Relationship with the Native Hawaiian Community," 59126.

60 US Department of the Interior, "Procedures for Reestablishing a Government-to-Government Relationship with the Native Hawaiian Community," 59126.

61 US Department of the Interior, Final Rule, "Procedures for Reestablishing a Government-to-Government Relationship with the Native Hawaiian Community, 1090-AB05," *Federal Register* 81, no. 199 (October 14, 2016): 71286.

62 Joanne Barker, *Native Acts: Law, Recognition, and Cultural Authenticity* (Durham, NC: Duke University Press, 2011), 32.

63 US Department of the Interior, Final Rule, "Procedures for Reestablishing a Government-to-Government Relationship with the Native Hawaiian Community," 71306.

64 US Department of the Interior, Final Rule, "Procedures for Reestablishing a Government-to-Government Relationship with the Native Hawaiian Community," 71307.

65 US Department of the Interior, Final Rule, "Procedures for Reestablishing a Government-to-Government Relationship with the Native Hawaiian Community," 71307, emphasis added.

66 Barker, *Native Acts*, 6.

67 Iwado, "Public Meeting Regarding Whether the Federal Government Should Reestablish a Government-to-Government Relationship with the Native Hawaiian Community," transcript of public comments, July 8, 2014, 89.

68 Plizga, "Public Meeting Regarding Whether the Federal Government Should Reestablish a Government-to-Government Relationship with the Native Hawaiian Community," transcript of public comments, June 28, 2014, 43.

69 Coulthard, *Red Skin, White Masks*, 109.

70 Iwado, "Public Meeting Regarding Whether the Federal Government Should Reestablish a Government-to-Government Relationship with the Native Hawaiian Community," transcript of public comments, July 8, 2014, 24–26.

71 Iwado, "Public Meeting Regarding Whether the Federal Government Should Reestablish a Government-to-Government Relationship with the Native Hawaiian Community," transcript of public comments, July 8, 2014, 26.

72 See Carl Schmitt, *Political Theology: Four Chapters on the Concept of Sovereignty*, translated by George Schwab (Chicago: University of Chicago Press, 1985).

73 Giorgio Agamben, *Homo Sacer: Sovereign Power and Bare Life*, translated by Daniel Heller-Roazen (Stanford, CA: Stanford University Press, 1998); Michel Foucault, *Society Must Be Defended: Lectures at the College de France, 1975-1976*, edited by Maura Bertani and Alessandro Fontana, translated by David Macey (New York: Picador, 2003).

74 Mark Rifkin, "Indigenizing Agamben: Rethinking Sovereignty in Light of the 'Peculiar' Status of Native Peoples," *Cultural Critique* 1, no. 73 (2009): 88–124.

75 Hanson, "Public Meeting Regarding Whether the Federal Government Should Reestablish a Government-to-Government Relationship with the Native Hawaiian Community," transcript of public comments, July 1, 2014, 64.

5

POSTCOLONIAL BIOPOLITICS AND THE HIEROGLYPHS OF DEMOCRACY

SHONA N. JACKSON

An ACT to provide for the recognition and protection of the collective rights of Amerindian Villages and Communities, the granting of land to Amerindian Villages and Communities and the promotion of good governance within Amerindian Villages and Communities.—AMERINDIAN ACT 2006

Sovereignty belongs to the people, who exercise it through their representatives and the democratic organs established by or under this Constitution.—CONSTITUTION OF THE CO-OPERATIVE REPUBLIC OF GUYANA

In earlier work focused on understanding Indigeneity and settler colonialism in the Caribbean, I argued that the descendants of formerly enslaved and formerly indentured peoples (Creoles) should be thought of as *involuntary* settlers.[1] They positioned themselves as such by seeking to link their reason for being in the region—labor—to rights. The labor performed under slavery and indenture became the labor of their own prior right to land and sovereignty, which constrained the prior rights of Indigenous peoples. That study included a brief discussion of Cap. 29:01, the Amerindian Act, the set of laws that govern Indigenous identity (delimiting who can be said to be Indigenous) and lands (setting out the rights to territory and the limits of those rights) in Guyana. It stems from the British ordinances—which superseded Dutch means of governing relations with Indigenous peoples in the Guianas—meant to manage the colonial relationship with the Indigenous peoples of Upper Amazonia, or the Guiana Shield.[2]

In looking at how the act regulated Indigenous lands and the category of the Indigenous, however, I had not considered the *what* and *where* of its governance. My limited focus on the juridical statements contained within the act missed how it captures and represents the actual bodies it governs and the specific intersections of those bodies with the state. Attention to the latter leads to several questions. How does the act attempt to suture the gap between Indigenous bodies and lands as threats, or excess, to the state and as citizens whose rights fall within the state? How can the act recognize Indigeneity as *ante*-colonial and cosmogonically charted while simultaneously representing Indigenous peoples in terms of a post-contact, secular, and biological life that can be governed as a state-defined, political, and juridical entity?[3] What if we viewed the act not only in terms of the rights it gives or takes away but as the enactment of a real space of power, a state of exception, through which the postcolonial nation-state can have control over lands and peoples that are always already surfeit? Moreover, what complexities come into focus if we view the act as a specific mechanism of power of postcolonial governance: the legal substitution of a space of excess at the limit of postcolonial state sovereignty for a space that can be governed and erodes the real *truth* of a territory and people who do not have their origin in the colonial state and the Atlantic crossings that helped generate it as such?[4] In looking at the form of exception that attains in Creole postcolonial rule over Indigenous peoples, what differences exist in the latter's regulation as a separate legal entity? Does the management of Indigenous life necessarily include the management of Indigenous death?

This chapter addresses these questions by focusing not on the freedoms the act presumably gives to, "recognizes," or assigns to Indigenous peoples. It also does not approach the act as a colonial hangover. Instead, it examines the power that Creoles actually claim over Indigenous peoples' lives and lands through the act to inhibit Indigenous sovereignty. I resituate the act as part of a broader

structure of biopolitical governmentality that achieves the management of Indigenous peoples, with the understanding that just as state constitutions regulate the actual *lives* of their subject populations, so does the act. As that which
achieves the reproduction of Indigenous space as always *within* the bounds of
the state, the act as a mechanism, or *how* of power, works through its ability to
effect a *where* of power. It constitutes a point of symbolic and material application by producing the location (Indigenous lands) that makes such governance
possible. It is, however, insufficient by itself to achieve the governance of Indigenous peoples. What had to be created first was the Indigenous body as an *object*
of power within and for the postcolonial (rather than colonial) state: a *what* of
governance (i.e., that which can be governed). In short, since its point of application is both Indigenous bodies and lands, the act both defines who Indigenous
peoples are to govern them and reproduces Indigenous space *as* governable.

The sections of the chapter first elaborate the concepts of hieroglyphs and
simulacrum that frame this interrogative of the biopolitical modes of governance in the postcolonial state, then turn to a limited genealogy of biopolitics
and, finally, to a closer examination of the Amerindian Act. In sum, I suggest
that the remaking of Indigenous pre-contact symbols, or petroglyphs, should
be understood as more than a containment of Indigenous culture or a rescripting of it for the postcolonial leadership. Instead, it is simulacrum, which I read
as a critical moment of biopolitical governance at work. It is the reproduction
of Indigeneity, which facilitates the legal mechanisms of control (the act) that
recast Indigenous peoples as the "bare life" of the Creole postcolonial subject.
This is a concept of bare life that manages the particular way in which racialized groups, even postcolonial ones, haunt the threshold of humanity as
conceived by the West. It is thus not transferable to all postcolonial contexts
or to postimperial ones. It is specific to the nonwhite, postcolonial state that
maintains within it a less materially developed Indigenous population that can
be made subject to the necessary continuation of the colonial project after independence, both in the service of the humanity of the formerly enslaved and
indentured and as a key part of postcolonial democracy.

Simulacra, or the Hieroglyphs of Democracy

In 1969, in a politically symbolic gesture, the administration of Guyana's first
postindependence leader, Forbes Burnham, changed the name of the Atkinson
Aerodrome, long used for US military purposes, to Timehri International Airport. Timehri, the town in which the airport is located, is so named for early
pictorial images or carvings on rocks, or petroglyphs, by Indigenous people.

The airfield's nominal change signaled a rejection of continued foreign interference and domination in the early postcolonial era. The renaming was part of a broad attempt to develop the Burnham regime's cultural nationalism, for which Indigenous symbolism was appropriated. In the 1970s, Burnham's administration sought to reframe the Guyanese economy and society through cooperative socialism, the cultural dimension of which was spelled out most cohesively in *Co-operative Republic, Guyana 1970: A Study of Aspects of Our Way of Life*.[5] Commissioned by the administration, *Co-operative Republic* is a collection of essays about Guyanese culture that link national culture to cooperativism as an economic and political practice of collective and democratic ownership, which Burnham hoped would take the country in a new direction.[6] It comprises selected works by those then recognized as the nation's cultural and intellectual elites.

Of significance is how the volume invites Guyanese to see its Indigenous population and their lands as an important part of the single postcolonial and (Afro) Creole national sovereignty Burnham sought. The volume's essays deliberately tie the cooperative development scheme to the development of the interior, or Hinterland, where the majority of the country's Indigenous population lives. They invite Guyanese to see the interior as a space of potential wealth, rather than waste, which will grow the national economy. As I demonstrate in an earlier piece, *Co-operative Republic* reinvents the Guyana interior not as an Indigenous space where the majority of the country's first inhabitants live and where the land rights of Indigenous peoples attach, but as a national, Creole space from which wealth can be extracted for the benefit of the nation—specifically, the Creole coastal regions.[7] In an effort to mitigate the colonial undertones of its project, the regime, in a separate document, distinguished this postindependence use of the interior from that of colonial British use by suggesting that the British did not have Indigenous peoples' well-being in mind.[8] Coextensive with *Co-operative Republic*'s imagistic transformation of the interior, was the effort by the then ruling party, the People's National Congress (PNC), to pull Indigenous peoples *out* of their lands by redefining their search for better services and land rights as a desire on their part for integration or assimilation. Thus, the symbolic rescripting of the country's Indigenous peoples as *proto*-Guyanese rather than as separate nationals denied sovereignty—much as the entire colony had been under European rule—represented the transformation and *continuity* of some modes of colonial power necessary for Creole sovereignty.

Burnham's cultural rewriting of Indigenous peoples as protonationals, prior to the 1976 act, was made urgent by the Rupununi rebellion in January 1969 in which, together with Indigenous peoples, a group of ranchers backed by Venezuela revolted against the Guyana government. A study of the rebellion conducted in 1981 for the Ministry of Information surmised that Indigenous peoples took part in the rebellion because they "have a vague sense of nationalism," fostering an "unawareness" of the border dispute with Venezuela, which "poses a threat to the defense of the territory."[9] As a people located not just in the Hinterland but also on, or in greater proximity to, the colonially determined legal boundaries of the state, Indigenous peoples clearly, for the administration, posed a threat to Guyana's sovereignty vis-à-vis Venezuela. Thus, the recasting of Indigenous peoples' sovereignty with documents such as *Co-operative Republic*, even as their rights to land were affirmed, became central in the struggle to maintain Guyana's own sovereignty.

With the publication of *Co-operative Republic* a year after the rebellion, Burnham revised the image of Indigenous peoples as an impediment to national sovereignty by appropriating their cultural symbols as palimpsest for Guyanese sovereignty and, necessary to that sovereignty, national economic gain. In one example from the collection, the poet and cultural and social critic A. J. Seymour's essay celebrates the government's adoption of "Timehri" as the airport's name by suggesting that "the way lies clear for some industrial printer to create fabrics where the timehri [*sic*] markings might be used on the cotton, as in the case of the afro prints, so that we in Guyana would have a distinguished textile material, which would certainly attract the attention of tourists."[10] In another example, Rory Westmass, then the chief architect with the Ministry of Works, argues that Amerindian architectural style, which was chosen for the construction of the Umana Yana, should influence the direction of postcolonial Guyanese architecture to replace the colonially "derivative culture" of the country.[11] Collectively, Indigenous peoples' lands, cultures, and bodies, are rescripted in *Co-operative Republic* as precolonial origin for postcolonial national culture and as essential to national decolonization. The Burnham regime thus preserved Indigenous peoples both as central for the state and simultaneously as necessarily displaceable within it.

In March 1997, five years after assuming the long-denied presidency of Guyana, the decades-long opposition leader Cheddi Jagan died. That May, without formal discussions with Indigenous peoples, an act was passed to rename the Timehri International Airport in Guyana after Jagan, with strong support from Vibert DeSouza, then the minister of Amerindian Affairs (now Indigenous Peoples Affairs).[12] DeSouza, who was appointed minister by the administration of the People's Progressive Party (PPP) according to the parliamentary system, and not elected by Indigenous peoples, endorsed the renaming because of what he saw as gains for Indigenous peoples under the leadership of the PPP. The airport celebrates Jagan's legacy, giving him a place at the gateway to the nation.

The nominal choice of "Jagan" for the Timehri airport should therefore be read as an attempt to cement Jagan's status as founder of the nation, equal to Burnham, as well as an affirmation of (Indo) Creole nationalism. With it, what once served as the Indigenous cultural element of Burnham's cooperative socialism came to function as the sign of the Jagan/PPP's short-lived democracy-cum-hegemony in which Indigenous peoples' sovereignties, self-determination, and well-being were continuously sacrificed to the (Afro and Indo) Creole nation-state and the well-being of its non-Indigenous citizens. The namings are, thus, functionally the same: Indigenous peoples' cultures and lands served as palimpsest for both Burnham/PNC and Jagan/PPP articulations of their right to rule. Within settler-colonial studies, this palimpsestic engagement with Indigenous peoples' cultural symbolism might be read, together with the aims of *Co-operative Republic* and the 1981 document, as part of the ameliorative dimension of the logic and method of elimination of Indigeneity that characterizes settler states. It might be read as an appropriation and strategic misreading or translation of Indigenous cultures under the settler logics that seek to disappear Native populations through force or assimilation, as Patrick Wolfe has argued.[13] While that might be true to the extent that Indigenous lands are held in reserve for the state, I suggest that in the *involuntary* settler state, the "negative articulation" between persons and objects—which, according to Wolfe, characterizes dominant settler-colonial relations and undergirds Fanonian dialectics in which the slave cannot compete on the same plane of being as the master—becomes a "positive articulation" that works from the productive ends of the logic of elimination.[14] This I read as a mechanism of control that is both tied to and disarticulated from the logic of elimination. It hinges on the *reproduction* or *representation* of Indigenous peoples themselves as protonationals rather than as *extra*-sovereigns resisting (post)colonialism under Creoles so that, again, it is now a positive articulation, and the postcolonial Creole subject can be apprehended as fundamentally different from the colonial British subject who does not have Indigenous peoples' well-being in mind. It, in other words, facilitates an ontological relationship between Indigenous peoples and Indo and Afro Creole postcolonials and the governability of Indigenous peoples within the state.[15]

Occurring in the same year as the rebellion and a year before *Co-operative Republic*, Burnham's renaming reflects the successful transformation of Indigenous petroglyphs of absolute difference to the postcolonial nation-state into the hieroglyphs of postcolonial sovereignty and cultural progress. In his appropriation of Indigenous *petro*glyphs, Burnham achieved a transformation of those images into logographic characters, or *hiero*glyphs, frequently dated to

Egypt and thus representable within or *as* the prehistory of the nation-state.[16] His was a rewriting of the pre-contact, cosmogonically based symbolic of Indigenous peoples as now representable within the secular time of the postindependence state and within the logos of man or the logos necessary for man as a sovereign subject of the state.[17] It is a rescripting of Indigeneity for the postcolonial state and its deployment of a set of rules—that is, the act—that govern and in so doing recognize Indigenous peoples as *capable of being* governed, as capable of logos and therefore representable within, and displaceable from, the historical rather than as prehistorical or ungovernable, and with rights to lands that originate outside of and prior to the geopolitical boundaries of the state. Moreover, this inscription into logos is now the full scripting of Indigenous culture within the terrain of the biopolitical, which I elaborate later. It cannot, therefore, be read just as a rewriting or appropriation of Indigenous signs. It must be read as a necessarily violent *first* writing of Indigenous men and women as fully biopolitical subjects within the time and logos of the colonial-cum-postcolonial state government.[18] The now painted words, rather than carved images, giving the name of the airport (figure 5.1) can better be understood in their appropriation not as signs but as simulacra, as a first writing that substitutes for what was prior, so that what was pre-logocentric and outside the nation (petro) can, again, be represented as its prehistory (hiero).

For the sociologist and cultural critic Jean Baudrillard, simulacra are substitutions or copies of the real that take the place of the real. He distinguishes this from representation, saying, "Whereas representation tries to absorb

FIGURE 5.1. Cheddi Jagan International Airport publicity photo. *Source*: Publicity material, Cheddi Jagan International Airport.

simulation by interpreting it as false representation, simulation envelops the whole edifice of representation as itself a simulacrum."[19] In other words, simulacra in late twentieth-century capital function as the real because it is only through them that the real can be apprehended as a sign of the simulation itself. For Baudrillard, the simulacrum is a sign that has a third form of value after and in relation to use and exchange value in political economy and is therefore embedded within a value system of meaning that is specific to the capitalist mode of production in the late twentieth century. Here, Baudrillard's elaboration of the political economy of the sign can be useful in thinking through what it means to appropriate and reproduce Indigenous cultural symbolism for the nation.[20] Not only are Indigenous petroglyphs appropriated as hieroglyphs, but this specific appropriation and translation is the new political economy of Indigenous culture as sign. The hieroglyphs should be apprehended as simulacra that displace/replace the original, and the fact that the original petroglyphs could mean, signify, or have values that were not coextensive or coterminous with the nation-state in its attempt to establish a cooperative mode of political economy in the face of the expansion of global capitalism. The substitution, in short, is a particular expression of and embedding within the political economy of signs in late twentieth-century capital and the condition of possibility for the management of Indigenous peoples within the postcolonial state. Despite Burnham's socialist-democratic leanings and the attempt of his administration to achieve a cooperative society in theory, if not in practice, the regime needed to relate to subjects within the terms set out by the parameters of the nation-state under global capitalism. That mode of relating, for Indigenous peoples, is simultaneously an inscription into what we can call the logos (read again sign) and value-system of capital.

The reproduced images by and for the nation are the recognition of the prior inalienability of Indigenous right and an abrogation of that right. They are, therefore, as I explore later, a substitution *necessary* for the governance of the Indigenous person as a biological being (a being that can be captured and displaced by logos) and thus should be read within political economy as part of a strategy of governance tied to the market. The transformation of petro- to hieroglyphs achieved the transformation of Indigenous peoples as cosmogonically charted into secularly biological subjects who could be governed by and within the word, by and within the law. This apotheosis of the petroglyphs was necessary not for the colonial state, which sought to manage Indigenous peoples as a separate sphere of influence outside the major social contract of the state with its inhabitants. However, unlike the power of the colonial state, which was tied to empire as an external check on and aggrandizement of colonial power, the sovereignty of the militarily limited postcolonial state in the economically underdeveloped Global South is necessarily and precariously within. Moreover, it is the hieroglyphic form of Indigenous culture that controls engagement with what the hieroglyphs themselves now serve as a sign of but always replace in doing so, the real as excess. Later I explore what the transformation of Indigenous culture into sign, rather than just symbol, means for the ability to govern Indigenous peoples. I approach the sign as the terrain of biopolitical governance in formerly colonized states, one that, again, facilitates the governing mechanisms of the Amerindian Act.[21]

Postcolonial Biopolitics

Writing about Caribbean states at independence in the 1960s, Sylvia Wynter argues that the more cooperative and socialist ideals of governments were undercut because the West forced these states to recognize themselves as "underdeveloped" and thus made the mimicking of the capitalist state essential to the sustaining of independence.[22] The demands of this economic mimicry, recognized previously by Frantz Fanon, would lead them to transform and keep, rather than reject, the colonial mode of governing Indigenous peoples, the British ordinances-cum-Amerindian Act.[23] Earlier, I suggested that the transformation of Indigenous symbolism under postindependence nationalism facilitated the application of the act as the legal document of a secular state that could govern the Indigenous body as well as Indigenous land. Here I frame the act as an *exception* within biopolitical governmentality, which works because of the earlier noted reproduction of Indigeneity within the symbolic. Giorgio Agamben theorizes the state of exception as a rule that is essential to the functioning of so-called democratic states, in part because, in delineating a subject who can be governed as a rational object of power within the state, biopolitical governmentality also achieves a necessary separation or break from that which is ungovernable: the body that cannot speak or be spoken for and is hence outside the sphere of rationality. I suggest that the Amerindian Act is a tool of exception that both suspends and simulates the rules of the state to recast Indigenous peoples as the bare life of the postcolonial Creole subject.

For this approach to the Amerindian Act, I rework Agamben's account of biopolitical subjecthood and the roles of states to make life and manage/engender death, in which he argues that to be recognized or inscribed as a political subject, one's bare, naked life, or *zoē*, must be excised. Moreover, in the state of exception that he says is the hallmark of so-called democratic governmentality, any restoration of this bare life is simultaneously an excision from the state as *homo sacer*.[24] While Agamben's subjects have been paradigmatically white/European, my approach follows Achille Mbembe's and Alexander Weheliye's work on the colonized and the Black body as paradigmatic for biopolitical analysis, respectively, to understand bare life as it relates to nonwhite, non-European subjects who are still experiencing the outcomes of enslavement and settler colonization.[25] Since Blacks were enslaved as beings denied full, if any, humanity, their status as chattel during slavery, as property, is not an inscription into the polis—the elevation of and simultaneous excision of bare life necessary for political subjecthood. Instead, it corresponds to the axis that governs the biopolitics of racialization as articulated by Weheliye and in which "the biological given is as such immediately racialized, and the political is as such immediately the racialized given."[26] In other words, while biopolitics isn't possible without racialization, as Weheliye argues, its modes of us versus them place the "dysselected" (read Black) on one side and Man, the human, on the other.[27] Thus, if Mbembe takes the colony as paradigmatic of the biopolitical, Blacks within the chattel colony always lived not a political subjectivity in slavery but existed as *zoē*, in terms of their naked life, but a mode of *zoē* that is not in relation to their political being as it begins to evolve from the sixteenth century on. As former chattel, newly emancipated Blacks literally lacked the moment of "birth" that is, according to Agamben in his reading of the 1789 *Declaration of the Rights of Man and Citizen*, necessary for man's "inscription" into the polis as a "bearer of rights."[28]

Although it can be taken away and one can lose this form of rights bearing political identity that reflects a shift from monarchic to modern state sovereignty, essentially becoming *homo sacer*—or racially dysselected, after Wynter and Weheliye—the latter condition can occur only if there has first been an inscription. While we can argue that at emancipation in the nineteenth century Blacks were thrust into the colonial polis where they could begin to be remunerated for their labor, they not only still lacked "birth," they also lacked a human status (in Christian and in evolving secular humanist terms) that is necessary for full political subjectivity. In contrast, Jews had to first be understood as Man, as human, *before* their own dysselection via the Holocaust. As Calvin Warren notes, as Holocaust victims Jews could "*still lay claim to Being* (and *human* rights)."[29] However, Blacks as irrational others—appearing below the threshold of being, as Fanon, Wynter, Warren, and George Ciccariello-Maher elaborate and, hence, incapable of History (Hegel) or Reason (Kant)—were not fully in the word and not represented by the word, by a declaration or constitution. In the United States, for example, emancipation occurred *after* both, thereby requiring later civil rights and voting legislation that sought to rectify the founding excision of Blacks as full rights-bearing subjects through a form of right that is not originary and that still forces Blacks to serve as liminal figures within the genre of man/human of the West.[30] The slow inclusion of Blacks as more full, but always incomplete, political subjects since emancipation is thus based on an a priori exclusion that is itself prepolitical.

My suggestion is that to achieve inscription in the postcolonial polis as becoming rather than being, which is always deferred for Blacks, at independence, Blacks and, later, South Asians (Indians) reimagined their bare life not as what I call an intimate or proximate exception but as an external one in the Indigenous body. Not only did they need to represent Indigenous lands as potentially colonizable to meet the demands of capitalist economic conscription/mimicry and the teleological ends of labor, as I have argued elsewhere; they also needed to both make the Indigenous body governable and representable within state law and position that body as the new limit/threshold of humanity within the state. Moreover, that body becomes the space/place of a disciplinary mode of regulation that is both necessary to and exceptional within the postcolonial state. It is for this reason that the initiation of a new discursive relationship to the Indigenous—via, for instance, the Timehri symbols—was necessary. The substitution and erasure performed by the symbols as hieroglyphs are functionally a writing. They are a writing in which the nonbiological or, again, cosmogonically charted Indigenous body is inscribed within the realm of the political, and its own bare life, of which the now transcended but recursive petroglyphs become a sign, can be both captured and excluded. It is the moment of becoming or biopolitical subjecthood within the postcolonial state for the Creole. With the 1976 act, seven years after the naming of Timehri, the postcolonial government invoked a state of exception in which the now fully inscribed Indigenous body/person could simultaneously be represented within the postcolonial polity and excluded from it.[31] Indigenous peoples were reduced to the bare life that is the ungovernable excess of Black humanity that needs to be outside the polis. Blacks, for instance, did not achieve the state of pure inclusion of *zoē* or exclusion of *zoē* in the polis, because this was tied to an account or a particular experience of being from which, to again recall Fanon, they were precluded. Thus, their governance under the state was not in terms of the excision of bare life. Yet to function as full political subjects of the state who are not full human beings, Creoles must *enact* this condition, and they achieve this through engagement with Indigenous peoples, who, as denizens of even more underdeveloped lands, become their own bare life now held up at that critical distance necessary for subjecthood in the polity.

To understand the workings of this other way of experiencing the inscription and distance from *zoē* in political life, we must work back through some gaps in both Agamben's and Mbembe's work. First, Indigenous peoples as an explicit category are left out of Mbembe's concept of necropolitics, while the slave who is supposedly in more intimate contact with Western modes of governance (read some Hegelianism here) is included. While Mbembe's gesture might make sense, we need to return to a flaw in the discussion of Jews in Agamben. In the late fifteenth century, well before the rise of the liberal state in the late eighteenth century (Foucault), Jews, and Muslims, were being expelled from Spain. They could convert to Christianity or leave. This is a particular form of expulsion from belonging/right in the evolving, monarchic state that precedes that of the totalitarian state (Hitler's Germany) within which their prior rights were stripped away. Thus, Agamben in fact ignores the prior liminality of Jews as political subjects as constitutive of any part of their liberal mode of sovereignty and thus misses where their condition exists as a parallel to that of enslaved Blacks to the extent that *both* share this prior moment of failure of the progression of subjecthood from monarchy to liberalism. Jews were already understood as others within Christendom, while a new mechanism of exclusion would eventually have to be deployed to deal with a now global set of others whose very locations challenged the Judeo-Christian geography on which the social order was built.[32]

Yet in this moment of being expelled from Spain, Jews were experiencing a truly modern phenomenon: expulsion from subjecthood. It is not the same as Black, cosmogonic expulsion, but it is, again, a parallel, occurring at the threshold of historical modernity and to a group whose religious cosmogony overlaps with but is not the same as that of the state in which they exist. This parallel reflects two strands of biopolitics, both of which impact or shape how Indigenous peoples and Blacks function as biopolitical subjects: (1) necessary expulsion or functional exclusion, such as is *zoē* for Mbembe; and (2) inclusion as limit—read Indigenous removal, death, and its endless narrative performance, then read enslavement, *encomienda*, *repartimiento*, Bartolomé de Las Casas, and so on. Moreover, in spite of the fact that Indigenous peoples were granted partial protections, placing them in a position different from that of Blacks with regard to humanity, this position is based on a prior liminality, another parallel of the liminal modes experienced by Blacks and Jews.[33] These two strands or parallels of liminality are what shape biopolitical subjectivity for whites and nonwhites, and they allow us to account for or make visible their particular modes of racialization.

Here, the positioning of Indigenous peoples as not integral to the market (discussed in my earlier work) or to the rise of capital in the Caribbean has broader significance. Their market marginalization is the reinstituting of a liminal position within politics and economics, allowing Creoles to move slightly from their position as that which was valuable but could be killed, a kind of *homo sacer* on the plantation, to their position in the postcolonial state in which they *might* die. Indigenous peoples can now both be killed and be allowed to die. (Though the state tries to govern via the latter, as a function of making life productive, the limit of black ontology requires the former.) Their inhabiting of this position is what allows Blacks to move ever so slightly into a less pointed position with regard to death. It is the symbolic that allows for this recasting of Indigenous peoples as *homo sacer*, but a version of *homo sacer* that is not the one intended by Agamben, in which one first has to be fully within humanity and fully captured by the state as citizen to be excised from it. It is not the same as the condition of being stateless that is crucial for Agamben, whose *Muselmann* exists outside the state in the camp. Rather, it is a condition of illegibility with regard to the state and, as such, a version of *homo sacer* that emerges from the precondition of liminality for Agamben's own formulation and, genealogically, from the chattel colony (and later adaptations such as the Congo Free State) and the particular reduction of the enslaved and the marginal to bare life outside the orbit of the political.

In sum, Indigenous peoples inhabit the role of a recapitulated (in the biological sense) *homo sacer*, so placed by the market in the necropolitical sense described by Warren Montag—hence, their status as a necessarily underdeveloped, internal South—and within the terrain of subjectivity and subjecthood: the ontological and the politico-economic.[34] The Amerindian Act, as a strategy of containment of Indigenous peoples, is the initiation of a state of exception. It is one based in simulacra and in which Indigeneity works for the humanity of Creoles for whom the sovereignty of the postcolonial state is what, to borrow from Warren, achieves the "structural adjustment" of Black infra-humanity so that state sovereignty, however achieved, is tied to the *possibility* of Black being.[35]

The Amerindian Act

The 1976 Amerindian Act, established under Forbes Burnham, emerged out of ordinances and laws used to control Indigenous peoples' interaction with the colonial state.[36] In a document from 1959 by the British Information Services, a brief section on Amerindian policy refers to what was then the most recent Amerindian Ordinance, passed in 1951, saying that it establishes "a new Amerindian policy based on the principle that it is possible and generally desirable to adapt Amerindians to Western civilisation so that they are able to take their place in the general life of the colony."[37] The Constitution of independent Guyana, however, sought to reframe integration as protection, and the most recent version holds that "Indigenous peoples shall have the right to the protection, preservation and promulgation of their languages, cultural heritage and way of life."[38] Burnham's efforts to adapt Indigenous symbolism and reform the ways in which Guyanese viewed Indigenous lands and peoples reveals not only that "protection" is paternalistic but also that the adaptation of the colonial logic of integration is a mechanism of control.

The ordinances should be read not simply as imperial or colonial documents but as the first deployment of a specific type of modern biopolitical strategy that emerges at the interstices of empire and colonial state formation. They emerge in a then colonial state moving toward greater self-definition after the end of slavery, and these documents are essential to that and the state's future sovereignty. The creation of the 1976 Amerindian Act on the cusp of neoliberalism's dominance as a late twentieth-century political-economic, global market strategy, as well as the act's 2006 revision, reveal a shift in that biopolitical strategy and how it constructs its object of power and the point at which the political and economic sovereignty of racialized peoples is necessarily undercut by the *continuity* of the modes of power that ushered in slavery and indenture.[39] While the act links the type of governance in Guyana with those of dominant and normative settler states such as the United States, it simultaneously represents the limits of the success of subaltern settler states, which must choose to maintain some modes of *colonial* biopower that worked to subordinate its entire population of nonwhite others. The twentieth-century ordinances that developed in Guyana specifically to control Indigenous populations are firmly a product of modern power and the rise of the colonial state as an extension and transformation of imperial forms of governmentality. Rather than being a hallmark of fully executed imperial power, the ordinances reflect the rationality and raison d'état of the colonial government in its deployment of separate strategies of control for Indigenous peoples as a group, as distinct from those who would become its fully enfranchised citizens.[40]

As an expression of the break and continuity between imperial and colonial forms of power, the ordinances cared less about Indigenous life (live and let die). However, the 1976 act, as a legal strategy of the now postcolonial state, actually sought to harness Indigenous peoples as a kind of labor power. While this may seem to contradict what I refer to as the need to continually delink Indigenous identity from the forms of labor (enslaved and indentured) that congeal in a right to rule, it is a different kind of labor. The act, and the concomitant program of cooperativism, made Indigenous peoples and their lands productive *for* the state where possible, as evidenced by their symbolic use as the country's Indigenous element and the rights contained within the act to both grant and *revoke* title where necessary for the good of the postcolonial nation-state. Put differently, the ordinances only had to contain and curtail Indigenous peoples' sovereignty to give the colonial state viability, but the act—established, again, under the first postindependence government and with a partial goal of establishing promised title to Indigenous lands—has to do more. It has to curtail sovereignty *and* delimit the space of Indigenous peoples' productivity so it will not threaten Creole well-being. In short, you can't have Indigenous peoples' communities and identities proliferate in such a way that they threaten the state and state-sponsored identities.

The act initiates "protection" as that "third space of sovereignty" between the postcolonial state and full Indigenous sovereignty.[41] Moreover, it makes the symbolic representation of Indigenous peoples a real mechanism of biopolitical control—hence, my previous discussion of the symbolic as a *first* writing. It is an internal limit placed on Indigenous peoples' identity and rights, as is evident in the framing of the 2006 version: "to provide for the recognition and protection of the collective rights of Amerindian Villages and Communities, the granting of land to Amerindian Villages and Communities and the promotion of good governance within Amerindian Villages and Communities."[42] Though the act upholds features of Indigenous, precolonial forms of governance, and its 2006 revision was a long sought-for change by Indigenous communities, the act is a revision of a contract that never came from an Indigenous world view, and it is based entirely on what we can read as the principle of Indigenous "recognition" of the postcolonial government as a limit to Indigenous sovereignty.[43] It forces reservations to be constructed as states in and of themselves and, at the same time, as objects of an external state power that through the act can be represented within it. This is reinforced by the power of the minister of Indigenous Peoples Affairs, a national governmental position, to enact different portions of the act according to the time of the Guyana government—the time of the state and its fully biological subjects—and not necessarily Indigenous desire, time, or right. I discuss more specific aspects of the 2006 act later and how they work to manage both Indigenous life and death.

According to the Ministry of Indigenous Peoples Affairs, the 2006 act has less say about what Indigenous peoples do on their land and less power to repossess than the 1976 act. In a propaganda piece put out by the ministry in 2005 and designed to essentially sell the act to Indigenous polities prior to its ratification, the ministry claims that the new act "removes the Minister's authority over Amerindian titled land" (although, of course, the Ministry still grants titles).[44] According to that document, the new act provides greater rights and protections for Indigenous peoples when it comes to mining on their lands (even the power to reject what are deemed "small-" and "medium-"scale mining projects) as well as forestry. However, if a village rejects a "large-scale" mining project, the project can still be carried out with the permission of the ministry if it is deemed in the "public interest."[45] By citing "public interest," Indigenous peoples are allowed greater access to mining rights precisely because their sovereignty remains subordinate to coastal Creole public good, and their lands are essentially held in reserve for that, despite the granting of titles. Moreover, both "mining" and "minerals" are actually determined, extra-culturally, by the Mining Act of 1989.[46]

The issue of mining rights demonstrates the particular tensions between Indigenous communities and the state government that persists with the 2006 act. It is also emblematic of how the conflict between the government of Guyana and Indigenous peoples hinges on the fact that there are two kinds of rights in play: what the act deems "traditional right," which falls under the purview of Indigenous peoples, and right that attaches to the ministry and, hence, the government. In the section defining what an Indigenous community or village is, as well as what a "traditional mining privilege is," among other things, the act defines "traditional right" as "any subsistence right or privilege, in existence at the date of the commencement of this act, which is owned legally or by custom by an Amerindian Village or Amerindian Community and which is exercised sustainably in accordance with the spiritual relationship which the Amerindian Village or Amerindian Community has with the land, but it does not include a traditional mining privilege."[47] Prior to this, the act defines "traditional mining privilege" (as distinct it seems from small-, medium-, and large-scale mining) as "any privilege to carry out artesianal mining which an Amerindian possess by virtue of being a member of an Amerindian or Amerindian Community."[48] Traditional right emerges as that which is delimited by custom, community, sustainability, and spirituality. In addition, it is the point at which the act recognizes and affirms Indigenous modes of life. However, by saying that "traditional right" refers to rights "in existence at the date of the commencement of this Act," we can understand that such right refers to what predates the act itself. It is thus a right determined not solely by the features listed (again, spirituality, community, etc.) but by how the *time* of the nation-state recognizes them and continuously locates them as antecedent. Moreover, the features indicated earlier are, I would suggest, a deliberate reframing of Indigenous prior arrival right, the term given for the rights to land that Indigenous peoples held prior to colonization. In this light, traditional right can be understood as a simulation of prior right. It is, in other words, both a recognition of Indigenous rights and the means by which those rights can be managed or interpreted by the state as a check on Indigenous sovereignty.

An example of the power of the terms *community* and *tradition* to act as a limit on Indigenous right emerges in the definition of *community* itself. The act defines an Indigenous community through tradition, communal culture, and the fact of "occupying or using the *State lands* which they have traditionally occupied or used."[49] Thus, while it affirms continuous occupation and use of lands, those lands simultaneously belong to the postcolonial state. In other words, *traditional* both works to affirm Indigenous right to lands and, at the same time, indicates how that right is always already and necessarily a right granted by the state, which it cannot contravene. The conundrum is baldly evident when we see how, exactly, the rights of the state work against those of Indigenous peoples. With regard to the former, not only does the minister of Indigenous Affairs "approve any rule made by a Village Council," but she or he can only do so if that rule does not "conflict with any law."[50]

This tension between right derived from tradition and governmental right is where we must read the translation of cosmogonically charted belonging *into* tradition, and tradition is precisely what the government can then manage through affirmation or rejection. As a permanent substitute without an original referent, tradition is the moment of simulacra into which the biopolitical erupts. These moments of translation/re-presentation don't simply undercut the power the act grants to Indigenous peoples, they are what in fact create or reproduce Indigeneity as secularly governable. Moreover, the governance is of lands and rights and of Indigenous life itself, since the fact that they are on "state lands" means that methods of state governance must be invoked to manage Indigenous bodies and to make Indigenous life governable within the act. This becomes most clear when the act defines Amerindians as "any citizen of Guyana who—(a) belongs to any of the native or aboriginal peoples of Guyana; or (b) is a descendent of any person mentioned in paragraph (a)."[51] And elsewhere, "this Act applies to all Amerindian Villages and Amerindian communities."[52] Again, Indigeneity here is indexed through state citizenship and it is the latter that makes Indigeneity subject to what Donna Haraway would refer to as the biopolitical strategy of the "informatics of domination" of the state.[53] In particular, the act specifies that the Village Council must keep records of "(i) the name of each resident; (ii) the date of birth of each resident; and (iii) the date of death of each resident," all of which "must be provided to the Minister."[54] While Indigenous peoples might record births and deaths for their own purposes, occurring within the act, these provisions also reflect the biopolitical codification of Indigenous peoples' lives. They make ALL Indigenous life subject to government control and representable within its modes of population management in their neo-/postcolonial expression.

The recording of Indigenous births and death is a biopolitical strategy of the nation-state used to maintain control over the Indigenous body through its constant reduction to its statistical representation as sameness, not difference, within the formal body of the nation-state. This delimiting of the Indigenous body and how it reproduces itself as such is coextensive with the limit placed on access to land in which a community can "apply in writing for a grant of State lands provided—(a) it has been in existence for at least twenty-five years," among other specifications.[55] While the minister of Indigenous Peoples Affairs must act in a more responsive time frame (six months) to grant or deny the title sought by a community, the fact that the ministry, as an office of the government, must still grant the title means that titles remain a negotiation between Indigenous peoples and the needs of the state. Thus, titles reflect Indigenous sovereignty, when conferred, and state power to grant or accept that sovereignty. The need for continuous twenty-five-year occupation of land at a time when Indigenous peoples are often made to move for work is a rejection of their contemporary and past movements, forced and volitional, and overidentifies them with fixed spaces. Moreover, where the state's need to supersede Indigenous rights results in unwanted mining, or other such checks on Indigenous self-determination, we must view it as enacting not only the productive ends of biopolitical governance that Foucault addressed (to grow the population so it can be productive for markets) but also the thanatopolitical dimension that subordinates life to market pressures.

As a juridical document, the act works through its transformation of Indigeneity into governable bodies that can be represented within the terms of state governance. For example, in 2015, under the new president, Junior Minister of Indigenous Peoples Affairs Valerie Garrido-Lowe claimed that the new national budget was finally a shift from the previous "one-party domination" in which the Hinterland was not treated as a part of the Guyanese nation. She asserted, "The hinterland is not a separate nation. . . . [O]ur indigenous brothers and sisters, despite their locations, should be provided with the same developmental apparatus as coastlanders."[56] According to Garrido-Lowe, "The fresh approach that our APNU+AFC [A Partnership for National Unity and Alliance for Change] Government is taking, the vision of our President, David Granger, the One Guyana concept . . . is the vehicle that is going to take our hinterland and indigenous brothers and sisters out of poverty. That is why the statement on page 4 in 'A fresh approach to the good life in a green economy' is so very important."[57] That statement reads: "'We share the same conviction that development must be for all our people, whether they are domiciled in urban or rural, hinterland or isolated areas.'"[58] Reading between the lines, the APNU+AFC position is essentially an application of a coastal concept of land and development that links Indigenous peoples with that of Creole populated areas. It assumes that when Indigenous peoples speak of development, it is within the same logic of the government, and thus not about their own self-determination or reproduction as sovereign beings beyond the constraint of the postcolonial state. Interior or Hinterland development (as a solution to these issues) should thus be read not as the same as coastal development but as its pessimistic form. This pessimistic form is where mining can be granted against the interests of Indigenous peoples, and mining itself, where concession is granted, can have destructive effects on Indigenous communities. A 2002 document, for example, cowritten by Jean La Rose, head of the Amerindian Peoples Association, holds that "mining represents one of the greatest threats to Amerindian welfare and survival."[59] It is here that we can plainly see where the management of life takes on a thanatopolitical dimension, but one more in line with Elizabeth Povinelli's concept of geontopower and the logic of elimination that, Wolfe argues, governs the interaction of Indigenous peoples with governments.[60] More specifically, if we read mining as solely a development strategy of the Guyana government, we underestimate the threat it poses to Indigenous peoples: it poses not just a health risk; it has the capacity to end Indigenous ways of life. It is here that we see the way in which Indigenous peoples become the bare life of the Creole subject and, as such, expendable.

Biopolitics as it is applied to Indigenous peoples allows their bodies to be read via the logics of state citizenship, which, in turn, means that as state citizens their lands can be held in reserve for the state and their lives (tied to those lands) are subject to the needs of the market. Moreover, the attempt to develop their lands, within the logic of the larger postcolonial state, is a form of assimilation that, after Wolfe, we must view suspiciously as part of the logic of elimination. While I have previously argued that elimination cannot be the singular goal of this type of postcolonial state, it nonetheless manifests at particular moments to facilitate governance and the well-being of the Creole population and reflects the way in which Indigenous peoples function as the bare life of Creoles.

Conclusion

I close with a final example of the abrogation of Indigenous prior right that the act achieves, one that is particularly difficult to read but that reveals the way in which the postcolonial settler state maintains both a putatively external (in regard to other states) border and an internal border that limits Indigenous sovereignty. The act recognizes the ability of the powers of the Toshao, or chief, but simultaneously delimits them by affirming that "a Toshao has the *powers* and immunities of a rural constable."[61] Here, the Toshao exists within the purview of Indigenous culture and sovereignty (read traditional right) but they are simultaneously translated as a functionary of the larger state (read state's right). As the Indigenous officer of the highest power, the Toshao is a definitive sign of Indigenous self-determination. Despite the considerable power that Toshaos have, the government cannot fully recognize the chief as an external state sovereign. Thus, the chief (as officer) is the precise simulation of sovereignty that makes Indigeneity manageable. This is the aporia between Indigenous right and Indigenous sovereignty that is captured in the quotations that frame this chapter. In the 2006 act, "rights" are what Indigenous peoples have, and in the Guyana Constitution, "sovereignty" is what the state and its citizens possess.[62] Thus, Indigenous peoples can exercise only a kind of nation-state sovereignty that is the very abrogation of their own. This undercutting of Indigenous sovereignty as the central issue behind Indigeneity in Guyana is further evinced by the 2005 propaganda piece that was meant to clarify the benefits of the 2006 act for Indigenous peoples. In that document, the government responds to efforts to have the term *Amerindian* replaced by *Indigenous peoples* in the name of the act. Such a move is not feasible, the document states, because "it means that other Guyanese would no longer be able to call themselves indigenous and this would breach the principle set by international law. All people have a right to call themselves 'indigenous peoples' if they want."[63]

The Constitution and the Amerindian Act reveal two sets of Indigeneity in conflict: one tied to sovereignty and the other tied to protection and articulated as right. It is in this tension between the Constitution as a normative juridical structure and the Amerindian Act as that which initiates a state of exception that we must understand the how, what, and where of the governance of Indigenous lands, lives, and bodies. As I have argued, what facilitates this governance is the symbolic. I therefore began by reading Timehri as the transformation of the extra-discursive symbolism of the petroglyphs—the excessive and potential threat of Indigenous cultures—into the symbolic antecedent of cooperativism, or hieroglyphs. Moreover, I suggested that this new symbolism was instrumental in creating the *what* of governance, in (re)producing a governable Indigenous body that could be managed and maintained as productive for rather than antagonistic to postcolonial state formation. While the original Timehri images signal occupation/belonging and existence outside

European coloniality, under Burnham they become palimpsest for the writing of the cultures of Creole Indigeneity. Moreover, with the name change, the PPP relied on this first writing and thus extended the coloniality of democratic, cooperative rule in the postcolony. Burnham's naming of Timehri was more than just cultural appropriation or containment. It was a specific biopolitical strategy necessary for the functioning of the labor episteme in which Creole prior time and rights are coextensive with their labor. In short, for the biopolitical to be deployed as a mode of governance that could encompass both the Creole citizen subject and the Indigenous as citizen and subject, a substitution or simulation had to occur so that the Indigenous body could be represented as just that—a body, a biologized figure that could then, if one follows Agamben, through the act of birth be governable within the state, by state laws. It is an inscription of the Indigenous body into secular peoplehood. The launch of an Afro-Creole cultural campaign and the (re-)creation of the Amerindian Act by the Burnham regime thus successfully transformed Indigenous peoples in Guyana and their lands into the staging ground for the new indigeneities of the postcolonial settler state, which has worked precisely because the labor of the formerly enslaved is now formally tied to the transformation of the state, and Indigenous peoples are not associated with the progressive ends of that labor, except where a Black—and, later, Indian—regime could extend its vision onto their lands.[64]

There are, however, limits to the power derived from biopolitical governance in the postcolonial state. Postindependence Creoles may have achieved constitutional sovereignty, but they still negotiate a world in which South Asian identity, Blackness, and Indigeneity collectively signal a degree of infra-humanity with regard to the wealthy First World nation-state. If the colonies, as Mbembe has argued, are the first space of the biopolitical, the act as it develops out of ordinances preceded by treaty and other arrangements is part of the same modern biopolitical modes of governmentality that managed Blacks and Indians under slavery and indenture, respectively. Thus, the act's function as a strategy to manage the difference, life, and death of its Indigenous or internal South population *as* and *at* the limit of Creole sovereignty is also reflective of the generalized politics of life and death. It is a politics that, from the colonial to the postcolonial era, holds the entire country and its population of nonwhite citizens at the threshold and limit of the sovereignties of the North and the humanity of the West, as the collective ontological underclass of modern European political and economic systems and their fully enfranchised rights bearers: Man.

A version of this chapter was first presented at the annual conference of the American Studies Association in November 2016.

1 See Shona N. Jackson, *Creole Indigeneity: Between Myth and Nation in the Caribbean* (Minneapolis: University of Minnesota Press, 2012).

2 For more on the ordinances, particularly the nineteenth-century ones, see Janette Bulkan and Arif Bulkan, "'These Forests Have Always Been Ours': Official and Amerindian Discourses on Guyana's Forest Estate," in *Indigenous Resurgence in the Contemporary Caribbean: Amerindian Survival and Revival*, edited by Maximilian C. Forte (New York: Peter Lang, 2006), 135–54. Crucially for my argument, they note that "the earliest laws that dealt with Amerindians specifically were two ordinances enacted in 1902 and 1910": Bulkan and Arif Bulkan, "These Forests Have Always Been Ours," 143. It is the twentieth-century ordinances that I read as a difference in strategies of governmentality that would produce the 1976 act.

3 Throughout, I use the term *cosmogonic* or *cosmogonically charted* to distinguish among Indigenous, pre-contact ways of life; the violent disruption of those by colonialism; and the eventual supplanting of these modes by biopolitics. Sylvia Wynter uses the term to refer to the "culture specific modes" of social and political organization that all societies develop and that are specific to each: see Sylvia Wynter, "Columbus and the Poetics of the *Propter Nos*," *Annals of Scholarship* 8, no. 2 (1991): 251–86.

4 The reference to "truth" here is from Jean Baudrillard's work: see Jean Baudrillard, "Simulacra and Simulations," in *Jean Baudrillard: Selected Writings*, edited by Mark Poster (Stanford, CA: Stanford University Press, 2001), 169–87.

5 L. Searwar, ed., *Co-operative Republic, Guyana 1970: A Study of Aspects of Our Way of Life* (Georgetown, Guyana: Government of Guyana, 1970), 82.

6 For a criticism of the Burnham plan and what it actually put in place as well as of the regime and Afro-Creole nationalism, see Percy Hintzen, *The Costs of Regime Survival: Racial Mobilization, Elite Domination and the Control of the State in Guyana and Trinidad* (Cambridge: Cambridge University Press, 1989).

7 For more discussion of the conception of the Guyana interior as a space of wealth, see Jackson, *Creole Indigeneity*.

8 Ministry of Information and Culture, *A Brief Outline of the Progress of Integration in Guyana* (Georgetown, Guyana: Ministry of Information and Culture, 1970), 5.

9 Wayne Jones, *Towards Further Amerindian Integration and Development: The Persuasive Approach* (Georgetown, Guyana: Ministry of Information, 1981), 54.

10 A. J. Seymour, "Cultural Values in the Republic of Guyana," in Searwar, *Co-operative Republic, Guyana 1970*, 82.

11 Rory Westmaas, "Building under Our Sun: An Essay on the Development of a Guyanese Architecture," in Searwar, *Co-operative Republic, Guyana 1970*, 158. The Umana Yana is an important cultural symbol in Georgetown. It was constructed by members of the Wai Wai peoples for the Conference of Foreign Ministers of Non-Aligned Countries (also called the Non-Aligned Foreign Ministers Conference) held in Guyana in 1976. It was burned to the ground in 2014 and has since

been rebuilt by members of the Wai Wai, who were not paid by the government of Guyana until they protested: see Denis Chabrol, "Wai-Wais Finally Paid for Re-building Umana Yana," *Demerara Waves*, March 11, 2016, accessed March 2, 2022, http://demerarawaves.com/2016/03/11/wai-wais-finally-paid-for-re-building-umana -yana.

12 See Government of Guyana, "Act No. 3 of 1997. Timehri International Airport (Change of Name) Act," *Laws of Guyana*, 1997, accessed March 2, 2022, http:// parliament.gov.gy/publications/acts-of-parliament/timehri-international-airport -change-of-name-act-1997. In an earlier work, I incorrectly said there were "barely recorded" protests of the naming by Indigenous peoples: see Jackson, *Creole Indigeneity*, 181. What I was referring to was that the major papers, such as the *Stabroek News*, covered the response of Indigenous peoples less adequately than organizations such as the Amerindian Peoples Association (APA) and the Guyana Human Rights Association. I originally cited the observations of an Indigenous writer/ journalist who wished not to be named: see, e.g., Hamilton Green, "The International Airport Was Renamed without Consultation," *Stabroek News*, September 28, 2010, accessed March 2, 2022, https://www.stabroeknews.com/2010/opinion/letters /09/28/the-international-airport-was-renamed-without-consultation.

13 See Patrick Wolfe, *Settler Colonialism and the Transformation of Anthropology: The Politics and Poetics of an Ethnographic Event* (London: Cassell, 1999); Patrick Wolfe, "Structure and Event: Settler Colonialism, Time, and the Question of Genocide," in *Empire, Colony, Genocide: Conquest, Occupation, and Subaltern Resistance in World History*, edited by A. Dirk Moses (New York: Berghahn, 2008).

14 Wolfe writes, "In the Indigenous case, it is difficult to speak of an articulation between colonizer and native since the determinate articulation is not to a society but directly to the land, a precondition of social organization. Since it is incoherent to talk of an articulation between humans and things, this social relationship can be conceived of as a negative articulation": Wolfe, *Settler Colonialism and the Transformation of Anthropology*, 2. For Fanonian dialectics, see George Ciccariello-Maher, *Decolonizing Dialectics* (Durham, NC: Duke University Press, 2017); Frantz Fanon, *Black Skin, White Masks*, translated by Charles Lam Markmann (New York: Grove, [1952] 1967); Calvin Warren, "ONTICIDE: Afro-pessimism, ~~Gay~~ Nigger #1, and Surplus Violence," *GLQ* 23, no. 3 (2017): 391–418.

15 For a discussion of Indigenous and Creole ontology, see Jackson, *Creole Indigeneity*. It is important to note that while, for Fanon, the white master does not need the slave for recognition, the relationship between Creoles and Indigenous peoples is closer to that of subalterns, though that term is problematic, so the latter are necessary as Creoles seek recognition, or what Denise da Silva calls transparency, through the state form: see Denise Ferreira da Silva, *Toward a Global Idea of Race* (Minneapolis: University of Minnesota Press, 2007).

16 This transformation is important because it is the logographic that becomes central for progress in world history, particularly as articulated by Enlightenment thinkers such as Hegel: see G. W. F. Hegel, *The Philosophy of History*, translated by John Sibree (New York: Prometheus, 1991). While *logographic* strictly means the representation

of words by symbols, I use it here (along with earlier references to logos) to suggest that the symbols now represent and defer the word—that is, they can be read within the interpretive context of Creole national culture.

17 For the centrality of "language" and writing to political representation and historicity, see Giorgio Agamben, *Homo Sacer: Sovereign Power and Bare Life*, translated by Daniel Heller Roazen (Stanford, CA: Stanford University Press, [1995] 1998); Hegel, *The Philosophy of History*.

18 An example of a violent first writing is Shakespeare's *The Tempest* and Aimé Césaire's adaptation, *A Tempest*, in which to be (re)cast in the word is to be so violently: see Aimé Césaire, *A Tempest: Based on Shakespeare's The Tempest, Adaptation for a Black Theatre*, translated by R. Miller (New York: TCG Translations, [1969] 2002); William Shakespeare, *The Tempest*, Folger Shakespeare Library, edited by Barbara A. Mowat and Paul Werstine (1623 ed.), accessed February 25, 2022, https://shakespeare.folger.edu/downloads/pdf/the-tempest_PDF_FolgerShakespeare.pdf.

19 Baudrillard "Simulacra and Simulations," 173. Crucially, Baudrillard writes, "Simulation is no longer that of a territory, a referential being or a substance. It is the generation by models of a real without origin or reality: a hyperreal. The territory no longer precedes the map, nor survives it. Henceforth, it is the map that precedes the territory—precession of simulacra—it is the map that engenders the territory and if we were to revive the fable today, it would be the territory whose shreds are slowly rotting across the map": Baudrillard "Simulacra and Simulations," 169.

20 See Jean Baudrillard, *For a Critique of the Political Economy of the Sign*, translated by Charles Levin (St. Louis, MO: Telos, [1981] 2011).

21 I want to suggest that there is a shift from peoplehood (by which I mean community) to personhood (by which I mean the form of possessive individualism associated with the liberal state) that Indigenous peoples undergo with the rise of the colonial state form. It is a shift that is, by extension, necessary for the postcolonial government that needed truly to present Indigenous peoplehood as personhood and, as such, governable within the social contract of parliamentary cooperativism. Moreover, it works as a substitution much the way the act does to represent Indigenous space and sovereignty as being contained within the law. Part of my thinking here is shaped by the discussion of Locke in Audra Simpson, *Mohawk Interruptus: Political Life across the Borders of Settler States* (Durham, NC: Duke University Press, 2014).

22 Sylvia Wynter and Katherine McKittrick, *Sylvia Wynter: On Being Human as Praxis* (Durham, NC: Duke University Press, 2015), 635.

23 See Frantz Fanon, *The Wretched of the Earth*, translated by Constance Farrington (New York: Grove, 1963).

24 See Agamben, *Homo Sacer*.

25 See Achille Mbembe, "Necropolitics," translated by Libby Meintjes, *Public Culture* 15, no. 1 (2003): 11–40; Achille Mbembe, "Provisional Notes on the Postcolony," *Africa* 62, no. 1 (1992): 3–37.

26 Alexander Weheliye, *Habeas Viscus: Racializing Assemblages, Biopolitics, and Black Feminist Theories of the Human* (Durham, NC: Duke University Press, 2014), 72. See also Agamben, *Homo Sacer*.

27 Weheliye borrows the term *dysselected* from Wynter's work.

28 Agamben, *Homo Sacer*, 75.

29 Warren, "ONTICIDE," 411. This lack of "birth" can be theorized through a host of work on slave breeding, the reproduction of previously sovereign Blacks as infrahumans, and work on (Black) sex/gender.

30 See Wynter's oeuvre for genres of the human.

31 I don't view the version of the act or the ordinances that were in existence prior to 1976 as constituting states of exception because, occurring during the period of colonial rule, they were exemplary of the different and always already exceptional ways in which nonwhite bodies had always been governed in the colonies.

32 See Wynter, "Columbus and the Poetics of the *Propter Nos*." See also Agamben's discussion in *Homo Sacer* on the shift from the monarchic state.

33 For more on the significance of Las Casas, see Sylvia Wynter, "New Seville and the Conversion Experience of Bartolomé de Las Casas, Part One," *Jamaica Journal* 17, no. 2 (1984): 25–32; Sylvia Wynter "New Seville and the Conversion Experience of Bartolomé de Las Casas, Part Two," *Jamaica Journal* 17, no. 3 (1984): 46–55. See also David T. Orique, *The Unheard of Voice of Law in Bartolomé de Las Casas's Brevísima Relación de la Destruición de las Indias* (New York, Routledge, 2021). In his discussion of Indigeneity and biopolitics, Scott Morgensen writes that the ability of Indigenous peoples to function as *homo sacer* has to do with inclusion and recognition via consanguinity: Scott Morgensen, "The Biopolitics of Settler Colonialism: Right Here, Right Now," *Settler Colonial Studies* 1, no. 1 (2011): 52–76. His work thus orients around the argument for Indigenous humanity by Las Casas. I, however, want to underscore the condition of prior liminality common to Indigenous peoples, Blacks, and Jews and to simultaneously recognize the difference posed by Blackness, since Blacks were denied recognition and struggled below a plane of being that both Indigenous peoples and Jews potentially achieved.

34 In taking up the thanato- and necropolitical arguments about biopower, Warren Montag Goes back to the providential function of the market as articulated by Adam Smith: Warren Montag, "Necro-economics: Adam Smith and Death in the Life of the Universal," *Radical Philosophy* 134 (2005): 7–17. In particular, he argues that in Smith's vision of the market, death was in fact necessary for the proper functioning of the market. In his so-called Hegelian reading of Smith, Montag does not discuss, however, spaces of death—for example, the plantation—and why its racialized others were subject to the necropolitical functioning of the market or the market as death dealer.

35 For more on structural adjustment and ontology, see Warren, "ONTICIDE."

36 Government of Guyana, "Act No. 6 of 1976: Amerindian Act 1976," *Laws of Guyana*, [1976] 1998, accessed March 2, 2022, http://www.guyaneselawyer.com/lawsofguyana/Laws/cap2901.pdf.

37 British Information Services, *British Guiana* (New York: Central Office of Information, 1959), 9. In some documents, there is mention of both a 1951 act and an ordinance, but the document itself is labeled "Ordinance."

38 Government of Guyana, "Act No. 2 of 1980: Constitution of the Co-operative Republic of Guyana Act," *Laws of Guyana*, [1980] 2012, 149G 103, accessed March 2, 2022, http://parliament.gov.gy/constitution.pdf.

39 In dating neoliberalism's dominance, I am relying on David Harvey's chronicling of neoliberalism's rise out of the ashes of the 1970s financial crisis; the strategies of Ronald Reagan, Margaret Thatcher, and other world leaders in the very late 1970s and early 1980s; and the global embrace of neoliberal strategies of governmentality: David Harvey, *A Brief History of Neoliberalism* (Oxford: Oxford University Press, 2005).

40 Here and later I make reference to concepts in Michel Foucault, *The Birth of Biopolitics: Lectures at the Collège de France, 1978-1979*, edited by Michael Senellart, translated by Graham Burchell (London: Palgrave Macmillan, [2004] 2008); Michel Foucault, *On the Government of the Living: Lectures at the Collège de France, 1979-1980*, translated by Graham Burchell (Hampshire, UK: Palgrave Macmillan, [2012] 2014); Michel Foucault, *Society Must be Defended: Lectures at the Collège de France, 1975-1976*, edited by Maura Bertani and Alessandro Fontana, translated by David Macey (New York: Picador, [1997] 2003); Michel Foucault, "The Subject and Power," in *Michel Foucault: Power, Essential Works of Foucault, 1954-1984*, vol. 3, edited by James D. Faubion, translated by Robert Hurley (New York: New Press, 2000), 326-48.

41 I find Kevin Bruyneel's framing of the US-Indigenous relationship here particularly apt: see Kevin Bruyneel, *The Third Space of Sovereignty: The Postcolonial Politics of U.S.-Indigenous Relations* (Minneapolis: University of Minnesota Press, 2007).

42 Government of Guyana, "Act No. 6 of 2006," 5.

43 For more on recognition, see Glen Coulthard, *Red Skin, White Masks: Rejecting the Colonial Politics of Recognition* (Minneapolis: University of Minnesota Press, 2014). For more on the desire of Indigenous peoples for the act to be revised, as well as some history, see Amerindian Peoples Association, "The Revision of the Amerindian Act," *WA-KII-WA*, December 1-2, 2002; Amerindian Peoples Association, "Indigenous Leaders Arrive at a Process to Revise the Amerindian Act 2006," December 4, 2017, accessed March 2, 2022, https://www.facebook.com/notes/amerindian-peoples -association-apa/indigenous-leaders-arrive-at-a-process-to-revise-the-amerindian -act-2006/1342839082493848.

44 See Ministry of Amerindian Affairs, *The New Amerindian Act: What Will It Do for Amerindians?* edited by G. G. I. Agency (Georgetown, Guyana: Guyana Government Information Agency, 2005).

45 Amerindian Act 2006, V.50.(1) (a), 24.

46 Amerindian Act 2006, I.2.(b), 5.

47 Amerindian Act 2006, I.2.(b), 6.

48 Amerindian Act 2006, I.2.(b), 6. Artesian mining refers to well drilling.

49 Amerindian Act 2006, I.2.(b), 5, emphasis added.

50 Amerindian Act 2006, IX. 81(1), 36.

51 Amerindian Act 2006, I.2., 5.

52 Amerindian Act 2006, I.3.(1), 6.

53 See Donna J. Haraway, *Simians, Cyborgs, and Women: The Reinvention of Nature* (New York: Routledge, 1991).

54 Amerindian Act 2006, III.19.(a) (b), 12.

55 Amerindian Act, 2006, VI.60.(1), 27.

56 See "Budget Debate 2015 . . . Hinterland Not a Separate Nation," *Kaieteur News*, August 19, 2015, accessed March 2, 2022, https://www.kaieteurnewsonline.com/2015 /08/19/budget-debate-2015hinterland-not-a-separate-nation.

57 "Budget debate 2015."

58 "Budget debate 2015."

59 See Marcus Colchester, Jean La Rose, and Kid James, *Mining and Amerindians in Guyana*, final report of the APA/NSI project "Exploring Indigenous Perspectives on Consultation and Engagement with the Mining Sector in Latin America and the Caribbean," North-South Institute, 2002. The APA frequently writes about the detrimental effects of mining in Amerindian villages.

60 See Elizabeth A. Povinelli, *Geontologies: A Requiem to Late Liberalism* (Durham, NC: Duke University Press, 2016).

61 Amerindian Act 2006, III.20.(2), 12, emphasis added.

62 Amerindian Act 2006, 5; "Constitution" II.9, 33. The 1976 version of the statement in the epigraph reads, "An Act to make provision for the good Government of the Amerindian Communities in Guyana": Amerindian Act 1976, 6.

63 Ministry of Amerindian Affairs, *The New Amerindian Act*, 7.

64 Bulkan and Bulkan reinforce this point about the marginalization of Indigenous labor when they write that "Amerindians did not provide direct labour power to the plantation economy": Bulkan and Bulkan, "These Forests Have Always Been Ours," 146.

6

FICTIONS OF LAND AND FLESH

Blackness, Indigeneity, Speculation

MARK RIFKIN

Black freedom struggles and Indigenous peoples' pursuit of self-determination occur at oblique angles. Their intellectual and political mappings, tropes, trajectories, and stakes remain somewhat incommensurable, with vocabularies and orientations that tend not to articulate well together. The two might be schematized, quite roughly, as imaginaries of flesh and of land, a contrast between the violence of dehumanization through fungibility and dispossession through domestication.[1] While both have been subjected to assaultive violence and dislocation, the ways in which those varied struggles tend to be articulated—prominent tropes, framings, and narrative strategies—differently address these concerns, with questions with respect to the (captured) body predominating in contemporary Black political imaginaries and issues of collective (self-governing) territoriality tending to guide Native ones. Movement between these (sets of) imaginaries involves acts of translation, recasting histories, trajectories, and configurations in ways that can generate potentially warping accounts of the other's aims and stakes. However, the dynamics of translation tend to be overlooked, inasmuch as (1) these various struggles are treated as if they readily could be situated within a neutral supervening structural analysis, rather than seeing such system narration as being oriented by particular political histories and goals; or (2) the conceptual framework guiding a particular account is treated as simply expressing the details of a particular event or social pattern rather than understanding the framing as itself arising from specific forms of political struggle, such that analysis generated out of other kinds of struggle might frame the event/relations/dynamics differently.

One might characterize the effort to track the translations performed by these varied political imaginaries in their engagements with each other as involving something like a speculative leap, in the sense of shifting out of extant ways of narrating the real.[2] In this vein, genres of speculative writing, such as science fiction and fantasy, open political possibilities. Not only do such texts lift off of the material embroilments and contentions of the factual world (What truly explains an occurrence or set of relations? Whose claims in this situation or this area should be given greater weight? Which issue is the more important one for public recognition and public policy consideration?), but in doing so they help make the use of particular tropes, framings, and narrative strategies more visible as such—as ways of making sense of the world and situating it in relation to particular histories and struggles instead of merely as the substance of what *is*. Moreover, speculative fiction creates "what if?" scenarios that enable forms of conceptual and representational experimentation, highlighting what happens when one set of political struggles gets translated into the terms of another.[3] In this vein, Octavia Butler's *Xenogenesis* envisions a future alien invasion/rescue that fuses the mass reduction of people to vulnerable flesh and the nativeness of humanity with respect to the Earth, cross-hatching figurations of Blackness and Indigeneity.[4] The novels take up the kinds of fungibility attributed to Blackness as a means of thinking about more capacious possibilities for embodiment that do not fit existing ideologies of propertied personhood and racial categorization.[5] In offering this opening onto "difference," the trilogy—*Dawn*, *Adulthood Rites*, and *Imago*—also repeatedly gestures toward sovereignty and self-determination, but in doing so, Butler largely translates them into the biopolitics of enslavement and its legacies, pursuing a mode of antiracist critique that defers robust engagement with Indigenous peoplehood.[6] Attending to these dynamics in the trilogy helps illustrate how such processes of transposition and refraction occur and how they influence possibilities for thinking across Black and Indigenous struggles.

The stakes of this kind of (mis)translation can be seen in the tendency within contemporary Black political and scholarly discourses to interpret modes of place-based peoplehood (including Indigeneity) in ways that cast it as a reactionary attachment to Euro-American ideologies of propertied selfhood. In this vein, work by Jared Sexton and Frank Wilderson has been particularly prominent. These scholarly accounts offer structural analyses of the centrality of anti-Blackness to global modernity, presenting such a conceptual framework as foundational in ways that tend to disallow the possibility of alternative framings, especially those grounded in collective territoriality. In "The *Vel* of Slavery," Sexton rightfully critiques the tendency within Indigenous studies to conceptualize Blackness in terms of an investment in belonging to the nation-state or as the failure to possess a conception/practice of place-based political collectivity (envisioned as lost through histories of colonization), but he goes on to suggest that the "preoccupation with sovereignty" that accompanies attention to Indigenous peoplehood(s) leads to "an elision of the permanent seizure of the body essential to enslavement" and an erasure of the fields of force to which the "captive body" is subjected.[7] Instead, he indicates that the political project of "abolition" lies "beyond (the restoration of) sovereignty" since "the slave's inhabitation of the earth precedes and exceeds any prior relation to land."[8] Indigenous sovereignty appears here as a commitment to the forms of propertied autonomy that characterize Euro-American systems of enslavement and their continuing effects in the wake of formal emancipation. By contrast, abolition involves a liberation of "the body" from its enthrallment to notions of possession, of which landownership is a key index. To identify as landed means to identify with ideologies of property and self-ownership. Thus, to defend a collective claim to place reinvests, in Sexton's terms, in *natality* and *nationality* in ways that cannot but fail to liberate "the body" from the force of enslavement.[9] From within this prism, collective potentials based in experiences of territoriality indicate a retrograde investment in propertied modes of being, implicitly reiterating the dominant notion of the human against which the antiracist undoing of boundaries gains meaning. Similarly, in *Red, White, and Black*, Wilderson distinguishes (Black) "fungibility" from (Native) "sovereignty." He suggests that Natives and settlers (by which he means whites) "can both practice cartography, and although at every scale their maps are radically incompatible, their respective 'mapness' is never in question," a territoriality that works to defer "the horrifying possibility that Black fungibility might somehow rub off of the Slave and stick to the 'Savage.'"[10] Following this logic, Native sovereignties invest in political cartography rather than attending to the violence done to racialized bodies via their being made fungible and murderable objects. "Mapness" per se appears as a deferral or denial of the effects of racialized corporeality, because cartographic visions of collective identity presumptively depend on becoming a subject through/of property, and reciprocally, to assert a collective claim to place is to desire to gain entry to the privileges of dominant personhood.

While these accounts illustrate the translation between Black and Indigenous political frameworks, Butler's trilogy in its speculative imagining offers a less pressurized means of tracing that process, of exploring in particular the effects of engaging Indigeneity within an account focused on the effects of racialized embodiment—of fungibility. The novels envision the subjection of humanity to alien rule, including profound reorganizations of social life. The aliens—called Oankali—arrive on Earth after a nuclear holocaust that results from the explosion of Cold War tensions. They preserve the surviving humans in suspended animation, and after 250 years they decide that one of the people they've awakened—an African American named Lilith—will guide and train other humans to become the nucleus of new human-Oankali settlements on an Earth restored/remade through Oankali intervention. However, humans will not be allowed to have children on their own and are physically altered so that they cannot do so. Instead, they will procreate through Oankali modes of kinship and reproduction, which involves gene mixing by a third-sex entity known as an ooloi, who combines genes from a human male and female and an Oankali male and female to produce a new kind of being—called a "construct." The novels cast the Oankali as offering an alternative to dominant human patterns of destruction and violence based on assertions of ownership and hierarchy. The trilogy, though, correlates this sense of possibility with traits often associated with Indigenous peoples, even as those qualities are dissociated from those peoples and Indigeneity as such.

Humans often charge that they are being enslaved by the Oankali. One of Lilith's earliest thoughts in *Dawn* in response to finding a "long scar on her abdomen" is, "She did not own herself any longer. Even her flesh could be cut and stitched without her consent or knowledge" (6).[11] While this laceration turns out to be due to Oankali surgery to treat emergent cancer of which Lilith was unaware, when assessing the veracity of what she's been told, she later thinks, "Why should they bother to lie? They owned the Earth and all that was left of the human species" (59). This sentiment is repeated at various points throughout the trilogy. In the next book, *Adulthood Rites*, readers learn that "Resisters," those humans who have been returned to the Earth but have fled from Oankali villages to create their own nonreproducing settlements, say of Nikanj, the ooloi to whom Lilith becomes mated, that it "sold" humanity to the Oankali (298). As Hortense Spillers argues, the presumptively self-contained, agential, property-owning body needs to be understood as fundamentally disjunct from the corporealities engendered by enslavement—penetrable and disposable Black flesh. She says, "Before the 'body' there is the 'flesh,' that zero degree of social conceptualization."[12] Building on Spillers's work and that of Sylvia Wynter, Alexander Weheliye conceptualizes this differential between the body and the flesh as a means of demarcating and policing "genres of the human," a division instituted by "a set of sociopolitical processes that discipline humanity into full humans, not-quite-humans, and nonhumans."[13] In this vein, the history of New World enslavement creates modes of social division through which whiteness is taken to index "full humans"—or "Man"—and Blackness marks not-quite-humanity, an absence of (the capacity for) self-possession inscribed through a "hieroglyphics of the flesh" that "are sociogenically imprinted."[14] In *Xenogenesis*, though, if there is a difference between the *embodied* and the *fleshly*, it takes the form of the distinction between human and aliens, with Oankalis seeking to inculcate humans into more capacious and less proprietary and insulating modes of relation. That process might be understood as seeking to turn the forms of fungibility attributed to Blackness toward other possibilities for understanding embodiment, identity, and personhood.

The Oankali insist not only that they do not aim to enslave humans but also that they never have done so to any species. At one point, Lilith insists to Nikanj, "You could kill us. You could make mules of our children," and it replies, "There was no life at all on your Earth when our ancestors left our original homeworld, and in all that time, we've never done such a thing" (55). Rather than making alien species (including humans) into commodities or servants, Oankali seek relations with them to stimulate and further catalyze an ongoing process of transformation through which Oankalis themselves continually are remade. When the Oankali male with whom Lilith initially engages (Jdahya) explains that Oankali means "Traders," and that they embarked on this interstellar "trade" billions of years ago, Jdahya elaborates: "We acquire new life—seek it, investigate it, manipulate it, sort it, use it. We carry the drive to do this in a miniscule cell within a cell—a tiny organelle within every cell of our bodies" (40–41). The Oankali seek less a unity, even a hybridized one, than a proliferation of potentials. As Naomi Jacobs suggests, Butler "posits an alien race whose very nature is premised upon metamorphosis and boundary-crossing by way of its practice of gene-trading. The Oankali's goal is not to preserve an essential species identity, but always to be transforming themselves into something else."[15]

Oankali trade does not so much subordinate humans by distinguishing them from a privileged Oankali bodily norm as enfold humanity within open-ended itineraries of becoming. As Tiffany King suggests, "the concept of fungibility denotes and connotes pure flux, process, and potential," adding, "Blackness is a form of malleable potential and a state of change in the 'socio-political order' of the New World" in that "Black fungible bodies have unlimited figurative and metaphoric value."[16] If Black fungibility historically has meant being positioned as an instrument in the service of someone else's worlding, Butler reframes such malleability as opening onto a radical reconceptualization of bodily possibility that is neither negatively contrasted with propertied personhood nor contained within racial taxonomies. In *Adulthood Rites*, Lilith's construct son Akin recalls Lilith telling him, "Human beings fear difference. . . . Oankali crave difference. Humans persecute their different ones, yet they need them to give themselves definition and status. Oankali seek difference and collect it. . . . When you feel a conflict, try to go to the Oankali way. Embrace difference" (329).[17] Oankali trade explores possibilities for collective modes of life not constrained by the (racialized) forms of selfhood, autonomy, and ownership currently recognized by/as the law. In depicting Oankali "difference," the trilogy implicitly invokes the fungibility attributed to Blackness as part of ongoing histories of anti-Black subjection—especially in terms of Black reproduction and motherhood—in ways that refigure such malleability as a way beyond dominant conceptions of the human. The novels describe Oankalis in ways that present them as "radical subjects-in-process," portraying the Oankali as "propagators of diversity."[18]

The trilogy's portrayal of various aspects of Oankali life shows how their privileging of networking and permeability undoes property-based understandings of identity (individual and collective). In these ways, the novels explore what Weheliye has termed the "political facets of enfleshment"—the possibilities for collective modes of life not constrained by dominant (racialized) forms of humanness.[19] In particular, their reciprocal relations with their environment and kinship dynamics evidence the absence of bourgeois modes of individualism. J. Adam Johns characterizes this vision as one of "a posthuman future."[20] However, the very qualities that for many signify *posthuman* potential—ways of getting beyond dominant, racializing Euro-American paradigms of humanness—can be seen less as a move beyond humanity than as a citation of dominant ways of depicting Indigenous peoples.[21] The novels' portrait of the Oankali resonates with prominent images, both historical and contemporary, of Indigenous peoples, suggesting that the possibilities represented by the Oankali might be read as translating knowledges, practices, and occupancies conventionally attributed to Indigenous peoples into an other-than-human register.

The intimacy of Oankali connections to their space of inhabitance offers perhaps the most easily recognizable allusion to dominant accounts of Indigeneity.[22] At one point, Lilith asks Nikanj whether Oankalis "ever build machinery," "using metal and plastic instead of living things," to which it responds, "We do that when we have to. We . . . don't like it. There's no trade" (85). Jdahya earlier observes of the relationship with their ships, "There is an affinity, but it's biological—a strong, symbiotic relationship. We serve the ship's needs and it serves ours. It would die without us and we would be planetbound without it. For us, that would eventually mean death" (35). In these moments, Butler suggests the absence of a clear dividing line between Oankalis and the environments they occupy, instead suggesting an organizing reciprocity in which these various kinds of entities participate within a complex, if shifting, matrix that provides the shared and indivisible context for their continuing development and well-being. Indigenous peoples often are expected to perform just this sort of ideal of seamless connection to "natural" surroundings to be intelligible as Indigenous and to argue for recognition of the legitimacy of their status and emplacements as polities. As Ronald Niezen observes, non-Natives "tend to perceive indigenous societies as living in perfect harmony with the natural world," and "to satisfy the public that can help them . . . , [Indigenous peoples] must also be noble, strong, spiritually wise, and, above all, environmentally discreet."[23] Attributions of environmental consciousness, then, regularly substitute for engagement with the politics of Indigenous self-determination. Karen Engle notes that "states even prohibit indigenous groups from using land in a manner that goes against what the state sees as the group's purported attachment to it": "When they do not behave toward the land in the idealized manner that has come to be expected of them, these groups might cease to be considered real Indians."[24]

Oankali genders and kinships further illustrate their ability to traverse the conventional boundaries of selfhood in ways that implicitly point toward longstanding conceptions of Indigeneity. The sense of Oankali sociality conveyed to readers emphasizes belonging to extended *families*. The extensive and intensive genealogical orientations of Oankali life provide a contrast to the kinds of atomization attributed to humans in the novels. Dominant liberal visions of privatized autonomy depend for their coherence on being distinguished from, in Elizabeth Povinelli's terms, "the genealogically determined collective," defined by its racialized image as "illiberal, tribal, customary, and ancestral[ly determined]."[25] In this way, the *Xenogenesis* trilogy draws on the legacy of ethnology, in which Indigenous modes of social organization and governance have been characterized as familial rather than properly political.[26] Furthermore, Butler literalizes the conception of a "third sex" often attributed to non-Western peoples as its own kind of body that functions as central in the process of propagation. As Jdahya cautions Lilith in their initial conversation, "It's wrong to assume that I must be a sex you're familiar with" (13). Through the ooloi, the novels allude to the ways gender roles may exceed the dimorphic binary instantiated by heteronormative models of personhood, drawing on the tradition of European and Euro-American observations of alternative social configurations among Indigenous peoples largely, but not exclusively, from the Americas.[27]

Signs of Indigeneity serve as the vehicles for marking Oankalis' deviance, for signaling the ways they represent an alternative to the enclosed and propertied modes of being attributed to humanity as such, but Oankalis have no determinate relationship to place. In fact, they are defined not simply by the absence of such a connection but by an innate imperative toward self-dislocation. As Jdahya notes, to be "planetbound . . . would eventually mean death" (35). For billions of years, that cycle of contact, trade, and emigration has persisted (36), and without any sense of a continuing connection to the world from which they came or to any subsequent one, their connection to the place they occupy at any given moment is merely anticipatory of the time they will journey again, never to return to any of the worlds they have inhabited. When Lilith asks Jdahya, "Do you remember your homeworld itself? I mean, could you get back to it if you wanted to?" he responds with evident amusement, "No, Lilith, that's the one direction that's closed to us," adding, "We left it so long ago . . . I doubt that it does still exist. . . . It was a womb. The time had come for us to be born" (36–37). Except for the ships themselves, which also provide their dwellings and village sites when on-planet, the spaces Oankalis occupy are nothing but collections of extractable resources that enable their further travel—including the Earth, which, after another few centuries, will be left behind "as lifeless as the moon" (365). Indigenously inflected forms of sociality, then, do not signal something like the potential for sovereignty or territorially determinate modes of governance; instead, they index possibilities for moving human social life away from propertied and privatizing notions of selfhood.

The trilogy does broach the issue of self-determination—but in rather ambivalent terms. In *Adulthood Rites*, Lilith's son Akin comes to decide that humans deserve the right to have their own existence distinct from the Oankali, and he devises a plan to move all those humans who desire such separation to Mars, where their reproductive abilities will be returned and the Oankali will provide terraforming technology to make the planet habitable. The principal objections offered to this plan by the Oankali have to do with the fact that they conceive of humans as inherently destructive due to humans' genetic "contradiction." In Lilith's initial set of conversations with Jdahya, he indicates, "Your bodies are fatally flawed. . . . You are hierarchical. . . . When human intelligence served it instead of guiding it, when human intelligence did not even acknowledge it as a problem but took pride in it or did not notice it at all . . . [, t]hat was like ignoring cancer" (38–39). The Oankali—and, to some extent, the novels themselves—offer this set of genetic tendencies as the explanation for the nuclear war that nearly ended the human race and the possibility for life on the planet.[28] Humans exist as a biological type, defined by their "contradiction," and that (racial) type innately moves toward (self-)annihilation. From within this framing, the Oankali insist that humans need to be altered as part of an effort to promote the potential for life, as against inborn tendencies toward self-destruction. During the deliberation on the prospective Mars colony, one Oankali highlights "the Oankali understanding of life itself as a thing of inexpressible value. A thing beyond trade. Life could be changed, changed utterly. But not destroyed" (470). The notion of restoring humans' independent reproductivity and allowing them to live on their own again appears as a "profoundly immoral, antilife thing"; even when the Oankali come to accept the need for it, it can only be characterized as "a cruelty" (475).

In being animated by the promotion of and the potential for life, Oankali collective thinking, action, and morality can be understood as enacting a biopolitical mode of governance. In *The History of Sexuality*, Michel Foucault defines biopolitics by sketching a shift from the prior location of (European) authority in the monarch's power to kill to a justification of the exertion of power based on "the right of the social body to ensure, maintain, or develop its life."[29] As Foucault suggests in *Society Must Be Defended*, though, the flipside of the positing and defense of this norm in the name of "life" lies in the emergence of "the internal racism of permanent purification," such that racialization operates as a necessary supplement to the production of modes of life enhancement—justifying targeting for containment/destruction those who deviate from the "norm" by understanding them as bearing biological incapacity/danger.[30] However, the Oankali do not have a privileged bodily norm as such. In the absence of a normative model of embodiment, processes of racialization work by defining a population as subjects of regenerative *incapacity*—as disabled. When initially explaining the human "contradiction" to Lilith, Jdahya says of it, "A complex combination of genes that work together to make you intelligent as well as hierarchical will still handicap you whether you acknowledge it or not" (39), and with respect to the Mars colony, Jodahs observes, "The Oankali *know to the bone* that it's wrong to help the Human species regenerate unchanged because it *will* destroy itself again," adding by way of further explanation, "To them it's like deliberately causing the conception of a child who is so defective that it must die in infancy" (532). Humans are genetically "handicap[ped]" and "defective" with respect to the promotion of life, which is what makes the notion of the Mars colony so "immoral" and "antilife" (475). In these ways, humans appear as the objects of Oankali pastoral care, and thus any effort to refuse such attentions itself serves as evidence of mental/emotional deficiency—as an expression of their genetic predisposition toward hierarchy and an attendant unwillingness to allow themselves to be aided and protected.[31] This orientation can be characterized, in Alison Kafer's terms, as "a *curative imaginary*, an understanding of disability that not only *expects* and *assumes* intervention but also cannot imagine or comprehend anything other than intervention," and within this imaginary, "the political nature of disability, namely its position as a category to be contested and debated, goes unacknowledged."[32] The understanding of humanity as an aggregation of individual disabled bodies in need of care thwarts the possibility of engaging with *the political nature* of Oankali rule, the ways it defers and dismantles the potential for human collective organization as such.[33] To refuse Oankali governance means choosing to be disabled; such collective repudiation signifies a will to "antilife" rather than a commitment to alternative *lifeways* and forms of (geo)political order other than those instituted by Oankalis. If "life" is "of inexpressible value" *because* it can be "changed, changed utterly" (470), then resistance to seeking "difference" through "change" indexes not opposition but recalcitrance born from infirmity (34, 329).

The novels register the *politics* of this attribution of disability—and the human desire for modes of sociality not superintended by the Oankali—in Akin's project of creating a Mars colony in which the resisters can live and reproduce free from Oankali intervention. The human characters all conceptualize humanity as a "people," not simply an aggregation of persons but a collective whose existence is threatened by Oankali modes of becoming. Such peoplehood serves as the basis of Akin's argument for humans' right to self-determination. He had "been among resister Humans long enough to being to see them as a truly separate people" (378). To the extent that resisters are, as Audra Simpson suggests in her discussion of Indigenous peoples' sovereignty, "using their territory in a manner that is historically and philosophically consistent with what [they] know, then, it is an incident of a failed consent and *positive refusal*."[34] The active, organized, and ongoing nonconsent of the resisters to Oankali overtures can be understood as refusing to live a "life" acknowledged as such by the Oankali. Simpson suggests of settler modes of engagement with Indigenous sovereignties that such terms of recognition are "politically untenable and thus normatively should be refused," earlier noting, "Refusal comes with the requirement of having one's *political* sovereignty acknowledged and upheld, and raises the question of legitimacy for those who are usually in the position of recognizing."[35] Akin raises such a question with respect to Oankali processes of becoming: "What are we that we can do this to whole peoples?" (443). What's at stake is political sovereignty, in terms of the ability of a collective entity to remain distinct (to refuse incorporation into the encompassing jurisdiction of another political entity) and to continue to govern itself. Thus, in these moments the novel foregrounds the ways Oankali exchange—the possibilities of Oankali fleshliness and fungibility—functions as a mode of settler colonialism. For humans to function as a "people" means having their relative autonomy acknowledged: their right to refuse absorption into the apparatus of Oankali biopolitics. The imaginary of Oankali-overseen "change" depends on a colonial disavowal of humans' right to autonomous development, including an effort to sever their collective relationship to place— the Earth. In critiquing an Oankali biopolitics of "life," the trilogy invokes humans' right to exist as a distinct, place-based "people," implicitly drawing on Indigeneity as an imaginative and ethical resource for challenging racist attributions of infirmity and incapacity and their use as a means of justifying extensive intervention and invasion.

Yet many critics have characterized resister assertions of rightful collective autonomy as merely replaying racializing visions of purity. Scholars have described the resisters as desiring to maintain a biologically imagined sameness that seeks to thwart Oankali attempts to institute a sense of relationality, the fleshly potential for adaptability, and an embrace of newness.[36] These interpretations reflect the novels' tendency to cast the desire for a version of human autonomy as the reactionary (and racialist) preservation of a kind of body. Lilith wonders in *Dawn*, "How could she Awaken people and tell them they were to be part of the genetic engineering scheme of a species so alien[?] . . . How would she Awaken these people, these survivors of war, and tell them that unless they could escape the Oankali, their children would not be human?" (117). Furthermore, after a brutal assault by humans on the Oankalis holding them captive aboard the ship, Lilith responds to Nikanj's surprise at the ferocity of humans' feelings: "What did you think would happen when you told us you were going to extinguish us as a species by tampering genetically with our children?" (231). The "human" becomes a function of a particular "genetic" profile, such that "tampering" with it induces an almost unbridled rage to maintain the intergenerational continuity of this biological typology. In *Adulthood Rites*, one of the resisters expresses her anger about the effects of the Oankali management of human procreation, asserting, "Oankali drove us to become what we are. If they hadn't tampered with us, we'd have children of our own. We could live in our own ways, and they could live in theirs" (399). Soon thereafter, she states, "We don't get old. We don't have kids, and nothing we do means shit" (402). The existential crisis marked here signifies in terms of the ongoing anxiety about the "genetic" coherence of the human race, such that to want to "live in our own ways" or to contest Oankali interventions cannot but bespeak a concern about retaining the physiological identity of humanness per se. Moreover, the resisters—those humans returned to Earth who have refused to live and mate with Oankalis—descend into a Hobbesian war of all against all, including waves of raiding, kidnapping, rape, and murder among resister communities. In addition, the question of the Mars colony, and of humans' right to live separately as a "people," arises in *Adulthood Rites* but then is dislocated from the narrative frame of *Imago*, the final novel in the trilogy, which focuses on the emergence of construct ooloi, their relations with humans, and the potentialities for "difference" and adaptation illustrated in this encounter.

On the whole, the trilogy retreats from the issue of political collectivity raised in *Adulthood Rites*. Instead, it tends to depict human refusal of Oankali care/ potential as a doctrinaire investment in maintaining species boundaries at the expense of enhancing quality of life through an embrace of the possibilities and ethics of relationality offered by the Oankali. Despite Butler's use of terminology associated with collective self-determination and self-governance, then, "people"hood continually appears in the trilogy as more or less expressive of the desire to maintain humanness as a particular discrete kind of embodiment. In this way, self-determination is corporealized—the (geo)politics of refusing alien occupation and intrusion can appear as a struggle to retain the integrity of a kind of body. Humans' apparent ongoing investment in atomized self-possession allows for the novels implicitly to portray the desire for territorial peoplehood—for what could be narrated as sovereignty—as a reactionary investment in (racial) purity.

The *Xenogenesis* trilogy envisions the potential for moving beyond the endemic forms of oppression and aggression that seem to characterize human history. In contrast to the pursuit of racialized and racializing modes of hierarchy, Butler offers an (alien) ethos in which positive modes of fleshliness and fungibility predominate, highlighting networks of interrelation in ways that challenge post-Enlightenment notions of personhood as self-possession and insular autonomy. The novels suggest a normative embrace of difference as an open-ended process of becoming through interaction with the unknown that generates new possibilities for being in the world, refiguring Blackness and the ongoing legacy of enslavement as an opening onto other genres of the human. This vision of ongoing transformation is juxtaposed with the ingrained human "contradiction" that drives people to mark boundaries (personal and collective) and to assert dominance, including in racial terms. However, in totalizing humanity, in terms of its capacity both for destruction and for fleshly engagement, the trilogy offers an antiracist framework whose conceptual coordinates render Indigenous self-determination unintelligible as such. The novels do not so much efface Indigeneity as cite it in ways that disarticulate it from place-based peoplehood.

The aspects of Oankali modes of sociality that seem most alien to the human characters can be understood as indexing conventional accounts of Indigenous difference. Yet if qualities so often attributed to Indigeneity serve as something of an aspirational horizon for the novels, indicating possibilities for becoming less driven to and by violence; they also appear disconnected from enduring connections to place. Reciprocally, humanity itself takes on qualities of Indigeneity, particularly in terms of the resisters' desire to remain a "people" separate from Oankalis with Earth as their shared home. Through Akin and the movement to recognize human collective autonomy, Butler offers an account of the ethics of self-determination, raising questions about the legitimacy of Oankali narratives of protection. However, (Indigenous) "people"hood in the texts appears less to mark the existence of a polity or set of polities than to index the desire to maintain forms of purity as the basis for membership—in this case, the normative human physiology that the Oankalis seek to transmute through trade.

In this way, the trilogy translates self-determination as a desire to maintain the identities, territorialities, and associated kinds of aggression that characterize the human "contradiction." Thus, although the novels present self-determination (or a people's sovereignty over themselves) as an important norm, the ethical force of that ideal is hollowed out by its implicit alignment with what is cast as an investment in property—both in (kinds of) bodies and land. In the absence of a robust conception of peoplehood, and the potential multiplicity of *peoples*, the trilogy's efforts to deracialize personhood (to envision possibilities for exceeding dominant, hierarchical Euro-American conceptions of what it means to be human) end up engaging Indigenous self-determination and territoriality as a kind of unfortunate, if ethically unavoidable, backwardness. The erasure of *peoples* limits the possibilities for acknowledging the actually existing multiplicity of ways of being human, in terms of belonging to separate collectivities, and for recognizing the normative value of such acknowledgment. Indigeneity provides a double ethics in the trilogy in ways that are incommensurate with each other: a vision of nonpropertied relationality attributed to the Oankali but divorced from placemaking, on the one hand, and on the other, a vision of emplaced human refusal of Oankali oversight that gestures toward a politics of sovereignty and self-determination yet also gets corporealized as a form of racial reactionism. This fissuring of Indigeneity illustrates the difficulties generated by approaching place-based peoplehood from within the frame of a biopolitics of racialization ordered around histories of enslavement and abolition. Butler's trilogy, then, offers a powerful prism for understanding the impasses that arise in seeking to move between political imaginaries of land and flesh.

NOTES

1   I should clarify that I'm not speaking about members of Native nations who are of African descent and the forms of anti-Black racism that they can face in being recognized as Native, including by other Native people(s): see James F. Brooks, ed., *Confounding the Color Line: The Indian-Black Experience in North America* (Lincoln: University of Nebraska Press, 2002); Sharon Patricia Holland and Tiya Miles, eds., *Crossing Waters, Crossing Worlds: The African Diaspora in Indian Country* (Durham, NC: Duke University Press, 2006); Brian Klopotek, *Recognition Odysseys: Indigeneity, Race, and Federal Tribal Recognition Policy in Three Louisiana Indian Communities* (Durham, NC: Duke University Press, 2011); Claudio Saunt, *Black, White, and Indian: Race and the Unmaking of an American Family* (New York: Oxford University Press, 2005).

2   While I am addressing efforts to think across these disparate struggles, there also is the complex politics of how to address the ways that non-Native people of color can participate within processes of settlement: see Zainab Amadahy and Bonita Lawrence, "Indigenous Peoples and Black People in Canada: Settlers or Allies?," in *Breaching the Colonial Contract: Anti-colonialism in the U.S. and Canada*, edited by Arlo Kempf New York: Springer, 2010), 105–36; Ikuko Asaka, *Tropical Freedom: Climate, Settler Colonialism, and Black Exclusion in the Age of Emancipation* (Durham, NC: Duke University Press, 2017); Jodi A. Byrd, *The Transit of Empire: Indigenous Critiques of Colonialism* (Minneapolis: University of Minnesota Press, 2011); Shona N. Jackson, *Creole Indigeneity: Between Myth and Nation in the Caribbean* (Minneapolis: University of Minnesota Press, 2012).

3   On histories of Black science fiction and speculative fiction, see Mark Bould, "The Ships Landed Long Ago: Afrofuturism and Black SF," *Science Fiction Studies* 34, no. 2 (2007): 177–86; André M. Carrington, *Speculative Blackness: The Future of Race in Science Fiction* (Minneapolis: University of Minnesota Press, 2016); Isiah Lavender

III, *Race in American Science Fiction* (Bloomington: Indiana University Press, 2011); Gregory E. Rutledge, "Futurist Fiction and Fantasy: The *Racial* Establishment," *Callaloo* 24, no. 1 (2001): 236–52. On Afrofuturism within sci-fi writing and beyond it, see also Mark Dery, "Black to the Future: Interviews with Samuel R. Delany, Greg Tate, and Tricia Rose," in *Flame Wars: The Discourse of Cyberculture*, edited by Mark Dery (Durham, NC: Duke University Press, 1994), 179–222; Alondra Nelson, "Introduction: Future Texts," *Social Text* 20, no. 2 (2002): 1–15; Lisa Yaszek, "Afrofuturism, Science Fiction, and the History of the Future," *Socialism and Democracy* 20, no. 3 (2006): 41–60. On the racial subtexts and trajectories of scientific and futurist imaginings in non-Black writing in the twentieth century, see De Witt Douglas Kilgore, *Astrofuturism: Science, Race, and Visions of Utopia in Space* (Philadelphia: University of Pennsylvania Press, 2003).

4   The novels in the trilogy—*Dawn, Adulthood Rites*, and *Imago*—originally were published separately over the course of three years, 1987–1989. They were published together as *Xenogenesis* in 1989, and the trilogy later was republished as *Lilith's Brood*, from which I cite: see Octavia E. Butler, *Lilith's Brood* (New York: Grand Central, 2000). I continue to refer to the novels as the *Xenogenesis* trilogy, though, since this name was the one first used for it, and is the one by which it largely is known. Further citations from this edition are in parentheses in the text.

5   On fungibility, Blackness, and the possibilities for thinking other formations of the human, see Tiffany Lethabo King, "The Labor of (Re)reading Plantation Land-scapes Fungible(ly)," *Antipode* 48, no. 4 (2016): 1–18; C. Riley Snorton, *Black on Both Sides: A Racial History of Trans Identity* (Minneapolis: University of Minnesota Press, 2017); Alexander G. Weheliye, *Habeas Viscus: Racializing Assemblages, Biopolitics, and Black Feminist Theories of the Human* (Durham, NC: Duke University Press, 2014).

6   The novels' use of the notion of "difference" resonates with Audre Lorde's theoriza-tion of it: see Audre Lorde, *Sister Outsider: Essays and Speeches* (Freedom, CA: Cross-ing, 1984). For a recent analysis of the work performed by Lorde's conception of difference, see Grace Kyungwon Hong, *Death beyond Disavowal: The Impossible Politics of Difference* (Minneapolis: University of Minnesota Press, 2015).

7   Jared Sexton, "The *Vel* of Slavery: Tracking the Figure of the Unsovereign," *Critical Sociology* 42, nos. 4–5 (2016): 592.

8   Sexton, "The *Vel* of Slavery," 593.

9   Sexton, "The *Vel* of Slavery," 593.

10 Frank B. Wilderson III, *Red, White, and Black: Cinema and the Structure of U.S. Antago-nisms* (Durham, NC: Duke University Press, 2010), 181, 235.

11 Lilith's Blackness is not revealed to readers until about a third of the way through the first book (85). On the allusions to slavery in the trilogy, see Éva Federmayer, "Octavia Butler's Maternal Cyborgs: The Black Female World of the *Xenogenesis* Trilogy," in *The Anatomy of Science Fiction*, edited by Donald E. Morse (Newcastle, UK: Cambridge Scholars, 2006), 95–108; Christa Grewe-Volpp, "Octavia Butler and the Nature/Culture Divide: An Ecofeminist Approach to the *Xenogenesis* Tril-ogy," in *Restoring the Connection to the Natural World: Essays on the African American Environmental Imagination*, edited by Sylvia Mayer (Münster: LIT, 2003), 149–73;

Lavender, *Race in American Science Fiction*; Cathy Peppers, "Dialogic Origins and Alien Identities in Butler's *Xenogenesis*," *Science Fiction Studies* 22, no. 2 (1995): 47-62; Jeffrey Tucker, "'The Human Contradiction': Identity and/as Essence in Octavia E. Butler's *Xenogenesis* Trilogy," *Yearbook of English Studies* 37, no. 2 (2007): 164-81.

12 Hortense J. Spillers, "Mama's Baby, Papa's Maybe: An American Grammar Book" (1987), in *Black, White, and in Color: Essays on American Literature and Culture*, by Hortense J. Spillers (Chicago: University of Chicago Press, 2003), 206.

13 Weheliye, *Habeas Viscus*, 2, 4.

14 Weheliye, *Habeas Viscus*, 71.

15 Naomi Jacobs, "Posthuman Bodies and Agency in Octavia Butler's *Xenogenesis*," in *Dark Horizons: Science Fiction and the Dystopian Imagination*, edited by Raffaella Baccolini and Tom Moylan (New York: Routledge, 2003), 95-96.

16 King, "The Labor of (Re)reading Plantation Landscapes Fungible(ly)," 3-4.

17 On how Butler's framing of the drive to "difference" draws on contemporaneous work in sociobiology, particularly that of E. O. Wilson, see J. Adam Johns, "Becoming Medusa: Octavia Butler's *Lilith's Brood* and Sociobiology," *Science Fiction Studies* 37, no. 3 (2010): 382-400.

18 Gabriele Schwab, "Ethnographies of the Future: Personhood, Agency, and Power in Octavia Butler's *Xenogenesis*," in *Accelerating Possession: Global Futures of Property and Personhood*, edited by Bill Maurer and Gabrielle Schwab (New York: Columbia University Press, 2006), 214; Aparajita Nanda, "Power, Politics, and Domestic Desire in Octavia Butler's *Lilith's Brood*," *Callaloo* 36, no. 3 (2013): 774. See also Nolan Belk, "The Certainty of the Flesh: Octavia Butler's Use of the Erotic in the *Xenogenesis* Trilogy," *Utopian Studies* 19, no. 3 (2008): 369-89; Jacobs, "Posthuman Bodies and Agency in Octavia Butler's *Xenogenesis*"; Peppers, "Dialogic Origins and Alien Identities in Butler's *Xenogenesis*"; Rachel Greenwald Smith, "Ecology beyond Ecology: Life after the Accident in Octavia Butler's *Xenogenesis* Trilogy," *Modern Fiction Studies* 55, no. 3 (2009): 545-65; Tucker, "The Human Contradiction."

19 Weheliye, *Habeas Viscus*, 116.

20 Johns, "Becoming Medusa," 382. For additional discussion of the trilogy's imagination as "posthuman," see Jacobs, "Posthuman Bodies and Agency in Octavia Butler's *Xenogenesis*"; Peppers, "Dialogic Origins and Alien Identities in Butler's *Xenogenesis*." On the posthuman—or parahuman—in relation to histories of enslavement, see Monique Allewaert, *Ariel's Ecology: Plantations, Personhood, and Colonialism in the American Tropics* (Minneapolis: University of Minnesota Press, 2013).

21 Schwab uncritically signals this fusion by referring to the novels' exploration of the need for "extraterrestrial or indigenous knowledges" while also (rather disturbingly) characterizing Oankali as like Indigenous peoples in being "precapitalist" and "preindustrialized": Schwab, "Ethnographies of the Future," 208, 213-15, 225. On histories of stereotyping Native peoples, see also Philip J. Deloria, *Playing Indian* (New Haven, CT: Yale University Press, 1998); Shari M. Huhndorf, *Going Native: Indians in the American Cultural Imagination* (Ithaca, NY: Cornell University Press, 2001); Nancy Marie Mithlo, *"Our Indian Princess": Subverting the Stereotypes* (Santa Fe, NM: School for Advanced Research Press, 2008); Michelle H. Raheja, *Reservation Reelism:*

Redfacing, Visual Sovereignty, and Representations of Native Americans in Film (Lincoln: University of Nebraska Press, 2010).

22 On Oankali relations with their environment, see Grewe-Volpp, "Octavia Butler and the Nature/Culture Divide"; Schwab, "Ethnographies of the Future"; Smith, "Ecology beyond Ecology"; Mary Wallace, "Reading Octavia Butler's *Xenogenesis* after Seattle," *Contemporary Literature* 50, no. 1 (2009): 94–128.

23 Ronald Niezen, *The Origins of Indigenism: Human Rights and the Politics of Identity* (Berkeley: University of California Press, 2003), 179, 186.

24 Karen Engle, *The Elusive Promise of Indigenous Development: Rights, Culture, Strategy* (Durham, NC: Duke University Press, 2010), 169–70.

25 Elizabeth A. Povinelli, *The Empire of Love: Toward a Theory of Intimacy, Genealogy, and Carnality* (Durham, NC: Duke University Press, 2006), 183, 226.

26 On this tradition, especially as circulated through the work of Lewis Henry Morgan, see Robert E. Bieder, *Science Encounters the Indian, 1820–1880: The Early Years of American Ethnology* (Norman: University of Oklahoma Press, 1986), 194–246; Adam Kuper, *The Reinvention of Primitive Society: Transformations of a Myth* (London: Routledge, [1988] 1997); Audra Simpson, *Mohawk Interruptus: Political Life across the Borders of Settler States* (Durham, NC: Duke University Press, 2014), 67–94; Thomas R. Trautmann, *Lewis Henry Morgan and the Invention of Kinship* (Berkeley: University of California Press, 1987).

27 On versions of the "third sex" and the ways it has been employed to (mis)translate Indigenous social roles and formations, see Sabine Lang, *Men as Women, Women as Men: Changing Gender in Native American Cultures* (Austin: University of Texas Press, 1998); Scott L. Morgensen, *Spaces between Us: Queer Settler Colonialism and Indigenous Decolonization* (Minneapolis: University of Minnesota Press, 2011); Will Roscoe, *Changing Ones: Third and Fourth Genders in Native North America* (New York: St. Martin's Griffin, 1998); Evan B. Towle and Lynn M. Morgan, "Romancing the Transgender Native: Rethinking the Use of the 'Third Gender' Concept," *GLQ* 8, no. 4 (2002): 469–97.

28 On the novels' adoption of this perspective, see Johns, "Becoming Medusa"; Jim Miller, "Post-apocalyptic Hoping: Octavia Butler's Dystopian/Utopian Vision," *Science Fiction Studies* 25, no. 2 (1998): 336–60; Mary E. Papke, "Necessary Interventions in the Face of Very Curious Compulsions: Octavia Butler's Naturalist Science Fiction," *Studies in American Naturalism* 8, no. 1 (2013): 79–92; Smith, "Ecology beyond Ecology"; Hoda M. Zaki, "Utopia, Dystopia, and Ideology in the Science Fiction of Octavia Butler," *Science Fiction Studies* 17, no. 2 (1990): 239–51. In a number of interviews, Butler herself seems to endorse this reading of the trilogy. For examples, see Conseula Frances, ed., *Conversations with Octavia Butler* (Jackson: University Press of Mississippi 2010), 19, 67.

29 Michel Foucault, *The History of Sexuality, Volume 1: An Introduction*, translated by Robert Hurley (New York: Vintage, [1978] 1990), 136.

30 Michel Foucault, *Society Must Be Defended: Lectures at the Collège de France, 1975–1976*, edited by Maura Bertani and Alessandro Fontana, translated by David Macey (New York: Picador, 2003), 62.

31 On the novel's critique of Oankali discourses of disability, see Megan Obourn, "Octavia Butler's Disabled Futures," *Contemporary Literature* 54, no. 1 (2013): 109–38.

32 Alison Kafer, *Feminist, Queer, Crip* (Bloomington: Indiana University Press, 2013), 3, 27. On the ways categories of disability and racializing and imperial differentiations historically work in and through each other in the United States, see Cassandra Jackson, "Visualizing Slavery: Photography and the Disabled Subject in the Art of Carrie Mae Weems," in *Blackness and Disability: Critical Examinations and Cultural Interventions*, edited by Christopher M. Bell (East Lansing: Michigan State University Press, 2011), 31–46; Michelle Jarman, "Coming Up from Underground: Uneasy Dialogues at the Intersections of Race, Mental Illness, and Disability Studies," in Bell, *Blackness and Disability*, 9–30; Ellen Samuels, *Fantasies of Identification: Disability, Gender, Race* (New York: New York University Press, 2014); Sami Schalk, *Bodyminds Reimagined: (Dis)ability, Race, and Gender in Black Women's Speculative Fiction* (Durham, NC: Duke University Press, 2018); Siobhan Senier and Clare Barker, "Introduction," *Journal of Literary and Cultural Disability Studies* 7, no. 2 (2013): 123–40.

33 As Lisa Stevenson suggests with respect to non-Native efforts to prevent suicides by Native people, particularly Indigenous youth, it "is no longer (if it ever was) only about the person on the other end of the line. It is about enlightenment, democracy, and a new social order. . . . [T]he binary logic of a biopolitical state means that you are either part of the great stream of life or outside of it": Lisa Stevenson, *Life beside Itself: Imagining Care in the Canadian Arctic* (Oakland: University of California Press, 2014), 90, 120.

34 Simpson, *Mohawk Interruptus*, 128.

35 Simpson, *Mohawk Interruptus*, 11, 22.

36 For examples, see Jacobs, "Posthuman Bodies and Agency in Octavia Butler's *Xenogenesis*"; Obourn, "Octavia Butler's Disabled Futures"; Papke, "Necessary Interventions in the Face of Very Curious Compulsions"; Wallace, "Reading Octavia Butler's *Xenogenesis* after Seattle."

7

"I WAS NOTHING BUT A BARE SKELETON WALKING THE PATH"

Biopolitics, Geopolitics, and Life in
Diane Glancy's *Pushing the Bear*

SABINE N. MEYER

In 1999, the Choctaw historian Donna L. Akers expressed her frustration about the dearth of historiography on Indian Removal from a Native perspective and the general framing of Indian Removal by non-Native historians as an official US policy, "an official, dry, legal"—and, as I would like to add, geopolitical—"instrument" to create a coherent national territory. "The story of the American policy of Indian Removal must be reexamined and retold," she demands emphatically, with a focus on "the human suffering it caused and the thousands of lives it destroyed."[1] As a historian, Akers naturally focuses on nonfictional Removal histories in her assessment of the field. Hence, she leaves aside the growing body of fictional literature on Indian Removal that Indigenous writers have been producing to unsettle the existing historiography and revise the official narrative.

Due to the massive impact of Indian Removal on the past and present lives of many generations of Native Americans and on its legal afterlives in the courts, Native American writers have returned to the subject in their poetry, short stories, and, even more so, novels. The Trail of Tears, in particular, has become "the narrative pivot, the focal point for a description of the hardships and cruelty of settler colonial oppression," as Gregory D. Smithers has recently pointed out.[2] Notable examples of Indigenous historical Removal novels from the twentieth and twenty-first centuries are Robert J. Conley's *Mountain Windsong: A Novel of the Trail of Tears* (1992), Diane Glancy's *Pushing the Bear: A Novel of the Trail of Tears* (1996), the Afro-Native author Sharon Ewell Foster's *Abraham's Well: A Novel* (2006), and Blake Hausman's and Daniel Heath Justice's speculative Removal novels *Riding the Trail of Tears: A Novel* (2011) and *The Way of Thorn and Thunder: The Kynship Chronicles* (2013).[3] All these novels share an intense interest in framing, and critiquing, US Indian policy in the Removal era not only as a forcible appropriation of Native lands but also as a biopolitical attack on the lives of Native American individuals and collectives.

My analysis of one particular example of Native Removal literature—the Cherokee writer Diane Glancy's *Pushing the Bear*—seeks to highlight the potential of Native American literature to render Removal as one of the central "technologies of biopolitics" in ways that complicate our understanding of biopolitics.[4] Resonating with the more recent critiques of biopolitics from a settler-colonial and Indigenous studies perspective formulated by Jodi A. Byrd, Tiffany Lethabo King, Scott Morgensen, Mark Rifkin, and others (outlined more fully in the introduction to this volume), the novel pushes against the limitations of the Foucauldian and Agambenian theoretical frameworks.[5] By emphasizing Indigenous practices and forms of living and conceptualizing the world, it reveals "bare life" and "biopolitics" to be "resolutely Europe-centered visions" that require denaturalizing.[6] Written at a time when scholarly interest in Indian Removal began to grow and literature on Indigenous sovereignty and rights proliferated in various fields, Glancy's *Pushing the Bear*—along with other works of Native American Removal writing—exposes the conditions Native Americans experienced under settler colonialism, lays bare settler colonialism's bio-geopolitical logics in order to disrupt it, and thus contributes to what has been called the "reconceptualization" and "systematic decolonization of American 'history.'"[7]

Indian Removal as a Biopolitical Assault

Writing in the tradition of Native authors who also fictionalized Removal, Glancy, as she explicitly states, sets out to rewrite Indian Removal from a Cherokee perspective by re-creating the story from the historical fragments at her disposal and by mingling historical fact and fiction.[8] This method results in her reframing of Removal as a carefully instituted biopolitical assault on Native lives and bodies rather than as a contingent and misguided act of forced relocation. Placing the Trail of Tears and the massive Cherokee suffering it produced at the center of her narrative allows Glancy to emphasize settler colonialism's systematic abandonment, reduction, and destruction of Native lives.

The novel's representation of Indian Removal as a biopolitical assault already becomes evident in its epigraph: "From October 1838 through February 1839 some eleven to thirteen thousand Cherokee walked nine hundred miles in bitter cold from the southeast to Indian Territory. One fourth died or disappeared along the way." The movement of Native bodies across the vast American territory; the bitter cold, hunger, pain, and violence experienced by these bodies; and the elimination of a great number of them immediately reveal to the reader the immensity of the attack on Native lives. The verb *disappeared* serves to trigger the readerly imagination: besides evoking the physical elimination and vanishing of a people through the workings of the settler state, it also suggests their elimination from the collective national memory to "naturaliz[e] domestic space."[9]

On the next pages, the novel spells out the ways in which the settler policy of Removal reduced the Cherokees to disposable bare life that could be violated, mutilated, and killed with impunity: along the Trail of Tears, Native women are raped by soldiers; Native men are beaten when they refuse to obey the soldiers' orders and are killed in cases of outright resistance (10, 12). Besides depicting acts of violence inflicted by the American soldiers, *Pushing the Bear* represents the Trail of Tears itself as undoing the integrity of the Native body. Hence, the novel's characters complain repeatedly about a number of bodily symptoms resulting from their forced relocation across the country. Maritole states: "'There is always someplace I hurt,' I told my father as we walked. 'I scraped the skin off my fingers starting a fire this morning. The burns on my hands are still tender. I dropped a log on my foot yesterday. My head aches and my legs cramp from walking. There are always blisters and my nose is raw. My shoulders hurt from the pack of some of Mother's things I carried on my back. I'm hungry'" (93). Other bodily symptoms do not result from physical attacks or the hardships of the walk but are directly linked to the Natives' loss of personal belongings and land. As Luthy complains: "They stole our land. It was as if they cut open my chest. Took my breath" (152). And Maritole describes her reactions to losing her cabin and belongings: "I cried about the white men in our cabins. I cried for the Cherokees who had lost everything. Hiccups rocked my body. I scratched at myself with my burned hands" (16).[10]

On the one hand, these passages evoke the strong links that exist between Native individual and collective existence and their land. Losing the land, for Luthy, means losing her breath—and hence, the force that keeps her alive. Maritole's loss of "everything," including her land, translates into bodily reactions and the need to inflict bodily pain on herself. *Pushing the Bear* emphasizes that, in the context of Indian Removal, the land itself was not merely the locus where biopolitical strategies were implemented. Removal did not solely mean a dispossession of real property in the Western sense of the term. The novel suggests that the act of dispossession created, as Akers points out with respect to the Choctaw, "moral and spiritual crises" due to Natives' "deep spiritual and physical attachment" to their land. The relocated peoples "saw themselves as part of the soil, an integral part of the ecosystem, tied inextricably to this specific part of the Earth. . . . Separation from [their homelands] meant their death," at least in spiritual terms.[11] By highlighting the strong links between land loss and the loss of bodily integrity, *Pushing the Bear* emphasizes the inextricable connection between *geos* and *bios* in Indigenous cultures. It expounds that in the context of settler colonialism, geopolitics and biopolitics were intimately intertwined and operated in tandem. Removing Indigenous people(s) from their land was not merely a geopolitical measure but also a biopolitical measure; it was an attempt to disrupt Native American individuals' and collectives' complex cultural and spiritual relationships to the land and hence deprive them of a sense of self/community. In the context of US settler colonialism, biopolitics and geopolitics were mutually enabling and cannot meaningfully be distinguished from each other.

On the other hand, by relating her bodily pain to the loss of her cabin and other personal belongings—which, according to Cherokee conceptions of property, constituted her individual possessions (in opposition to the communally owned land)—Maritole draws a connection between her personal property and her sense of self.[12] In her oft-quoted contribution "Property and Personhood," Margaret Jane Radin proposes that, "to achieve proper self-development—to be a *person*, an individual needs some control over resources in the external environment."[13] Since personhood is inextricably tied to personal property (which she contrasts with purely fungible property), Radin continues, the loss—or, in the case of Removal, theft—of such personal objects occasions pain.[14] From the numerous kinds of personal property, she singles out the home as being "affirmatively part of oneself."[15] Radin's theory is, of course, based on Western ideas of personhood and property. If one takes into account, however, that long before, but at least by the time of Indian Removal, Cherokees participated in the Anglo-American capitalist economy and "recognized extensive and well-developed rights in personal property," Radin's emphasis on the significance of personal property for self-identification and self-development may be a useful interpretive avenue to Glancy's novel.[16] Maritole's sense of self is bound to her cabin and other personal belongings. By depriving her of the farm and the improvements that signify Native permanence on the land and that constitute her sense of self, the colonizers deprive Maritole of her identity. In her own view, by losing her property she has also lost personhood and what the colonizers construe as civilization. She has finally turned into the propertyless, unsettled, rootless, uncivilized "savage" of settler-colonial discourse, who, according to Western theorizations of property, could be rightfully dispossessed of her land.[17]

Glancy heightens the cataclysmic nature of Removal by using numerous homodiegetic narrators, the majority of them clearly identifiable Cherokee characters but also indistinct Cherokee "voices." By revealing these narrators' thoughts mostly through interior monologues, she provides the reader with a collage of viewpoints, experiences, and emotional responses and thus with a high degree of subjective introspection. In this polyvocal narrative, the executioners of Removal (i.e., the soldiers) also have a voice. Readers learn about "their fear and hatred of the Indians, and the sense of power from having them under arms" (42), their discussions about their violent behavior toward the Cherokees, and their debates about whether to kill them all, thereby "do[ing] the country a favor" (70). The evocative question by one soldier—"How can we push them off the end of the earth?" (79)—is posed to highlight the eliminatory intent of the Indian Removal policy. Moreover, as all their conversations imply, the soldiers act outside of what Giorgio Agamben terms "the normal juridical order."[18] Along the trail, their arbitrary subjugation and violation of Native bodies goes unpunished, with the Cherokees having been abandoned to the status of *homines sacres*, whose (bare) lives can be taken with impunity.[19] The entire trail is thus represented in the novel as a state of exception, in which bare life is produced systematically and that is "independen[t] from every judicial control and every reference to the normal judicial order." To quote Agamben: "*The camp is the space that is opened when the state of exception begins to become the rule.*"[20]

In *Pushing the Bear*, as well as in many other Native Removal writings, the camp is also represented as a concrete material and physical space in which the exception signified by the Native *homo sacer* is spatialized and becomes a "thanato-political norm."[21] Chapter 2 is the only chapter in the novel that does not carry a geographical name. It is titled "The Stockade," and the reader soon learns that "there were stockades all over the Cherokee nation. You couldn't count them on two hands" (32). An excerpt from James Mooney's ethnological studies on the Cherokees from around the turn of the twentieth century lists the great number of camps by name and emphasizes that they were built "on [the Cherokees'] own land" (34). The camps, this long list suggests, were an integral part of a systematic machinery of elimination, and the fact that this machinery was established on tribal land signifies the completeness of Cherokee degradation and dispossession. It was in the context of Removal, Glancy and other writers of Native American Removal literature suggest, that the camp emerged as a settler-colonial practice of elimination. Native American Removal literature thus reveals a blind spot in Agamben, who traces the history of the camp to the Spanish colonial efforts in Cuba in 1896 and the British conquest of the Boers at the beginning of the twentieth century and hence does not consider colonialism as a context for the emergence of biopower.[22]

The way in which Glancy describes the operation of the camp during Removal foreshadows Agamben's conceptualization of the Nazi camps as "the most absolute biopolitical space ever to have been realized, in which power confronts nothing but pure life, without any mediation."[23] Before entering the stockade, the Cherokees are dispossessed for a second time. When driven away from their homes, they were deprived of their land, cabins, and improvements. Now, at the camp, they are forced to part with everything valuable they carry with them (32). Moreover, in the camp their bodies suffer from utter deprivation due to malnutrition and cold (35, 45, 68). The only thing they have left are their bare lives, their biological existence, as Maritole's mother declares ("We have our lives" [35]). Glancy backs up her fictional account of the camp as an absolute biopolitical space by inserting a non-Native voice (also fictive)—that of the physician. He confesses to spending his days "tending measles, whooping cough, pleurisy, bilious fevers." The presence of one doctor for the several thousand Cherokees in the stockade, the physician admits, is a drop in the ocean (34). Later in the novel, Maritole adds other diseases to the doctor's list, such as "dysentery, diarrhea, fever, toothaches, gonorrhea, constipation, and frostbite." She emphasizes that the children are particularly affected: "Many children were dying of whooping cough and measles. I felt my flesh shrivel when I heard the rattle of their breath" (83). The novel's repeated emphasis on the death of Native children marks the camp as a space instituted to decimate the Cherokees' offspring and thereby bar the path to an Indigenous future.

Decimation is also achieved through the systematic exertion of sexual violence: to violate Native women's bodies, disrupt familial relations, and break the morale of both Cherokee men and women, the soldiers take Native women to the woods at night to rape them (41).

In a state of exception such as the camp, Agamben emphasizes in *Homo Sacer*, the life of the sacred man is "a threshold of indistinction." It is "the life of the *loup garou*, the werewolf, who is precisely *neither man nor beast*, and who dwells paradoxically within both while belonging to neither."[24] *Pushing the Bear* similarly represents the Native *homines sacres* walking the trail to be in a constant flux between human being and animal. When the soldiers grab Anna Sco-So-Tah, she thinks for a moment that she is a hen: "For a moment I thought I was a hen. I flopped on the ground. My brown feathers in the dust" (7). And while the novel's eponymous hero, the bear, has been interpreted in various ways (as a symbol for greed, self-centeredness, trauma, etc.), it is indisputable that the longer she walks, the more the bear becomes a part of Maritole's body and thus of herself, eating her body, stomach, and chest, finally getting down to her bones (114, 183).[25] During the Trail of Tears, Maritole reflects on the nakedness of her life and the utter subjugation of her body by the colonial power: "The cold sat upon my bones. It was as though I had no clothing. It was as though I had no skin. I was nothing but a bare skeleton walking the path. I felt anger at the soldiers. I felt anger at the people in my cabin. They were using my plates and bowls. Sleeping under my quilts! I cursed them. There was something dark and terrible in the white man" (58).[26] The "bare skeleton," deprived of property, clothing, and skin, stands for bare life itself, a life "damaged . . . , stripped of its political significance, of its specific form of life."[27] By conceptualizing Native life in the context of Indian Removal as bare life, *Pushing the Bear* establishes a genealogy of biopower that reaches back much further than either Agamben or Michel Foucault are aware of or willing to grant. Glancy's novel theorizes the state of exception with relation to Native Americans and thereby suggests that "modern biopower is the product and process of a colonial world," as Morgensen phrases it elsewhere, referencing Ann Laura Stoler's work on "the colonial order of things."[28]

Naked life, as Agamben postulates, "is a product of the [biopolitical] machine and not something that preexists it"—that is, naked life is produced by sovereign power.[29] *Pushing the Bear* similarly conceptualizes the biopolitics of Removal as the result of collaborative machinations of settler state politics and law. Throughout the novel, the various Native characters explain to one another the significant role of individual government officials (Andrew Jackson, John Schermerhorn), Georgia's extension laws, the Indian Removal Act, the Treaty of New Echota, and the Marshall Trilogy for the implementation of Removal (20–22, 41, 60, 64, 186, 224).[30] They also talk about Indian Removal's geopolitical dimensions and hence suggest that, in the context of US Indian policy, bio- and geopolitics invariably fold into each other, becoming so entangled that it is appropriate to speak of a settler-colonial biogeopolitics.

Settler-Colonial Biogeopolitics in Pushing the Bear

Pushing the Bear expounds the deep entanglement between biopolitics and geopolitics in the context of Indian Removal. Differentiating between the set- tler state's biopolitical and geopolitical measures in effecting the forced reloca- tion of Native Americans turns out to be impossible because of Indigenous understandings of land and the significant role it plays in the construction of Indigenous self- and peoplehood. It is through the act of depriving Native Americans of their land that biopolitical measures, such as the elimination of Native American individuals and peoples, become effective. As Luthy and Maritole emphasize, the loss of land causes bodily harm and often leads to the individual's spiritual, and potentially even physical, death. The intimate con- nection between geopolitics and biopolitics also becomes visible on a collective scale. While walking, Quaty Lewis, another Cherokee character in Pushing the Bear, remembers her husband saying how a whole nation was on the move (6). But looking at the Constitution of the Cherokee Nation from 1827, one real- izes that, according to tribal law, the Cherokee Nation could not have been on the move: by clearly outlining the boundaries of the nation, Article I, Sec- tion 1 of the Constitution links Cherokee nationhood "forever hereafter" to a distinct territory in the East. Thus, by depriving the Cherokees of their na- tional territory through forced relocation, the United States transforms them from a "people," as the character Chief John Ross conceptualizes the Chero- kee Nation in the novel, all united under a Constitution and a body of laws, into a landless, nationless, uncivilized agglomerate of individuals, as Maritole astutely observes (23, 201).[31] Glancy's novel thus traces how the US measures taken to create a coherent national territory lead to what Rifkin has called "the biologization of peoplehood"—to the transformation of Native peoples into populations.[32]

Pushing the Bear also makes a strong case for the intimate connection be- tween biopolitics and geopolitics by addressing, albeit very tentatively, the complex relationship between Black dehumanization and commodification and Indigenous dispossession in the context of US settler colonialism, a topic that has only very recently entered scholarly discourse.[33] Five times the novel briefly mentions the fact that some Cherokees, especially the "rich landowners," had adopted chattel slavery and took enslaved Black people with them on the Trail of Tears (46; see also 31, 47, 56, 78). Ewa Plonowska Ziarek has theorized the commonalities and differences between slavery and the *homo sacer*: "What both slavery and the *homo sacer* have in common is the production of bare life stripped of its historically specific form of life, and yet what distinguishes them is the contrast between the sovereign ban and the marginal inclusion of enslaved life. If the sovereign decision on the state of exception captures bare life in order to exclude it, the biopolitics of slavery is confronted with the profitable inclusion of socially dead beings."[34] Despite the fundamental difference between enslaved people's "liminal incorporation" and the *homo sacer*'s sovereign exclusion, enslavement, according to Ziarek, "produces another instance of bare life, violently stripped of genealogy, cultural memory, social distinction, name, and native language, that is, of all the elements of Aristotle's *bios*."[35] By embedding the reduction of Blacks to bare life by one privileged group of Cherokees in a narrative on Cherokee dispossession, *Pushing the Bear* suggests that the settler-colonial biogeopolitics of Removal and the Native engagement in a biopolitics of Black enslavement are deeply entangled. The novel's repeated emphasis on the Cherokees' attachment to their private possessions (14–15, 60–61, 72, 151)—among them their slaves—serves to unmask the colonizers' conceptualization of them as nomadic and as strangers to the idea of private property as a fabrication geared toward legitimizing dispossession and expulsion. At the same time, it gestures toward the strategies the Cherokee elite employed to avert Removal and to preserve political autonomy. By owning slaves—that is, by fashioning themselves as property-owning individuals—the novel suggests, members of this elite strive to be identified as both civilized and white. Such identification might have been viewed by leading Cherokees as a particularly efficient means to ward off Removal.

Agamben argues that "the production of bare life is the originary activity of sovereignty."[36] Seen from this theoretical angle, the Cherokee Nation's practices of enslavement can be read as an attempt to signify an "activity of sovereignty" before a colonial power intent on eroding Indigenous sovereignty. Just as the settler-colonial policy of Removal reduced Native Americans to bare life through biogeopolitics, Glancy's novel suggests, it encouraged the biopolitical production of Black bare life—socially dead beings marginally included by categorizing and listing them as the individual property of those "removed."[37] That eventually the Cherokees had to make room for a southern plantocracy—despite their attempts to assert their sovereignty, arguably in part by turning Black people into property—further speaks to the deep entanglements of geo- and biopolitics in the operations of a colonial slaveholding state. *Pushing the Bear* does not expound these entanglements in more detail. It would take another decade until the African Cherokee and African Choctaw novelists Sharon Ewell Foster and Zelda Lockhart returned to the history of Removal in their works of fiction to reflect, as Justin Leroy phrases it, "on the slippages and ambiguities" of the projects of slavery and settler colonialism, and to engage more directly with the complex linkages between US Removal policy and the production of enslaved bare life within these Native communities.[38]

The intertwining of biopolitics and geopolitics during the Removal era is also represented formally and visually in *Pushing the Bear* through the geographical structuring of the narrative as well as through the inclusion of maps at the beginning of each chapter. The novel's single chapters—titled after the states the Cherokees passed through on their forced march to Indian Territory—as well as the maps inserted underneath the single chapter headings emphasize that the Native *homines sacres* walk across a territory that has already been divided up and named and hence been taken into possession by the colonizer. On the novel's first pages, Maritole puts these settler-colonial acts of taking possession into her own words: "The white men had divided our land among their states and called most of our places by English names" (9; see also 17). The repeated appearance of state names and maps throughout the novel constantly reminds the reader that "the geopolitical project of defining the territoriality of the nation" was the underlying rationale for the biopolitical treatment of Native Americans.[39] Geopolitical objectives clearly motivated and enabled biopolitical measures, Glancy's geographic locations and cartographic visualizations suggest. It could, however, also be the other way around. By narratively depicting the Cherokees' gradual transformation from a people into a population and their reduction to bare life through the settler state's acts of violence, all the while visualizing their walk across already surveyed territory, *Pushing the Bear* demonstrates that biopolitical forms of power serve to legitimize acts of appropriation and geopolitical dominance and, as Rifkin put it, "to render national space self-evident."[40] A population deprived of their individual and collective property, the Cherokee characters are forced to live up to settler-colonial categorizations of Natives as uncivilized, savage, and illegitimate occupants—rather than as owners—of the land.[41] The racial discourse of savagery is considered by the novel's characters the key to their dispossession. Maritole states: "They called us savages. Then it was all right to drive us from our land" (112). And her husband, Knobowtee, quotes from the speech held by Wilson Lumpkin, then the US Commissioner to the Cherokees: "'*The earth was formed for cultivation and none but civilized men could cultivate it*'" (136, emphasis in original). "Savagery" was defined by the colonizer through the absence of property. The figure of the savage as construed by the American imagination and implemented by legal-political rhetoric allowed the settler nation to represent Native peoples as an exception, as anomalous populations merely with rights of occupation rather than rights to title over the land.[42]

In "Indigenizing Agamben," Rifkin criticizes Agamben's work for emphasizing the "production of race" at the expense of the "production of space."[43] While he encourages us to always think of biopolitics and geopolitics together and highlights their "dynamics," emphasizing "that the biopolitical project of defining the proper 'body' of the people is subtended by the geopolitical project of defining the territoriality of the nation," Rifkin still suggests that a distinction can be made between the former and the latter.[44] Through exposing the simultaneous workings of bio- and geopolitics, and by representing them as mutually enabling and as invariably folding into one another, Native writings on Indian Removal such as Glancy's *Pushing the Bear* call into question such distinction. In the context of the US Indian policy of Removal, geopolitics was biopolitics, and vice versa, so that it is indeed appropriate to speak of a settler-colonial biogeopolitics or geobiopolitics.

Bare Life versus Indigenous Lives

While *Pushing the Bear* frames Native life during Removal as being subject to settler-colonial biogeopolitics, the novel also introduces a second line of narration that grapples with the first. This second narrative within the narrative of Removal serves as a reflection on how Native Americans thus depoliticized and dehumanized can maintain their status as human beings and as peoples.[45] It is through this second narrative that *Pushing the Bear* advances alternative conceptions of Native existence that challenge Western conceptions of *bios* and serve to empower Native Americans to resist the biogeopolitics of the settler nation. The remaining pages of this chapter will not suffice to do justice to the complex reflections by the novel's Cherokee characters on what "life" means for them and in what way their respective ideas of life differ from categories of life in Western thought. Their considerations particularly revolve around their intimate relationship to the land as well as its flora and fauna, which is so strong that even forced relocation fails to dissolve it. Along the Trail of Tears, the Cherokee characters realize that they have interiorized the land and the animals: they have become such integral parts of the Cherokee individual and collective body and life that the settler state's acts of depoliticization and dispossession may have succeeded in creating coherent national space but have failed to oppress, if not eliminate, Indigenous modes of placemaking and collectivity (10, 95, 98, 105, 113, 179, 214).

In what follows, I limit myself to *Pushing the Bear*'s representation of language, written and oral, as a way to politicize bare life and to disrupt settler-colonial rule. Throughout the novel, the Cherokee characters reflect on the power of language. They associate written language, as used in treaties and court rulings, with treason and distortion, and consider it the agent of their dispossession.[46] The novel also directs the reader's attention to the written word's treacherous and distortive potential by placing its own account of Native physical suffering in conversation with the historical archive in the form of official documents drafted by the agents of Removal. In the proclamation by General John Wool, for instance, which Glancy inserts into her fictional account, Wool explains to the Cherokees that he has been sent by the president "to cause you by the Treaty of 1835 to join the pact [*sic*] of your people already established in prosperity on the other side of the Mississippi" and asks them to "make preparations for emigration." He then announces: "Hasten to Calhoun, where you will be received in kindness by officers selected for this purpose. You will find food, clothing, and will in comfort be transported to your new homes" (46). By presenting to the readers historical documents voicing the US government's rhetoric of paternal care alongside the account of so far largely untold Native suffering, Glancy exposes settler-colonial writings as camouflaging colonial reality and as mere instruments of colonialism.

In contrast to written language, oral language is considered by the novel's Cherokee characters to be powerful in a good way. Knobowtee contrasts spoken versus written language:

> The spoken words were the real trees. The written words were merely their reflection in the creek. I'd seen the waves as pages. Pages of written words. Distorting the real trees. That was the trouble with written words. They dealt with reflections. There was treachery in writing. The country had found it. The government had turned the written word to expediency. They had cheated with their written words. Therefore they wouldn't have the power of the spoken word to use. It would become meaningless, something that couldn't be trusted. Something that couldn't make anything happen. The trees along the creek bank would not look the same to them. They would prefer their reflection. Muddied by their feet. (228)[47]

The spoken word, the quote suggests, has great potential for the Cherokees. Stories in particular, the novel emphasizes time and again, have the power to rebuild the world, to order the disorder, and to weave back together what was unwoven (158). Stories, as the basket maker explains, hold meaning. They help the Cherokees relate themselves to the new land and to come to terms with the experience of the Trail of Tears. "The trail needs stories," he claims (153–54).[48]

Despite the tainted nature of the written word, *Pushing the Bear* makes a strong argument in favor of Indigenous writing. Such a tremendous amount of power inheres in written words, Tanner muses, that the Cherokees cannot afford not to employ them for their own benefit. He states:

> We had changed from the old ways. Even our prayer. We used to dance on the square grounds. That was our prayer. Now we used words. They had changed everything.
>
> The white man had a way with words. The men remembered the laws that came into being with words. The Cherokee couldn't mine gold on his own land. He couldn't testify against a white man in court about the continual raids on Cherokee farms. The white man even got us to agree to our own removal.
>
> We could do anything with written words. We had to be careful we didn't us them that way. Our words would turn on us. Like summer into winter. (224)

It is not surprising that as a work of Native literature, *Pushing the Bear* highlights the potential of the written word. It presents Indigenous writing as the key to countering the dehumanization and depoliticization of Native peoples. At the end of the novel, Glancy has her characters put these insights into action. Below Knobowtee's name, the reader finds a reprint of the Cherokee Act of Union between Eastern and Western Cherokees from July 12, 1839, in the preamble of which the Cherokees assert to *"have existed as a separate and distinct nation, in the possession and exercise of the essential . . . attributes of sovereignty, from a period extending into antiquity, beyond the records and memory of man."* It also emphasizes that *"these attributes, with the rights and franchises . . . remain still in full force and virtue"* and that they, *"the people"* from the Western and Eastern branches of the Cherokees, *"agree to form ourselves into one body politic, under the style and title of the Cherokee Nation"* (231–32).[49] The inclusion of this Cherokee political document in a biopolitical narrative of dehumanization and depoliticization is a powerful act of individual and collective refusal that challenges the settler state's reduction of Native peoples to "savage" populations during the trail and its conceptualization of all Native American tribal communities "which reside within the acknowledged boundaries of the United States" as "domestic dependent nations" and "wards" under the protection of the United

States.[50] Knobowtee is skeptical about the effectiveness of the Cherokee Act of Union in their contestations with the colonizers. "We're still nothing to them," he argues in council. He then adds, "But we can be a nation to ourselves" (232). *Pushing the Bear* thus emphasizes that even if this assertion of political autonomy is not recognized by the colonizer, it is significant for the Cherokees themselves, as it is a rejection of settler-colonial modes of governance and, as such, as Audra Simpson has put it, it "is an option for producing and maintaining alternative structures of thought, politics and traditions away from and in critical relationship to states."[51] Through language, written and oral, bare life can be repoliticized and rehumanized. The Act of Union (re)combines the individual voices along the Trail of Tears—the "Voices as They Walked" or "Voices in the Dark" (69, 132, 188, 189), as Glancy terms them to emphasize the settler state's biopolitical transformation of Indigenous peoples into populations—into a people who, through language, assert "a politics of sovereign living."[52] The novel thus gestures at the possibility and necessity of—to quote Glen Coulthard—"generat[ing] rehabilitated Indigenous subjectivities" and decolonizing those "forms of life that make settler-colonialism's constitutive hierarchies seem natural."[53]

While *Pushing the Bear* primarily envisions the reconstruction of a national body—the Cherokee Nation—it also takes the potential of transnational collaborations into consideration. Several times in the novel, various characters express their doubts about whether it was the right decision in 1811 not to join the Shawnee chief Tecumseh, who wanted to form an alliance with the southeastern tribes to fight against the US government. The Cherokees' decision against joining Tecumseh, these passages imply, might have been responsible for their inability to counter the settler-colonial attacks on their sovereignty and for their eventual expulsion (97, 186, 223). One should certainly not place too much evidentiary weight on these passages. However, considering that Glancy wrote her novel in the midst of the United Nations International Decade of the World's Indigenous People, which was itself the result of a Pan-Indianism that had emerged in the 1960s, and during the negotiation of the United Nations Declaration on the Rights of Indigenous Peoples, such passages might be not coincidental but, rather, expressive of a general trend toward greater transnational collaboration and self-identification of Indigenous people.[54] Thus, the novel does not merely reflect on the meaning of Native *life*; it also tentatively positions itself in favor of Indigenous *lives*—a transnational category that opens new vistas for an Indigenous disruption of settler-colonial biogeopolitical logics.

Native literature on Indian Removal serves as a critical lens through which to recalibrate this nineteenth-century US Indian policy as a conquest of

Native lands *and* bodies, to reflect on the entanglements between biopolitics and geopolitics, and to challenge and disrupt the sociolegal formations and forms of life that have become naturalized through the state's implementation of bio- and geopolitical regimes of power. By negotiating Indigenous existence under the US American settler state's biogeopolitical modes of governance, Native American Removal literature contributes to the theorization of biopower. Most significantly, it establishes a revised genealogy of biopower. In its historical recalibration, colonialism becomes an important context for the emergence of biopower. Native American Removal literature hence gestures toward the significance of scholars' returning to colonial history in their efforts to fully grasp modern state biopolitics.

Native Removal literature, as well as other works of Native American fiction engaged with colonial history, can and should therefore be considered important tools for intervening in, and recalibrating, Foucauldian and Agambenian theories of biopolitics. Grounded within Indigenous epistemologies, such texts have the capacity to make visible the Eurocentrism of these theories and their investment in, as Morgensen has so succinctly put it, "the naturalisation and continuation of settler colonialism."[55] What Byrd has stated with respect to Indigenous critical theory is also true for Native American historical fiction: "Steeped in anticolonial consciousness, [it] has the potential . . . to offer a transformative accountability" and is thus an invaluable tool for Indigenous studies scholars in their task to "deconstruct [ ] and confront [ ] the colonial logics of the settler state."[56]

As my analysis of Glancy's *Pushing the Bear* has demonstrated, Native American Removal literature can also be transformative in a different sense. Despite its focus on the intense physical and emotional suffering of its Native characters, it is deeply affirmative of Indigenous ways of being in the world. Rather than limiting itself to narrating the reduction of Native Americans to bare life, Glancy's novel, along with most other Native works on Indian Removal, is an intense reflection on the category of life itself; on the shortcomings of Western conceptions of *bios*; and on how alternative conceptions of existence can be employed, adapted, and reconfigured to cope with, if not to overcome, settler-colonial efforts to obliterate Native lands and lives. Native American Removal literature is concerned with the question of how Native collectives can define and assert their own Indigenous social, cultural, and legal-political forms of living, being, and belonging within the settler-colonial legal-political order. They go back to the past not only to reframe that past from the perspective of those silenced and obscured but also to shed light on the Indigenous present and to map out "an after to empire"—an Indigenous future.[57]

1 Donna L. Akers, "Removing the Heart of the Choctaw People: Indian Removal from a Native Perspective," in *Native Historians Write Back: Decolonizing American Indian History*, edited by Susan A. Miller and James Riding (Lubbock: Texas Tech University Press, 2011), 116.

2 Gregory D. Smithers, *The Cherokee Diaspora: An Indigenous History of Migration, Resettlement, and Identity* (New Haven, CT: Yale University Press, 2015), 249.

3 Robert J. Conley, *Mountain Windsong: A Novel of the Trail of Tears* (Norman: University of Oklahoma Press, 1992); Diane Glancy, *Pushing the Bear: A Novel of the Trail of Tears* (New York: Harcourt Brace, 1996); Sharon Ewell Foster, *Abraham's Well: A Novel* (Bloomington, MN: Bethany House, 2006); Blake Hausman, *Riding the Trail of Tears: A Novel* (Lincoln: University of Nebraska Press, 2011); Daniel Heath Justice, *The Way of Thorn and Thunder: The Kynship Chronicles* (Albuquerque: University of New Mexico Press, 2011). Writings on Indian Removal include other genres, as well. Within poetry, it extends at least from Ruth Margaret Muskrat, "The Trail of Tears," *University of Oklahoma Magazine* 10, February 1, 1922, 14, to Linda Hogan, "Trail of Tears: Our Removal," in *Dark. Sweet.: New and Selected Poems*, by Linda Hogan (New York: Coffee House, 2014), 357–59. Native family histories and autobiographical texts on Removal include Glenn J. Twist, "The Dispossession" and "The Promised Land," both in *Boston Mountain Tales: Stories from a Cherokee Family* (New York: Greenfield Review, 1997) as well as in Wilma Mankiller, *Mankiller: A Chief and Her People* (New York: St. Martin's, 1993). More recently, a number of works of Native young adult Removal fiction have been published, including Beatrice Harrell, *Longwalker's Journey* (New York: Dial Books for Young Readers, 1999), and Tim Tingle, *How I Became a Ghost: A Choctaw Trail of Tears Story* (Oklahoma City: Roadrunner, 2013). For a conceptualization and analysis of the genre of Native Removal writing in light of domestic settler-colonial, international, and tribal law, see Sabine N. Meyer, *Native Removal Writing: Narratives of Peoplehood, Law, and Politics* (Norman: University of Oklahoma Press, 2022).

4 Jodi A. Byrd, "Introduction to Indigeneity's Difference: Methodology and Structures of Sovereignty Forum," *J19* 2, no. 1 (2014): 134.

5 Jodi A. Byrd, *The Transit of Empire: Indigenous Critiques of Colonialism* (Minneapolis: University of Minnesota Press, 2011); Tiffany Lethabo King, "New World Grammars: The 'Unthought' Black Discourses of Conquest," *Theory and Event* 19, no. 4 (2016), http://muse.jhu.edu/article/633275; Scott Lauria Morgensen, "The Biopolitics of Settler Colonialism: Right Here, Right Now," *Settler Colonial Studies* 1, no. 1 (2011): 52–76; Mark Rifkin, "Indigenizing Agamben: Rethinking Sovereignty in Light of the 'Peculiar' Status of Native Peoples," *Cultural Critique* 73 (2009): 88–124.

6 Alexander G. Weheliye, *Habeas Viscus: Racializing Assemblages, Biopolitics, and Black Feminist Theories of the Human* (Durham, NC: Duke University Press, 2014), 29–30.

7 Donna L. Akers, "Decolonizing the Master Narrative: Treaties and Other American Myths," *Wicazo Sa Review* 29, no. 1 (2014): 72–73. For works from the 1990s indicating scholarly interest in Indian Removal, see, e.g., Akers, "Removing the Heart of the Choctaw People"; Theda Perdue, *Cherokee Editor: The Writings of Elias Boudinot*

(Athens: University of Georgia Press, 1996); Theda Perdue and Michael D. Green, *The Cherokee Removal: A Brief History with Documents* (Boston: Bedford, 1995). For two seminal works of the 1980s and 1990s on questions of sovereignty and Native rights, see Vine Deloria and Clifford Lytle, *The Nations Within: The Past and Future of American Indian Sovereignty* (New York: Pantheon, 1984); Robert A. Williams, *The American Indian in Western Legal Thought: The Discourses of Conquest* (Oxford: Oxford University Press, 1990).

8   For Native authors who also fictionalized Removal, see, e.g., Conley, *Mountain Windsong*; John Milton Oskison, *The Singing Bird: A Cherokee Novel*, edited by Timothy B. Powell and Melinda Smith Mullikin (Norman: University of Oklahoma Press, 2007); John Rollin Ridge, *The Life and Adventures of Joaquín Murieta: The Celebrated California Bandit* (Norman: University of Oklahoma Press, 1969). Glancy, *Pushing the Bear*, 236 (hereafter, page numbers from this work are cited in parentheses in the text).

9   Mark Rifkin, *Manifesting America: The Imperial Construction of U.S. National Space* (Oxford: Oxford University Press, 2009), 4.

10 For another example of Maritole's anger about her loss of personal property, see Glancy, *Pushing the Bear*, 14–15.

11 Akers, "Removing the Heart of the Choctaw People," 108, 110.

12 For Native conceptions of property, see Kenneth Bobroff, "Retelling Allotment: Indian Property Rights and the Myth of Common Ownership," *Vanderbilt Law Review* 54, no. 4 (2001): 1559–1623. For Cherokee conceptions of property around the time of Removal, see also Article 1, Section 2 of the Constitution of the Cherokee Nation from 1827, "Constitution of the Cherokee Nation," *Cherokee Phoenix*, February 21, 1828, 1–2, Special and Digital Collections, Hunter Library, Western Carolina University, Cullowhee, NC, https://www.wcu.edu/library/DigitalCollections/CherokeePhoenix/Vol1/no01/constitution-of-the-cherokee-nation-page-1-column-2a-page-2-column-3a.html.

13 Margaret Jane Radin, "Property and Personhood," *Stanford Law Review* 34 (1982): 957, emphasis in original.

14 Radin, "Property and Personhood," 959–60.

15 Radin, "Property and Personhood," 992, 1013.

16 Bobroff, "Retelling Allotment," 1583. Bobroff's findings are affirmed in Matthew L. M. Fletcher, *American Indian Tribal Law* (Frederick, MD: Aspen, 2011), 478.

17 Patrick Wolfe, "Settler Colonialism and the Elimination of the Native," *Journal of Genocide Research* 8, no. 4 (2006): 396. Maritole's self-identification through what she owns is presented in *Pushing the Bear* as the rule rather than as an exception in the Cherokee community. For an extensive analysis of the novel's representation, and critique, of Cherokee conceptions and practices of property, see Meyer, *Native Removal Writing*, chapter 3.

18 Giorgio Agamben, *Homo Sacer: Sovereign Power and Bare Life* (Stanford: Stanford University Press, 1998), 96.

19 Agamben, *Homo Sacer*, 47.

20 Agamben, *Homo Sacer*, 96, emphasis in original.

21 See, e.g., Conley, *Mountain Windsong*; Hausman, *Riding the Trail of Tears*; Stephen Graham Jones, *The Bird Is Gone: A Monograph Manifesto* (Tallahassee: FC2, 2003); quote from Ewa Plonowska Ziarek, "Bare Life," in *Impasses of the Post-global: Theory in the Era of Climate Change*, vol. 2., edited by Henry Sussman (Ann Arbor, MI: Open Humanities, 2012), 197.

22 Giorgio Agamben, *Means without End: Notes on Politics*, translated by Vincenzo Binetti and Cesare Casarino (Minneapolis: University of Minnesota Press, 2000) 37; Morgensen, "The Biopolitics of Settler Colonialism," 55.

23 Agamben, *Homo Sacer*, 97.

24 Agamben, *Homo Sacer*, 63, emphasis in original.

25 Agamben's theory is highly anthropocentric and speciesist, hierarchizing all life-forms and placing humans at the top. Citing Aristotle, Agamben reiterates that only humans can live a "politically qualified life" that differs from "the simple fact of living," which he attributes to all other life forms: Agamben, *Homo Sacer*, 9. Native modes of living reject such an anthropocentric understanding of the world, emphasizing instead the connectedness of all life-forms and their nonhierarchical engagement with one another. Hence, one could also interpret the quoted passages as a challenge to non-Native ways of knowing and ordering the world, or, as René Dietrich has phrased it, as a rejection of "settler fantasies of naturalized hierarchies and a naturalized politics of hierarchization": René Dietrich, "The Biopolitical Logics of Settler Colonialism and Disruptive Relationality," *Cultural Studies ↔ Critical Methodologies* 17, no. 1 (2017): 9.

26 See also Tanner talking about the Cherokees' nakedness without their farms and council fires (181).

27 Ziarek, "Bare Life," 195.

28 Morgensen, "The Biopolitics of Settler Colonialism," 55; Ann Laura Stoler, *Race and the Education of Desire: Foucault's History of Sexuality and the Colonial Order of Things* (Durham, NC: Duke University Press, 1995); see also Byrd, *The Transit of Empire*, 191.

29 Giorgio Agamben, *State of Exception*, translated by Kevin Attell (Chicago: University of Chicago Press, 2005), 87–88.

30 The Marshall Trilogy remains the Removal era's most significant and far-reaching set of rulings, determining the geographical, political, and legal contours of Native America until the present day. In *Johnson v. M'Intosh* (1823), *Cherokee Nation v. Georgia* (1831), and *Worcester v. Georgia* (1832), the Supreme Court, headed by Chief Justice John Marshall, defined forms of Indigenous belonging, including the legal status of Native American collectives and their property rights (Meyer, *Native Removal Writing*, 28–43).

31 "Constitution of the Cherokee Nation"; see Rifkin, "Indigenizing Agamben," 99. The Cherokee characters in the novel seek to counter such settler-colonial efforts at depoliticization by determining to keep both their constitution and their laws on the trail and in the new territory (63). Historical sources also reveal the Cherokees' efforts to maintain nationhood. As one of its last acts before being forcibly relocated, the Cherokee National Council passed a resolution declaring the tribal government to be transferred intact to the new homeland. It thus sought to ensure the re-creation of the Cherokee Nation in the West according to the legal and political

structures established in the East: Andrew Denson, *Demanding the Cherokee Nation: Indian Autonomy and American Culture, 1830–1900* (Lincoln: University of Nebraska Press, 2004), 41.

32 Mark Rifkin, "Making Peoples into Populations: The Racial Limits of Tribal Sovereignty," in *Theorizing Native Studies*, edited by Audra Simpson and Andrea Smith (Durham, NC: Duke University Press, 2014), 152, 155.

33 Within the past two decades, the scholarship on the history of African-Native relations—in particular, on the question of practices of enslavement among the Cherokees, Seminoles, Creek, Choctaw, and Chickasaw—has proliferated. See, e.g., David A. Chang, *Race, Nation, and the Politics of Land Ownership in Oklahoma, 1832–1929* (Chapel Hill: University of North Carolina Press, 2010); Barbara Krauthamer, *Black Slaves, Indian Masters: Slavery, Emancipation, and Citizenship in the Native American South* (Chapel Hill: University North Carolina Press, 2013); Tiya Miles, *Ties That Bind: The Story of an Afro-Cherokee Family in Slavery and Freedom* (Berkeley: University of California Press, 2005); Claudio Saunt, *Black, White, and Indian: Race and the Unmaking of an American Family* (Oxford: Oxford University Press, 2005). Justin Leroy encourages scholars of Indigenous and Black studies to explore the tangled terrain of slavery and settler colonialism: see Justin Leroy, "Black History in Occupied Territory: On the Entanglements of Slavery and Settler Colonialism," *Theory and Event* 19, no. 4 (2016), https://muse.jhu.edu/article/633276. For a similar argument, see King, "New World Grammars"; and Tiffany Lethabo King, *Black Shoals: Offshore Formations of Black and Native Studies* (Durham, NC: Duke University Press, 2019).

34 Ziarek, "Bare Life," 202.

35 The idea of "liminal incorporation" is taken from Orlando Patterson, *Slavery and Social Death: A Comparative Study* (Cambridge, MA: Harvard University Press, 1982), 45; Ziarek, "Bare Life," 200–201.

36 Agamben, *Homo Sacer*, 53.

37 See, e.g., the historical property list of Chief John Ross that Glancy inserts in the novel; the list includes four "Negro houses" and their value. As Glancy indicates in a footnote, the property lists are taken from the Cherokee Register of Valuations that is part of the Records of the Bureau of Indian Affairs housed in the National Archives in Washington, DC (78).

38 Foster, *Abraham's Well*; Leroy, "Black History in Occupied Territory"; Zelda Lockhart, *Cold Running Creek* (Hillsborough, NC: LaVenson, 2007). For a theorization and analysis of the inextricable connection between Black enslavement and Native dispossession in Native Removal fiction, see Meyer, *Native Removal Writing*, chapter 4.

39 Rifkin, "Indigenizing Agamben," 94.

40 Rifkin, "Making Peoples into Populations," 158.

41 "Discovery," as Chief Justice John Marshall argued in *Johnson v. M'Intosh*, 21 US 543 (1823), "gave title to the government by whose subjects or by whose authority it was made against all other European governments, which title might be consummated by possession." The power of settlers, as well as their acts of consummating possession, are also felt by the Cherokees during their march when even in the far west they encounter white settlements, markers, churches, and fences. Looking at the

farms along the trail, Knobowtee realizes: "They would even come to Indian Territory. Push the Cherokees over there, too. It would only be a matter of time" (221).

42 Brenna Bhandar, "Title by Registration: Instituting Modern Property Law and Creating Racial Value in the Settler Colony," *Journal of Law and Society* 42, no. 2 (2015): 266, 274–75; Rifkin, "Indigenizing Agamben," 98.

43 Rifkin, "Indigenizing Agamben," 90.

44 Rifkin, "Indigenizing Agamben," 94–95.

45 Agamben, *Homo Sacer*, 12.

46 See the debates about the Marshall Trilogy and treaties (20–21, 121, 224).

47 Knobowtee, in another passage, states that "writing was the beginning of our end" (224).

48 The novel also emphasizes the significance of the Cherokee language: Luthy's telling of a story both in Cherokee and in English because translation is not able to capture all of its facets (194–95). Glancy's use of written Cherokee language throughout the novel similarly points to the significance of the Cherokee language and the limits of translation (239).

49 Emphasis in original. As it appears in the novel, the Act of Union is not simply a written document. Its placement underneath the caption "Knobowtee" is to suggest that the act is thought of or orally recited by Knobowtee. It thus works at the intersection of orality and writing—it combines the power of the spoken word with that of written word.

50 *Cherokee Nation v. Georgia*, 30 US (5 Pet.) 1 (1831), https://supreme.justia.com/cases/federal/us/30/1/case.html.

51 Audra Simpson, "The Ruse of Consent and the Anatomy of 'Refusal': Cases from Indigenous North America and Australia," *Postcolonial Studies* 20, no. 1 (2017): 2.

52 René Dietrich, "Biopolitics and Indigenous Literary Studies: Settler Colonial Hierarchies, Relational Lives, and the Political Potential of Native Writing in N. Scott Momaday's *The Way to Rainy Mountain*," in *Comparative Indigenous Studies*, edited by Mita Banerjee (Heidelberg: Winter, 2016), 8.

53 Glen Coulthard, *Red Skin, White Masks: Rejecting the Colonial Politics of Recognition* (Minneapolis: University of Minnesota Press, 2014), 109, 152.

54 Ronald Niezen, *The Origins of Indigenism: Human Rights and the Politics of Identity* (Berkeley: University of California Press, [2003] 2010), 24, 42.

55 Morgensen, "The Biopolitics of Settler Colonialism," 70.

56 Byrd, *The Transit of Empire*, xxix–xxx.

57 Byrd, *The Transit of Empire*, 229.

8

UNSEEN WONDER

Decolonizing Magical Realism in Kim Scott's
Benang and Witi Ihimaera's "Maata"

MICHAEL R. GRIFFITHS

Red Shoes and Floating Archons

He floats over the papers of the Native Affairs report, suspended in an uncanny act of levitation above the archive of his family's colonial subordination. Stolen, removed, an Aboriginal child, a Noongar child taken from family and kin, he begins life in a world ungrounded. Scholars have argued that, in Kim Scott's novel *Benang: From the Heart* (1999), a form of magical realism narrates the protagonist Harley's levitation as he undertakes research into family history.[1] These scraps of paper that make up his archive—Native Affairs dispatches, photographs, and telegrams—are technologies of settler-colonial biopower that describe an identity to be undone.[2] As Harley narrates matters, this archive is "mine and my grandfather's skin, my only kin, these pieces of paper."[3] Yet two opposed causes of "magic" emerge in the text: colonial biopower with such innumerable "pieces of paper" and Noongar storytelling with its association with grounding and earth.[4] The archival obsession that indexes colonial biopower causes Harley's levitation; it is for this reason that Harley's Noongar uncles Jack Chatalong and Will Coolman must produce a grounded storytelling. What springs forth in *Benang*, then, can be read as quite a peculiar form of magical realism—if it is indeed that. In this space, I suggest that the word *magic* operates relationally, between the legacy of colonial power and the desire for survivance.[5]

In a comparable vein to *Benang*, Witi Ihimaera's novella "Maata" (1989) describes a Māori journalist's vision of a mysterious woman's red shoes, the truth of which emerges only through a telepathic communication with their eventual owner at the text's denouement. The mysterious woman is a vision of Maata, a Māori woman of great status and power. Maata, little known to modernist readers, has in literary history been the silenced voice beside the Pakeha (European) New Zealand writer Katherine Mansfield, her friend in adolescence. In the geopolitics of postcolonial literature, Mansfield has always been explained as the figure of the oppressed Antipodean, an outsider to London literary society. Virginia Woolf excused herself for "despis[ing]" Mansfield "as a colonial" by referring to her uncouth impropriety; to Woolf, Mansfield "stank like a civet cat that had/taken to street-walking."[6] However anxious and colonially inflected this resentment of "the only writing I was ever jealous of" may be, nonetheless, such a geopolitics of center and periphery abandons Maata, forgetting the relation between Indigenous agents that can reconstitute the fabulation of the literary modernist archive through trans-Indigenous practices of reading and relation. Within studies of magical realism, "magic" is often an othering device for that which is not conceivable by Western empiricism. This essay seeks to show how the reduction of Indigenous practice—say, Noongar belief in *boodja/* Country or Kaupapa Māori—to "magic" by modernity and colonialism is deconstructed in *Benang* and in "Maata."[7] Through this deconstruction, these texts show Western empiricism and Indigenous knowledge to be contrasting relational modes of observation and thinking that cannot be positioned in an epistemic hierarchy, the one over the other.

There remains a trans-Indigenous and trans-temporal production of knowledge that is invisible to the center-periphery distinction, wherein Auckland-London (say) relations constitute the geopolitics of the transnational, as it did with Woolf and Mansfield.[8] This subversion of center and periphery emerges through a recursive narrative evocation of *whakapapa* in Mahaki's story. Through a gradual return to the performance of genealogical recitation, Mahaki learns through the course of the novella that his journalistic training—an empiricist mode—must be complemented by an embrace of such Māori practices as *whakapapa* for him to truly uncover the secret history of Maata and the meaning of his encounter with her red shoes.

Homi Bhabha notably baptized magical realism "the literary language of the emergent postcolonial world."[9] But what of the texts that come from the figurative archipelago of settler colonies—from Indigenous cultural contexts and not from the "emergent postcolonial" world? What does the magical narration look like when it comes from peoples still living under settler-colonial occupation?[10] How does this awareness of ongoing occupation intensify a pervasive sense of colonial biopolitics and the peculiar force—or, indeed, "magic"—embedded in its archives? In this essay, I suggest a trans-Indigenous reading of magical realism as a concept under erasure (*sous rature*) when it is undertaken by Indigenous writers from the Fourth World.[11] By positioning such a genre as magical realism under erasure I mean to evolve a reading strategy that makes itself available by what has been said about magical realism in the colonized world but in such a way as to gradually dispose of this reading strategy. By unpicking the inherent hierarchies in the notion of magical realism I hope to restore epistemologies of Indigenous-colonial relationality and ultimately to exalt the Indigenous epistemologies through which these texts position themselves. For Chadwick Allen, such trans-Indigenous reading involves "staging purposeful Indigenous juxtapositions" to locate analysis "in the specificity of the Indigenous local while always remaining cognizant of the relevant Indigenous global."[12] I focus on the Noongar writer Scott's *Benang* and the Māori writer Ihimaera's "Maata" as a trans-Indigenous conjugation in part either because they have been explicitly named magical realist by extant criticism (in the case of *Benang*) or because the one ("Maata") is comparable to the other and can do some work of comparative analysis by being placed adjacent to the former. In doing so, I want to take some first steps in providing an alternative to the reception of the magical realist canon from Gabriel García Márquez through Salman Rushdie to Ben Okri, not by simply denying the salience of this generic category but by showing the limits of its application. Indeed, where magical realism is seen as a unifiable world genre, connected by genealogies and anxieties of literary influence, Indigenous representations of what exceeds the norm can provide pause to too ready generic categorization.

Daniel Heath Justice has recently provided a succinct yet comprehensive set of caveats to the application of labels such as "speculative," "fantasy," and "magical (realist)" as they are applied to Indigenous fiction while not foreclosing the stories and novels that are sometimes (mistakenly) read in these ways. He suggests:

For secular, post-Enlightenment readers of the industrialized West, the very ideas of spirit beings and little people, individualized and speaking animals, stones and plants with powers to shape the reality around them and motivations of their own, human actions changing weather and affecting various elemental forces, and other worlds of being and kinship with the other-than-human peoples, are the stuff of childish make-believe or even pathology, not generally understood as the mature, experimental realities they are in most traditional Indigenous systems. . . . Even the category of "magical realism" fails to fully meet this challenge, given its basic assumptions about the ultimate artificiality of the "magic" part of the definition.[13]

Instead, Justice offers the notion of "wonderworks" as an alternative to the hegemonic transnational category of magical realism. As he describes it, "Etymologically 'wonder' is of uncertain origin, but always keeps astonishment, admiration, and even a bit of mindful fear at its core. Wondrous things are *other* and *otherwise*. . . . Wonderworks, then, are those works of art—literary, filmic, etc.—that center this possibility within Indigenous values and towards Indigenous, decolonial purposes."[14] Thus, for Justice wonderworks tell narratives of "spirit beings and little people" emergent from the specific Indigenous cultural context from which they arise not through a dismissive form of the otherwise but, rather, through a reverent one. Wonderworks, Justice says, "insist on difference not as deficiency but as *distinction*."[15]

If a recourse to representing the so-called magical as paradoxically continuous with the empirical subsists in Fourth World texts—including not only *Benang* and "Maata" but also, for instance, Tomson Highway's *Kiss of the Fur Queen* and James Welch's *Fools Crow* (texts that similarly invest in the relation with both Indigenous belief and modes of colonial power)—then this recourse may tell us more about wonder as a category than the paradox it appears (to Western readers) to, at first, offer. Such wonderworks can be said to tell us more about empiricism as it operates in settler-colonial space than about historical realism, more about the nature of colonial enchantment than the consideration of literary self-consciousness that has pervaded much criticism, and all because each of these wonderworks opens a pathway between competing ideas about the empirical and the real. *Benang* and "Maata," enact what Scott calls "the most local of histories" (10). I take this invocation of the local to mean, in part, the way global and national forms of biopolitical power are localized and experienced by the colonized subjects who find themselves its objects of intervention. Scott's and Ihimaera's texts are perhaps peculiar as Indigenous wonderworks in that they find unseen forces emerging not only in Indigenous culture (though they do find them there) but also in the colonial-Indigenous relation. In both texts, the "magical" tropes are, to varying degrees, not simply a reproduction of Noongar or Māori cultural apparel in isolation. The grounding of Scott's Harley through Noongar kinship and story or the presence of Maata's red shoes are produced through Noongar culture and Kaupapa Māori, respectively. Similarly, in both texts emphasis is given to the modes of settler-colonial archiving by which Indigenous difference is indexed and targeted even as settler-colonial modes of knowledge must be overcome in the texts (and more widely) to recenter the restorative power of Indigenous knowledge. In this essay, I remain with the concept of magic to erase it in favor of wonder. I do so because each of the texts I am working with proffer a fictional magic arising from the archive of colonial biopolitics that, in each case, has to be healed by Noongar or Kaupapa Māori wonder—whether through reverence for and grounding in *boodja* or through the practice of *whakapapa*.

In the pharmakon of coloniality, archives untether the subject from Indigenous conceptions of groundedness in land and kin—particularly here, the Noongar concept *boodja* (meaning "Country" or land) and the Māori concept of *whenua* (meaning "land" but also connection to kin through literal and symbolic connection mediated by the placenta). Scott and Ihimaera underscore the archive's reduction of Indigenous knowledge in many receptions to simply "the archaic itself [as] a function of the new" (in Theodor Adorno's words).[16] Adorno, here writing to Walter Benjamin, designated the way, as Michael Taussig puts it, "the surfacing of 'the primitive' within modernity [is] a direct result of modernity, especially of its everyday rhythms of montage and shock."[17] This is to say that the rendering of wonder as "magic" is a result of the misapprehension of colonial modernities. And, I would add, the complex workings of modernity's archives on bodies condition how colonized peoples can intervene in, appropriate, and redeploy such modes of power as practices of decolonization. If we read *modernity* here not only as colonial but also as Indigenous modernity, then a whole dialectical inversion of settler logics is sublated by Indigenous presencing. To recognize how, as Taussig puts it, "alterity is every inch a relationship, not a thing in itself," is not to deny the moral force of Indigenous autonomy and resistance but to accept that settler-colonial interventions in "alterity" or "the primitive," which anthropology and colonial policing undertake, are interventions that invent and then target a false but forceful discursive thing.[18] This recognition of relation is not, I insist, a dismissal of the salient autonomy of Indigenous culture, but it does foreground how Indigenous culture, from the moment of contact, exists in a dynamic interplay with the colonial culture. What Marcia Langton calls "Aboriginality" is, she argues, a "social thing" in Émile Durkheim's sense, produced in discursive relations between colonizing and colonized social positions.[19] Taking modernity for coloniality *as* modernity subordinates an Indigenous modernity, reducing it to a social thing that becomes, at turns, unseen and forceful. This social thing does not encapsulate Indigeneity—far from it! Rather, Indigenous modernity emerges to the settler reader at the level of a reception that always withholds—a re-presencing that always insists on tactical rights to refusal.[20]

The Unseen

It is commonly accepted that one key characteristic of magical realism is that it is structured, as Wendy Faris has it, around "an irreducible element of magic" constituted by "something we cannot explain according to the laws of the universe as they have been formulated in Western empirically based discourse."[21] However, one immediate question that is raised in this definition is the mode by which this other order—this "irreducible element"—is distinct from such empirical discourse. How is magic an other of empirical modernity? Rather, is "magic" not simply a name for another order of empirical practice or perception? The designation "magic," then, becomes a way of othering a relation to the sensible and knowable, or their invisible inversions—to the wondrous; to turn a different way of seeing into one with, as Justice had it, a deficit. I wish to put pressure on this assertion by suggesting that what is called magic may be distinct from Western empiricism in appearance but is also, ironically, affected by its relation to the normative epistemology that privileges such empiricism. For Brenda Cooper, "The relationship between the magical and the scientific . . . is the narrative space where the educated writer's simultaneous ironic distance from, and acceptance of, pre-scientific worldviews negotiate the magical realist stance."[22] I depart from Cooper insofar as the "archaic is a function of the new" and submit that the so-called prescientific worldviews represented in Indigenous wonderworks that are mislabeled magical realist are not simply the organic cultural paradigms of the premodern but something else. Rather than simply the return of the precolonial, magical realist engagements from the Fourth World often engage the Indigenous presencing of an alternative modernity precisely by drawing on and exceeding the distinction between the putatively premodern and the ostensibly modern. Liam Connell has suggested that magical realism is not generically distinct from modernism even as it is often distinguished purely on the basis of anthropological and cultural difference.[23] According to the common sense rightly critiqued by Connell, the "premodern" is vested in the magical while European modernism experiments with psychological modes of alterity that do not invest in their onto-logical points of emergence. This is a significant problem, though noting such binary division introduces further difficulties. Connell himself perceives the difficulty with reconciling this problem by annexing magical realism to mod-ernism when he suggests:

> While it is fair to say that the writers who are categorized as Magic Real-ists are writing forms of Modernism, this assertion is potentially reduc-tive, suggesting once again that they are simply reinscribing pre-existing Western forms. In no way am I proposing that they are only re-working the prior literary project of European writers. What I am suggesting, as a response to Jameson's proposition that "magic realism depends on a con-tent which betrays the overlap or the coexistence of precapitalist with nascent capitalist or technological features," is that we are dealing, in both cases, with attempts to negotiate rapid modernization.[24]

I don't, I submit, think we gain much (or, perhaps, enough) by insisting on modernization as the common factor between so-called magical realist texts (when they are, in fact, Indigenous wonderworks) and modernist works except insofar as it may, indeed, be highly useful to retain the notion of Indigenous temporality as thoroughly modern in its own right. I would assert instead that wonderworks labeled magical realist, in taking seriously what is normally dis-missed as an "other" system of belief and practice, invest not only in Indigenous belief systems but also in the conflict that arises between these belief systems and colonial modernity's own forms of mimesis, which themselves could be seen to be the source of magic. In this relation, colonial biopower is not simply a trace or vestige but an ongoing imposition.[25] Nor, however, can colonial biopower and its transgenerational inheritances be parsed simply as "modernization." Rather, a more nuanced reading of modernity might be useful here—one that, as a be-ginning condition, does not conflate modernity and modernization with the coming of European technology, epistemology and the colonial projects that bear them. In *Benang* in particular, a dialectical gesture foregrounds conflict between Indigenous modernity grounded in technologies of kin and Country, on the one hand, and colonial modernity's archival drive, on the other. The fact that colonial modernity seeks to represent and eliminate Indigenous pres-ence reveals the perverse dimension of its biopolitical taxonomies.

The birth of an ostensibly disenchanted colonial modernity relies on the othering of the unseen. By *unseen*, I mean that which is literally or symbolically invisible, that which cannot be rendered meaningfully visible within Western empiricism because it defies the causal logic that undergirds that system's modes of verification. The excess produced by this disenchantment I read as the production of an othered figure named "magic" by representatives of colonial comparison, from Marcel Mauss onward.[26] In this way, what is labeled "magic" is dialectically produced as the other of empirical science. Thus, what comes to be called the "magic" of magical realism in Western logics of reception covers over the unseen presencing of Indigenous knowledge. Adorno is aware of this when he writes, "I have come to realize that just as the modern is the most ancient, so too the archaic itself is a function of the new: it is thus first produced historically as the archaic, and to that extent is dialectical in character and not 'pre-historical,' but rather the exact opposite."[27] This dialectical sense of colonial modernity's relation to structures of knowing that it reproduces as "archaic" functions as a better mode of beginning if we are to understand Ihimaera and Scott's re-presencing of Indigenous knowledge within prose.

Sympathetic magic was defined by J. G. Frazer at the end of the nineteenth century as fomented by contact between the body of the shaman and the person to be affected. But what if such magic involved the recursive knowledge of shamans and not their credulity? What if the shaman, too, is an empiricist? If sympathetic magic (for instance) is, itself, a form of empiricism, then its labeling as archaic supernatural magic is a mode of othering that would seek to hierarchize forms of empirical investigation on the basis of their cultural position.[28] Systems of empirical observation that situate cause and effect—for instance, when vested in forms of kin-based genealogical relation, as in Kaupapa Māori practices such as *whakapapa*—often function as means to explain unseen phenomena. Yet these systems of knowledge frequently have been not only dialectically related in an open exchange of alterities but also hierarchized according to race. As Christopher Bracken notes, "For centuries, but with particular intensity in the later nineteenth century, scholars in the so-called Western tradition have taken it for granted that some concepts are not just culturally but *racially* superior to others. . . . [A] difference between races was projected onto an enduring scholarly debate about the relation between signs and things."[29] In a minimal way, some such attempts to taxonomize magical realism as a genre have, at times, risked smuggling back this hierarchical (if not explicitly racialized) distinction between ideas of connection and disconnection between signs and things.

Within magical realism scholarship, investment in modes of knowing that accept that which cannot be seen or measured via Enlightenment accounts of the relation of signs and things has seen problematic ascriptions of indulgence in the exoticization of alterity even in its literary, secular reception. Jean Franco has labeled magical realism "little more than a brand name for exoticism."[30] Maria

Takolander, following Amaryll Beatrice Chanady, worries that "its mobilisation for ex-centric identity politics" means that its "hybrid worldview simultaneously transgresses and supplements Western ratiocinative epistemologies."[31] Christopher Warnes negotiates between diverging modes of engaging the magic of magical realism. He identifies two modes of doing so, one he calls "anthropological (in the broad sense of the term)," which "seeks to interpret the magic in magical realism culturally, as a particular belief system or way of seeing the world."[32] The other "sees magical realism as akin to a form of epistemological scepticism, a productive fictional mode of critique."[33] Warnes provides perhaps the most rigorous account of what Bhabha called the "literary language of the postcolonial world," even, I argue, as his taxonomy nonetheless risks smuggling back the risk of hierarchizing worldviews.

Warnes argues that what makes a text, in broad terms, classifiable as magical realist is "that each treats the supernatural as if it were a perfectly acceptable and understandable aspect of everyday life."[34] While Warnes distinguishes between the "anthropological" and "skeptical" modes of magical realism, he also aims to bring them together precisely to reintroduce an ostensibly more effective form of what emerges as an equivalent distinction. Drawing on Stanley Tambiah's adaptation of the anthropology of Lucien Lévy-Bruhl, Warnes describes two attitudes to empiricism. In one such view, a "mystic" mentality (Lévy-Bruhl's term) undergirds the naturalization of the "supernatural" in the practice of magic and in magical realism more particularly. This mysticism is vested in "a belief in forces and influences and actions which, though imperceptible to sense, are nevertheless real."[35]

Following Tambiah and Lévy-Bruhl, Warnes distinguishes "two modes of ordering the world": "causality" and "participation." In so doing, he produces a novel taxonomy of magical realism.[36] Aligned with empirical science, causality, for Tambiah (and for Warnes), denotes "the paradigm of evolution in space and time" and the "successive fragmentation of phenomena" in "the construction of scientific knowledge."[37] However, participation is defined by the consensual, social practice of and assent to shared beliefs involving "the language of solidarity, unity, holism and continuity in space and time," and "intersubjective understandings, the telling of myths and the enactment of rituals."[38] Both causality and participation emerge, in Warnes's account of Tambiah's anthropology, as distinct modes of empirical investigation. Initially, they are not hierarchized. Warnes writes, "Magical realism may represent an attempt to supplement, extend or overwhelm causality with the terms of participation."[39] Further, he rightly notes that causality has been "tainted by association with colonialism and neo-colonialism."[40] Nonetheless, I would insist that Warnes's taxonomy risks reinscribing a binary division between Western ideas of "causality" and non-Western modes of "participation" when, instead, a recourse to relation and dialectical interplay better describes the pervasively intertwined conflict of these epistemic modes.

What, then, if magic (and therefore magical realism) is not "hybrid," as Takolander and many others would put it, or subject to a segregated binary, as Warnes risks depicting it, but, instead, following Adorno and Bracken, something that emerges from the dialectic between worlds—an excess produced by the tense desire to both other and name modes of empiricism that do not conform to "causality"? What if the distinction between causality and participation is, in fact, a particular conjuring of the relation between signs and things and, therefore, a form of participation? What if we emphasized the intersubjective consensus that conditions both causality and participation rather than pragmatically privileging scientific empiricism vested in causality? This would not be to deny the pragmatic import of each form of knowledge; instead, it would be an acknowledgment of the shared role of practice and community across both modes of empiricism, each of which, arguably, makes participatory ritual functional in a different but comparable way to causally focused forms of investigation.

Warnes himself seems to recognize as much when he notes that an irreverent form of magical realism insists that "the truth claims of causality are seen as contingent on consensus, founded in language, and driven by discourse about reality rather than reality itself."[41] Nonetheless, the hardening of the distinction between causality and participation risks occluding the relation between cultures, which characterizes both a dialectics of coloniality and the drive of Indigenous peoples toward decolonization. When compared across two modes of wonder, such as those that become apparent in the Noongar-Māori conjugation that proceeds in this essay, this comparison reveals how Indigenous writers and storytellers produce modes of presencing that exceed center-peripheral relations, producing temporal and recursive accounts of returning and remaining on the land that can be further understood when compared with one another. This does not mean that they do not also deconstruct the colonial archive, but it does mean that such recursive accounts of remaining are more concerned with returning presence than with critiquing the colonizer alone.

The Factish

The drive to mimesis and mimicry is present in both the sympathetic magic of the so-called primitive and the empirical systems that Western modernity establishes to ostensibly capture, catalogue, and describe it. As Taussig puts it, "Mimicry corrodes the alterity by which [anthropological] science is nourished."[42] Similarly, Bruno Latour has shown that the logic of the fetish—that which is made and constructed even as it holds mimetic power on which the maker depends—traverses the arbitrary divide between modern and ancient, science and Indigenous knowledge, Western and non-Western.[43] For Latour, there is a false separation between non-Western modes of fetish making and Western empirical practices of fact making: "Thanks to the fetish, in a single wave of a magic wand, its creator can turn himself from a cynical manipulator into an ingenious dupe. Thus, even though the fetish is nothing but what a human makes of it, it nevertheless adds a little something: it invents the origin of the action, it dissimulates the human work of manipulation, and it transforms a creator into a creature."[44] Thus, Latour coins the term *factish* (*fétiche*), a portmanteau in English derived from a French pun on the word for make/made and from the word for fetish itself. Isabelle Stengers succinctly designates factishes as "those beings we fabricate and that fabricate us."[45] The idea of the factish serves to designate the way, under modernity, transcendent facts are derived from constructions that are made under particular conditions. Many foundational facts in Western science possess quite an affinity with fetishes in, so-called archaic society—at least insofar as they craft intersubjective participatory communities.

For Stengers, this proceeds even to the hard sciences. The inevitability that, in quantum physics, the neutrino is observed under experimental conditions even as its truth claims are understood as transcendent means that the neutrino—as a factish—does not inhabit a substantively different order of participation from, say, a fetish arising in a so-called archaic society, designed to assist in functional and symbolic tasks. As Stengers puts it: "It is not fetishistic belief that needs to be defended, but rather a 'cult of fetishes' in all their diversity, modern and nonmodern. . . . [T]he beings fabricated by physics may nonetheless be referred to as 'real,' endowed, no matter that they are 'fabricated,' with an autonomous existence: 'factishes,' as Latour calls them."[46] Latour and Stengers, then, aim to overturn a peculiar hierarchization of factishes in an economy of distinct entities. Archaic fetishes are not designated as lesser because they are less effective than the facts of the Western scientific laboratory. Indeed, in certain located contexts, their efficacy might be pragmatically superior. Rather, the construction of certain kinds of modern *factish* as *fact* depends on the designation of Indigenous practices of wonder and story making as a difference with a deficit (as Justice had it), as primitive, other, or archaic— as Bracken had it, "a difference between races . . . projected onto an enduring scholarly debate about the relation between signs and things."[47] This is, at least in part, what is meant in Adorno's pithy formula, "The archaic itself is a function of the new." What I mean by "the unseen," then, resists the arbitrary and hierarchical distinction—based on ethnic and cultural difference—between ritual, participatory practices derived from or deriving factishes, and scientific fact. Whether in the observation of the neutrino, the practice of *whakapapa*, or the knowing of *boodja* (Country) through story, aspects of the process of deriving knowledge engage with something unseen and postulate transcendent intersubjective facts about it. Similarly, each allows the practitioner—scientist or clever person—to *do* things with this unseen product of knowledge. Magical realism in the texts of Scott and Ihimaera problematizes this gap not only by revealing the truth of Indigenous belief (though the texts do so at key moments) but also by showing how colonial biopolitics produces perverse, participatory beliefs in hierarchy and difference that—however false in their racially derived thinking—*work* to produce traumatic effects in Indigenous lives. Indigenous modes of empirical knowledge are revealed to be equivalent ways of understanding the facts of self, kin and genealogy as lived experiences connecting past and present. In such magical realist texts as *Benang* and "Maata," Indigenous knowledge, then, is not only employed to resist colonialism (though it is). It also rescripts a false image of the "primitive."

In *Benang* and "Maata," Scott and Ihimaera differently insist on the force of the modernity and biopower as producing its own form of magic—or perhaps, better, of factish—derived from its practices of surveilling and ordering. What each text differently narrates (among much else) is how Harley and Mahaki have to locate themselves in a participatory Indigenous knowledge system—a form of wonder—that can be maintained in spite of their encounters with (and participation in) the invasive magic of colonial modernity that has attempted their erasure.

Tapping into Benang's Magic

What makes Harley float? A whole intertextual play of tropes undergirds this magical realist trope of levitation refracted in Scott's novel. Harley's floating is linked explicitly to the archive through which he is researching his Aboriginality. He finds himself "rising and falling in all that flurry" of papers as he reads through the words and images that his grandfather Ernest Solomon Scat has compiled along with the fictionalized (though, not fictional) Chief Protector of Aborigines A. O. Neville (27). Scat and Neville, having collaborated in a eugenic experiment on Harley, are revealed to have framed the very episteme by which Harley has access to his Aboriginality. The pair represent instances of what Jacques Derrida calls the "archon": the keeper of archival knowledge.[48]

Scott describes Neville's archival documents as a "continual—albeit perverse—source of inspiration" from which he draws to rescript their relation to Noongar lives like Harley's (497). This relation between perversity and inspiration describes a frequent, though not all-encompassing, relation that Aboriginal people can and do have with colonial archives. While these archives are the sources of trauma, records produced by perpetrators of biopolitical surveillance and attempted genocide, they also often provide access to knowledge that either is otherwise lost or confirms what was lived and continues to be remembered and orally passed down. I do not mean, then, to suggest that Indigenous storytelling or resistance is limited to the colonial archive. Rather, I wish to underscore the degree to which the former has taken inspiration ("perverse" inspiration, as Scott describes it) from the latter and that understanding the Fourth World magical realism deployed in Scott's novel relies in part on an engagement with the relation between Indigenous survival through memory and the archive that emerged from colonial modernity and its eugenic project. As the Indigenous writer and scholar Natalie Harkin notes, "Through my own archive-fever I [am] compelled to resist, subvert and write."[49] For Harkin, as for Scott, the colonial archive is a potential space from which resistance and subversion can be drawn, even as it also emerges as a site of trauma.

As I have argued elsewhere, Scott's text redeploys the language of "raising," "uplifting," and other such metaphors of biopolitical regulation that purport to undertake a civilizing mission from Neville's published and archived writings to deconstruct their premises.[50] *Benang* narrates the trauma that is produced by such colonial violence as it is associated with supposed civilizational uplift, and it does so through an engagement with the archive. Uplift becomes Harley's magic power, but one he cannot control and one that signifies his own investment in a perverse system that emerges from colonial modernity and its eugenic project. Indeed, Harley's floating is related via a repetition of tropes to Ern's own untethered nature: "Ernest Solomon Scat was up in the air, back then, and looking around. He had touched jetty, railway, electrical and telegraph wires, sealed road. He had rarely touched the land. Ernest Solomon Scat floated all his life, in a different way to myself, and never even realised it" (52–53). Scat's metaphorical floating is etiologically connected to what becomes literal for Harley. His figural drift between various projects and professions becomes solidified in the archive that seems to invest Harley in the uncontrollable power to levitate, particularly when he scours the archive's papers and files. In this way, the empirical dryness of Scat's projects is associated with the archive's biopolitical project of modernity, and Harley's suspension literalizes the way this project injects a magical otherness into its Indigenous targets and products. The archive is composed of factishes that provide knowledge—often traumatically so—but they also offer the potential for a subversive and resistant engagement. Thus, magical realism in *Benang* is identified not in modernity or Indigenous knowledge (though the text displays a different form of reverence for the latter, as I address shortly) but, instead, through the dialectical relation (and, indeed, conflict) between Indigenous cultural modernity and that of the colonial archive. Harley floats because he is learning about his heritage, but the perverse and untethered dimension of this floating becomes apparent insofar as his source of learning is an archive whose original project was biopolitical—indeed, genocidal. As Uncle Jack Chatalong tells him, his floating—when it is vested in an obsession with the archive alone—is *kaartwarra*, Noongar for mad, foolish or, indeed, mentally unstable (162). Intervention in the archive cannot come untethered. If it does, it risks producing an experience of cultural sickness—of being *kaartwarra*.

The trope of "tapping" in *Benang* is a key motif that reveals the interplay between Noongar culture and Harley's relation to the colonial archive as well as—crucially—the overcoming of the latter by the former. Scott onomatopoetically evokes Harley's attempt to write the family history with the "tap tap" of the keyboard and of his tapping of the wall of the house built by Ern:

> Tap tap. I began chipping the render from the stone walls of the old house. I hesitate to mention it; in the context of this story it may seem dreadfully *symbolic*. But what can I do? It is the truth. Tap tap. There were many walls to do, and I was only doing a very little at a time. I was very listless, but the task, the tools I was using, and the fragments of render I stuffed in my pockets kept my feet on the ground. . . . Tap tap. Fingers on the keyboard now. Long after then. (24–25)

The archive, etymologically, refers not only to a repository of papers but also to the house of the magistrate (*archon*) who manages it.[51] Tapping, then, figures Harley's destruction of the house of Ern—the archon, symbolically designating the house as archive in turn. In doing so, the trope of tapping away render figures a deconstruction of the seat of the archive itself. Similarly, it is by dismantling the archive that Harley becomes grounded, as he places "fragments of render" in his pockets to weigh him down. Here, the deconstruction of the archive diegetically produced within and through Scott's text provides the figurative ballast to anchor Harley to the ground—symbolically resisting the magical floating associated with archive fever. Indeed, weight and grounding are connected to Noongar logics of Country (*boodja*) and connectedness in the text. Just as tapping signifies the archival storytelling of the keyboard and the removal of the render from the walls of the archon, Scat's house, so Noongar uncles Will Coolman and Jack Chattalong offer grounding to Harley, and this grounding is figured through a parallel tapping: "Tap tap. Uncle Will tapping me on the shoulder" (24). Jack taps Harley on the chest as he instructs him in Noongar modes of grounded being: "Uncle Jack, tapping me on the chest (as, more and more others would later do). 'You feel it in your heart? Say it like you feel it'" (148).This is proleptically referred to early in the text when Harley, dancing and floating—though now in a way acceptable to Noongar kin—in the campfire notes the uncles who approach, "and tapping their fists on my chest," advise him to "speak it from the heart'" (8). Tapping, then, is resignified as a mode of storytelling that draws both from the archive and, more urgently, from the Noongar practice of "speaking it from the heart."

The archive is composed of factishes. Do not such archons as Ernest Solomon Scat and A. O. Neville invest in the magic of the archive in precisely such a mystical mode as we find in such Western constructions of Indigenous belief as, for instance, in Lévy-Bruhl? Does Harley not also do so for a time—until he becomes regrounded in Noongar culture by Jack and Will? If this is so, then colonial modernity is subject to precisely the magic that it would evacuate from the Aboriginal lives and bodies that it biopolitically manages. What *Benang* narrates is the demystification of this magic and its resignification not via a causality with eugenic and genocidal ends but, rather, as a participatory logic of Noongar cultural practice that, while drawing from the archive, vests itself in the living logic of memory and participation toward which Harley gradually becomes oriented in the text. With this unworking of the colonial magic of the archive, in part through the archive itself, the wonder of *boodja* (Country) is restored.

The Whakapapa *of the Red Shoes*

Just as Scott critically mines and mimes the Western Australian Native Affairs archive in order to subvert it, so Ihimaera positions the ethnographic work of Elsdon Best as both a source of inspiration and a locus of critique. Midway through "Maata," Ihimaera has Mahaki encounter an extant text by P. A. Lawlor about the existence of Mansfield's Māori friend. Ihimaera reproduces a whole chapter of Lawlor's text, including the text's forceful assertion (drawn from the intertext of Elsdon Best, the ethnographer employed by Ihimaera) that Māori thought is essentially distinct from that of the Pakeha (European): "The mentality of the Māori is of an intensely mystical nature. . . . We shall never know the inwardness of the native mind."[52] It is possible, as long as we retain a hermeneutic of suspicion, to unpack Best's writing as an intertext for Ihimaera's text—a kind of archive. While insisting on the inextricable and inexplicable difference of Māori "mentality" and while (as elsewhere) hierarchizing European modes of knowledge as superior, Best nonetheless, in wider writings, asserts that Māori modes of abstraction are complex and multiple. Best argues in *Spiritual and Mental Concepts of the Maori* (1922) that Māori "mentality" is not only open to abstraction but given to a higher multiplicity of abstractions than that of Europeans. His opening sentence is telling, inscribing an essential difference around "barbarism" while, ironically, debunking racist assumptions about the absence of Indigenous cultural complexity: "The mental concepts of a barbaric race must ever possess an element of interest to the ethnographer, and in studying those of the Māori folk we encounter evidence to show that they had evolved a belief in many singular abstractions."[53] While Best's texts accomplish the opening of a cultural relation—Indigenous and non-Indigenous, Māori and Pakeha—they then foreclose this potential relation by arbitrarily insisting on the superiority of the Pakeha mode of factish over that of the Māori.

For Best, the Māori possessed not a dearth of abstraction in their cultural practice but, instead, an abundance of it. Best, indeed, would note in Māori culture and "mentality" the "amazing genius for personification, his powers of introspective thought, his long developed faculty of abstraction." And yet, Best nonetheless sets out to explain how this multiple mode of abstraction remains somehow "primitive."[54] For Best, while the complexity of Māori cultural modes of abstraction was remarkable, this other mode of engagement with the seen and unseen, with its difference in mode of participation—this other factish—ultimately had to be relegated to a subordinate position in a hierarchical binary. Best's text belies a barely concealed desire to ascribe cultural superiority to a peculiarly Western mode of abstraction: monotheism. That the Māori have multiple names for the spirit and ascribe these spiritual aspects to humans, animals, plants, and even inanimate objects is seen not as a source of complexity but as a deficit in knowledge. Complexity, when it comes to belief, is produced by Best as inferior to the ostensibly improved simplicity of monotheism—a point that is hardly self-evident. Best also subtly insists that the very virtue of contact lies in the reification of so-called civilized belief. To meet an Indigenous person is, it would seem, to fix in place the superior religious beliefs of the non-Indigenous: "Thus the lot of people of the higher culture-plane, when brought into contact with those of an inferior grade, is not to cultivate their sense of the abstract but to curb it."[55]

However, Ihimaera subtly critiques Lawlor's use of Best. While in some sense avowing a wondrous thought that could be described as "mystical"—for instance, with his narration of Mahaki's telepathic communication with the old woman—Ihimaera also shows that it is the capacity for narrative, shared between cultures, that offers Mahaki access to blood memory as an act of the imagination. This trope of "blood narrative" derives from the thought of the Kiowa writer N. Scott Momaday and is explicitly connected to narratives that engage with the archive by Natalie Harkin. As she argues, drawing on Chadwick Allen's work on Momaday:

> Blood memory . . . can respond to . . . collective loss. It can be understood as both a way of thinking and a literary-method framed and underpinned by a series of "narrative tactics" (Allen) that can achieve many things: writing back to the State's colonial discourses and fixed imaginings on blood, race and identity; and contributing to larger narratives of history through constructing and reconstructing personal narratives. This writing back to colonial discourses on blood can expose the very essentialism embodied in State-constructed ideas of indigenous blood-quantum identity, thereby disrupting the racial economy, or the fixed stability of bloodlines which determines Indigenous blood as the abject contaminating threat to white colonial genetic purity.[56]

Ihimaera's depiction of *whakapapa* and its relation to the telepathic power embodied in the relation between Mahaki and the old "madwoman" works to rescript such ideas of blood as essential colonial identity.

Mahaki, the protagonist of Ihimaera's "Maata," is occupied with genealogical and historical investigation in multiple ways. First, there is his search for the story behind Mansfield's friendship with a Māori woman named Maata. Second, the text portrays the modern mimetic magic of journalism, in which Mahaki participates to uncover the secrets of Maata. The novella is framed by two forms of textual reproduction of archival motifs: in the teletype of headlines that frames each chapter and through his investigation into Mansfield and Maata's friendship, the encounter Mahaki has with the ethnographic archive of Best and Best's attempt to typify Māori modes of wonder. Mahaki is, in part, designated a mimic man insofar as he tends to reject Māori practices in favor of Western knowledge. As his Aunt Iris notes when writing to Mahaki about her research into his *whakapapa*: "I know you've never been interested in this but it is something we try to keep up as Māoris" (47). For Ihimaera, as for Iris, Mahaki must be unmade as a mimic man of the journalistic investigation of facts to be remade as a wielder of the relational power of factishes. Mahaki, in this way, must come not only to see the archive of facts about Mansfield and Maata but also to experience the unseen through Māori practice. Through *whakapapa*, Mahaki comes to see the full wondrous diversity of factishes available as including not only Western modes of mimesis but also the Māori modes of knowing and being with kin that he has ignored.

The magic of the text is also echoed through the teletype paper which opens each of the text's chapters. The plot is contextualized in relation to the settler-colonial context that is aimed at further fragmenting Māori society, and this is presented as a series of potential headlines mirroring the teletype printouts of newspaper offices. For instance, the opening chapter is framed by one such teletype epigraph:

> 1953 ... CORONATION YEAR ... NORDMEYER MAKES BID TO RE-PLACE WALTER NASH AS LEADER OF THE OPPOSITION ... GOVERNMENT PASSES MAORI AFFAIRS ACT ... EISENHOWER BE-COMES NEW U.S. PRESIDENT. (11)

The novella begins in 1953, the year of the introduction of the Maori Affairs Act by the New Zealand Parliament. This is directly referred to in the list of headlines given in the opening teletype epigraph. The act was a means for compulsory acquisition of Māori land, which operated by labeling Māori land use unproductive and permitting land employed for such ostensibly unproductive use to be taken by the New Zealand government.[57] By presenting this information through the mode of newspaper archivization, Mahaki's community is shown to be a potential victim of settler-colonial exploitation even as he himself finds agency by participating in this system of journalistic reporting and the mimetic magic of Pakeha print culture.

Late in the story, Mahaki learns not only that Maata is, in fact, a Māori woman who knew and inspired Mansfield but also that she is a distant relative of his. He and his Aunt Iris visit the home of an old woman who may or may not be Maata herself. During this encounter, the old woman takes Mahaki's hand, and "then he began to hear the voice in his head, and it was like the voice of a *madwoman*" (53). In this way, the text deploys the trope of telepathy as a way to give force to Māori knowledge about kin and connection. It is only by acknowledging the force of *whakapapa* that Mahaki comes to understand not only the facts behind Mansfield's relation to Maata and the transit of the red shoes from Maata through her kin (they are at this point being worn by the madwoman's daughter) but also his own embedding in this system of relation.

Mahaki is instructed to speak only English, not Māori, to the old woman, positioning her as, perhaps, an assimilated subject. Yet the way in which Mahaki is able to communicate with the old woman reveals the resilience of Māori cultural practices in spite of this trajectory of assimilation. Like Harley, Mahaki is engaged in the restoration of traditional knowledge in the wake of a history of attempted cultural fragmentation.

Coda

In *Benang* and "Maata" we encounter archival technologies as colonial empirical investigation that is then resignified through relation to Noongar and Māori cultural practices. What emerges here is not, however, a hybrid between colonial archival knowledge, with its modes of biopower, and Indigenous cultural knowledge. Instead of such a third space, we encounter in these texts an ecology of factishes, each with potentially complementary power; in each case, it is Indigenous knowledge that has been devalued historically and must be apprehended anew. Thus, if such Indigenous texts as Scott's and Ihimaera's are to be seen as magical realist, they should be seen as such only under erasure. According to this way of apprehending things, what in fact exists is a network of relational factishes—of efficacious constructions of knowledge and practice from *whakapapa* to Noongar storytelling. These would be recognized as othered but not other. That is to say, they have experienced a historical record of having been othered by Western modes of empiricism (and therefore are seen as "magical"), but that they are not themselves in any way lesser. They are merely alternative modes of observation and representation. By drawing out the magic of modernity, *Benang* renders it, with its biopolitics, perversely other. Each protagonist is positioned to turn to Noongar or Māori culture to ground their practice and identity, insisting on the necessity to exalt wondrous Indigenous knowledge as a way to unmake the hierarchical privilege of Western modes of empiricism, with their biopolitical effects. Yet finally, even with all this multiplicity of factishes emergent from the archive and elsewhere, traditional modes of Indigenous cultural practice win out in both texts. In *Benang*, Harley must learn to reground himself in *boodja* (Country), and similarly, in "Maata" Mahaki must relearn *whakapapa* vested as it is, for him, in blood memory. In this way, while I have insisted on the relative magic of colonial modernity and Indigenous modernity in all its wonder, these narrative texts are not at all uncertain about which wins out. I leave you to read and wonder.

NOTES

1 Maria Takolander, for instance, has made a forceful case for the novel's investment in magical realism as a genre: see Maria Takolander, "Magical Realism and Irony's 'Edge': Rereading Magical Realism and Kim Scott's *Benang*," *Journal of the Association for the Study of Australian Literature* 14, no. 5 (2014): 1–11.

2 For a discussion of technologies of biopolitical surveillance in absorption- and assimilation-era Native Affairs discourse, see Michael R. Griffiths, "The White Gaze and Its Artifacts: Governmental Belonging and Non-Indigenous Evaluation in a (Post)-Settler Colony," *Postcolonial Studies* 15, no. 4 (2013): 415–35.

3 Kim Scott, *Benang: From the Heart* (Fremantle, Australia: Fremantle Arts Centre, 2000), 108 (hereafter, page numbers from this work are cited in parentheses in the text).

4 On the relation between Michel Foucault's notion of biopolitics and settler colonialism, see, e.g., René Dietrich, "The Biopolitical Logics of Settler Colonialism and Disruptive Relationality," *Cultural Studies* ↔ *Critical Methodologies* 17, no. 1 (2017): 67–77; Scott L. Morgensen, "The Biopolitics of Settler Colonialism: Right Here, Right Now," *Settler Colonial Studies* 1 (2011): 52–76.

5 Gerald Vizenor, "Aesthetics of Survivance: Literary Theory and Practice," in *Survivance: Narratives of Native Presence*, edited by Gerald Vizenor (Lincoln: University of Nebraska Press, 2008), 1–24.

6 Quoted in Gerri Kimber, "'To Hell with the Blooms Berries': Katherine Mansfield in *Mansfield* and the Work of C. K. Stead," in *Bloomsbury Influences: Papers from the Bloomsbury Adaptations Conference, Bath Spa University, 5–6 May 2011*, edited by E. H. Wright (Newcastle upon Tyne, UK: Cambridge Scholars, 2014), 122. I thank Joshua Lobb for reminding me of this quotation.

7 Kaupapa Māori as a concept refers to the aspiration, vision, and community of Māori communities collectively.

8 Chadwick Allen, *Transindigenous: Methodologies for Global Native Literary Studies* (Minneapolis: University of Minnesota Press, 2012).

9 Homi Bhabha, "Introduction: Narrating the Nation," in *Nation and Narration*, edited by Homi Bhabha (London: Routledge, 1990), 7. See also Lois Parkinson Zamora and Wendy Faris, eds., *Magical Realism: Theory, History, Community* (Durham, NC: Duke University Press, 1995).

10 Ben Holgate engages this question differently in "Unsettling Narratives: Reevaluating Magical Realism as Postcolonial Discourse through Alexis Wright's *Carpentaria* and *The Swan Book*," *Journal of Postcolonial Writing* 51, no. 6 (2015): 634–47.

11 Jacques Derrida, *Of Grammatology*, translated by Gayatri Chakravorty Spivak (Baltimore: Johns Hopkins University Press, 1976), 60–66. See also Gayatri Spivak's cogent explanation of Derrida's concept of erasure in her translator's preface to the same volume, ix–lxxxviii.

12 Allen, *Transindigenous*, xix.

13 Daniel Heath Justice, *Why Indigenous Literatures Matter* (Waterloo, ON: Wilfred Laurier University Press, 2018), 141–42.

14 Justice, *Why Indigenous Literatures Matter*, 153.

15 Justice, *Why Indigenous Literatures Matter*, 155.

16 Theodor W. Adorno and Walter Benjamin, *The Complete Correspondence, 1928–1940*, edited by Henri Lonitz, translated by Nicolas Walker (Cambridge, MA: Harvard University Press, 1999), 38.

17 Michael T. Taussig, *Mimesis and Alterity: A Particular History of the Senses* (London: Routledge, 1993), 20.

18 Taussig, *Mimesis and Alterity*, 130.

19 Marcia Langton, "Aboriginal Art and Film: The Politics of Representation," in *Blacklines: Contemporary Critical Writing by Indigenous Australians*, edited by Michele Grossman (Carlton: Melbourne University Press, 2003), 118.

20 Audra Simpson, "On Ethnographic Refusal: Indigeneity, 'Voice' and Colonial Citizenship," *Junctures* 9 (2007): 78.

21 Wendy B. Faris, *Ordinary Enchantments: Magical Realism and the Remystification of Narrative* (Nashville, TN: Vanderbilt University Press, 2004), 8.

22 Brenda Cooper, *Magical Realism in West African Fiction: Seeing with a Third Eye* (New York: Routledge, 1998), 221.

23 Liam Connell, "Discarding Magic Realism: Modernism, Anthropology, and Critical Practice," *ARIEL: A Review of International English Literature* 29, no. 2 (1998): 95–110.

24 Connell, "Discarding Magic Realism," 108.

25 Taussig talks of "the magic of mimesis" manifesting in those instances "wherein the replication, the copy acquires the power of the represented": Taussig, *Mimesis and Alterity*, 20.

26 Marcel Mauss, *A General Theory of Magic* (London: Routledge, [1902] 2005).

27 Adorno and Benjamin, *The Complete Correspondence*, 38.

28 On J. G. Frazer's notion of "sympathetic magic," see Taussig, *Mimesis and Alterity*, 250–56.

29 Christopher Bracken, *Magical Criticism: The Recourse of Savage Philosophy* (Chicago: University of Chicago Press, 2007), 6.

30 Cited in Christopher Warnes, *Magical Realism: Between Faith and Irreverence* (London: Palgrave Macmillan, 2009), 1.

31 Takolander, "Magical Realism and Irony's 'Edge,'" 1.

32 Warnes, *Magical Realism*, 6.

33 Warnes, *Magical Realism*, 6.

34 Warnes, *Magical Realism*, 2–3.

35 Lucien Lévy-Bruhl, quoted in Warnes, *Magical Realism*, 9.

36 Stanley Tambiah, quoted in Warnes, *Magical Realism*, 10.

37 Tambiah, quoted in Warnes, *Magical Realism*, 10.

38 Tambiah, quoted in Warnes, *Magical Realism*, 10.

39 Warnes, *Magical Realism*, 11.

40 Warnes, *Magical Realism*, 12.

41 Warnes, *Magical Realism*, 13.

42 Taussig, *Mimesis and Alterity*, 8.

43 Bruno Latour, *On the Modern Cult of the Factish Gods*, translated by Catherine Porter and Heather MacLean (Durham, NC: Duke University Press, 2010).

44 Latour, *On the Modern Cult of the Factish Gods*, 9.
45 Isabelle Stengers, *Cosmopolitics I*, translated by Robert Bononno (Minneapolis: University of Minnesota Press, 2010), 23.
46 Stengers, *Cosmopolitics I*, 19.
47 Bracken, *Magical Criticism*, 6.
48 Jacques Derrida, *Archive Fever: A Freudian Impression*, translated by Eric Prenowitz (Chicago: University of Chicago Press, 1995), 9.
49 Natalie Harkin, "The Poetics of (Re)Mapping Archives: Memory in the Blood," *Journal of the Association for the Study of Australian Literature* 14, no. 3 (2014): 10.
50 Michael R. Griffiths, "Need I Repeat? Settler Colonial Biopolitics and Postcolonial Iterability in Kim Scott's *Benang*," in *Postcolonial Issues in Australian Literature*, edited by Nathanael O'Reilly (Amherst, NY: Cambria, 2010), 165.
51 Derrida, *Archive Fever*, 2.
52 Witi Ihimaera, "Maata," in *Dear Miss Mansfield* (Auckland: Viking, 1989), 41 (hereafter, page numbers from this work are cited in parentheses in the text).
53 Elsdon Best, *Spiritual and Mental Concepts of the Maori* (Auckland, New Zealand: Government Printer, [1922] 1986), 5.
54 Best, *Spiritual and Mental Concepts of the Maori*, 56.
55 Best, *Spiritual and Mental Concepts of the Maori*, 5.
56 Harkin, "The Poetics of (Re)Mapping Archives," 8. Allen, *Blood Narrative: Indigenous Identity in American Indian and Maori Literary and Activist Texts* (Durham, NC: Duke University Press, 2002), 26–40.
57 Maori Affairs Act 1963 (1953 No. 94) (Auckland, New Zealand: Government Printer, 1953).

9

AGENCY AND ART

Survivance with Camera and Crayon

JACQUELINE FEAR-SEGAL

Schools for Indigenous children were an integral part of the United States' broader biopolitical agenda. In the final quarter of the nineteenth century, the US government conquered and confined on reservations all the Native nations of the Plains, incorporating their lands into the expanding United States. As part of this national project, Indigenous children were enrolled in government boarding schools for reeducation and transformation from "savages" into "civilized" individuals "worthy of American citizenship." Studies of settler colonialism illuminate how processes governing the settler-colonial project in the United States, and in all other settler nations, were inherently violent and destructive for Indigenous peoples.[1] Schooling was a distinctive and disturbing genre of violence and destruction, and by targeting children, it cut to the very heart of Indigenous cultures and identities.

The Australian anthropologist and ethnographer Patrick Wolfe (1948–2016) has elucidated how, unlike traditional forms and definitions of colonialism that exploit Indigenous labor and extract Indigenous resources, the paramount goal of settler colonialism is always the acquisition of land; the settler colonist has come to stay. Settler colonialism is therefore "premised on displacing indigenes from (or replacing them on) the land," and a key associated objective is always the destruction of Native societies. "The ruling logic of elimination" is the essential characteristic of the settler-colonial project, Wolfe argues, because it always seeks to eliminate rather than incorporate Indigenous peoples.[2] To achieve the nation's continental geo- and biopolitical goals, the United States needed to subjugate all Natives nations, expunge their legal title to lands, and then completely eliminate all traces of their traditional cultural heritages. To achieve this end, the final "Indian" war was fought in the classroom, against children.

The campaign to school "Indians" was articulated in the upbeat American educational rhetoric of progress and possibility, but its underlying objective was always cultural genocide, or what the historian David Adams has called "Education for Extinction."[3] The little red schoolhouse, so long acclaimed in the United States as a benign institution underpinning the foundations of democracy, was co-opted in the late nineteenth century and transformed into a military boarding institution, organized to target Indigenous youth and extinguish all aspects of their inherited cultures. Although still referred to as "schools," these large residential establishments, which were completely severed from the communities they ostensibly served, had little in common with America's idealized local schoolhouse. Such schools were vital to the objectives of the wider settler-colonial project, so comparable institutions were also established in Canada during the same period. Analogous programs of "reeducation" would be conducted in all settler-colonial nations.

Only recently have the abuses (physical, psychological, sexual) that were inflicted on residential school students in Canada been publicly acknowledged and discussed. The Canadian Truth and Reconciliation Commission (2008–15), set up by the government, created a forum that empowered more than seven thousand Canadian First Nations survivors to come forward to tell their painful stories. The opening lines of the summary section of the commission's seven-volume report unequivocally stated that residential schools had been part of a long-term, deliberate policy of cultural genocide.[4] Prime Minister Justin Trudeau was present at the report's release in Ottawa on December 15, 2015, and reiterated his predecessor's apology for "one of the darkest chapters in Canadian history."[5] In the United States, there has been no similar public apology or investigation, but the legacies of the boarding schools have begun to be acknowledged, and organizations such as the National Native American Boarding School Healing Coalition have begun to "break the silence" to "begin the healing."[6]

The discovery in 2021 of hundreds of unmarked student graves at a succession of residential schools in Canada brought the horror of this issue to international attention. Something that First Nations people have long spoken about is now impossible to deny, with ground-penetrating radar helping to provide indisputable evidence. The flag over Canada's Parliament flew at half-mast as a national sign of respect for the tragedy that was coming to light. In the United States, Secretary of the Interior Deb Haaland (Laguna Pueblo) announced a Federal Indian Boarding School initiative to review the troubled legacy of boarding schools in her nation. She announced a comprehensive review, with investigation into records of cemeteries and burial sites as well as examination of the intergenerational impact of Indian boarding schools and the unacknowledged and unspoken traumas of the past that have carried forward into the present of every Native American community.[7] It has taken more than a century for the destructive and enduring impact of the schools to begin to be acknowledged.

In the final decades of the nineteenth century, when Indigenous children from across the Plains were being transported from their homes to faraway residential institutions, the communities they left behind were already in deep crisis. The rapid and deliberate destruction of the buffalo herds in the second half of the nineteenth century, on which all the Plains tribes had depended, devastated their economies and, now restricted within reservation boundaries, forced them to depend on government rations to survive. Proud Native leaders who had once fought and negotiated for their people were reduced to paupers and suppliants. And once the tribes were conquered and confined, "Indian affairs were no longer matters of executive importance" in Washington.[8] It is within this broad historical context that the establishment and all activities of the federal Indian school system must be framed and analyzed. It is also within this context that the responses of the students and their communities must be interpreted and understood.

Young, far from home and family, and living among strangers in an unfamiliar landscape while being subjected to a relentless program of cultural demolition, the students were extremely vulnerable and defenseless. All aspects of their lives were regulated, controlled, and surveilled: the times that they ate, slept, studied, worshiped, worked, and played were ruled by the bell; the clothes they wore were standard uniforms; and even their compulsory letters home were read and censored. We know from the scholarship that some students demonstrated open revolt against the rigors of the school—for example, by running away or even committing arson.[9] Many others engaged in less overt forms of rebellion, asserting their agency in veiled ways that James C. Scott, an American scholar of subaltern politics, has helped us to understand as "hidden transcripts" of resistance, or "critiques of power spoken behind the back of the dominant."[10]

This chapter explores some of the visual "hidden transcripts" created by Native students who were transported to the Carlisle Indian Industrial School (1879–1918). These students came from a wide variety of cultural backgrounds and spoke many different languages. Although they were made to learn English at school, their voices only rarely speak out in the written archive, and their words come to us—in commentary, school newspapers, or letters home— refracted through the rigid prism of official power structures.[11] Such student-authored documents need to be read with care to see beyond the one-sided range of thoughts and opinions they often seem to present. Some of these written accounts have been vigilantly analyzed by scholars, bringing insight into the children's and their parents' thoughts and responses to boarding schools and revealing the complex and sometimes contradictory ways these Native authors engaged with the assimilationist and progressive rhetoric of the time.[12] The visual record, however, has been studied for these purposes more rarely and perhaps presents even greater challenges for interpretation. Pictures, like writing, do not carry a single, unambiguous, or indisputable truth, but their great fluidity of meaning also brings possibilities. This chapter examines the visual archive to reveal some of the creative ways that Native students expressed agency and asserted their identities through their claims to pictorial sovereignty in two quite different media: drawing and photography. The resilience and resourcefulness that are encapsulated in their visual assertions need to be understood within the historical context of the mission of the Carlisle Indian School.

The Carlisle Indian School Photographs

The founding of Carlisle, the first US government boarding school, marked the beginning of a coordinated, state-run campaign of cultural genocide through schooling. Carlisle was an experiment in cultural transformation, and it was here that the blueprint for the federal system of Indian schools would be developed. It was deliberately established far from Indian Country in a disused US Army barracks in Pennsylvania. Nearly eight thousand Indigenous children and young adults from across the United States were transported to Pennsylvania during the thirty-nine years that the school was in operation (1879–1918).

Thousands more would be enrolled in the lookalike institutions Carlisle spawned across the American West.

Carlisle's founder and first superintendent, Lieutenant Richard Henry Pratt, was a man with a mission. During three years (1875–78) as the jailer of imprisoned Kiowa, Comanche, Cheyenne, and Arapaho leaders and warriors at Fort Marion, Florida, he had set up a fortress school for the younger prisoners and become convinced that "education" offered the best solution to the nation's vexed "Indian problem." He argued that, if Native children could be treated in the same way as the prisoners and transported to schools far from their reservation communities and the "debasing influences of camp life," they could be stripped of all vestiges of their traditional cultures and readily reeducated in the religion, language, values, and behavior of mainstream settler society. Pratt projected that at schools such as Carlisle, this transformation of the "Indian" from "savagery" to "civilization" could be accomplished in a single generation.[13]

Just three years after the combined forces of the Northern Cheyenne and Lakota nations had wiped out George Armstrong Custer's Seventh Cavalry, the federal government was keen to support an educational experiment that promised to pacify and "civilize" Native children. This would enable the peaceful settlement of the West, while Native children were held as "hostages for the good behavior of their people."[14] Many white Americans, however, were doubtful that "savages" could ever be educated and made fit for "civilization." Pratt's goal at the Carlisle Indian School was therefore twofold: to "civilize" Native children from across the nation and to demonstrate to Americans that this was possible.

From day one, Pratt recruited the new medium of photography to provide visual "proof" that the dramatic transformation he promised could, indeed, be rapidly achieved. A visual record was vital to his purpose. When he arrived at the Carlisle Barracks with the first party of eighty-six students from Dakota Territory, the buildings of the disused facility were in a state of total disrepair; the rooms were not furnished with beds or desks; and the promised food and clothing for the children had not been delivered by the Office of Indian Affairs.[15] Pratt thus faced a large number of urgent practical issues. Nevertheless, the day after the children's midnight arrival, he made certain that a local photographer, John Nicholas Choate, was on the campus with his stereoscopic camera and mobile studio to make a series of photographs of the new students, to begin recording and documenting this audacious experiment. It is significant that the opening of the Carlisle Indian School coincided with a decade in which, as the visual anthropologist Christopher Pinney has observed, "photography . . . reached a new evidentiary crescendo."[16] Photography, a medium claimed internationally as a means to supply evidence for phenomena as apparently dissimilar as race and criminality, was consciously and deliberately employed at Carlisle to chronicle and exhibit this experiment in racially inflected cultural transformation.

The photographic images Choate made on the students' first day were designed to display their "savagery," which was the school's so-called point of departure, and to demonstrate the "civilizing" mission of the school already at work. If we look at this first photograph of the boys, newly arrived from the Rosebud and Pine Ridge agencies, they have been very carefully positioned in front of the brick building that was to be their dormitory (figure 9.1). Quite deliberately, the building has been incorporated into the picture, complete with white-painted porch columns. It provides the context as well as a "civilized" backdrop for the picture. The boys have been lined up in two rows, denoting order and discipline, with the smaller ones seated in front, as in modern school photographs, hinting at care and succor. More rows with less of the building in sight would have made a very different picture. The two interpreters, Charles Tackett and Louis Roubidoux, dressed in black suits, flank the group on the extreme right (with Tackett's wife, Sarah Spotted Tail, standing between them); and on the left, with a measured space between him and the group, Pratt stands in commanding profile, with hat in hand and legs separated and braced, holding the group under his surveilling gaze. The alien exoticism of the boys' "savagery" is thus visually enclosed and contained by suited figures of white, male authority. In this carefully constructed picture, the voyeuristic white eye is invited to gaze on this seemingly motley group, with feathers and blankets clearly visible, while also seeing these "savage" children as already living reassuringly under the order and discipline of the "civilizing" school controlled by agents of the Euro-American biopolitical regime.

A similar strategy was used for the first photograph of the girls (figure 9.2). In it, they are carefully placed under the watchful eye of a white woman in middle-class attire: Sarah Mather. She had accompanied Pratt to Dakota to help recruit the girls. Her upright, respectable, surveilling presence signals that even though the Carlisle student body included both boys and girls (on the orders of General William Tecumseh Sherman), the girls would be properly safeguarded and "civilized" according to the gender roles and doctrines of white women's middle-class respectability.[17]

Far from their home communities, the Carlisle students in these photographs are shown to have found new parental figures in Pratt and Mather and, by implication, a new "family" at Carlisle. These "before" photographs were not taken out West on the reservations of Pine Ridge and Rosebud, which

FIGURE 9.1. Sioux boys as they appeared on arrival at Carlisle Indian School, October 6, 1879. Photograph by J. N. Choate. Courtesy of Cumberland County Historical Society, Carlisle, PA.

were the children's genuine "point of departure." Instead, they construct the children as being without kith or kin. In their new institutional "home" (as noted by Jolene Rickard), they are also without a land base or any aspect of their own communities or cultures, apart from the clothes they stand in.[18] Photographing them on their own lands might have risked suggesting not just residence but also ownership; placing them within the school grounds wiped any reference to their homes or communities from the viewers' awareness. Visually absent, the land could be deemed unnecessary and thus legitimately appropriated. The students' severance from their homelands makes clear the conjoined relationship between schooling and Native land dispossession—between the state's biopolitics and its geopolitics.

These first photographs of the children newly arrived from the West would later be paired with images of them dressed in their Carlisle uniforms. The visual narrative embedded in these before-and-after duos powerfully suggests that a dramatic change had taken place in the children, deftly implying that their exhibited exterior changes had been matched by analogous interior changes. The boys' "after" image uses their dormitory as a display case (figure 9.3). Lined up with caps in hand, they present a studied, repetitive sameness, dressed in their

FIGURE 9.2. Sioux girls as they appeared on arrival at Carlisle Indian School, October 6, 1879. Photograph by J. N. Choate. Courtesy of Cumberland County Historical Society, Carlisle, PA.

Army-style uniforms and positioned too far from the camera's lens for facial features to be easily recognized. Here, the viewer's eye is invited not to identify the exotic characteristics of their Native garb but, instead, to take in the reassuring military regularity and sameness of the three lines of students. Carefully organized by size, with smaller boys in front, the whole group has now melded into and is held in place by the straight lines and military architectural structures of the Carlisle Barracks. White viewers' fear of what they regarded as the chaos, wildness, and ferocity of "savagery" is reassuringly countered by an image that presents order, composure, and regularity. The boys are well on their way to becoming "civilized"; the overt surveillance visible in the previous photograph is no longer necessary and so has been withdrawn.

These were the first of many hundreds of photographs Choate made of Carlisle students and the school's activities. More than a dozen of these images (including small and large groups as well as individuals) were presented as before-and-after pairs to provide visual proof of the ongoing success of Carlisle's "civilizing" program.[19] The most iconic and best known of these duos was of Tom Torlino (Diné). It was widely circulated and used as propaganda for Carlisle long after Torlino had returned to his home in the Navajo Nation.

FIGURE 9.3. Indian boys from sixteen different tribes in first uniforms on the porches and balcony of the Carlisle Indian School residence building, 1880. Photograph by J. N. Choate. Courtesy of Cumberland County Historical Society, Carlisle, PA.

If we read these before-and-after images within their wider historical context and, instead of acquiescing with Pratt's insistence that they offer proof of Carlisle's success consider them as evidence of Wolfe's "ruling logic of elimination," then we can engage with and understand them as part of what Ted Jojola, from Isleta Pueblo, describes as "a magic act called 'The Vanishing American'" and what the Anishinaabe poet and writer Gerald Vizenor calls "the evidence of a vanishing race, the assurance of dominance and victimry."[20]

Photographic Portraits of Carlisle Students

The Carlisle photographs constitute a very carefully choreographed colonial archive that was deliberately created and used by school officials to sanction and advance the United States' national biopolitical agenda. Some of these photographs, nonetheless, hold meanings and implications that are far more complex and multilayered than their makers intended. "What can we see in the photographic representations of the racial other that is not dominance?" Vizenor demands. Answering his own question, he says, "Portraiture as evidence . . . must be more than the eternal silence of a fugitive pose; there, in the stare of the shadows, is an elusive native presence."[21] Vizenor's observation about photographs is echoed and corroborated in a different register by the British historian and visual anthropologist Elizabeth Edwards, who also notes that photographs produced in a colonial context have fault lines where alternative histories can be detected: "Even the most dense of colonial documents can spring leaks if we 'keep our theory close to the ground' and interrogate not the sweep of abstractions, but the distinctions and points of fracture in the image."[22]

Focusing on these "points of fracture," a guiding assumption underpinning this analysis is that the inconclusive quality of photographs and their infinite recodability means that, despite the political and visual sovereignty that empowered Euro-American educators to choreograph, make, disseminate, and sell these images of "Indians," Native students and their parents were able to engage with, interpret, and use the photographs in very different ways and to view them from radically different perspectives.[23] Photographs, as Vizenor, Edwards, and others remind us, cannot fully be understood at a single point of their existence. They are socially salient objects that operate in time, space, and culture.[24] So they are available to be claimed and reframed by their Native subjects in what Vizenor defines as "acts of survivance," and those who perform such acts are, for Vizenor, "warriors of defiance." The concept of survivance (combining the notions of survival, endurance, resistance) was delineated and developed by Vizenor to characterize all acts of Native assertion and affirmation. He explains that "the character of survivance creates a sense of native presence over absence, nihility, and victimry. Native survivance is an active sense of presence over absence, deracination, and oblivion; survivance is the continuance of stories, not a mere re-action however pertinent. Survivance is greater than the right of a survivable name."[25] The "warriors of survivance" who asserted "a sense of Native presence over absence, nihility, and victimry" demonstrate, for Vizenor, the same courage that "their ancestors once evinced on horses," and in so doing, they create what he regards as the "new stories of tribal courage."[26]

We have seen how Carlisle's carefully created "colonial" photographic archive provides visual evidence of the school's aggressive and uncompromising campaign of cultural genocide. Now, with Vizenor's concept of survivance in mind, I turn to the students' and parents' active engagement with the Carlisle photographic project to explore how, when claiming photographs for their own agendas, these warriors of survivance often succeeded in destabilizing and subverting the original purposes of the images by asserting visual sovereignty over a medium that was created and controlled by Euro-Americans. Recent discussions of sovereignty have contributed to this study by opening up new ways to consider how the visual can, in Michelle H. Raheja's words, be "a germinal and exciting site for exploring how sovereignty is a creative act of self-representation that has the potential to both undermine stereotypes of indigenous peoples and to strengthen what Robert Warrior has called the 'intellectual health' of communities in the wake of genocide and colonialism."[27]

From the opening of the Carlisle Indian School until his sudden death in 1902, John Nicholas Choate was the school's photographer.[28] The majority of the photographs he made are portraits. They display a monotonous regularity in composition, presenting the supposedly "civilized" students posed in their Carlisle uniforms, surrounded and buttressed by the props and rituals of the late nineteenth-century photographer's studio. A photographic portrait from this era was generally the product of a conscious collaboration between photographer and subject. As Eric Homberger has shown, the technology of photography at this time dictated long exposures that were necessarily arranged and agreed on. The subject had to consciously consent to the occasion, except in the case of "involuntary or culturally unequal portraits."[29] The extreme asymmetries in power relations within the Carlisle Indian School raise the question of *how* the students were involved in the photographic process and in what ways this varied on different occasions. Having looked at the carefully choreographed early photographs, over which the students could exert very limited agency, I now focus on instances in which some students, able to engage with photographic encounters on their own terms, even if minimally, became active participants in a larger transcultural interchange or performance. In such circumstances, it can be argued, the photographic encounter at Carlisle operated as a visual "contact zone," to use the term developed from its ethnographic foundation by the literary critic Mary Louise Pratt. She uses it to designate a place where disparate cultures come together and the subordinate group actively and selectively borrows from the dominant group.[30] At Carlisle, in a variety of different ways, some students succeeded in contributing a special resonance to Pratt's observation when they claimed photographs for their own agendas. Reflecting more broadly on the readiness of Native Americans to embrace photography, Paul Chaat Smith positions the camera in a long line of technological innovations, "along with horses, rifles, flour and knives," that Native people have enthusiastically adopted, and explains wryly: "We have been using photography for our own ends as long as we have been flying, which is to say as long as there have been cameras and airplanes."[31]

At Carlisle, most straightforwardly, students used photographs as a visual means to communicate and maintain contact with family and community on the reservation, recruiting for their own purposes photographs that were generally made as part of Carlisle's assimilating mission. Letters written in English could not be read by family members on the reservation without the help of a literate interpreter. Photographs carried a more immediate message and could be viewed at home without the help of an interlocutor. So students made voluntary trips to Choate's studio on Carlisle's Main Street to pose for their portraits and sent these photographs home. Complex cross-cultural interactions, these pictures were identical in structure to portraits of whites, but these photographic encounters were often very complex, even though not forced.

Parents often sent money and requested their children's portraits. A photograph of Wica-Karpa offers one poignant example of the many complex histories and meanings carried in these apparently straightforward portraits. Wica-Karpa, known at Carlisle as Ernest White Thunder, arrived in Pennsylvania with the first group from Dakota. He wrote home to tell his father, the Brulé leader White Thunder (Wakinyan Ska), that he was unhappy and terribly homesick. Meanwhile, Pratt told the boy's father that Ernest was being troublesome and uncooperative, so White Thunder wrote to his son urging him to attend to his books. But in the same letter he also asked his son for a photograph: "You wrote me that you were all soldiers and had uniforms. I send you $2.00 for you to get a large picture in your uniform so that I can see it. . . . I sent you there to be like a white man and I want you to do what the teacher tells you."[32]

A magnificent photograph was indeed made of Ernest, showing off his uniform to full effect (figure 9.4). But once we know more of the story, it turns out to be a problematic, convoluted image, with Ernest's performance for the camera fraught with contradictions and his uniform becoming his later burial garment. While White Thunder was visiting Carlisle with a delegation of leaders from Dakota in spring 1880, Ernest tried to run away from the school to return home. He stole aboard the delegation's departing train but was discovered and immediately sent back to the school.[33] Shortly after this he fell ill. Pratt wrote daily letters to tell White Thunder that his son was sick—"He would not eat and he would not take his medicine"—and then, tragically, on December 14, 1880, little more than fourteen months after Ernest's arrival, Pratt wrote that he had died. Pratt buried Ernest in the school cemetery, "dressed in his uniform, with a white shirt and a nice collar and tie."[34] After describing the boy's funeral, he ended his final letter to White Thunder: "I find I have two pictures of Ernest, which I think you will like to have."[35] The complex history of Ernest's uniformed portrait, White Thunder's last memento of his son, was almost certainly unknown to the Euro-American people who eagerly purchased the photograph. This image, originally made for the boy's father, was sold as "number 8" on Choate's popular commercial list, long after its subject's tragic death and burial.

FIGURE 9.4. Studio portrait of Ernest White Thunder (a.k.a. Wica-Karpa [Knocks Off]) wearing a school uniform, 1880. Photograph by J. N. Choate. Courtesy of Cumberland County Historical Society, Carlisle, PA.

While white Americans were buying cabinet and boudoir albumen prints of Carlisle students to arrange and view in the plush, photographic albums that were popular at the time, photographic viewing of a quite different kind was taking place in the regular exchange of photographs between Pennsylvania and the reservations of the US West.[36] Not only did Native parents delight in receiving pictures of their children, but students also openly welcomed the solace offered by a photograph from home. One student wrote, "You must not send me any money. You just keep it and help yourself. But I do ask your picture and I will send my picture some day."[37] Out in the West, Native people joined the many Americans who visited local photography studios to have their portraits made, and they, too, became adept at performing for the camera.

One Indigenous leader who deliberately and consistently used the camera to help craft a public identity was the Oglala Lakota Red Cloud (Maȟpíya Lúta). Frank H. Goodyear III, former curator of photographs at the National Portrait Gallery, describes him as "the most photographed Native American in the nineteenth century." Goodyear suggests that after Red Cloud moved his campaign of resistance to the negotiating table, "the photographer's studio became one of [his] most important [alternative] battlegrounds."[38] It was here that Red Cloud creatively worked to maintain his status among the Oglala as well as among the Euro-Americans.[39] Goodyear suggests that Red Cloud's active participation in the ritual of portrait photography shows that he was consciously and carefully fashioning his own public identity. He posed for the camera fifty times and appears in more than a hundred photographs, skillfully recruiting a medium very different from traditional Lakota storytelling and pictographic drawing.

Other Native leaders adopted a similar, if less public, strategy when they visited local photography studios to pose for portraits to send to their children at Carlisle. Among them was Cloud Shield, another important Oglala leader and keeper of one of the Lakota Winter Counts.[40] In 1880, he sent a carefully crafted portrait to his son at Carlisle, and although that photograph, sadly, has not survived, we do have Cloud Shield's letter, which was published in *Harper's Magazine*:

> My Dear Son, I send my picture with this. You see that I had my War Jacket on when taken, but I wear white man's clothes, and am trying to live and act like white men.[41]

Cloud Shield could neither speak nor write English, so this letter was undoubtedly written for him by someone else. His photograph—showing his face, war jacket, and, perhaps, war bonnet—must surely have created a stronger impression on his son receiving this package in Carlisle, than his letter, written in a foreign tongue in another's hand. All Cloud Shield's brave deeds as a warrior would have been incorporated into his war shirt's design, and thus would have been instantly visible to his son. The photograph would have served as a more powerful reminder of Cloud Shield's high standing and the brave warrior past that buttressed his status, than his claimed efforts to "live and act like white men."

The vast majority of photographs taken of Carlisle students were crafted to serve the school's mission and reflected the asymmetry in power relations already discussed. But remarkably, some Carlisle students succeeded in finding ways to use the camera as a medium of self-expression and self-representation. In so doing, they subtly and ingeniously realigned the purpose of the Carlisle photographic project, asserting an "elusive native presence" (to use Vizenor's words) and so claiming part of the project as their own. One student who displayed this creative ability was the Brulé Lakota boy Óta Kté, or Plenty Kill, who arrived in Pennsylvania with the first group of students.[42] He is seen sitting in the middle of the front row of the photograph analyzed at the start of this chapter (see figure 9.1). At Carlisle, Óta Kté would become known as Luther Standing Bear. He chose his first name by pointing blindly at a list on the blackboard that he could not read; his father's name was then added by the school to serve as his last name.[43] Luther Standing Bear would become one of Pratt's star Carlisle pupils. After six years, in 1885, he returned to his reservation and found work at the government school there. Later he would tour England as the interpreter for Buffalo Bill's Wild West Show. He would witness the Ghost Dance at Pine Ridge and become a spokesman for Native peoples, a critic of government policies in his speeches and writings, and the author of two autobiographical works.[44] Vizenor suggests that Luther Standing Bear's writings mark him out as the first post-Indian "warrior of survivance." For Vizenor, "The postindian warriors encounter their enemies with the same courage in literature as their ancestors once evinced on horses, and they create their stories with a new sense of survivance."[45]

At Carlisle, before he had published any of his writings, Standing Bear's confidence and composure in front of the camera confirm that he was already able to construct visual renderings of the "new stories of tribal courage," which, Vizenor insists, are the hallmark of any "warrior of survivance."[46] Luther Standing Bear's capacity to claim for himself and exploit the power of the camera is already evident in one of his portraits, made by Choate. Wearing a jaunty boater and pocket watch with chain, the photograph displays Luther Standing Bear's love of Euro-American clothes, which he writes about enthusiastically in his autobiography.[47] It simultaneously demonstrates his poise and ability to claim as part of his own identity these Euro-American middle-class clothes, which, he admitted, he at first found "cumbersome and awkward."[48] Luther Standing Bear was also photographed with his father, Chief Standing Bear, at the same photo session in Choate's Carlisle studio. Chief Standing Bear wore citizen's dress and a pocket watch, too, along with his braids and a string of beads. Luther would later include this image in his second autobiographical volume, in which he was highly critical of Carlisle, thus positioning his visit to Choate's studio as a pivotal moment in his life.[49] For able and confident students such as Luther Standing Bear, photography provided an opportunity to explore new identities, to perform for the camera, and, by consciously constructing and owning these images, to use self-representation as a means of empowerment.

For Vizenor, "survivance is a practice, not an ideology," and, he insists, it is "the practices of survivance" that "create an active presence."[50] So it is noteworthy that photography, the medium Carlisle officials used consciously and assertively to visually reshape and publicize Native students' apparently transformed identities, was also employed by students, such as Luther Standing Bear, to practice and display their confidence in shaping their own changing identities.

It is worth mentioning the stark contrast between the ebullience of the Choate portrait under discussion and the austere paired photographs that were made of Luther Standing Bear (wearing his Carlisle uniform) as part of a series designed to exhibit the physiological characteristics of the "Indian race." In those he is photographed in front and side view, as a scientific specimen of a Brulé Sioux, for the Bureau of Ethnology. None of his evident flair for self-presentation was permitted in that structured, "scientific" photographic encounter.

Students' Drawings and Visual Systems of Meaning

One explanation for why both adult Native Americans and Carlisle students such as Luther Standing Bear felt confident to lay claim to the medium of photography was their cultural familiarity with visual systems of meaning and the different ways these could be used to define the public self. For generations, young men of the Plains had used hides, robes, and tipis as surfaces on which to draw and paint their successes in war and visually assert their prowess and status. As the United States had rapidly and progressively destroyed the buffalo herds and confined Native Nations on reservations, Natives peoples' daily lives were suddenly and dramatically changed and curtailed. But one result of this was that, in agency towns, paper as well as pencils and ink became available, and the men now began to draw their stories in ledger books. Artistic conventions remained the same, but in these ledger books, materials, subject matter, and layout were altered as the men adapted their art to their new situation.[51]

These cataclysmic social and economic transformations happened on all reservations across the West, and it is noteworthy that photography and ledger art emerged during the same period. As Goodyear observed, "Native peoples learned to use both mediums for their own purposes."[52]

At Carlisle, too, some students turned to drawing, actively employing the artistic traditions of the Plains, using pencil and crayon to explore and express aspects of their identities. Small pictographic drawings sketched in the margins of students' school slates (recorded in photographs), and Luther Standing Bear's observation that drawing gave solace to Ernest White Thunder when he was homesick, provide evidence that many students brought with them both a knowledge and a love of drawing.[53]

While acting as jailer at Fort Marion, Pratt had encouraged the adult prisoners to draw using their Plains tradition. He allowed them to sell their work to tourists, but no instruction in art was given to the prisoners.[54] It seems clear that Pratt's encouragement of drawing continued at Carlisle, but there, as part of his "civilizing" program, Pratt also organized art classes to teach the children about perspective and the Euro-American representational style of drawing.[55] Some of these representational images have survived in the archive.[56] But more remarkably, a small collection of student art, drawn in the pictographic Plains style and dating from the 1880s, has also been preserved in the collections of the Cumberland County Historical Society.[57] This is a unique record in a medium with direct links to visual modes of representation developed on the Plains over generations. Gayatri Spivak, in her seminal *Can the Subaltern Speak?*, reminded us that the reclamation of the pure "native text" in a postcolonial or settler-colonial context is a utopian ideal.[58] Nevertheless, these students' drawings, although hard to interpret, offer a rare firsthand record that was created by students while at the school. These drawings have received very limited scholarly attention.[59] Yet they carry clear evidence of the students' knowledge of traditional modes of representation, as well as their ability to execute drawings in the Plains style.

Modern scholars writing about Plains Indian art make clear that Plains pictographic drawing and ledger art was a sophisticated form of communication. Working within a tight set of rules, it used a visual code to convey very clear and precise meanings that could be read and interpreted only within the context of its own cultural production. Karen Daniels Petersen explains that "without a knowledge of the basic rules of Plains Indian drawing, the language of the pictures is a foreign tongue."[60] There was, in all drawings, an economy of detail. Backgrounds and all irrelevant details were omitted. Clothing, however, was very important and frequently drawn in great detail, to indicate both status and individual identity. Focus was always on the exploits or actions of an individual or group, generally male. Movement, which was important, was from right to left, and every detail in the drawing or painting carried an unambiguous and precise meaning.

While they are obviously the work of children, some of the Carlisle drawings share many similarities with the ledger art being produced on the reservations of the West at this time. Yet included in the Carlisle student ledger art is a small group of four drawings that stand out as being different from the more traditional action images and can perhaps even be classified as portraits. Each shows a single, full-length figure, accompanied by a student's name and tribal affiliation. In these four Carlisle portraits, unlike in traditional Plains art, focus is on the individual himself. All action is absent, and in this respect these drawings have an affiliation with static patterns of representation more familiar to Western traditions of portraiture. But the figures are dressed traditionally, and in all of the drawings very careful attention has been paid to the details of clothing and regalia. Whether they were drawn spontaneously or as part of a school exercise, all these portraits display the students' clear memory of specific items of regalia as well as their capacity to reproduce them. These portraits can, I suggest, be deemed student alternatives to the photographic portraits produced at Carlisle.

The most elaborate of these portrait drawings was made by McKay Dougan (Osage) (figure 9.5). His accomplished portrait presents a spectacular image of an Osage leader, whose identity is made known by the pictographs on his shield.[61] Covering most of a seven-inch square page, the image has been inked with assiduous care and precision. From the archival record we can learn very little about McKay Dougan. A student record card gives his dates of arrival (June 9, 1982) and departure (July 6, 1985), his age on arrival (seventeen), and the fact that he left Carlisle because he was "sick."[62] But from his drawing we can find out a little more. In it, Dougan displays intimate knowledge of both the appearance and construction of Osage regalia. From this we can infer that he had an understanding of the Osage cosmos and its full spiritual complexity. The two-row bone hairpipe breastplate, worn on special occasions, signals the wealth and status of its wearer. And the rare Osage split-horn headdress indicates this leader's authority during "ritual preparations for the hunt."[63] A sacred object, the headdress was made from materials that represented the creative forces of the cosmos. As was usual in pictographic art, the facial features of this man are rudimentary. It is his *regalia* that carries the story, along with the ceremonial lines of red paint on his cheeks. McKay Dougan drew a powerful warrior who, with his ceremonial regalia and red face paint, was quite literally dressed to kill.

FIGURE 9.5. *McKay Dougan, Osage*, crayon and ink drawing, ca. 1882–85. Courtesy of Cumberland County Historical Society, Carlisle, PA.

This drawing does not comply with one of the main ledger art traditions, because there is no action. There is, however, a clear assertion of individual worth. The artist has matched the intricate detail of his drawing with the elaborate writing and decoration of his own name: large, strong red letters that run parallel with the lance and the warrior and an additional outline of red dots decorating each letter.[64] In this way, McKay Dougan has spatially aligned and chromatically integrated himself with the powerful Osage figure he has drawn, and in so doing he has perhaps asserted and confirmed his own personal sense of being Osage. McKay Dougan would have been old enough to have participated in the last Osage buffalo hunts and to have witnessed the ceremonial preparations beforehand.[65] The full meanings of this image are not obvious and knowable. What we *can* conclude, however, is that McKay Dougan was confident in his own cultural heritage, carried within him very exact memories of the precise detail of how a great warrior would dress in preparation for the hunt, and openly claimed a personal relationship with these traditions. Drawings such as this carry intricate messages that can be read and interpreted in different ways. By depicting a named individual from the Osage tribe and writing his own name alongside him, McKay Dougan was perhaps inscribing a version of himself that linked him to a high-ranking, respected, and powerful Osage. The spirit of rebellion implicit in McKay Dougan's drawing, at a school dedicated to destroying Indigenous cultures, was probably not fully grasped by his Euro-American teachers, because its meaning was hidden to all except those with a knowledge of Osage culture. It can thus be read as a "hidden transcript" of the type delineated by Scott, and evidence of "the elusive native presence" understood by Vizenor. It seems likely that if there was an intended audience, it was the Native students at Carlisle, and particularly the Osage.

Ironically, at Carlisle, drawings whose style and content challenged the school's mission to destroy all aspects of "Indianness," and might therefore have been deemed subversive, were apparently permitted and promoted. These drawings raise a puzzling question: If Carlisle was intent on obliterating all elements of Native cultures, why were such drawings in the pictographic style permitted, even if their deeper meanings could not be readily understood? And equally important, why were they preserved? One part of the answer may lie in the comparative purposes for which they were used by the school. A school newspaper report on the Carlisle Indian School exhibit at the Cumberland County Fair in 1882 explains how, among the items of the children's work on display, were "rude and grotesque paintings, side by side with very fine specimens of . . . drawing, showing what rapid progress the boys and girls have made."[66] This suggests that on such occasions, the students' drawings were used as the artistic equivalent of the before-and-after photographs and were both permitted and preserved to provide evidence of the children's supposed progress from "savagery" to "civilization."

Conclusion

Photography was a Euro-American medium whose early development occurred in a time frame that corresponded almost exactly with the dispossession of Native nations of the American West. Despite the medium's newness, Native people on the Plains were quick to become active subjects in the photographic encounter, presenting themselves for the camera in ways that expressed their own agency, choosing poses, gestures, and, in particular, clothing to exert an impact on the photographic images made of them by Euro-American photographers.[67] Within the power structures of a boarding school Native students had fewer freedoms, so it is remarkable that some demonstrated an ability to recruit photography for their own purposes and agenda. Drawing was different: it had a long tradition of development on the Plains and operated according to a set of well-established conventions. Yet even in a school dedicated to expunging all "Indianness," some students who arrived at Carlisle in the early years were able to engage in "practices of survivance" (Vizenor) by creating images that linked them epistemologically, imaginatively, and visually to traditional knowledge systems. The visual archive of the Carlisle Indian School—photographs and drawings—carries within it the invitation to study the "points of fracture" (Edwards) to discover how, even at a school dedicated to eliminating all aspects of Indigenous cultures, some students found subtle ways to protect and assert their identities by making creative claims to visual sovereignty.

NOTES

Parts of this chapter were previously published in "Owning the Image: Indigenous Children Claim Visual Sovereignty Far from Home," in *Art, Observation, and an Anthropology of Illustration*, edited by Max Carocci and Stephanie Pratt (London: Bloomsbury, 2022), 95–113. They are republished in this volume with permission of the publisher, Bloomsbury Visual Arts, an imprint of Bloomsbury Publishing Plc.

1 Fiona Bateman and Lionel Pilkington, eds., *Studies in Settler Colonialism* (London: Palgrave Macmillan, 2011); Walter L. Hixson, *American Settler Colonialism: A History* (London: Palgrave Macmillan, 2013).

2 Patrick Wolfe, *Settler Colonialism and the Transformation of Anthropology: The Politics and Poetics of an Ethnographic Event* (London: Bloomsbury, 1999), 1.

3 David Wallace Adams, *Education for Extinction: American Indians and the Boarding School Experience, 1875–1928* (Lawrence: University Press of Kansas, 1995).

4 Truth and Reconciliation Commission of Canada (TRCC), *Honouring the Truth, Reconciling for the Future: Summary of the Final Report of the Truth and Reconciliation Commission of Canada*, vol. 1, 2015, 1, accessed March 14, 2018, http://www.trc.ca/websites/trcinstitution/File/2015/Findings/Exec_Summary_2015_05_31_web_o.pdf.

5 "Prime Minister Trudeau Receives TRC Report," *NationTalk*, December 15, 2015, http://nationtalk.ca/story/prime-minister-trudeau-receives-trc-report-promises-action-net-newsledger.

6 See the National Native American Boarding School Healing Coalition's website at https://boardingschoolhealing.org.

7   U.S Department of Interior, "Secretary Haaland Announces Federal Indian Board-ing School Initiative," press release, June 23, 2021.

8   Hermann J. Viola, *Diplomats in Buckskin: A History of Indian Delegations in Washington City* (Norman: University of Oklahoma Press, 1995), 111.

9   Adams, *Education for Extinction*; Genevieve Bell, "Telling Stories out of School," PhD diss., Stanford University, 1998, https://trove.nla.gov.au/work/17745331?q&versionId =20816673; Jacqueline Fear-Segal, *White Man's Club: Schools, Race, and the Struggle of Indian Acculturation* (Lincoln: University of Nebraska Press, 2007); K. Tsianina Lomawaima, *They Called It Prairie Light: The Story of Chilocco Indian School* (Lincoln: University of Nebraska Press, 1994).

10 James C. Scott, *Domination and the Arts of Resistance: Hidden Transcripts* (New Haven, CT: Yale University Press, 1992).

11 Luther Standing Bear was a Carlisle student and in later years wrote two autobio-graphical texts in which he reflects on his schooling: *My People the Sioux* (Lincoln: University of Nebraska Press, [1928] 2006) and *Land of the Spotted Eagle* (Lincoln: University of Nebraska Press, [1933] 1978). They are invaluable sources; nevertheless, it is significant that Standing Bear wrote with the benefit of hindsight, years after he left the school.

12 Brenda Child, *Boarding School Seasons: American Indian Families, 1900–1940* (Lincoln: University of Nebraska Press, 1998); Jacqueline Emery, *Recovering Native America Writings in the Boarding School Press* (Lincoln: University of Nebraska Press, 2017); Lomawaima, *They Called It Prairie Light*; Robert Warrior, *The People and the Word: Reading Native Nonfiction* (Minneapolis: University of Minnesota Press, 2005).

13 For Pratt's account of his founding and running of Carlisle, see Richard Henry Pratt, *Battlefield and Classroom: Four Decades with the American Indian, 1867–1904* (Lin-coln: University of Nebraska Press, 1964).

14 Pratt, *Battlefield and Classroom*, 220.

15 Pratt, *Battlefield and Classroom*, 231.

16 Christopher Pinney and Nicholas Peterson, eds., *Photography's Other Histories* (Durham, NC: Duke University Press, 2003), 1.

17 Pratt, *Battlefield and Classroom*, 218.

18 Jolene Rickard, "The Occupation of Indigenous Space as 'Photograph,'" in *Native Nations: Journeys in American Photography*, edited by Jane Alison (London: Barbican Art Gallery, 1998), 60–61.

19 Jacqueline Fear-Segal, "Facing the Binary: Native American Students in the Cam-era's Lens," in *Before-and-After Photography: Histories and Contexts*, edited by Jordan Bear and Kate Palmer Albers (London: Bloomsbury Academic, 2017), 153–73.

20 Ted Jojola, "Photographs from Hell," in *Beyond the Reach of Time and Change: Native American Reflections on the Frank A. Rinehart Photograph Collection*, edited by Simon J. Ortiz (Tucson: University of Arizona Press, 2004), 79; Gerald Vizenor, *Fugitive Poses* (Lincoln: University of Nebraska Press, 1998), 155.

21 Vizenor, *Fugitive Poses*, 152, 156.

22 Elizabeth Edwards, *Raw Histories: Photographs, Anthropology, and Museums* (Oxford: Berg, 2001), 12.

23   Edwards, *Raw Histories*, 256.

24   Edwards, *Raw Histories*; Chris Gosden and Yvonne Marshall, "The Cultural Biography of Objects," *World Archaeology* 31, no. 2 (1999): 169–78; Igor Kopytoff, "The Cultural Biography of Things," in *The Social Life of Things*, edited by Arjun Appadurai (Cambridge: Cambridge University Press, 1986), 67; Daniel Miller, *Material Culture and Mass Consumption* (Oxford: Blackwell, 1987); Daniel Miller, *Material Culture: Why Some Things Matter* (London: UCL, 1998); Vizenor, *Fugitive Poses.*

25   Gerald Vizenor, "Aesthetics of Survivance," in *Survivance: Narratives of Native Presence*, edited by Gerald Vizenor (Lincoln: University of Nebraska Press, 2008), 1.

26   Gerald Vizenor, *Manifest Manners: Postindian Warriors of Survivance* (Hanover, NH: Wesleyan University Press, 1994), 4.

27   Raheja's observation about film can also be productively applied to still photographs: Michelle H. Raheja, "Reading Nanook's Smile: Visual Sovereignty, Indigenous Revisions of Ethnography, and Atanarjuat (The Fast Runner)," *American Quarterly* 59, no. 4 (December 2007): 1161.

28   There was no Native eye behind the camera lens at Carlisle, except briefly and remarkably between 1894 and 1896, when a Puyallup student, John Leslie, was apprenticed to J. N. Choate. Some of Leslie's photographs were sold as part of Choate's commercial list; Leslie also contributed most of the images for Carlisle's 1895 catalogue. By the mid-1890s, cameras were more readily available, and there is evidence that they were sometimes used by students informally on campus.

29   Eric Homberger, "J. P. Morgan's Nose: Photographer and Subject in American Portrait Photography," in *The Portrait in Photography*, edited by Graham Clarke (London: Reaktion, 1992), 115–31.

30   Mary Louise Pratt, *Imperial Eyes: Travel Writing and Transculturalism* (New York: Routledge, 1992), 7.

31   Paul Chaat Smith, "Every Picture Tells a Story," in *Partial Recall*, edited by Lucy R. Lippard (New York: New Press, 1992), 97.

32   White Thunder to Ernest White Thunder, reprinted in *Eadle Keahtah Toh* 1, no. 2 (April 1880): 3.

33   Pratt, *Battlefield and Classroom*, 239.

34   Richard H. Pratt to White Thunder, December 15, 1880, Pratt Papers, Beinecke Rare Book and Manuscript Library, Yale University, New Haven, CT.

35   Pratt to White Thunder.

36   Elizabeth Siegel, *Galleries of Friendship and Fame: A History of Nineteenth Century American Photograph Albums* (New Haven, CT: Yale University Press, 2010).

37   *Morning Star* 6, no. 3 (October 1885): 8.

38   Frank H. Goodyear III, *Red Cloud: Photographs of a Lakota Chief* (Lincoln: University of Nebraska Press, 2003), 8.

39   Goodyear, *Red Cloud*, 10.

40   Cloud Shield's Winter Count is published in Garrick Mallery, "Pictographs of the North American Indians," *Fourth Annual Report of the Bureau of Ethnology to the Secretary of the Smithsonian Institution, 1882–1883*, https://archive.org/details/PictographsOfTheNorthAmerican86Pages3256GarrickMallery.

41 Reprinted in Helen Wilhelmina Ludlow, "Indian Education at Hampton and Carlisle," *Harper's Magazine*, April 1881, 675.

42 "Descriptive and Historical Record of Student—Luther Standing Bear," Carlisle Indian School Digital Resource Center, Archives and Special Collections, Waidner-Spahr Library, Dickinson College, Carlisle, PA (hereafter, CISDRC), http://carlisleindian.dickinson.edu/sites/all/files/docs-ephemera/NARA_1327_b060_3019_0.pdf.

43 Standing Bear, *Land of the Spotted Eagle*, 233–34.

44 Standing Bear, *Land of the Spotted Eagle*; Standing Bear, *My People the Sioux*.

45 Vizenor, *Manifest Manners*, 5.

46 Vizenor, *Manifest Manners*, 4.

47 Standing Bear, *My People the Sioux*, 142–43.

48 Standing Bear, *Land of the Spotted Eagle*, 232.

49 Standing Bear, *Land of the Spotted Eagle*, 235.

50 Vizenor, "The Aesthetics of Survivance," 11.

51 Janet C. Berlo, ed., *Plains Indian Drawings, 1865–1935: Pages from a Visual History* (New York: Harry N. Adams, 1996); Colin G. Calloway, *Ledger Narrative: The Plains Indian Drawings in the Mark Lansburgh Collection at Dartmouth College* (Norman: University of Oklahoma Press, 2012); Joyce N. Szabo, *Howling Wolf and the History of Ledger Art* (Albuquerque: University of New Mexico Press, 1994).

52 Goodyear, *Red Cloud*, 6.

53 Standing Bear, *My People the Sioux*, 159; John N. Choate, "Slate, Belonging to Luther Otakte, with Math Exercise and Drawing of Man Shooting Bird out of Tree with Bow and Arrow," 1879, photo lot 81-12 06814000, National Anthropological Archives, Smithsonian Institution, https://learninglab.si.edu/collections/carlisle-indian-industrial-school/mCa9fK9iuz6EHWa9#r/68245; John N. Choate, "Carlisle Student Slate with Vocabulary Exercises, Drawings of John Williams? on Horseback, and Letter to His Father, Written by Rutherford B. Hayes," June 25, 1880, photo lot 81-12 06813900, National Anthropological Archives, Smithsonian Institution, https://learninglab.si.edu/collections/carlisle-indian-industrial-school/mCa9fK9iuz6EHWa9#r/68246.

54 Joyce Szarbo, *Howling Wolf and the History of Ledger Art* (Albuquerque: University of New Mexico Press, 1994), 70.

55 For a discussion of the teaching of art at Carlisle, see Joyce Szarbo, "Drawing Life's Changes: Late Nineteenth-Century Plains Drawings from Hampton Institute and Carlisle Indian School," *Native American Studies* 18, no. 1 (2004): 41–51. For an excellent broader study of the use of art as an instrument of Americanization/colonization in the Indian school system, see Marinella Lentis, *Colonized through Art: American Indian Schools and Art Education, 1889–1915* (Lincoln: University of Nebraska Press, 2017).

56 See esp. Joshua Given (Kiowa), "Still Life," pencil on paper, Cumberland County (PA) Historical Society.

57 This collection of drawings at the Cumberland County Historical Society has not yet been made accessible digitally.

58 Gayatri Chakravorty Spivak, *Can the Subaltern Speak?* (Basingstoke, UK: Macmillan, 1988).

59 Szarbo, "Drawing Life's Changes," is an excellent, preliminary exploration of this topic.

60 Karen Daniels Petersen, *Plains Indian Art from Fort Marion* (Norman: University of Oklahoma Press, 1971), x.

61 So far it has not been possible to identify this warrior. The exactitude of the rich pictographic traditions of the Osage was recognized and chronicled by Euro-Americans in the early nineteenth century: see Tahuska et al., *Osage Indian Pictographs, Signs and Emblems, with English Translations*, American Philosophical Society Digital Collections, https://diglib.amphilsoc.org/islandora/search/osage%20 indian%20pictographs?type=dismax.

62 McKay Dougan, "Student Information Card," CISDRC, http://carlisleindian .dickinson.edu/sites/all/files/docs-ephemera/NARA_1329_b005_c00d_0029.pdf.

63 There is another similar split-horn headdress in the Brooklyn Museum that was owned by the Osage leader Shunkahmolah. According to Osages consulted by the museum, the split-horn headdress was used in "ritual preparations for the hunt" and was worn as a symbol of authority: *Osage Split Horn Headdress*. Photo: Brooklyn Museum, 11.694.9050.jpg, http://epoc2.cs.uow.edu.au/brooklyn_r_1000_ws /similarity/index.php?o=130426.

64 Although it is possible that the dots are guidelines for the writing and were put there by a teacher, I conclude that this is not the case because (1) they are not in a straight line; (2) they are not in pencil, as in the case in two of the other portraits; and (3) they do not shape the letters but, instead, top and tail them.

65 John Joseph Mathews, "Chief Fred Lookout Saw Great Changes Come to His Tribesmen of the Osage," *Daily Oklahoma*, April 23, 1939.

66 *Eadle Keatah Toh* 2, no. 12 (July 1882): 3.

67 Martha A. Sandweiss, *Print the Legend: Photography and the American West* (New Haven, CT: Yale University Press, 2004), 217; Carol J. Williams, *Framing the West: Race, Gender, and the Photographic Frontier in the Pacific Northwest* (Oxford: Oxford University Press, 2003).

10

LAND THROUGH THE CAMERA

Post/Colonial Space and Indigenous Struggles
in *Birdwatchers* (*Terra Vermelha*)

KERSTIN KNOPF

Imagine this scene at the beginning of a film: in a small motorboat, white Anglophone tourists glide along a calm rain-forest river in Mato Grosso do Sul, Brazil,
on a bird-watching tour, then the camera shows hostile-looking Indígenas (Indigenous people)—naked, with loincloths, traditional jewelry, face painting, and
weapons—standing by the shore and watching the tourists (figure 10.1). This is
an uncanny moment of being watched while watching—a masterful repetition
of colonial contact situations. It is put into relief in the next scene, when we see
the Indígenas in a clearing behind the river put on modern clothes and receive
a scant payment for their playacting primitive people for the tourists. Such relief is short-lived, though, since we learn that these Indigenous people are dispossessed of their land and cooped up in small reserves. The complex relation
between Indigenous people and Brazilian landowners is the central focus of the

FIGURE 10.1. *Birdwatchers* (*Terra Vermelha*), film still. Rai Cinema/Karta Film/ Gullane Filmes.

film *Birdwatchers* (*Terra Vermelha* [2008]), by the award-winning Chilean Italian director Marco Bechis.[1] The film, a Brazilian and Italian coproduction, presents a plot around the cultural and political struggle of the Guaraní-Kaiowá to regain control over their culture, lives, and traditional lands, and specifically around the *retomadas*, the growing Indigenous land reclamation movement.

This chapter develops a concept of dispossessed Indigenous homelands in post/ colonial settler societies as post/colonial space that is produced through colonization, non-Indigenous settlement, gradual dispossession, displacement, and elimination of Indigenous populations who understand these territories as their homelands. These territories are necessary for sustaining Indigenous lifeways and cultural traditions, which have been adapting to modern developments and influences of non-Indigenous cultures since contact; Indigenous modernity is thus produced by post/colonial conditions; settler-state policies; and traditional Indigenous, non-Indigenous, and subsequently hybrid ways of life and understandings of reality. I wish to rethink the concepts of deterritorialization and reterritorialization and to employ them for the purpose of theorizing Indigenous lands as post/colonial space informed by Indigenous and settler-colonial ontologies and epistemes, settler-colonial bio- and geopolitics, and Indigenous modernities and resistances in postcolonial settler states. To point toward the simultaneity and confluence of colonial bio- and geopolitics and Indigenous and non-Indigenous lives, practices, and epistemes in modern post/colonial settler states (colonial from Indigenous perspectives; postcolonial from perspectives of settlers who have gained independence from the British mother state) for the construction of space on place, I use the term *post/colonial* when referring to space, place, and modernities. Deterritorializing Indigenous people is a simultaneous process that reterritorializes colonial settler groups on the same lands and produces post/colonial space implicated in a hierarchized matrix of power-space-economics with differing Indigenous and non-Indigenous sociopolitical, economic, ontological, and epistemological realities and approaches. In connection with these ideas, the chapter discusses the film *Birdwatchers* and its representation of the conditions that de- and reterritorialization produce for Guaraní people and of their struggles to reclaim parts of their homelands.

Land Reclamation Struggles in Birdwatchers

Walter Mignolo argues that Europe's massive colonization of space and concomitant economic and religious expansion that began at the end of the fifteenth century went hand in hand with the need to expand geographical knowledge and the creation of maps of the Americas.[2] After Edmundo O'Gorman, he says that "America was not an existing entity . . . waiting to be discovered. . . . [I]t was a European invention."[3] This invention was and is taken as "truth" because "one takes maps as true representations of the earth . . . and not as cognitive and culture-relative artifacts used not only for way-finding but also for the colonization of space and of the mind. Briefly, maps were tools that, historically, played a crucial role in European expansion and territorial control of its colonies."[4] By the last quarter of the twentieth century, he argues, "the early colonial process designed to 'modernize,' Christianize, and civilize the world was transformed . . . into a process with an aim to 'marketize' the world. Coloniality continues to be, in this global domain, an unnamed, unspoken driving force of modernization and the market."[5] The redefinition of colonized lands as belonging to European settler nations—basically, the understanding that North America, Latin America, Australia, and New Zealand, for example, are "white" lands with Indigenous minority populations—was also an unnamed process of modernization. Mignolo and Paul Gilroy (and others) insist that European colonization of world territories and Atlantic enslavement of Black people are modernity's well-concealed darker sides and are, in essence, the most fundamental influences on modernity. Mignolo holds: "Coloniality . . . is constitutive of modernity—there is no modernity without coloniality."[6] Gilroy stresses that slavery is irreducibly entangled with modern capitalism, plantation slavery being "capitalism with its clothes off."[7]

The film *Birdwatchers* takes issue with Guaraní modernity and with how modernity and entangled economic and spatial relations privilege some groups of people at the cost of other groups' dismal ways of living. The film unrelentingly presents the daily reality of the Guaraní, who have lost their entire homeland during the past one hundred years. Deforestation has transformed large parts of the Guaraní homeland into a huge network of cattle ranches, soy farms, and sugarcane plantations.[8] The goods produced on Guaraní homelands are consumed largely in mainstream settler societies and in Europe, societies that in this way are indirectly involved in the dispossession, oppression, and impoverishment of Indigenous people in Brazil such as the Guaraní. Survival International states that today there are approximately 51,000 Guaraní living in seven Brazilian states, the largest Indigenous group in Brazil.[9] More Guaraní live in the neighboring countries of Paraguay, Bolivia, and Argentina. Some Guaraní now live in small, overcrowded reserves surrounded by cattle ranches and sugarcane and soy fields, and some have no land to use at all and live in makeshift plastic tents beside freeways and roads, in squalid conditions without access to clean water and food. Malnutrition, hunger, poverty, disease, substandard sanitary conditions, low health levels, and youth suicide are rampant in these devastated communities. Wild animal populations have been severely decimated because of increasing rain-forest clear-cutting, and land and rivers have been slowly polluted by agro-industrial pesticides; the Guaraní cannot continue to collect and hunt for sustenance because of destroyed forests and restricted access to traditional territories.[10] Because of massive dispossession, Guaraní were forced to take up temporary paid labor on plantations and in a fast-growing number of ethanol refineries for biofuels, where they are exposed to unfair treatment, exploitation, and structural health risks. In general, they face high rates of unfair imprisonment, violence, and homicide.[11] Those who take part in the *retomadas*—the land reclamation movements and struggles to get legal recognition of their rights to their dispossessed homelands—are constantly threatened by ranchers' gunmen. Attacks on *retomada* camps and the murder of Guaraní people seems to be one method to undermine the movement; forty-four Indigenous people were assassinated in Mato Grosso do Sul in 2007, and forty-two were murdered in 2008. One camp and one group in the process of relocating were attacked by ranchers and their guards. Several leaders of *retomadas* have been assassinated in the past years. Survival International lists the names of ten murdered people in its report to the United Nations (UN) Committee on the Elimination of Racial Discrimination, their deaths presumably linked to gunmen working for local ranchers.[12] Such is the daily reality of only one dispossessed Indigenous population in Latin America. James Anaya, UN Special Rapporteur on the situation of human rights and fundamental freedoms of Indigenous people, stated: "Tensions between indigenous peoples and non-indigenous occupants have been especially acute in the state of Mato Grosso do Sul, where indigenous peoples suffer from a severe lack of access to their traditional lands, extreme poverty and related social ills; giving rise to a pattern of violence that is marked by numerous murders of indigenous individuals as well as by criminal prosecution of indigenous individuals for acts of protest."[13]

Also, Brazilian senator and former environmental minister Marina Silva proclaimed after her visit to Mato Grosso do Sul that the Indigenous people face "social apartheid" in the state since they cannot exercise their rights.[14] The Guaraní-Kaiowá Indigenous Rights Commission holds: "At the root of the situation is the lack of land, which is the consequence of the history of theft and destruction of our traditional territories, of the policy to confine us in reserves, of the loss of our liberty and even the loss of a will to live."[15] This statement clearly points toward the major reason for deteriorating life and culture of Guaraní— the lack of land that provides physical and spiritual sustenance. Gastón Gordillo explains that, in terms of land, (most) Indigenous people have a "stable spatiality, which emphasizes that their identities are grounded in, and defined by, well-defined territories saturated with meanings produced throughout generations."[16] Aline Frey discusses the Guaraní concept of *tekohà* as sacred territory that must be taken care of and that grants the Guaraní life and their particular way of life. She says:

> As such, more than a mere place of origin or residence, the notion of *tekohà* has a fundamental role in giving meaning to social, economic, politic, religious and cultural aspects of the community. While there is a tendency to view these Indigenous relations to land as a given persisting as they do through time, there is an important way in which these relations are proposed as knowledges and understandings that need to be taken account of—adjusted and calibrated in the polity at large for new circumstances. Rather than being static they are present here as emergent.[17]

Marco Bechis designed a plot for his film that fictitiously presents the struggle of a Guaraní-Kaiowá community that suffers from despicable living conditions, malnutrition, lack of job opportunities, and a general lack of future prospects for young people, with youth suicide rampant. They intend to relocate to their traditional homeland since they cannot be a healthy community away from their *tekohà*, and they force land reclamation processes to begin. Frey states that reserves are usually too small and overcrowded to allow economic and cultural survival and opportunities; at the same time, the *tekohà* is an extension of the community, as people and land are inseparably bound together.[18] The Guaraní establish a makeshift camp between a road and the fence of a field that is part of a large farm established on their deforested former homeland. The farmer Moreira and his wife also sell the bird-watching tours and pay the Guaraní-Kaiowá to play the "primitive" Natives. They now regularly cross the field to haul water from the river and go hunting in the adjacent rain forest—or, better, in what is left of it. However, they are continually hunted by armed guards and driven off the land that the "landowner" now claims as his by title. An armed guard is put up in an old trailer in the middle of the field to prevent the people from entering it, and their camp is sprayed with pesticides from a plane. More people and shamans from the surrounding areas arrive and support the movement to reclaim their traditional land. But the *retomada* movement is weakened by the influences of alcohol, internal strife, the need to work for money on neighboring plantations, stubbornness of the *cacique* (a term for an Indigenous leader in territories colonized by the Spanish and Portuguese), and yet another suicide: that of the *cacique*'s son Ireneu. Finally, in a symbolic act of claiming the land, the people move onto the field, physically reoccupying their dispossessed land. Police and a lawyer are brought in to deal with the situation. In a face-to-face encounter, both the *cacique*, Nádio, and the farmer, Moreira, explain their claim to the land. No solution is found, and the issue is transferred to the courts. The farmers "solve" the issue according to their interests: Nádio is insidiously killed by agribusiness henchmen after being betrayed by one man in the camp. The young Osvaldo, who has the gift to communicate with the spirits and is trained to become a shaman, is torn between two worlds: that of Indigenous modernity adapted to settler-colonial realities in their former territories and the world of traditional spirituality. He is also driven to suicide by the evil spirit Anguè after Nádio's death but resists killing himself and, as the film suggests, succeeds in negotiating a traditional and modern Guaraní existence.

Bechis is wise enough not to reduce the conflict to a black-and-white opposition; instead, he presents complex entanglements underneath the surface of the big landowner-Guaraní conflict: there is a budding romantic relationship between Osvaldo and Maria, the farmer's daughter; the Indígena Lia strategically seduces the guard on the field to get food and disarm him; the white store owner supports the people *and* the landowners; a man from the *retomada* camp is paid to betray Nádio; Ireneu leaves the *retomada* camp along with others to earn money through plantation work and spends it on flashy sneakers instead of food for the camp and is scolded by his father, which drives him to suicide; the land conflict remains unsolved. With this extraordinary film, Bechis critically presents the dispossession of Indigenous peoples in Latin America and their continuing dehumanization, impoverishment, and paternalistic treatment through the settler-colonial state, conditions that are intensified by the increasing clear-cutting of rain forests; business interests of multinational companies; and the world's hunger for precious wood, beef, sugar, soy, wood, and biofuels.

Theoretical Thoughts on Dispossessed Indigenous Land as Post/Colonial Space

In this chapter, I rethink the concepts of "deterritorialized" and "reterritorialized" in connection to Indigenous lands, colonial processes, and the redefinition of land to employ these modified concepts for the analysis of settler-colonial realities of dispossessed lands and the construction of these lands as settler-colonial space. My ideas are not localized so as to look at specific Indigenous territories, but I think through the relationship of land, Indigenous people, and settler-colonial people in a general sense. Thus, I bring together ideas from North American and Latin American scholars and then use them to analyze the Brazilian film. Settler colonialism, according to Glen Coulthard, "refers to contexts where the territorial infrastructure of the colonizing society is built on and overwhelms the formerly self-governing but now dispossessed Indigenous nations; indeed, settler-colonial politics are predicated on maintaining this dispossession."[19] Gilles Deleuze and Félix Guattari introduced the concepts of "deterritorialization" and "reterritorialization" in their two-volume *Capitalism and Schizophrenia* (1972, 1980), while describing social and cultural processes that accompany the development of global capitalist modernity. "Deterritorialization designated the motor of permanent revolution," argues Eugene W. Holland, "while reterritorialization designated the power relations imposed by the private ownership of capital."[20] Gil-Manuel Hernàndez i Martí writes, "Deterritorialization speaks of the loss of the 'natural' relation between culture and the social and geographic territories, and describes a deep transformation of the link between our everyday cultural experiences and our configuration as preferably local beings."[21] In the second volume, *A Thousand Plateaus*, Deleuze and Guattari deconstruct the dichotomy between the concepts and explain their entanglements. Deterritorializing of spaces involves reterritorializing in the very same process—a reordering and redefining of a place, territory, or cultural space within a matrix of power relations imposed on that place:

> *Theorem Five:* deterritorialization is always double, because it implies the coexistence of a major variable and a minor variable in simultaneous becoming (the two terms of a becoming do not exchange places, there is no identification between them, they are instead drawn into an asymmetrical block in which both change to the same extent, and which constitutes their zone of proximity). *Theorem Six:* in nonsymmetrical double deterritorialization it is possible to assign a deterritorializing force and a deterritorialized force, even if the same force switches from one value to the other depending on the "moment" or aspect considered; furthermore, it is the least deterritorialized element that always triggers the deterritorialization of the most deterritorializing element, which then reacts back upon it in full force.[22]

Hernàndez i Martí reminds us to see these processes not as "impoverishment of cultural interaction" but as transformations of local cultural relationships and experiences as results of globalization and transnational flows and their imprint on the local.[23] And he makes clear that the idea of "deterritorialization" cannot be based on notions of fixed, isolated cultures, and that all individuals experience cultural deterritorialization in different ways and within the framework of unequal conditions and contexts.[24] Deterritorialization and reterritorialization thus result in changed and more complex and varied cultural spaces. Arjun Appadurai defines deterritorialization with respect to global migration "as one of the central forces of the modern world, since it brings laboring populations into the lower class sectors and spaces of relatively wealthy societies, while sometimes creating exaggerated and intensified senses of criticism or attachment to politics in the home-state."[25]

Postcolonial scholarship has intensely engaged with Deleuze and Guattari's ideas to critique colonialism and postcolonial conditions.[26] For the discussion of Indigenous lands, I follow Bruce B. Janz's suggestion to forget Deleuze and "not look to see whether he gives us a new tool to solve an old problem."[27] Instead I apply these ideas and "then strike . . . out on a new path."[28] Robert C. Young focuses attention on "lands" when he describes territorialization, deterritorialization, and reterritorialization as "geographical processes linked to subject-formation."[29] These are processes of "the appropriation of land and its confiscation from those who have formerly worked it, with or without legal title. . . . A third moment of 'reterritorialization' describes the violent dynamics of the colonial and or imperial propagation of economic, cultural, and social transformation of the indigenous culture, at the same time as characterizing the successful process of resistance to deterritorialization through anti-colonial movements."[30] I want to follow suit and move away from Deleuze and Guattari's ideas of deterritorialization and reterritorialization bound to psychological processes and processes of mediatization, migration, and the production of cultural space and center them instead on their semantic and conceptual base—"territory." Then Indigenous populations, dispossessed of territories they believe they belong to according to Indigenous philosophies and narratives, are rendered a deterritorialized group, while colonizing groups are rendered a reterritorialized group.[31]

Theoretical interventions by postcolonial geographers—foremost, Edward Soja—have triggered a reconceptualization of space in postcolonial studies. Following Henri Lefebvre, Soja argues that all social relations in history also have a spatial existence.[32] Concrete places are implicated in what he theorizes as the space-time-being trialectics. Social practices in concrete places, in consequence, produce space in time, or "Thirdspace," which Soja defines as "lived social space with its multifaceted inclusiveness and simultaneities."[33] Social space is thus produced by myriad spaces, or sets of relations.

With Lefebvre's and Soja's theoretical ideas on social space in mind, I turn to Gordillo, who uses Deleuze and Guattari's ideas to discuss deterritorialization processes that involve Guaraní, with a focus on their dislocation from Bolivian territories as a result of capitalist encroachment on their lands and their subsequent migration to northern Argentina, where they worked largely on sugarcane plantations and built a Guaraní diaspora. In Gordillo's argumentation, these Guaraní experienced deterritorialization from their homelands and reterritorialization on Argentinian land that was dictated by the interests of agribusinesses and, decades later, again experienced deterritorialization from these diasporic lands due to the establishment of more plantations.[34] Gordillo applies Deleuze and Guattari's ideas but does not perceive these processes as dictated by the state. Following Lefebvre, he uses the idea of "reterritorializations as *spatially productive* processes that, rather than simply unfolding on a fixed spatial matrix, transform and reconstitute the social and physical texture of the geography."[35] Unlike Gordillo, I do not focus on Indigenous diasporas generated through processes of dislocation and the establishment of plantations on different lands, which "became machines of capitalist deterritorialization that transformed vast geographies on both sides of the border as they recruited thousands of permanent and seasonal workers."[36] I want to concentrate on traditional homelands of Guaraní—here, Brazil—and understand the deterritorialization of Indigenous people and reterritorialization of the settler culture as a simultaneous process happening on the same territory, in which the Indigenous people are not completely driven away from their homelands but are dislocated to fringe territories such as reserves and roadside places.

Akhil Gupta and James Ferguson argue that spaces are not autonomous but are marked by discontinuities and power relations that produce their relationships; colonialism displaces local interconnections between place and community by newly imposed interconnections as much as it has dislocating effects on existing communities.[37] They hold that cultural difference is not a given but construed and produced in the process of cultural contact, which "occurs in continuous, connected space, traversed by economic and political relations of inequality."[38] During the colonizing process, the colonizing group is construed as the normative or naturalized localized culture in the colonial episteme and master narrative, whereas the Indigenous culture is gradually displaced and denaturalized as the "other," not belonging to this place in the same episteme. It is construed as the "other," a deterritorialized group tolerated in the place, whereas the colonizer is produced as the naturalized, located, or reterritorialized group. With Aileen Moreton-Robinson, René Dietrich argues in the introduction to this volume that biopower functions as a normalizing force that produces whiteness as the norm; hence, in their entangled operationality, biopolitics and geopolitics produce white settlers as the normalized inhabitants and the dispossessed territories as white land. Mark Rifkin argues similarly when he says that "U.S. national policy and identity fundamentally is animated by and enacts an imperial dynamic—naturalizing domestic space by foreclosing countervailing political geographies."[39] Existing Indigenous geographies are superimposed by imperial or colonial geographies and orders of space, as Mishuana Goeman makes clear: "Mistranslations of Indigenous notions of space, implementation of European binaries to define space, and the erasure of Indigenous practices of making place existed since contact with European countries."[40] Colonial geographies then reordered Indigenous space physically through surveying, marking, and fencing and legally by establishing nations, borders, and rigid spatial categories.[41] They also transformed it into propertied space, as Goeman suggests: "the simultaneous unmarking of the area as Native land with a mapping of it as private corporate property" and private individual property or public property.[42] And colonial geographies reordered Indigenous space symbolically and discursively through the unbridled practice of naming and renaming Indigenous lands, mapping the lands, maps being "the narrative backbone of conquest,"[43] and defining land according to function and value— for example, farmland, industrial land, recreational land, national parks, (sub)urban land, reservation land, and wasteland. These entangled processes that Goeman would call "colonial spatial violence" construe the renamed, reordered, mapped, and marked place as "self-evident" settler-colonial space and produce Indigenous life ordered by this space: "Colonial spatial constructs, such as that of borders or private/public land for instance, materially impact daily lives by constructing a lived reality. From tribal jurisdiction to access to healthcare by off-rez individuals, the language of borders demarcates space by enclosing land and excluding bodies. Borders also, as many living on demarcated Indigenous land would attest, control the flow of resources and economics."[44] Difference thus emerges as a category of distinction in terms not only of culture and life-forms but also of spatial and economic inequality and domination. Cultural difference becomes a marker of naturalized/reterritorialized versus denaturalized/deterritorialized space—in fact, a hierarchized space—leading toward changes in collective and individual identities and cultural habits and, moreover, changes in economic and social conditions and conduct. This globalized world, according to Gupta and Ferguson, is "a world where identities are increasingly coming to be, if not wholly deterritorialized, at least differently territorialized. Refugees, migrants, displaced and stateless peoples—these are perhaps the first to live out these realities in their most complete form."[45] Displaced or dispossessed Indigenous people then experience a literal imprisonment within economic spaces that are "zoned . . . for poverty [e.g., urban ghettoes, reserves]."[46] In other words, the physical territory of the Americas was gradually naturalized as an imagined "white" America, Canada, Mexico, or Brazil, whereas the original inhabitants were gradually dispossessed of their physical territories, denaturalized from them, and "zoned" into small places. Epistemic, political, social, and economic power hierarchies produce these former Indigenous territories as "Eurocentric" spaces with settler-colonial regimes that continue to dominate and control interactions of community and place. Indigenous inhabitants are, in a sense, often incarcerated in specific zones (reserves, ghettoes, so-called Indian flats and Indian skid rows, no-man's-land) through political, social, economic, and epistemic conditions and practices and become physically and imaginatively deterritorialized. Former traditional Indigenous homeland, in this line of thought, becomes denaturalized Indigenous space and naturalized non-Indigenous space at the same time with a colonial-settler regime of control and domination. The "specific spatial logics" operating in settler-colonial nations, Goeman holds, set up certain conditions for Indigenous communities and people while simultaneously allowing the continual repetitions and performance of naturalized settler life on Indigenous lands. She says: "Foundational to normative modes of settler colonialism are repetitive practices of everyday life that give settler place meaning and structure. Yet space is fluid, and it is only in the constant retelling and reformulating of colonial narratives that space becomes place as it is given structure and meaning"—what she calls "settler grammar."[47]

I argue that Indigenous lands are reconfigured through settler spatial logics and practices as post/colonial space with colonial histories and settler-colonial political, social, economic, and epistemic relations in post/colonial settler-colonial states. This post/colonial space is produced through colonial politics of dispossession and displacement of people; historical and ongoing domination of cultural habits, life, and sustenance patterns; the regulating, manipulating, and disciplining of bodies and minds; control and domination of economic and social development and structures; and representation of the "other"—in this way, creating an imaginary "other." Jodi Byrd says: "Indigenous peoples and lands became recognizable as they were conscripted into Western law and territoriality and then disavowed from the space of actor into that space which is acted upon within the systems of colonial governmentality that continue to underwrite the settler empires that have emerged through the direct benefit of lands stolen from peoples who could not maintain territoriality or humanity in the face of the grinding appropriations of modernity."[48] One could twist Byrd's statement a bit by stressing the simultaneity of such processes on the same physical lands and arguing that dispossessed Indigenous lands acquire two different spatialities or lived social spaces. They would be the space of the displaced Indigenous and that of the naturalized colonizer, where both construe an imagined homeland with differing sets of relations and ties that are conditioned by the oppositional states of nonpropertied and propertied being on land as results of colonial geopolitics. The two different lived social spaces on the same lands are ordered according to colonial and postcolonial power relations—that is, the settler state has established legal and political control of the lands, and the idea of the naturalized/reterritorialized settler space overrides the idea of the once territorialized Indigenous space that must emerge in the settler narrative as deterritorialized Indigenous space. Whereas the history and the political, economic, and legal realities of dispossessed Indigenous lands precondition the imagined colonizer's naturalized spatiality and official representation of this land as, for example, urban, industrial, mining or farming area, the same history and political, economic, and legal realities of dispossessed Indigenous lands suppress the former Indigenous naturalization in this space and produce imagined and lived Indigenous deterritorialized spatiality.

However, the traditional spatiality can never be completely suppressed or reconfigured, as there are narratives and cultural habits tied to particular lands that remain part of the imagined and lived denaturalized Indigenous identity. Goeman explains: "Native stories speak to a storied land and storied peoples, connecting generations to particular locales and in a web of relationships."[49] And Patrick Wolfe holds that "settler colonialism does not simply replace native society *tout court*. Rather, the process of replacement maintains the refractory imprint of the native counter-claim."[50] In this sense, the process of settler-colonial reterritorialization must be seen as an inherently incomplete process that is continually contested with regard to physical, legal, symbolic, and discursive configurations of land. Most often, Indigenous people continue to see themselves as the stewards of lands and assert their sovereignty as many protests against industrial development show (e.g., the Caledonia, or Grand River, land dispute near Toronto in 2006 and protests against the Keystone XL and Dakota Access Pipeline in 2016-17). A differentiated discussion is necessary with regard to the legal definitions of reservations and reserves, so-called crown land, and land legally redefined in land claim settlements (e.g., the Nisga'a Treaty and Nunavut in Canada). However, as these are comparably small areas within the larger dispossessed territories in the Americas and do not apply to the land represented in the film *Birdwatchers*, this discussion must remain wanted. Likewise, due to the struggle over land between Guaraní and a Brazilian landowner, the chapter concentrates on Indigenous and settler positionalities in relation to land, where both are understood as changing and dynamic cultures, and neglects processes of Indigenous migration to different lands and urban areas, non-European immigration to settler nations, and non-Indigenous support of Indigenous land rights struggles.

Sarah Radcliffe holds that Indigenous spaces are defined by the colonizing culture, which appears as beneficial, neoliberal, and multicultural as it provides education, health care, social services, and the like.[51] Through multiculturalist concepts and policies, the inclusion of the Indigenous is proclaimed, and yet, as Goeman puts it so succinctly, "The national space does not become imagined as Native space."[52] In the settler-colonial context, disturbing issues of stewardship, usage, and control of land and exploitive neoliberal economies are usually bracketed and excluded from political discourse. This happens exactly because the settler state, Nicholas Dunlop holds, assigns value to Indigenous lands in purely economic terms, ignoring their cultural and spiritual value.[53] Thus, land is usually defined as either usable (urban, industrial, agricultural, or mining land) or unusable and expendable (desert, barren land, or wasteland). Radcliffe says: "Relations of colonialism established colonial power over 'unnamed' territories, and incorporated them into a system of meaning that makes them visible only under the terms of colonial inscription."[54] Producing the space of the post/colonial nation-states, Radcliffe argues, relies on the erasure of Indigenous presence and Indigenous cultural, cosmological, and geographical knowledges through colonization and colonial politics.[55] The settler-colonial desire for land on which the settler state's existence is predicated, "produces," as Audra Simpson argues, similar to Coulthard, "'the problem' of the Indigenous life that is already living on that land."[56] Both Radcliffe and Simpson thus echo Wolfe, who demonstrates that elimination of the Indigenous is an organizing principle of settler-colonial society rather than a singular and superseded occurrence. Such practices of elimination include "officially encouraged miscegenation, the breaking-down of native title into alienable individual freeholds, native citizenship, child abduction, religious conversion, resocialization in total institutions such as missions or boarding schools, and a whole range of cognate bicultural assimilations."[57] They are premised on, as Wolfe reminds us, "the securing—the obtaining and the maintaining—of territory," and vice versa, hinting at the connection between biopolitical and geopolitical measures of the settler state.[58] "The present-day reality for many indigenous and black populations" as a consequence, says Radcliffe, "is to be dispersed across a series of overlapping, fragmented and often insecurely titled lands, in material geographies that dis-empower and restrict their access to resources."[59]

In his article "Indigenizing Agamben," Rifkin looks at Giorgio Agamben's concepts of *homo sacer* and "bare life" and applies them to the biopolitics of settler nations and the Indigenous life and existence they produce. He explains that, "for Agamben, the generation of 'bare life' makes thinkable the consignment of those who do not fit the idealized 'biopolitical body' to a 'zone' outside of political participation and the regular working of the law but still within the ambit of state power."[60] The excluded is simultaneously exterior to the sphere of government and law but remains a reference point for the state's practices of government and law—an "inclusive exclusion."[61] Morgan Brigg would call this an "excluded-inclusion."[62] Policies that target Indigenous people or biopolitics in settler states have produced Indigenous existence outside of *bios* and meaningful participation in qualified political life but still under state control: the legitimacy of state rule is grounded in the exclusion of the Indigenous body from *bios*, or, as Rifkin says, the "axiomatic negation of Native peoples' authority to determine or adjudicate for themselves the normative principles by which they will be governed."[63] In terms of Australian settler colonialism, Brigg holds that biopolitical dominance designates and governs Aboriginal people by simultaneously excluding and including them in the Australian political community: "Life is marked apart but included—an excluded-inclusion—in the same way that speech is marked apart from voice. . . . Aboriginal people are constituted vis-à-vis the state and its law, and are simultaneously exposed to violence. Their exclusion is also an inclusion; an excision or excluded-inclusion of the type diagnosed by Agamben."[64] Rifkin argues further that the production of national space (e.g., the United States, Canada, Paraguay, Brazil) depends on defining Indigenous people and their lands as an exception reduced to bare life and deprived of any rights—in a sense, being reduced to bare life like inmates of a concentration camp. They live in a continuous state of exception: subjects of the power of the state to be killed or allowed to live and controlled in terms of their political and natural life. Shona Jackson, in this volume, corroborates the notion of the Indigenous as the *homo sacer* with the caveat that Indigenous people were never assigned that subjectivity and meaningful life—*bios*—but were occupying a liminal position within the emerging settler-colonial logic and state from which they are excised and can be killed or allowed to die. She says, as well: "Indigenous peoples inhabit the role of a recapitulated (in the biological sense) *homo sacer*, so placed by the market in [a] necropolitical sense . . . hence their status as necessarily underdeveloped, internal South."[65]

Rifkin thinks settler states' biopolitics that regulate Indigenous peoples (e.g., assimilation, education, administration, representation, definition of identity, surveillance and disciplinary regimes) together with the states' historical and contemporary geopolitics (e.g., dispossession, displacement, herding people into defined zones such as reservations and ghettoes) as entangled conditions and practices. He says: "I am suggesting, then, that the biopolitical project of defining the proper 'body' of the people is subtended by the geopolitical project of defining the territoriality of the nation, displacing competing claims by older/other political formations as what we might call *bare habitance*."[66]

The logic here is that, when bodies are placed outside meaningful political and social life and are reduced to bare life, then bodies being dispossessed, displaced, and herded into specific zones are excluded from meaningful territorialized existence and are reduced to bare habitance. Likewise, Goeman astutely pinpoints the entanglement of geo- and biopolitical practices of the settler state: "Bodies are organized, categorized, surveilled, and made readable to the state by mapping national and non-national spaces and appointing the appropriate bodies in those spaces. In the case of Native people, this has supported genocide, containment on the reservation, or imprisonment in controlled spaces such as boarding schools or prisons."[67] Rifkin corroborates this notion, explaining that "biopolitical discourses perform geopolitical work [that] the state's assertion of its own territorial self-evidence is critical to the exertion of settler authority over Indigenous peoples-cum-populations" and that "biopolitics works to render national space self-evident."[68]

Guaraní Homeland as Post/Colonial Space in Birdwatchers

Birdwatchers is a very local, low-budget film without technical gimmicks and produced in close cooperation with the Guaraní-Kaiowá. Bechis almost exclusively casts nonprofessional Guaraní-Kaiowá as actors; they are cultural advisers and have considerable influence on the film product, having been encouraged by Bechis to collaborate on the script.[69] In this way, the film helps their autonomous self-representation and supports Indigenous political struggles for survival and reclamation of homeland in Brazil that has not yet seen the release of a feature film by an Indigenous director.[70] Bechis, as a non-Indigenous director, employs appropriate cultural sensitivity; he immersed himself for two months in a Guaraní community, living with Ambrósio Vilhava (who plays Nádio), and he centralizes the Guaraní perspective in the film. Right at the beginning, the film introduces the land with aerial shots of a river meandering through rain forest for twenty-one seconds, accompanied by the rich sound of birdsong in the forest. The next shot features the sound of the motor boat, showing the forest from the perspective of the river before cutting to the tourists in the boat, who stand in for the land-grabbing and exploitive non-Indigenous culture. In various scenes, Bechis represents the abject poverty and living conditions of the Guaraní on the reserve and in their makeshift camp. Figure 10.2 shows a scene in the camp, with wooden constructions wrapped in dark-green plastic serving as accommodations. The shot is symmetrically composed, with the vanishing point almost in the center of the image. The plastic tents are grouped on either side, and an outdoor cooking place constructed over a small fire is placed in the foreground. Deep-space photography permits three different actions on three planes to take place on one axis between the camera lens and the vanishing point: the shaman Nhanderu drives away the power of the gun of the guard who is approaching; a woman sweeps the dirt outside her tent; and two people stretch green plastic over a wood structure to make a new tent. Taking in these actions at once, the shot visually stresses the poverty of the Guaraní and their contested state on their homeland (here the roadside strip) that is defined by the settler state as belonging to a farmer. Figure 10.3 shows the inside of a tent with a coughing toddler swinging in a hammock in the center, a woman by its side preparing food, and Nhanderu sitting on the ground on a mattress on the other side. This shot effectively visualizes Indigenous worldviews that place children at the center of society, with adults, elders, and the community surrounding them. It also visualizes the main conflict of the film, with the Guaraní in abject poverty in the foreground and the contested traditional homeland, which is now a field generating prosperity and

FIGURE 10.2. *Birdwatchers* (*Terra Vermelha*), film still. Rai Cinema/Karta Film/ Gullane Filmes.

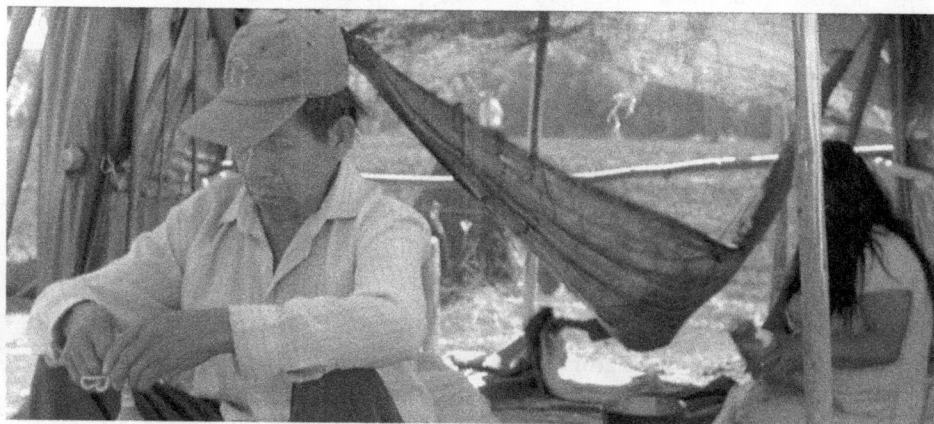

FIGURE 10.3. *Birdwatchers* (*Terra Vermelha*), film still. Rai Cinema/ Karta Film/Gullane Filmes.

a meaningful life for the farmer and his family, in the background, with the guard walking across it. These images also echo the photographs of Guaraní roadside camps Survival International include in its report.[71]

Both the film and images in the Survival International report show makeshift dwellings, outdoor cooking places, dilapidated chairs, clothes racks, and old plastic buckets used as containers for water and other things. They document the "economic spaces zoned . . . for poverty" of which Gupta and Ferguson speak.[72] These images represent the settler state's production of what Rifkin theorizes as bare life and bare habitance of Brazilian Indigenous people in presenting squalid conditions of the landless Guaraní, who have made makeshift homes on the side of the road on their traditional homeland. On the reserve and beside the road, they are subjected to an existence of bare life and bare habitance since their older/other claims to these territories, as Rifkin would have it, were displaced in the process of the settler state Brazil defining its territoriality.[73] At the same time, the violence against the Guaraní—the pesticide spraying, armed guards shooting at men, and Nádio's death, all of which are deliberately included in the plot—illustrate the farmers' self-appropriated power of the sovereign to let live or to kill. Their colonial spatial practices and violence withhold from the Guraní the right to *zoē* (non-qualified, natural life) and to *bios* (qualified, political life) and reduce them to bare life: "life exposed to death."[74]

The film also visualizes and verbalizes the restriction of access to resources in a scene in which Ireneu and Osvaldo go hunting, cross a farmer's field, and are followed by his guard. The guard, who cannot catch the fast-running young men, shouts after them: "Indians! Get out of here! Sooner or later I'll shoot you!"[75] Also the farmer Moreira voices his conviction that the appropriated land belongs to him and the Guaraní on the reserve. In a first encounter after the Guaraní have relocated outside "his" field, he says: "You can't camp out here. Your place is in the Reserve! Why don't you go back to the Reserve? That's your place. What are you doing here? You'll just cause problems. Why are you here?" He represents the general notion that the settler culture is the normative and naturalized localized culture and the Indigenous culture is the displaced and denaturalized culture in territories deemed useful land, here for agricultural purposes. In his understanding the land is settler space, with space for the original inhabitants on the fringes, in the reserve. The three questions he asks show that he is actually puzzled and worried about the *retomada* occupation; he apparently has no sense of the settler-colonial character of the land he claims as his. Bechis makes very clear that in the national imaginary "usable" land is defined as belonging to mainstream settler society and that the deterritorialized traditional homelands of Indigenous people are reterritorialized as "white" settler space. He thus illustrates a tendency among the non-Indigenous population to fiercely oppose any process of recognition of Indigenous rights to land and food, which has generated strong forms of prejudice, racism, and violence against the Guaraní.[76] While the guard is established on the field, some Guaraní haul water from the river across the field to their camp. Moreira says to the guard, while handing him a gun, "Look at that. They're already bringing water in. We can't let that happen. You have to be a scarecrow, you gotta scare them." The camera is trained in close-up on the gun, visually underlining the risk of violence and murder that the farmer consciously takes. The murder of Nádio at the end of the film reflects the practice of using assassination as a method to weaken the land rights movement and intimidate land rights activists. Here the film pinpoints the notion of expendability of Indigenous life, or "worthless life" that is entangled with the division of land into useful and useless land in settler-colonial thought. Sadly, Ambrósio Vilhava also belonged to the group of Indigenous leaders murdered as means to intimidate the *retomada* movement.[77]

In the *retomada* scene, the Guaraní emerge from the forest and the roadside camp (figures 10.4 and 10.5). Accompanied by songs and rattles, they move onto the farmer's field and take the guard hostage to occupy their former homeland. They plant a feathered stick to manifest their reclaiming of the land, the camera showing the stick in the red earth in close-up, visually emphasizing this act. The people thus reverse the much performed colonial act by seafaring explorers of planting a stake to claim the new land for European crowns. In these scenes, the Guaraní are portrayed as embedded in the land. They emerge from the forest and their camp, hardly noticeably at first; they move onto the reddish soil that is placed in the middle foreground in low-angle shots that put visual emphasis on the land. In figure 10.5, the feathered stick features in blurry focus in the immediate foreground and indicates the spiritual connection between land and people. The Guaraní in this scene use mainly traditional weapons such as bows and arrows, possibly to stress their move of reclaiming

FIGURE 10.4. *Birdwatchers* (*Terra Vermelha*), film still. Rai Cinema/Karta Film/ Gullane Filmes.

FIGURE 10.5. *Birdwatchers* (*Terra Vermelha*), film still. Rai Cinema/Karta Film/ Gullane Filmes.

traditional land. They are also aligned with the land through careful color composition. The organic green, reddish, brown, and ochre tones of the forest, river, and soil echo the skin of the Indígenas; they echo their red and black face paint and their clothing, which is often coated in dust. The dust of the earth even makes blue jeans and red and yellow clothing items appear in organic color. The camera further creates a compelling effect by filming the silent, defiant faces of the Indígenas (figure 10.6).

One could even argue that their paid playacting as hostile Indígenas on the river shore (see figure 10.1) visually aligns the Guaraní with the land in terms of their traditional clothing and jewelry, weapons, and scant clothing. They make this appearance of their own free will, as they earn money through the act and are agents of their actions. But the playacting is also part of an exploitative business scheme of the farmer's wife in which the Guaraní are made into "primitive" decorations on land from which they are dispossessed in an objectifying gesture of "order and pay" that the farmer's wife controls. While playacting, the naked bodies and traditional clothing are "reterritorialized" with settler-colonial discourse (the idea of the primitive Indigenous person) through a settler-colonial gaze and the appropriating scheme of the farmer's wife. At the same time, however, limited agency in this playacting articulates claims to the land and defiant Indigenous presence, buoyed by the hostile gazes and calls of the Guaraní as well as by arrows shot in the direction of the boat. In the *retomada* scene, scant traditional clothing, weapons, and face paint are redefined as Indigenous paraphernalia that support the self-conscious act of reclaiming land and

FIGURE 10.6. *Birdwatchers* (*Terra Vermelha*), film still. Rai Cinema/Karta Film/
Gullane Filmes.

undoing settler-colonial reterritorialization of land. The film has a rather slow
pace, employing long takes and no fast cuts. Bechis says he avoided a mobile
camera and preferred stable shots, as in western movies.[78] But here the "shoot-
out" involves not guns but the soil. In the encounter on the occupied land, a
lawyer directs clear restraining orders to both sides and does not "want justice
violated." Moreira counters: "I don't see how you can talk of justice when this
land has been invaded, a land duly recorded at the land office," thus repeating
his understanding of reterritorialized land as his and accusing the Guaraní of
land theft. He discursively establishes the Indigenous move as invasion and
reverses the responsibility for land appropriation. Facing Nádio, he takes some
red earth into his hands to underscore his statement and says, "This land. My
father arrived here more than sixty years ago. That's three generations. I was
born here. My daughter grew up here. I work this land from dawn to dusk, so
that it gives fruit. I sow nourishment so that people can eat." Nádio silently
takes some red earth, as well, and puts it into his mouth to eat it—meaning
his people have always been of this land that directly nourishes them. While
Moreira exhausts and pollutes the land (with pesticides) to produce food, the

Guaraní have used the land in responsible ways and have concepts of steward-ship in place for the land that gives them food. The encounter also highlights that the prosperity and food production of one group involves the demise and hunger of another group, while both claim connections to the same piece of land—the reconfigured post/colonial land that is denaturalized Indigenous and naturalized settler land. This is another pivotal scene, as it demonstrates a settler-colonial definition of land in material and economic terms. It demon-strates this definition through legal ownership acquired through dispossession and settler-colonial land politics versus Indigenous understandings of belong-ing to the land, which has cultural, spiritual, and nourishing value. It illus-trates the imagined colonizer's naturalized spatiality versus Indigenous efforts to renaturalize their spatiality and reterritorialize their existence. The land conflict in the film will be settled in the courts, again emphasizing that Indig-enous lands are post/colonial spaces that are controlled by the settler culture and that the double post/colonial spatiality is hierarchized through existing power relations. Guaraní land is posited within the state juridical power and order, whereas the people are exteriorized and are not protected by the law.

In the end, the film again presents the dense and rich green forest from a bird's-eye view for twenty seconds. The camera then pans left to show the adjacent clear-cut fields, with both rain forest and field on the screen together for ten seconds, the boundary shifting toward the right. The same aerial shot continues showing the red field for twenty-six seconds. This composition of aerial shots visually supports the film's main conflict between Indigenous life depending on the healthy forest and land and the settler-colonial destruction and exploitation of that forest and land. While the plot provides a rather posi-tive ending, with Osvaldo resisting suicide, the visuals at the end transmit a different message. The rain forest is slowly replaced by a deforested field now used by a non-Indigenous farmer; this image has more screen time than the forest, which indicates that more Indigenous land is now deforested and used for agro-industry than is left as intact rain forest. The slowness of the camera movement also implies that the settling of the land conflict may take several years, while the Guaraní have no means of existence. Here Bechis hints at the current situation in Mato Grosso do Sul, where land reclamation processes are slowed by farmers. In 2007, Brazil's government and twenty-three Indigenous leaders signed an agreement, the Termo de Ajustamento de Conduta, which stipulated the identification of thirty-six Guaraní ancestral lands, the demar-cation of seven large territories encompassing them, and the return of these lands by 2010.[79] These endeavors have been sabotaged by concerned farmers, who stall all processes with endless court orders and appeals and threats of violence toward employees of the Fundação Nacional de Indio who came to demarcate Guaraní land.[80]

Film, in general, creates meaning on several levels: with images, with perspective, with camera work, and with dialogue and sound. Bechis adjusted his filmmaking style to the local Indigenous people: he employs mainly their perspective, filming from within the community, observing and presenting their daily lives in squalid conditions and often shooting their faces in close-up. He reserves more screen time for the struggles of the Indígenas. This might be expressive of a film style that moves from Hollywood-style fictional scripts, costumes, artificial sets, seamless presentation, and so on, toward one that is closer to documentary, with local nonprofessional actors who at times wear their own clothing and reenact life and struggles as they experience them in reality. Furthermore, he aligns the camera with the land and the people with subdued organic colors, as opposed to the bright colors of things related to western society. Examples include shots of a blue and green pool at the farmhouse; blue bikinis on Maria and her friend as they lounge at the pool and swim in the river; a blue tractor plowing a field; Maria's red motorbike in the forest; and the bright artificial colors in a mall where Ireneu buys sneakers and where he encounters four girls in pink promoting an item. Much of the story is set in the rain forest and on the clear-cut land, thus creating a visual presence of contested Indigenous land. The camera work is adapted to the slow-paced life of the Indigenous Brazilians, as opposed to mainstream Brazilians, whose world is filmed with faster cuts. Bechis uses a fast-moving mobile camera only when he emulates the point of view of the evil spirit Angué that threatens Osvaldo. The soundtrack mixes the intriguing soundscape of the rain forest, maraca rattles, the noises of an industrialized country, and the accentuated placement of Italian baroque music, which stresses colonization and the changes in Indigenous lives. Moreover, all dialogue among the Indígenas is presented in the Guaraní language.

The film calls to mind that in the twenty-first century, Indigenous people still face difficult living conditions caused by the violent dispossession of their land; and they are under various sorts of threats from post/colonial settler societies and world trade, of which people in industrialized countries, including the author, are part—even if they are aware and critical of the situation. The *retomadas* are an Indigenous attempt to reclaim post/colonial space, which is a palimpsestic space that includes Indigenous land and settler and Indigenous claims to this land, as well as Indigenous and non-Indigenous narratives and life-forms that are dynamic in themselves. The *retomadas* will unsettle the settlers' reterritorialization of Indigenous lands and the notion that Brazilian land is naturalized "white" land. They will compel the beginning of a process that redefines this land as space where settlers' and Indigenous peoples' interests, lifeways, claims to land, and epistemologies have to be negotiated. The film supports this struggle by raising awareness not only about Indigenous dispossession and exploitation by settler-colonial states such as Brazil but also about Western entanglement in this exploitive relationship with Indigenous people such as the Guaraní.

NOTES

1   For a discussion about the three titles in English, Portuguese, and Italian, cf. Aline Frey, "Resisting Invasions: Indigenous Peoples and Land Rights Battles in *Mabo* and *Terra Vermelha*," *Ilha Desterro* 69, no. 2 (May–August 2016): 157–58, http://dx.doi.org /10.5007/2175-8026.2016v69n2p151.

2   Walter Mignolo, "Putting the Americas on the Map (Geography and the Colonization of Space)," *Colonial Latin American Review* 1, no. 1 (1992): 34–36.

3   Edmundo O'Gorman, *The Invention of America: An Inquiry into the Historical Nature of the New World and the Meaning of Its History* (Bloomington: Indiana University Press, 1961); Mignolo, "Putting the Americas on the Map," 36.

4   Mignolo, "Putting the Americas on the Map," 59.

5   Walter Mignolo, *Local Histories/Global Designs* (Princeton, NJ: Princeton University Press), 220.

6   Walter Mignolo, "Coloniality: The Darker Side of Modernity," in *Modernologies: Contemporary Artists Researching Modernity and Modernism*, edited by Sabine Breitwieser, Cornelia Klinger, and Walter Mignolo (Barcelona: Museu Dart Contemporani de Barcelona, 2009), 39.

7   Paul Gilroy, *The Black Atlantic: Modernity and Double Consciousness* (Cambridge, MA: Harvard University Press, 1993), 15.

8   Survival International, "Violations of the Rights of the Guaraní of Mato Grosso do Sul State, Brazil: A Survival International Report to the UN Committee on the Elimination of Racial Discrimination (UN CERD)," 3, accessed May 2, 2017, http://assets .survival-international.org/documents/207/Guaraní_report_English_MARCH.pdf.

9   Survival International (https://www.survivalinternational.org) is an international nongovernmental organization that supports struggles of Indigenous peoples around the world.

10 Cf. Richard Robbins, who explains Guaraní sustenance in Paraguay as a combination of sustainable collection of commercial products such as yerba mate leaves and small-game hunting for sustenance. He argues that traditional Guaraní agroforestry practices are severely inhibited through the destruction of forests and their biosphere, which in turn obliterates Guaraní lifeways, social structures, and lives: Richard H. Robbins, "The Guaraní: The Economics of Ethnocide," in *The Indigenous Experience: Global Perspectives*, edited by Roger C. A. Maaka and Chris Andersen (Toronto: Canadian Scholars' Press, 2006), 154–56.

11 Survival International, "Violations of the Rights of the Guaraní of Mato Grosso do Sul State, Brazil," 5, 16; cf. Frey, "Resisting Invasions," 156–57.

12 Survival International, "Violations of the Rights of the Guaraní of Mato Grosso do Sul State, Brazil," 10–11; cf. Frey, "Resisting Invasions," 160.

13 Survival International, "Violations of the Rights of the Guaraní of Mato Grosso do Sul State, Brazil," 1.

14 Survival International, "Violations of the Rights of the Guaraní of Mato Grosso do Sul State, Brazil," 1.

15 Survival International, "Violations of the Rights of the Guaraní of Mato Grosso do Sul State, Brazil," 5.

16 Gastón Gordillo, "Longing for Elsewhere: Guaraní Reterritorializations," *Comparative Studies in Society and History* 53, no. 4 (2011): 857.

17 Frey, "Resisting Invasions," 152.

18 Cf. Frey, "Resisting Invasions," 157.

19 Glen Sean Coulthard, *Red Skin White Masks: Rejecting the Colonial Politics of Recognition* (Minneapolis: University of Minnesota Press, 2013), 184.

20 Eugene W. Holland, "Deterritorializing 'Deterritorialization'—From the *Anti-Oedipus* to *A Thousand Plateaus*," *SubStance* 20, no. 3, 66 (1991): 58.

21 Gil-Manuel Hernàndez i Martí, "The Deterritorialization of Cultural Heritage in a Globalized Modernity," *Transfer* 1 (2006): 95.

22 Gilles Deleuze and Félix Guattari, *A Thousand Plateaus: Capitalism and Schizophrenia*, translated by Brian Massumi (Minneapolis: University of Minnesota Press, 1987), 307.

23 Hernàndez i Martí, "The Deterritorialization of Cultural Heritage in a Globalized Modernity," 95.

24 Hernàndez i Martí, "The Deterritorialization of Cultural Heritage in a Globalized Modernity," 95.

25 Arjun Appadurai, "Disjuncture and Difference in the Global Cultural Economy," *Theory Culture Society* 7 (1990): 301.

26 See, e.g., Simone Bignall and Paul Patton, eds., *Deleuze and the Postcolonial* (Edinburgh: Edinburgh University Press, 2010); Lorna Burns and Birgit M. Kaiser, eds., *Postcolonial Literatures and Deleuze: Colonial Pasts, Differential Future* (Houndmills, UK: Palgrave Macmillan, 2012).

27 Bruce B. Janz, "Forget Deleuze," in Burns and Kaiser, *Postcolonial Literatures and Deleuze*, 24.

28 Janz, "Forget Deleuze," 24.

29 John K. Noyes, "Postcolonial Theory and the Geographical Materialism of Desire," in Bignall and Patton, *Deleuze and the Postcolonial*, 47.

30 Robert J. C. Young, *Postcolonialism: A Very Short Introduction* (Oxford: Oxford University Press, 2003), 52.

31 Cf. Jeannette Armstrong's and Richard E. Atleo's writings on Indigenous philosophy and land ethics, the understanding that people belong to land and are part of it at the same level as plants and animals while all beings and land together produce life. This understanding is expressed in oral narratives (now also transformed into "oraliture") that also belong to a territory and place and thus create a cultural

space: Jeannette Armstrong, "Constructing Indigeneity: Syilx Okanagan Oraliture and tmixʷcentrism" (PhD diss., University of Greifswald, Germany, 2010, http://ub -ed.ub.uni-greifswald.de/opus/volltexte/2012/1322); Richard E. Atleo, *Principles of Tsawalk: An Indigenous Approach to Global Crisis* (Vancouver: University of British Columbia Press, 2011); Richard E. Atleo, *Tsawalk: A Nuu-chah-nulth Worldview* (Vancouver: University of British Columbia Press, 2004).

32 Henri Lefebvre, *The Production of Space*, translated by Donald Nicholson-Smith (Malden, UK: Blackwell, 1991), 129; Edward Soja, *Thirdspace: Journeys to Los Angeles and Other Real-and-Imagined Places* (Malden, UK: Blackwell, 1996), 1, 46.

33 Soja, *Thirdspace*, 58.

34 Gordillo, "Longing for Elsewhere," 859–61.

35 Gordillo, "Longing for Elsewhere," 859.

36 Gordillo, "Longing for Elsewhere," 860.

37 Akhil Gupta and James Ferguson, "Beyond 'Culture': Space, Identity and the Politics of Difference," *Cultural Anthropology* 7, no. 1 (1992): 8.

38 Gupta and Ferguson, "Beyond 'Culture,'" 16.

39 Mark Rifkin, *Manifesting America: The Imperial Construction of U.S. National Space* (New York: Oxford University Press, 2009), 3–4.

40 Mishuana Goeman, "From Place to Territories and Back Again: Centering Storied Land in the Discussion of Indigenous Nation-building," *International Journal of Critical Indigenous Studies* 1, no. 1 (2008): 30.

41 Mishuana Goeman, *Mark My Words: Native Women Mapping Our Nations* (Minneapolis: University of Minnesota Press, 2013), 38.

42 Goeman, *Mark My Words*, 30.

43 Goeman, *Mark My Words*, 35. For a critical analysis of naming and renaming Indigenous territories, cf., e.g., Kerstin Knopf, "Exploring for the Empire: Franklin, Rae, Dickens, and the Natives in Australian and Canadian Literature," in *Postempire Imaginaries? Anglophone Literature, History and the Demise of Empires*, edited by Barbara Buchenau and Virginia Richter (Leiden: Brill/Rodopi, 2015), 69–100.

44 Goeman, *Mark My Words*, 11; Goeman, "From Place to Territories and Back Again," 30–31.

45 Gupta and Ferguson, "Beyond 'Culture,'" 9–10.

46 Gupta and Ferguson, "Beyond 'Culture,'" 17.

47 Mishuana Goeman, "Disrupting a Settler Colonial Grammar of Place: The Visual Memoir of Hulleah Tsinhnahjinnie," in *Theorizing Native Studies*, edited by Audra Simpson and Andrea Smith (Durham, NC: Duke University Press, 2014), 236–37.

48 Jodi A. Byrd, "Mind the Gap: Indigenous Sovereignty and the Antinomies of Empire," in *The Antinomie of the Earth: Philosophy, Politics, and Autonomy in Europe and the Americas*, edited by Frederico Luisetti, John Pickles, and Wilson Kaiser (Durham, NC: Duke University Press, 2015) 121.

49 Goeman, *Mark My Words*, 37.

50 Patrick Wolfe, "Settler Colonialism and the Elimination of the Native," *Journal of Genocide Research* 8, no. 4 (2006): 389.

51 Sarah A. Radcliffe, "Third Space, Abstract Space and Coloniality: National and Subaltern Cartography in Ecuador," in *Postcolonial Spaces: The Politics of Place in Con-*

temporary Culture, edited by Andrew Teverson and Sara Upstone (Basingstoke, UK: Palgrave Macmillan, 2011), 136.

52 Goeman, *Mark My Words*, 35.

53 Nicholas Dunlop, "A Few Words about the Role of the Cartographers: Mapping and Postcolonial Resistance in Peter Carey's 'Do You Love Me?'," in Teverson and Upstone, *Postcolonial Spaces*, 33.

54 Radcliffe, "Third Space, Abstract Space and Coloniality," 140.

55 Radcliffe, "Third Space, Abstract Space and Coloniality," 141.

56 Audra Simpson, *Mohawk Interruptus: Political Life across the Borders of Settler States* (Durham, NC: Duke University Press, 2014), 19.

57 Wolfe, "Settler Colonialism and the Elimination of the Native," 388.

58 Wolfe, "Settler Colonialism and the Elimination of the Native," 402.

59 Radcliffe, "Third Space, Abstract Space and Coloniality," 141.

60 Mark Rifkin, "Indigenizing Agamben: Rethinking Sovereignty in Light of the 'Peculiar' Status of Native Peoples," *Cultural Critique* 73 (2009): 92.

61 Giorgio Agamben, *Homo Sacer: Sovereign Power and Bare Life*, translated by Daniel Heller-Roazen (Stanford, CA: Stanford University Press, 1998), 27.

62 Morgan Brigg, "Biopolitics Meets Terrapolitics: Political Ontologies and Governance in Settler-Colonial Australia," *Australian Journal of Political Science* 42, no. 3 (2007): 404, https://doi.org/10.1080/10361140701513554.

63 Rifkin, "Indigenizing Agamben," 91.

64 Brigg, "Biopolitics meets Terrapolitics," 407, 413.

65 See Shona N. Jackson's chapter in this volume.

66 Rifkin, "Indigenizing Agamben," 94.

67 Goeman, *Mark My Words*, 36.

68 Mark Rifkin, "Making Peoples into Populations: The Racial Limits of Tribal Sovereignty," in Simpson and Smith, *Theorizing Native Studies*, 158.

69 Frey, "Resisting Invasions," 156.

70 Frey, "Resisting Invasions," 156.

71 Survival International, "Violations of the Rights of the Guaraní of Mato Grosso do Sul State, Brazil," 4, 5, 18.

72 Gupta and Ferguson, "Beyond 'Culture,'" 17.

73 Rifkin, "Indigenizing Agamben," 94.

74 Agamben, *Homo Sacer*, 88.

75 This and following quotations are taken from the English subtitles of the film.

76 Survival International, "Violations of the Rights of the Guaraní of Mato Grosso do Sul State, Brazil," 10.

77 Frey, "Resisting Invasions," 160.

78 Cristina Nord, "Edle Wilde gibt es nur für Touristen," *taz*, July 15, 2009, http://www.taz.de/!5159853.

79 Survival International, "Violations of the Rights of the Guaraní of Mato Grosso do Sul State, Brazil," 6.

80 Survival International, "Violations of the Rights of the Guaraní of Mato Grosso do Sul State, Brazil," 6.

CONTRIBUTORS

RENÉ DIETRICH is a senior lecturer in American Studies at the Catholic University of Eichstätt-Ingolstadt and was a visiting scholar at the American Indian Studies Center at the University of California, Los Angeles. He is the author of *Revising and Remembering (after) the End: American Post-apocalyptic Poetry since 1945 from Ginsberg to Forché* (2012), editor of the *American Indian Culture and Research Journal* special issue "Settler Colonial Biopolitics and Indigenous Lifeways," and has published in venues such as *Amerikastudien/American Studies*, *Anglia Cultural Studies-Critical Methodologies*, and *Journal of Transnational American Studies*. Currently he is working on a monograph on US settler-colonial biopolitics and Indigenous life writing.

JACQUELINE FEAR-SEGAL is a professor of American and Indigenous histories at the University of East Anglia (UK). Her research centers on Indigenous American histories, with a particular interest in Indian boarding schools, photography, and Native North American travelers to Europe. *Carlisle Indian Industrial School: Indigenous Histories, Memories, and Reclamations* (2016) is her most recent book. *Beyond the Spectacle: Native North American Presence in Britain* and *Indigenous Mobilities: Travellers through the Heart(s) of Empire* are two ongoing book projects, resulting from the research project Beyond the Spectacle. In 2006, she cofounded the Native Studies Research Network UK, which she continues to codirect.

MISHUANA GOEMAN, Tonawanda Band of Seneca, is a professor of gender studies and American Indian studies and affiliated faculty of critical race studies in the Law School, University of California, Los Angeles, and Community Engagements Program. She is also the author of *Mark My Words: Native Women Mapping Our Nations* (2013), coeditor of *Keywords in Gender and Sexuality Studies* (2021), and a co-principal investigator on the community-based digital projects Mapping Indigenous LA (2015), Carrying Our Ancestors Home (2019), and California Native Hubs.

ALYOSHA GOLDSTEIN is a professor of American studies at the University of New Mexico. He is the author of *Poverty in Common: The Politics of Community Action during the American Century* (2012), the editor of *Formations of United States Colonialism* (2014), and the coeditor of *For Antifascist Futures: Against the Violence of Imperial Crisis* (2022). He has coedited special issues of *Critical Ethnic Studies*, *Social Text*, *South Atlantic Quarterly*, and *Theory and Event* and is completing a book on US colonialism, racial capitalism, genealogies of Black and Native dispossession, and the politics of law and redress in the colonial present.

SANDY GRANDE is a professor of political science and Native American and Indigenous studies at the University of Connecticut, with affiliations in American studies; philosophy; and women, gender, and sexuality studies. She is the author of *Red Pedagogy: Native American Social and Political Thought* (2004), which has been published in a tenth-anniversary edition. In addition to publishing numerous articles and book chapters, she is a founding member of New York Stands for Standing Rock. She has also provided eldercare for her parents for more than ten years and remains the primary caregiver for her ninety-four-year-old father.

MICHAEL R. GRIFFITHS is a senior lecturer in English literatures at the University of Wollongong (Australia). He is the author of *The Distribution of Settlement: Appropriation and Refusal in Australian Literature and Culture* (2018) and the editor of *Biopolitics and Memory in Postcolonial Literature and Culture* (2016). His essays have appeared in *Australian Humanities Review*, *Discourse*, *Settler Colonial Studies*, *Journal of Commonwealth Literature*, *Postcolonial Studies*, *Textual Practice*, and many other venues. Griffiths is an active member of Jindaola, a curriculum decolonizing project founded at the University of Wollongong.

SHONA N. JACKSON is an associate professor in the Department of English at Texas A&M University. She is the author of *Creole Indigeneity: Between Myth and Nation in the Caribbean* (2012). Her publications include journal articles and book chapters in *American Quarterly*, *Atzlán: A Journal of Chicano Studies*, *Callaloo*, *Caribbean Quarterly*, *Keywords for African American Studies*, *The Oxford Handbook of Indigenous American Literature*, *Small Axe*, and *Theory and Event*, among others.

KERSTIN KNOPF is a professor of North American and postcolonial literary and cultural studies at the University of Bremen (Germany) and director of the Institute for Postcolonial and Transcultural Studies and the Bremen Institute for Canada and Quebec Studies. She is currently president of the International Council for Canadian Studies (2021–23). Her main research interests are Indigenous film and literature worldwide; postcolonial studies focusing on North America, Australia, New Zealand, and Papua New Guinea; epistemological power relations and postcolonial knowledge systems; American and Canadian romantic literature; and American prison literature.

SABINE N. MEYER is a professor of American studies and codirector of the North American Studies Program at the University of Bonn (Germany). Her research focuses on Native American writing and law from the nineteenth century onward and on representations of Native Americans/Indigenous peoples in North American popular culture. She is the author of *We Are What We Drink: The Temperance Battle in Minnesota* (2015) and *Native Removal Writing: Narratives of Peoplehood, Politics, and Law* (2022) and has published articles in *American Indian Quarterly, Eighteenth-Century Studies, Journal of American History*, and *Law and Literature*. She is the coeditor of the monograph series Routledge Research in Transnational Indigenous Perspectives.

ROBERT NICHOLS is an associate professor of political theory at the University of Minnesota, Twin Cities. He is the author of *The World of Freedom: Heidegger, Foucault, and the Politics of Historical Ontology* (2014) and *Theft Is Property! Dispossession and Critical Theory* (2020).

MARK RIFKIN is the Linda Arnold Carlisle Distinguished Excellence Professor of Women's, Gender, and Sexuality Studies and a professor of English at the University of North Carolina, Greensboro. He is the author of seven books, most recently *Fictions of Land and Flesh: Blackness, Indigeneity, Speculation* (2019) and *Speaking for the People: Native Writing and the Question of Political Form* (2021). His work has won the John Hope Franklin Prize for Best Book in American Studies, the Best Subsequent Book Prize from the Native American and Indigenous Studies Association, and the Best Special Issue award from the Council of Editors of Learned Journals. He also has served as president of the Native American and Indigenous Studies Association.

DAVID UAHIKEAIKALEI'OHU MAILE is a Kanaka Maoli scholar, organizer, and practitioner from Maunawili, O'ahu. He is an assistant professor of Indigenous politics in the Department of Political Science, University of Toronto, and an affiliate faculty with the Centre for Indigenous Studies and Centre for the Study of the United States.

INDEX

Kanaka Maoli (Native Hawaiians), 29, 107–25; federal recognition of, 110–21, 124 (*see also* Advanced Notice for Proposed Rulemaking [ANPRM]; 'a'ole); government-to-government relationship with, 110–11, 115; Indigeneity of, 28, 114. *See also* Native Hawaiian Governing Entity (NHGE); Office of Hawaiian Affairs (OHA); resistance; *Rice v. Cayetano*

Kauanui, J. Kēhaulani, 112, 114–15, 118

Kavanaugh, Brett, 28, 108–10

King, Tiffany Lethabo, 10–11, 164, 178

labor, 97, 102n15, 141, 151, 248; force, 70; incarceration and, 60; Indigenous, 132, 157n64, 220; power, 69, 144; prisoners as surplus, 90; slave, 140; wage, 71

LaPointe, Charlene Ann, 53–54

Las Casas, Bartolomé de, 49, 142, 155n33

Latin America, 11, 14, 247, 249, 251

ledger art, 234–37

Lévy-Bruhl, Lucien, 205, 211

Lewis, Jordan P., 77, 79, 80n8

liberalism, 142; modern, 11, 78; settler, 21–22

Madley, Ben, 49–50

magic, 30, 198–206; archive and, 199, 211; in *Benang: From the Heart* (Scott), 198, 208–9, 215; biopower and, 31, 208; in "Mataa" (Ihimaera), 213–14; of mimesis, 217n25; modernity and, 198, 202, 208, 213, 215; sympathetic, 204, 206, 217n28

magical realism, 30, 197–200, 202–6, 208–10, 216n1. *See also* Scott, Kim: *Benang: From the Heart*

Manpower Demonstration Research Corporation (MDRC), 71, 81n17

Māori, 211–12; cultural apparel, 201; practices, 199, 204, 214–45. *See also* Ihimaera, Witi: "Mataa"

Marshall, John, 194n30, 195n41

Marshall Trilogy, 50, 184, 194n30, 196n46

Mato Grosso do Sul, 245, 248–49, 266

Mbembe, Achille, 73, 140, 142, 151

mestizaje, 11, 14

Mignolo, Walter, 247–48

mimesis, 203, 206, 214, 217n25

mimicry, 206–7; economic, 139, 141

Miranda, Deborah, 47–51, 58, 62–63

Missouri River, 20, 26

Mitchell, Katharyne, 72, 82n19

mni wiconi, 19–26

modernity, 248, 256; anti-Blackness and, 161; biopolitics and, 73, 142, 209; capitalist, 251; colonial, 203–4, 208–9, 211, 215; factish and, 207; Indigenous, 31, 201–3, 210, 215, 246, 250; magic and, 198, 202, 208, 213, 215; Western, 12, 206

modernization, 203, 247

Montag, Warren, 143, 155n34

Monture-Angus, Patricia, 88, 94, 99

Moreton-Robinson, Aileen, 3, 11, 254

Morgensen, Scott, 3, 155n33, 178, 183, 191

mutuality, 68–69, 77

nation-states, 38n31, 51, 73, 138, 148; Blackness and, 161; Creole, 136; postcolonial, 132, 136, 145, 258; prehistory of, 137; settler, 5, 7–8; sovereignty of, 28, 150; subaltern, 14; time of, 146

Native Americans, 113, 119–23, 178, 184–87, 191; photography and, 229, 234; state of exception and, 183

Native Hawaiian community, 113–14; government-to-government relationship with United States, 110–11; as Indian tribe, 122; as Indigenous population, 109; special political and trust relationship with United States, 112, 115, 120

Native Hawaiian Governing Entity (NHGE), 121–23

Native Hawaiian government, 111, 114, 120–21. *See also* Advanced Notice for Proposed Rulemaking (ANPRM)

Native Hawaiians. *See* Kanaka Maoli (Native Hawaiians)

Native peoples, 47–48, 61, 123, 172n1, 184, 187, 189, 258–59; archive of refusal and, 31; as deficit subjects, 51; dispossession of, 40n53; gendered violence and, 63; governance and, 60; photography and, 229, 232, 235; stereotyping of, 174n21; suicide and, 176n33

Native women: dispossession and, 47, 52; gendered violence and, 63; justice and, 27, 46, 52–53, 56–58, 61–62; sexual violence against, 46–47, 49–55, 57, 60–62, 179, 183; violence against, 27, 46, 51; writers, 49

naturalization, 6; of domestic-vs.-foreign distinctions, 95; Indigenous, 256; of national space, 36n22; of the supernatural, 205

necropolitics, 32, 73, 142

neoliberalism, 73, 76–77, 91, 95, 144, 156n39

New Zealand, 4, 26, 104n31, 247; Maori Affairs Act, 214

Nixon, Rob, 14–15, 17, 40n53

Notice for Proposed Rulemaking (NPRM), 119–21

occupation, 93, 98, 147–48, 150, 170; of Hawai'i, 4, 116–17, 124; *retomada*, 262; rights of, 187; settler-colonial, 199

Office of Hawaiian Affairs (OHA), 107–8, 110

Oliphant v. Suquamish Indian Tribe, 56, 58

overrepresentation, 87–89, 92, 100, 103n24

peoplehood, 24, 168; Indigenous, 8, 25, 154n21, 160–61, 184; place-based, 25, 161, 171–72; secular, 151; territorial, 170

personhood, 154n21, 163, 171; heteronormative models of, 166; propertied, 160, 164; property and, 180–81; of water, 20

petroglyphs, 29, 133, 136, 138, 141, 150

Pine Ridge, 46, 95, 224, 233

sovereignty, 37n27, 52, 100, 229; American, 73; bare life and, 185; bodily, 49, 51, 53, 57; Cherokee, 189–90; Creole, 134, 151; critical, 47; geopolitical, 36n22; Guyanese, 135, 144; Kanaka Maoli/Native Hawaiian, 29, 107–8, 110, 113, 115, 117; liberal mode of, 142; nation-state, 28, 150; Native rights and, 193n7; pictorial, 222; political, 169, 228; postcolonial, 136, 139, 143; reason and, 78; settler, 59, 111; slavery and, 132; state, 3, 51, 92, 124, 132, 140, 143; territoriality of, 98; territorialized, 87, 92, 94, 96, 99–100; tribal, 56, 62; US, 117, 120–22, 124; visual, 31, 228, 239; Western, 6; *Xenogenesis* trilogy (Butler) and, 160–61, 166, 170–72. *See also* Indigenous sovereignty

Spillers, Hortense, 11–12, 163
Spivak, Gayatri, 216n11, 235
Standing Bear, Luther, 31, 233–35, 240n11
Standing Rock, 1, 18–20, 33n1, 34n5, 45, 59
Stanley, Gerald, 2, 16, 33n1
Stasiulis, Daiva, 9–10
state of exception, 6–8, 22, 36n22, 132, 139, 141, 143, 150, 181, 183, 185; continuous, 259; settler, 124
Stevenson, Lisa, 15–16, 77, 176n33
survivance, 31, 198, 228, 233–34, 239

Takolander, Maria, 205–6, 216n1
Taussig, Michael, 201, 206, 217n25
territoriality, 19, 22, 96–98, 100, 159, 171, 186, 187, 256, 259; Brazil's, 262; collective, 161; of conquest, 52; of Hawai'i, 121; settler-state, 7, 123; of the US settler state, 113
third sex, 162, 166, 175n27
Todd, Zoe, 20, 25

traditional right, 146, 150
Trail of Tears, 30, 178–79, 183, 185, 187, 189–90
translation, 138, 147, 160–62; of Indigenous cultures, 136; limits of, 196n48

US Department of the Interior (DOI), 28, 94, 109–13, 115–24
US Supreme Court, 50, 56, 107–8, 110, 194n30

Vizenor, Gerald, 227–28, 233–34, 238–39

Wacquant, Loïc, 91, 102n12, 103n17
Warnes, Christopher, 205–6
Warren, Calvin, 140, 143
Washburn, Frances A., 47, 58, 60, 63
Weheliye, Alexander, 11–12, 140, 155n27, 163–64
whakapapa, 198–99, 201, 204, 208, 213–15
whiteness, 3, 11, 14, 38n35, 163, 254
white supremacy, 41n73, 69
White Thunder, Ernest/Wica-Karpa, 230, 231f, 235
Wolfe, Patrick, 9–10, 15, 22, 41n73, 136, 153n14; logic of elimination, 9, 35n18, 38n32, 61, 68, 136, 149, 220, 227, 258; on settler colonialism, 19, 37n28, 38n32, 220, 257; on territoriality, 97
wonderworks, 30, 200, 202–3
Worcester v. Georgia, 122, 194n30
Wynter, Sylvia, 11–12, 39n36, 139–40, 152n3, 155n27, 155n30, 163

Yuval-Davis, Nira, 9–10

zoē, 22, 139–42, 262. *See also* bare life